Marine Policy for America

Marine Policy for America

The United States at Sea

Gerard J. Mangone
University of Delaware

Lexington Books
D.C. Heath and Company
Lexington, Massachusetts
Toronto

Library of Congress Cataloging in Publication Data

Mangone, Gerard J.
    Marine policy for America.

    Includes bibliographical references and index.
    1. Marine resources and state—United States. 2. United States. Navy.
3. Merchant marine—United States. I. Title.
GC1005.2.M36   333.9'164'0973   77-243
ISBN 0-669-01432-x

Published simultaneously in Canada

Printed in the United States of America

International Standard Book Number: 0-669-01432-x

Library of Congress Catalog Card Number: 77-243

For **Stephen Kemp Bailey**

Distinguished scholar in politics and education,
Creative administrator of universities and public affairs.
Pricelessly endowed with poetry and wit
In his ceaseless search for justice and beauty. . .

Contents

Preface

In July 1970 I was the first Fellow to arrive at the new Woodrow Wilson International Center for Scholars located in the castle of the Smithsonian Institution on the Mall in Washington, D.C. Created by Congress as a "living memorial" to Wilson, the most scholarly President after Thomas Jefferson, the Center, under the extraordinarily able guidance of its first director, Benjamin H. Read, was an ideal haven for unhurried research. Graced with the title of Coordinator of the Ocean Affairs Program, I was thereafter fortunate in welcoming to the Center such splendid colleagues of marine law and public policy as Ram Anand and S. Rao from India, Edward Brown from the United Kingdom, Lucius Caflisch from Switzerland, Arvid Pardo from Malta, Albert Koers from The Netherlands, Jorge Vargas from Mexico, F. Krüger-Sprengel from West Germany, and Seabrook Hull, Zdenek Slouka, J. Lawrence McHugh, George Reedy, and Athelstan Spilhaus from the United States. Their painstaking research, lively discussions, and warm friendship contributed much toward my education in the issues and problems of marine affairs to be found in this book.

My writing, interrupted by various administrative appointments, began at the Woodrow Wilson International Center and was completed at the new College of Marine Studies of the University of Delaware, the first graduate professional interdisciplinary school for marine studies in the United States. Here my colleagues in engineering and marine biology, chemistry, physics, and geology have instructed me on the science of the oceans while I have benefitted from the counsel of associates in marine affairs from the disciplines of law, economics, history, and political science. William S. Gaither, Dean of the College, has been a constant source of encouragement and assistance to marine policy research, for which I am most grateful.

Two outstanding secretaries, Gaenor Willson at the Woodrow Wilson International Center, and Gloria Cresswell at the College of Marine Studies, worked with me constantly on this book, suffering many pages of manuscript with patience and skill. To them I owe a great debt. Finally I wish to express in print my appreciation to Dr. Charles Mason and his colleagues in the Documents Department of the Morris Library of the University of Delaware for their help and hospitality during my erratic hours of research.

Essentially I have tried to provide an overview of the development of American marine policy for national security, the merchant marine, fisheries, seabed minerals, and pollution of the ocean environment. History, tempered by economic sense and political reality, should help in the formulation of sound laws to govern America's precious marine environment. Certain contemporary problems and issues that will require wise political decisions have been delineated, bearing in mind that both domestic and international factors must be considered in the choice of U.S. marine policy. In the future the oceans, the seabed, and the coastal zone will need vigilant public attention, and I trust this book may provide both factual background and an analytical framework for those who care about the marine environment.

Gerard J. Mangone

Newark, Delaware
7 July 1977

1 The United States as a Maritime Power

The European discoverers of North America—Leif Ericsson, Christopher Columbus, John Cabot, Giovanni da Verrazzano, and Jacques Cartier—came sailing bravely across the vast unchartered Atlantic ocean to touch a wild coast-
land, offset with islands and indented with unspoiled rivers. Subsequent English
voyagers who settled along the shores from Maine to Georgia crossed the heaving seas in frail vessels, with more guidance from God than from maritime
science. For most of their rugged history these settlers clung to the rim of the
ocean for security, food, and trade. All the original colonies that formed the
United States had a seacoast, and the small centers of population clustered
around the ports of Boston, New York, Philadelphia, Baltimore, and Charleston.[1]

Since 1789 the United States has grown to a great world power, with a land
area of more than 3,600,000 square miles and a population exceeding 210 million, but it has never lost close contact with the oceans. Although America
turned inward in the nineteenth century to develop its land mass, World War I
and World War II emphasized the importance of the seas to national defense.
Moreover, by the 1960s the republic began to perceive new values in the surrounding seas. In addition to the traditional uses of the marine environment for
national security, for trade, and for food, both government and industry realized
the potential of further exploitation of the seabed's resources, which new
scientific knowledge and technological developments had made possible. About
the same time the American people began to appreciate the worth of the marine
environment to the balance of nature and the quality of human life.

A host of presidential proclamations and orders, Congressional legislation,
and international conventions have been shaping U.S. policy for the oceans and
the seabed in complex and controversial ways. Indeed, without a wise use of
the oceans and the seabed that cover some 70 percent of the surface of the
earth, prospects for the future security and prosperity of the United States
appear dim. Few countries of the world have been so attached to the sea in the
past and have such a great stake in its future as the United States.

American Streams, Rivers, and Seas

More than 75 percent of the population of the United States lives in states that
are bounded by the oceans and the Great Lakes. Within thirty coastal states,

1

almost half the urban counties of America touch the seas. Close to 90 percent of the increase in the population during the 1960s and 1970s occurred in coastal states. More and more Americans have been moving nearer to large bodies of water for their livelihood and their leisure. Including Alaska, Hawaii, four island groups in the Atlantic ocean, and nine island groups in the Pacific ocean, the United States has a general coastline of 12,283 statute miles. The shoreline of all the coasts, offshore islands, sounds, bays, rivers, and creeks washed by tidal waters amount to 88,633 miles. From Maine to Florida the Atlantic coast sweeps southwestward more than 2000 miles; the Gulf of Mexico coastline of the southern states is 1631 miles long; while California, Oregon, and Washington front 1300 miles to the Pacific ocean. Alaska alone has a coastline of 6640 miles with a shoreline touched by tidal waters totaling 33,904 miles.[2]

The continental shelf of the United States, that submerged rim of the land mass, that geologically forms part of the American continent, contains many exploitable resources of sand, shell, phosphates, petroleum, and minerals. But the continental shelf is irregularly shaped, underlying various depths of water. Extending outward under the seas from the dry land, dropping sharply at the margin of the continental slope toward the deep seabed, the American shelf from Maine to New Jersey reaches up to two hundred miles from shore. Southward it narrows to only about twenty miles at Cape Hatteras, widening again to about seventy miles off Georgia, then narrowing to a few hundred yards off the southeastern coast of Florida. In the Gulf of Mexico about 135,000 square miles of continental shelf lie under water that is less than 350 feet in depth. But on the west coast from California to Washington the edge of the shelf drops precipitately and reaches only ten miles from shore, although there are shoals and rises as far out as 150 miles that could be considered as part of the continental shelf. Off Alaska, however, the Bering Sea is very shallow, and the underlying shelf is quite flat, extending as far out as four hundred miles from the shoreline. None of these measurements is static. A continuing rise in sea level has been recorded by tide gauges along the coasts of the United States. From 1930 to 1970, along the northern Atlantic shores, for example, the ocean may have risen almost a foot.

Oceanographers study the complex movement of the heaving tides and the currents of the oceans, and analyze the properties of sea water. Much remains to be learned about the seabed, its contours, shifts in the tectonic plates of the earth's crust, and sedimentary composition as well as the habits of the teeming crustacea and fish that inhabit the marshlands and salt oceans. But even a brief description of the physical dimensions of the coastline and the water currents that hem the United States reveal the dynamic interface of land and sea, the daily interaction of man with the marine environment, and the prevailing need for constructive national policies.

Great ocean currents, affecting climate, marine organisms, shipping, recreation, and the dispersal of pollutants, sweep along the eastern and western coasts of the United States. The trade winds that propelled Columbus to the New World in 1492 also moved water across the equatorial North Atlantic ocean into the Caribbean sea, through the Gulf of Mexico and the Straits of Florida, to enter the mighty Gulf Stream flowing northeastward along the Atlantic coastline. In the Pacific, the current from Japan meets the polar streams from Oyashio, the Aleutians, and Alaska, then drifts southward along Washington, Oregon, and California to be further cooled by the updrafts of deep water in that area, moderating the climates of Seattle, San Francisco, and Los Angeles.

From the brooks, streams, and rivers of the continental United States, moreover, 360 cubic miles of water pour into the surrounding seas and oceans each year. This water carries tons of silt containing the natural ingredients of soil and rocks as well as the washings, deposits, and dumpings of people, the wastes and residues from their bodies, their agriculture, and their industrial life. The chemical composition of runoffs from the land into the sea varies considerably, depending not only on population density and economic activity, but also on other factors, such as the type of soil and rocks over which the water flows and its rate of evaporation. North Atlantic waters receive a chemical load from rivers and streams nearly four times greater than western gulf basins.[3]

As the following chapters will show, the rivers of the United States and the oceans bounding America form a vital system for the safety, economic development, and health of American society. Yet for centuries after the first settlements on the North American continent the oceans and their bottoms were a dark terror-filled mystery to the navigators who bravely sailed across the heaving surface of the seas.

Scientific Expeditions and Oceanography

Although men had used the seas since the beginning of history, knowledge about the depth and profile of the ocean floor, the currents and temperature of the briny water, and the habits of marine life was hardly organized until the nineteenth century. While closely connected to the oceans, the United States was as ignorant of marine science as any other maritime state when the federal government was formed in 1789.

During the early years of the American republic the Congress could find nothing in the U.S. Constitution to support appropriations for "science," yet commerce was clearly within the purview of federal powers. How else could President Thomas Jefferson obtain funds from the Capitol for the Lewis and Clark expedition, which probably contributed more to natural history and ethnography than to instant trade? Under the same wise and perpetually curious intellect of Jefferson the first federal agency to advance science was created in 1807, the Coast Survey, in the Treasury Department, although its mandate was to improve commerce by mapping the American coastline and surveying the adjacent territorial waters.

Headed by an extraordinary man, Ferdinand R. Hassler (who had emigrated from Switzerland to Philadelphia, brought thousands of books with him, and attracted the attention of the American Philosophical Society with his meteorological ability), the Survey got off to a slow start for political reasons. Actual surveying did not begin until 1816, and it soon ground to a halt when Congress required all Survey employees (including Hassler) to be military or naval officers. Not until 1832, when the law was rescinded, did Hassler and the Survey begin to gather data continuously and systematically. Within the next decade enough data had been collected to chart the waters between Rhode Island and the Chesapeake Bay. In 1837 the great fishing grounds of Georges Bank east of Cape Cod, visited by European and American boats for centuries, were first sounded in detail, and the Survey's work contributed enormously to a delineation of the Atlantic coast and nearby waters.[4]

The second, tentative step of the United States into the science of oceanography grew out of a complaint by a Navy officer in 1830 that the navigational instruments and charts of the service were improperly stored, rarely tested, and inadequately maintained. In 1830, therefore, the Secretary of the Navy authorized the establishment of a Depot of Charts and Instruments and appointed the complaining officer, Lt. L. N. Goldsborough, as Superintendent. Among the responsibilities of the Depot was the collection and issuance of nautical charts to U.S. vessels, but during its first years the Depot emphasized astronomical work, testing ship's chronometers by astral observation, and it built an observatory in Washington.

The Depot of Charts and Instruments jumped into the limelight of the history of oceanography in the United States when in 1842 Lt. Matthew Fontaine Maury took charge of the Depot as its third Superintendent. He radically changed the direction, tempo, and magnitude of the Depot's work. Maury began a systematic study of the winds and currents of the oceans through an analysis of old log-books and sea journals. From these records he developed charts, and eventually was receiving from more than a thousand American navigators all over the world additional abstract logs of their voyages according to a general plan of observation from which new and more useful charts with sailing directions were drawn, a copy going to each of the contributors.

Following an international conference in Brussels in 1853, Prussia, Spain, Hamburg, Bremen, Chile, Austria, and Brazil offered their cooperation in Maury's plan, which resulted in safer and faster voyages along the navigation tracks of the world. For example, through Maury's work the passage between New York and San Francisco was shortened by forty-seven days. Maury also began deep ocean surveys of the North Atlantic with the vessels *Taney* and *Dolphin* that had been assigned to the Depot, and in 1854 he published the first bathymetrical chart of the North Atlantic basin with contour lines at one, two, three, and four thousand fathoms. Although drawn from only some 200 soundings, some of them highly dubious, it was clearly an original chart. It was of great interest to the organizers of the Atlantic Telegraph Company who were planning to lay a submarine cable between Newfoundland and Ireland. A year later, moreover, Maury's major book, *The Physical Geography of the Sea,* was published. Systematically organized into chapters on currents, atmosphere, winds, salt composition, temperatures, climates, and drifts, it justly obtained credit as the first textbook in oceanography, running through six editions in the first four years and translated into six languages.[5]

Although many of Maury's statements and theories about the nature and behavior of the oceans were widely disputed by scientists and, in later years, disproved, his contribution to navigation by sail and the study of the seas stands out sharply above the surface of nineteenth century work. In the years immediately preceding the Civil War Maury continued to gather data at the Depot, particularly observations from the unknown Arctic region. But in 1861 he joined the Southern cause with his home state of Virginia, spent some time as a Confederate agent in England, went to Mexico, and finally became a professor of meteorology at the Virginia Military Institute.

Meanwhile, in 1843, Ferdinand Hassler had died.[6] Alexander Dallas Bache, great grandson of Benjamin Franklin, a graduate of West Point with highest honors at 19, professor of chemistry and physics at the University of Pennsylvania, active in scientific affairs at the Franklin Institute and American Philosophical Society, and first President of Girard College in Philadelphia, was appointed second Superintendent of the Coast Survey. Bache brought a knowledge of science, energy, and an art of political persuasion to the Survey. He expanded the sounding of offshore waters and, most importantly, undertook a thorough study through more than a dozen transects of the Gulf Stream between Florida and New Jersey, revealing for the first time the alternate bands of warm and cool waters of that complex mighty river in the oceans. Another important contribution to oceanography in conjunction with this study of the Gulf Stream was the collection and classification of the sea floor sediments. Between 1844 and the late 1860s some 9000 sediment samples were collected off the east coast of the United States. Louis Francois de Portualès, another Swiss who had joined the Coast Survey, drew the first map of the American continental shelf from Cape Cod south to Florida, showing the distribution of the various rocks, gravel, sands, clays, and mud.

No love was lost between the Coast Survey and the Depot of Charts and Instruments of the Navy, nor between the scholarly, polished, affable Bache and the practical, bold, brusque Maury—especially since both agencies competed for Congressional funds to support their activities. After Maury's departure the work of the Depot soon faltered. In 1863 Bache, as the head of the new National Academy of Science, reported that the publication of Maury's charts in their contemporary form ought to be discontinued for want of practical use and for lack of scientific soundness. In 1866 the Depot was renamed the Hydrographic Office, separated from the Naval Observatory, and it contributed little thereafter to the progress of oceanography.

The activities of the Coast Survey also declined despite the adroitness of

Bache. He had succeeded in (1) maintaining up to the Civil War what had been started as a temporary agency to make a coastal survey of the United States; and (2) undertaking essentially scientific studies of the Gulf Stream and seabed sediments under the guise of surveying. But by 1865 he had become seriously ill, and in 1867 he died. Under the Harvard mathematician, Benjamin Pierce, the work of the Survey on land became more important while Congress took an ever-dimmer view of the agency's scientific research in marine zoology and geophysics. In 1878 the name of the Coast Survey was changed to the Coast and Geodetic Survey. Except for another pioneering study of the Gulf Stream in the 1880s, initially by the sailing ship *Drift* and then by the steamship *Blake*, which for the first time measured the current from a meter suspended from an anchored ship, the Survey's oceanographic research work for the rest of the century was nominal.

Another early thrust forward to the study of the seas had been given by the U.S. Congress when, on 14 May 1836, it authorized the first scientific ocean expedition to explore and survey the lands and waters of the "Southern Ocean." Some sixty-nine years earlier the Chevalier de Bougainville, the first Frenchman to manage a circumnavigation of the world, accompanied by a botanist and an astronomer, had reached Tahiti, explored many exotic islands, and collected data, specimens, and ethnographic materials of incalculable value to knowledge. And the great Captain James Cook, with his three epoch-making voyages of discovery that bore scientific investigation to the Pacific and the Antarctic, had demonstrated brilliantly in Great Britain the mixture of political-economic motives and scientific interest that could win public support.

As early as 1821 the U.S. Congress had passed a resolution calling for a small public vessel to be sent to the Pacific ocean and South Seas "to examine the coasts, islands, harbours, shoals and reefs, in those seas, and to ascertain their true situation and description." In 1824 President John Quincy Adams also tried to obtain funds for exploration of the southern ocean to advance science, a project strongly and tirelessly supported by John R. Reynolds, editor of a Wilmington, Ohio newspaper, but the Senate, in 1828, refused to back the project. Eight more years of importunities by Reynolds—joined by the sealing captain, Edmund Fanning—to stir public opinion with the promise of new whaling grounds and rich trade routes to China finally induced Congress to authorize a United States Exploring Expedition and to appropriate $300,000 for the venture.[7]

The organization of the Expedition started badly. Reynolds had sought the full participation of scientists and the fledgling American scientific societies in the project, with an emphasis on Antarctic exploration. The Secretary of the Navy, Mahlon Dickerson, however, saw the Expedition as a Navy operation. He was skeptical about civilian scientists and their participation, and he intended to place more effort on the Pacific explorations than on the Antarctic. From 1836 to 1838 polemics filled the air of Washington. Delays were chronic, several officers resigned from participation in the Expedition, scientists complained, corruption was alleged, and the Expedition seemed a disaster even before it started. But in March 1838 Charles Wilkes was given command of the Expedition and ordered to reorganize it. The number of scientists, some of whom were already disgusted by the delays and backbiting, was reduced. John R. Reynolds was pointedly dropped from the list. Finally, with two "naturalists," an assistant botanist, an assistant taxidermist, a mathematical instrument maker, and an artist aboard, the warship *Vincennes*, commanded by Wilkes, accompanied by the warships *Peacock* and *Porpoise*, as well as the *Relief*, carrying supplies, and two tenders set sail out the Chesapeake Bay from Hampton Roads at 3:00 p.m. on Saturday, 18 August 1838, bound for Madeira, Rio De Janeiro, and Tierra del Fuego.

The Expedition of six ships had hardly been designed for scientific ocean exploration, and they were poorly fitted for the demanding voyages that lay ahead. Three ships were crippled by storms soon after the Expedition entered the Pacific. But despite the adversities the vessels, in pairs or singly, sailed the Pacific from Valparaiso to the Fiji Islands and Sydney, and from the Sandwich (Hawaiian) islands to northwest America. They also made two bitter journeys to the southern polar seas that included the charting of some 1500 miles of ice-bound coast and led Wilkes to claim the first sighting of land of the Antarctic Continent. Almost four years and 90,000 miles later after leaving Hampton Roads, two remaining ships of the United States Exploring Expedition sailed back to the United States via Japan, Singapore, and Cape Town. Some 280 islands had been surveyed; 2,800 geographic positions had been fixed; and an atlas of 106 charts had been compiled. Moreover, the Expedition had ransacked large and wonderful collections of plants, animals, and other items of scientific interest from its years of exploration. A large part had been packed in jars, boxes, and crates and shipped to the United States. But much was lost or destroyed by accident, ignorance, and mishandling either in transit or upon arrival in Washington at the National Institute, which had been given responsibility for receiving and organizing the collection of the Expedition.

Ironically very little public enthusiasm greeted the return of the Expedition despite its stupendous achievements. The entire organization and conduct of the voyages from beginning to end had been filled with rancor. Congress procrastinated in making appropriations for the publication of the findings, insisting that only American scholars should be employed in the work. And Wilkes himself faced court-martial immediately on landing for his harsh and illegal treatment of subordinates. In 1842 under continuous pressure from Wilkes, Congress finally approved funds for the publication of twenty-four volumes (only one hundred copies of each volume!). Eventually five volumes of narrative written by Wilkes, ten volumes on natural history, three volumes on ethnography, one on hydrography, and one on meteorology were published over a thirty-two-year period. Wilkes, a brave man, but hardly an amiable character, kept pressing Congress for more money. But both House and Senate were exasperated by the incessant pleas for the advancement of science, and in 1874 Congress terminated all appropriations for the work of the Expedition.[8]

North Pacific and Arctic surveying expeditions had followed in the wake of Commodore Matthew Perry's diplomatic mission to Japan from 1852 to 1854, but the Civil War in the United States generally interrupted oceanographic research, except for surveys and charts required for the hostilities. Nevertheless in 1871 the U.S. Congress established the U.S. Fish Commission. Spencer Fullerton Baird, a naturalist and the assistant secretary of the Smithsonian Institution, had advocated such a commission. With the traditional boat-and-line fishers blaming the new trap-and-weir fishers for the decline of the stocks along the coasts of the northeastern United States, Congress sought a political compromise by establishing the Commission. Baird was named Commissioner, and given a mandate to investigate whether any diminution of the food fishes of the lakes and coasts had occurred, what the causes might be, and what could be done about it, if verified. With his assistants, he began his work at Woods Hole, Massachusetts in 1871, and although the government intended his work to be "commercial," Baird, as a scientist, had obtained an instrument for sustained and far-ranging investigations of habitats, species, life-cycles, and other data about marine plants and animals.

After a decade of summers along the New England coast, Baird decided to make Woods Hole the place for a permanent marine laboratory. He obtained private gifts and expressions of support for this enterprise, and he persuaded Congress to appropriate $117,000 for a laboratory and a dormitory for visiting scientists. Although the main and practical work of the Commission over the years became the raising and stocking of fish in ponds, lakes, and rivers, as well as the collection of statistics, Baird worked tirelessly to expand the Commission's contributions to science. He persuaded Congress to fund the first vessel especially designed and built by any government for oceanographic research, the *Albatross*.

A 234-foot steamer, displacing 1074 tons, the *Albatross* was built in Wilmington, Delaware, in 1882, and it was possibly the first public vessel to be equipped throughout with electric lights, which were powered by a dynamo designed by Thomas A. Edison. For thirty-nine years the *Albatross* cruised along the North Atlantic coast and made several long voyages, including trips to the Pacific ocean, to gather evidence of marine flora and fauna, their habits and environment. They also studied the effects of salinity, temperature, and currents on marine life.

Of course progress toward the science of oceanography was not confined to the United States. In fact, from 1870 to 1900 the combined efforts of scientists and governments in western Europe and America brought to light more information about the oceans, the sea bottom, and the creatures of the deep than all the previous history of civilization. Modern oceanography may be dated from the sailing of the 2300-ton British naval corvette, *Challenger*, on 21 December 1872 from Portsmouth. This was the forerunner and model of many deep-sea expeditions to follow. Captained by George S. Nares, who had previous experience with a scientific cruise, *Challenger* crisscrossed the Atlantic and Pacific oceans for three years and five months, traveling some 69,000 miles and touching the Canaries, the West Indies, Bermuda, South America, the Hawaiian Islands, Japan, the Fiji Islands, New Zealand, Australia, and even the ice floes of Antarctica. Only five scientists, led by Charles Wyville Thompson, were aboard the ship, and only one of these was a physical scientist, yet the expedition brought back some 13,000 species of animals and plants, more than 1400 water samples, and several hundred sea floor deposits. Moreover, *Challenger* provided the first full and modern foundation for knowledge of the physical, chemical, bathymetric, geological, and biological conditions in the open oceans. The expedition yielded fifty large volumes that reported and analyzed the voyage including soundings, samples, and collections in splendid scientific detail.[9]

Following the heralded voyage of the *Challenger,* other deep ocean expeditions were launched by the Russians, Italians, Germans, and Scandinavians. During the last decades of the nineteenth century Prince Albert of Monaco began to promote oceanic research. And the British continued to support other deep sea exploration expeditions after the success of the *Challenger.*[10]

In the United States the brilliant Alexander Agassiz, son of the great naturalist Jean Louis Agassiz, devoted some thirty-three years of his life to the study of the world's oceans, lakes, and streams. At the age of twenty-four, with a fresh Harvard degree in natural history, as well as special studies in geology and mining, Agassiz attached himself to the U. S. Survey of the Washington Territory and used the opportunity in 1859 to collect marine animals from San Francisco to Panama. Made wealthy by the fabulous Calumet mine in Michigan, which he superintended in 1867 and developed into a fantastic profit-making enterprise, he devoted himself to laboratory and museum work at Harvard. In 1887 he was invited by the Coast Survey to take charge of a dredging cruise of the *Blake,* the first of three in the Atlantic and Caribbean. This again offered him an opportunity for gathering marine flora and fauna. Other cruises in the Pacific took him to Peru, Easter Island, and the Great Barrier Reef of Australia. In 1899–1900 Agassiz, aboard the *Albatross* on a voyage from San Francisco to the Marquesas, made thousands of soundings and dredgings in the Pacific, including a haul at 4173 fathoms, the deepest recovery ever made up to that time. Certainly no person at the end of the nineteenth century had contributed more than Agassiz to knowledge of the configuration of the ocean bottom and the continental shelves of the world or knew as much about marine life in the Caribbean and Gulf Stream.

All science, of course, has been limited by the technology or instrumentation at hand. The telescope opened the celestial spheres; the microscope revealed an entirely new cosmos of teeming miniscule life within and about the human species. At the beginning of the nineteenth century there was little more available for the study of the seas than the ancient sail, the hand-cast lead on a line of hemp, and thermometers that could only register, at shallow depths, maximum and minimum temperatures. In 1843 Georges Aimé in Algiers had designed a *sondeur à plomb perdu*, a device for detaching the lead weight when it hit bottom and recovering a cupful of sediment. In 1853 John Brooke's "Patent Sounding Lead" was first used aboard the *Dolphin*, one of the Depot of Charts and Instruments' vessels acquired by Maury for oceanographic research. The use of the steam engine, moreover, which had still been auxiliary to the main sailing power of the *Challenger*, gradually changed the power of vessels, not only for navigation, but also for dragging, dredging, and lifting samples of the ocean floor. Wire displaced cords and rope. The *Challenger* utilized wire lines on a new type of double-edged dredge that proved much more efficient for seabed collections. From 1874 onward the reversing thermometer came into use (the *Challenger* had some), an arrangement that could record the water temperature at any depth by flipping the thermometer over and stopping the mercury column at that point. But they were not too reliable until the beginning of the twentieth century. As already noted, the measuring of currents had been improved by Pillsbury in 1876, and new propeller and pendulum meters were invented after the turn of the century. To record the temperature of deep ocean waters insulated bottles were also used, and in 1910 the great Arctic explorer Fridtjof Nansen mounted both reversing thermometers and insulated bottles into one frame.

During the early 1900s the U.S. Navy obtained a great deal of hydrographic data in the Caribbean sea and the Pacific ocean for nautical charts to be added to the more abundant collections of information about the Atlantic. In 1905 the privately endowed Carnegie Institution of Washington, using the wooden sailing vessel *Galilee*, began a three-year comprehensive study of the magnetic, electric, and chemical properties of the ocean. This endeavor was continued in 1909 by a new nonmagnetic ship *Carnegie*, the second American ship constructed especially for marine reserach. Interest in the deep-ocean circulation system, moreover, was aroused by the *Titanic* disaster in 1912; however, World War I limited the opportunities of scientists for oceanographic research from 1914 to 1918.

In 1921 an entirely new and priceless invention, the sonic depth-sounder, gave the United States the first opportunity to publish (1923) a bathymetric chart compiled from sonic soundings rather than lengths of wire lowered into the sea. Until the development of the sonic depth-sounder, only 15,000 recorded soundings had been taken from all the ocean floors of the world deeper than 3300 feet, or an average of only one sounding for each 5500 square miles in the Atlantic, one for each 10,000 square miles in the Pacific, and one for each 10,500 square miles in the Indian ocean. Within the following twenty years, hundreds of thousands of sonic soundings provided a greatly improved picture of the ocean floor with its plains, valleys, and mountains.[a]

About the same time scientists were beginning to understand better the circulation of the water masses of the ocean by the systematic measurement of salinity and temperatures, coupled to computations of density, that could be gathered as mathematical equations and used to calculate both rates and directions of flow. Between 1925 and 1927 the German *Meteor,* headed by Dr. Alfred Merz of the Oceanographic Institute of the University of Berlin, completed more than a dozen giant profiles of the Atlantic water circulation taking several thousand temperature and salinity measurements and tens of thousands bottom soundings. No oceanic expedition had been more thorough and systematic, more rigorously analytical in approaching the massive water movements on and below the surface of the Atlantic. They showed how the ocean was fed by cold floods from both the Antarctic and the frigid Newfoundland-Greenland seas.

But men had not actually seen much below the surface of the seas during the whole history of navigation, fishing, and oceanography. As late as 1934 Navy divers had gone no further than 308 feet under water, and the deepest submarines had descended no further than 386 feet below the crushing seas. On 11 August 1934, however, William Beebe and Otis Barton squirmed into a 4 ft.-9 in.-diameter hollow steel ball, with a shell 1.25 in. thick, which was tied to a 7/8 in. steel cable. Near Bermuda they were lowered down 3028 feet into the sea. This phenomenal record for descent into the ocean lasted fifteen years.

At the same time scientists wanted to know more about the composition of the sea floor, especially the geological stratification underlying the oceans. They had learned to dig and dredge near shore and to gather bottom samples in deeper water with coring devices. But as late as the 1930s no method had been found to obtain vertical cores more than nine to twelve feet long even in shallow seas. No core at all more than 2.5 ft. had ever been retrieved from the lower depths of great oceans. In 1935, however, Dr. Charles S. Piggot invented a new device that drove a corer into the sea bottom with explosive force rather than dead weight. Soon thereafter a series of cores, averaging ten feet in length, were obtained from the Atlantic ocean basin between Newfoundland and Ireland, yielding a picture of the sea floor and its sediments never before available to science. Ten years later the Piggot device was further improved by the Swede, Börje Kullenberg, to obtain even better cores of the ocean bottom.

By the 1930s, therefore, science could measure rather accurately the depths of the sea, calculate with reasonable precision the major water circulation patterns of the ocean, and drag up bottom samples as well as cores of the seabed a dozen or so feet thick. But what about the geological structure underlying the oceans, the layers of sediments and bedrock that formed the ocean floor?

---

[a]On 2 July 1923 the Naval Experimental and Research Laboratory was established following suggestions made by Thomas A. Edison in 1915 that the Navy should have its own scientific staff and a laboratory to test ideas and inventions of naval significance. Among other achievements of the laboratory was the development of a system for detecting a submarine by signal echoes reflected from its hull. This was invented by Dr. Harvey C. Hayes, following principles by the renowned French physicist, Paul Langevin.

Were there strata of different compositions, how thick were they, when were they formed, and how?

The search for petroleum in the 1920s had led to the introduction of seismic techniques for analyzing the underlying rock formation of the earth. Since sound waves travel at different velocities through rocks of different densities and are also reflected at interfaces, explosions in drilled holes could be recorded by microphones at various distances and locations to give a rather good picture of the size, contour, and layers of the hidden rock structures. By the 1930s, as the oil companies prospected marshlands in Louisiana for petroleum deposits, seismic techniques began to be used in shallow waters. Maurice Ewing, as a graduate student in physics at Rice Institute, had been employed in this work for a summer, and in the early 1930s joined the faculty at Lehigh University. He first attempted a seismic sounding of the seabed off Cape Henry, Virginia, in 1935. Improving his techniques over subsequent years, Ewing by 1940, working out of the Woods Hole Oceanographic Institution and aboard the *Atlantis* was able to measure layers of sediment of the U.S. continental shelf more than a thousand feet deep. In 1944 Ewing accepted a chair in geophysics at Columbia University and a few years later became director of the Lamont (Lamont-Doherty since 1969) Geological Observatory. In 1953 Columbia purchased the *Vema* for the Observatory, and Ewing continued his seismic patterning of the sea floor with hundreds of deep water measurements, constantly revealing new information about the oceanic crust of the planet and opening bold new inquiries about its origins and dynamics.

By the eighteenth century the maps of the world had already revealed to even a casual observer some peculiarities about the shapes of the continents: notably, the neat way in which the gross form of the western coast of Africa and the eastern coast of South America seemed to be congruent. In 1912 a German geophysicist, Alfred Wegener, had first set forth a hypothesis that once upon a time the earth's mantle had borne a single mass of land, but that over eons the one continent had cracked and its pieces had moved apart. In 1915 his book, *The Origins of Continents and Oceans,* launched the "continental drift" theory into wide and often acrimonious scientific debate. However, the shapes of land masses or even the evidence of fossils, minerals, plants, and animals related to each other across the seas, evidence adduced by geologists or biologists, was hardly enough to convince the physicists. They wanted to know *how* the continents moved across or through the oceans—if they did.

In the early 1930s Arthur Holmes, a British geologist with remarkable intuition, had suggested that the continents might be drawn along the moving mantle of the earth on the backs of convection currents, leaving behind them a trough in which oceans formed. Here was a bold embryonic theory of the sea floor spreading, but the author had little conviction about his own idea. He failed to develop it, nonplussed by both the fantasy and the difficulty of any proof.

Meanwhile, at the opening of the twentieth century a great leap forward in the determination of the age of rocks and artifacts had been taken when it was discovered that the magnetism of the earth over geological time had reversed itself several times. This enabled scientists to calculate more exactly not only the age of rocks, but their original position or orientation to the magnetic poles—assuming the poles themselves had not wandered over the eons. By the mid-1950s ample scientific evidence attested to a "wandering" of the poles, but the findings also seemed to verify that the continents too had "drifted." Still the question remained about the force that moved the crust or crusts of the earth.

During the early 1950s measurements of heat in the ocean floor had been made in both the Atlantic and Pacific oceans by Sir Edward Bullard of Cambridge, as well as by Roger Revelle and Arthur Maxwell of the Scripps Institution of Oceanography. These measurements strengthened the theory of some scientists that heat from the deep interior of the planet was being radiated outward in convection currents through the earth's mantle. Further experiments showed that the heat seemed to be greatest at the ridges rising above the ocean floor. It was also found that these ridges, which contained rift valleys along their parallel crests, were essentially earthquake belts, unstable and active areas of the fissured mantle. By 1956 more than 34,000 miles of earthquake belts under the seas had been identified. Moreover, the American marine geologist, Bruce Heezen, advanced the notion at the end of the 1950s that the formation of these ridges was related to the splitting apart of the continents. He argued that the ridges themselves were the rocks of the original rifts between the drifting continents that were left behind as the continents moved apart.

The stage was then set for some of the most recent theories about continental drift, sea floor spreading, and plate tectonics. In 1960, Harry Hess, chairman of the department of geology at Princeton University, who had been influenced by the ideas of both Arthur Holmes and Felix Andries Vening-Meinesz on the force of convection currents in the earth's mantle and the possibility that deep ocean trenches might be the downward curve of such currents, wrote an extraordinary theoretical paper. Hess suggested that the earth's mantle was convecting at the rate of about one centimeter a year, and that rising currents accounted for the oceanic ridges while descending currents made the trenches into which the cover of oceanic sediments and volcanic seamounts were riding down "into the jaw crusher of the descending limb." Thus, mantle material would come to the surface of the crest of oceanic ridges, spread out, and virtually sweep the ocean clean every 300 to 400 million years. According to Hess, the continents were carried passively on the mantle with convection and did not plough through the ocean crust. But the edges of a continent could be deformed, as illustrated by the west coast of South America, when they impinged on the downward thrusting mantle. In brief, the oceanic basins were impermanent features, for the ridges themselves were ephemeral over 300-400 million years as the convection currents altered, while the continental masses were permanent, although they could be either torn apart or welded together. Hess concluded that the demonstrable uniformities of the earth's topography, static or dynamic, could be accounted for by the mantle convection system.

In the early 1960s such a theory was hardly greeted with scientific approbation; indeed, it was ridiculed by many. Hess himself considered his paper on the "History of Ocean Basins" as an essay in "geopoetry," and he modestly acknowledged that many of his assumptions might prove incorrect. For proof, there could be no substitute for actual drilling and physical examination of the deep seabed mantle, especially at the rifts and their allegedly moving edges in order to make comparisons of the ages of the rocks. It would be necessary to demonstrate that the rocks of the mid-oceanic ridges were the youngest and that they were increasingly older *on both sides* of the ridge as the sea floor spreads under the force of the convection currents. L. W. Morely, a Canadian geologist, as well as Frederick Vine and D. H. Matthews of Cambridge University, England had made important contributions to the testing of the hypothesis by suggesting that magnetic anomalies—the reversing of magnetic fields over the history of the earth—could help prove the comparative ages of the rocks on either side of rifts. And data slowly began to accumulate showing the pattern of magnetic anomalies along the oceanic ridges, which permitted a computation of the rate of spreading of the ocean floor. Nevertheless, there were problems. For example, the South Atlantic sediments seemed more or less uniform over the seabed, a paradox if sea floor spreading were a fact.

Only extensive drilling in great water depths through the sediments could help give answers, and in 1964 the U.S. National Science Foundation began supporting scientists from four American oceanographic institutions in a Joint Oceanographic Institutions Deep Earth Sampling Program (JOIDES). On 20 December 1968, after some years of planning, the *Glomar Challenger,* held in fixed position by an acoustic beacon, a shipboard computer, and auxiliary motors, started drilling into the seabed floor 2.5 miles under the South Atlantic on the side of the mid-oceanic ridge. After boring into the seabed for 360 feet, the drill encountered the basaltic basement and the hole was abandoned. Fossil samples drawn from the cores from his hole and several others along the Mid-Atlantic ridge clearly indicated that the rocks closest to the crest of the ridge were some million years younger than rocks at the edge of the ridge areas, and they confirmed the rate of spreading that had been suggested by the magnetic anomalies. Subsequent years of research have further proved the phenomenon of sea floor spreading and gave rise to the theory of plate tectonics, the notion of six or more mammoth rigid plates of earth rising at the oceanic ridges and crumbling in trenches, with both the ridges and the trenches as manifest earthquake centers.

In 1972 an international project called FAMOUS (French-American Mid-Ocean Underseas Study) was initiated to examine in detail the tectonic and volcanic processes accountable for the formation of new oceanic crust. During the following years surface ships, including the *Glomar Challenger,* from the United States, Canada, England, and France made over twenty-five cruises for exploration and drilling to a small area on the Mid-Atlantic ridge at 36°50'N. Then, in 1973 and 1974 the first manned submersibles—the French *Archimede* and *Cyana* and the American *Alvin*—actually explored a valley, about 20 km. long and 1 km. wide at the center, which opened to 8 km. at either end. The valley lay from 1400 to 1700 fathoms under the sea. Direct observation revealed the episodic volcanic activity in the valley center and the continuous faulting along the rift that slowly leads to an accretion of oceanic crust and the edge of the tectonic plate.[11]

All these advances in the science of "oceanography" (a word which came into English usage in 1883 and which embraced functions that had previously been subsumed under hydrography) became more and more costly, rising from tens of thousands to tens of millions of dollars for research projects. The expenses for vessels, instruments, cruises, collections, experiments, analyses, and publication could hardly be met by private contributions alone, although they had played an important role in several expeditions. Also, the rightful interest of the public in naval defense, ocean commerce, and marine resource development could not completely be divorced from pure scientific research. Yet the formulation of public policy in the United States for the use of the seas tended to be sporadic and largely couched in the interests of the Navy. Institutional growth, both for the development of oceanography and the implementation of American marine policies, was sluggish, often starved for financial support as the fickle interest of Congress and the President vacillated from year to year.

Institutional Development and National Marine Policy

The Depot of Charts and Instruments in the U.S. Navy that had flourished under Maury became the Hydrographic Office in 1866. Then in 1878 the name of the Coast Survey, first organized by Hassler, was changed to the Coast and Geodetic Survey to express its greater emphasis on land surveys, and in 1903 both the Survey and the U.S. Fish Commission, renamed the Bureau of Commercial Fisheries, were placed under the Department of Labor and Commerce. Both these agencies remained under Commerce when the Department was separated from Labor in 1913.

Meanwhile private and educational resources began to flow more generously into marine studies. By 1885 Baird had established his marine laboratory at Woods Hole, patterned on ideas from the famed *Stazione Zoologica* in Naples that had been started a decade earlier by a German zoologist. Two years after Baird's death the Marine Biological Laboratory, which was privately financed, began its summer program for visiting scholars and students from all over the

United States. The Marine Biological Laboratory proved to be extraordinarily seminal in spreading American interest in coastal and ocean research.

In 1892 Stanford University opened its first marine laboratory on the Pacific coast at Pacific Grove in a two-story frame building only twenty-five feet wide and sixty feet long. At the same time William Emerson Ritter, who had studied at Harvard University during the very years that the Marine Biological Laboratory had been established on Cape Cod and had become an instructor of biology at the University of San Diego, was seeking a permanent marine laboratory on the coast. For some years he used temporary headquarters, but fortunately one summer met Edward W. Scripps, a wealthy newspaper tycoon, and his half-sister Ellen Browning Scripps. Ritter captured their interest and opened their generous purse to marine research. In 1905 the Scrippses provided money for some buildings in La Jolla cove, north of San Diego, and also donated their yacht *Loma* for research. Disaster followed when, a year later the yacht was wrecked and the town council approved an outfall of sewage pipes into the cove. Again the Scrippses were generous, offering funds to purchase land and establish a laboratory north of the cove as well as helping to build and equip a new research vessel, the *Alexander Agassiz*. In 1909 the first building of the "George H. Scripps Memorial Marine Biological Laboratory" was erected, which became part of the University of California three years later as the Scripps Institution for Biological Research. Gradually Ritter guided the work of the Institution toward marine physics and chemistry in addition to biology, and in 1925, two years after Ritter's retirement, it became the Scripps Institution of Oceanography.

Despite the historical dependence of the United States on the seas and despite the growth of both public agencies and private organizations with marine interests at the turn of the twentieth century, as late as the 1920s there had been no comprehensive analysis of America's interests in the oceans by the federal government. The first General Conference on Oceanography was held at the Hydrographic Office of the U.S. Navy in 1924, largely to discuss a proposed research expedition. With the State, War, and Treasury departments participating, as well as the Carnegie Institution of Washington, the Conference recommended that one or more new vessels be permanently assigned to oceanographic work and that their activities be called the Maury United States Navy Oceanographic Research Program. Although there was general acknowledgment of the importance of U.S. interagency and private cooperation with regard to the oceans, no concrete results came from the Conference.

The need for financial support for oceanography, however, was strongly felt by the scientists. On 27 April 1927 the National Academy of Sciences (NAS), which had been organized by a statute of Congress and approved by President Abraham Lincoln in 1863, adopted a resolution requesting its president to appoint a Committee on Oceanography "to consider the share of the United States of America in a world wide program of oceanic research" and to report to the Academy. Dr. Henry B. Bigelow, Curator of Oceanography in the Museum of Comparative Zoology at Harvard University, was engaged as Secretary and later became Chairman of the Committee. In consequence of this Committee's work and recommendations, the Rockefeller Foundation provided $6 million for the establishment of the Woods Hole Oceanographic Institution; gave support (50,000 British pounds) for the Bermuda Biological Station for Research to work with Woods Hole; assisted in building Ritter Hall at the Scripps Institution of Oceanography; and provided funds for a laboratory building and an oceanic research boat for the University of Washington.[12]

While the private oceanographic laboratories were being developed in the 1930s, the U.S. Navy created in 1933 a separate oceanographic section of the Hydrographic Office and maintained a very modest program of permitting civilian scientists aboard certain vessels for the observation of marine phenomena. Essentially, however, the Hydrographic Office continued as a printing and distribution center for navigational charts. With a worldwide economic depression, funds for basic research and bold new development programs in oceanography in the United States suffered.

World War II dramatically changed the focus of Americans on the seas. President Franklin D. Roosevelt made a vivid plea for a two-ocean Navy in January 1938—barely four years before the Japanese attack on Pearl Harbor, Hawaii. After the traumatic sinking of American battleships in the Pacific on 7 December 1941, a rampant torpedoing of merchant vessels and tankers by German submarines in the Atlantic followed in 1942. The President exhorted the nation to build a "bridge of ships" to Great Britain as a life-line for Allied supplies and an American expeditionary force. More details on U.S. naval operations of World War II will be found in the next chapter. During this period both the naval agencies and the civilian laboratories engaged in military oceanography, emphasizing research on water acoustics, wave propagation, underwater explosive phenomena, and geophysics, and accelerating and expanding their activities in the war effort. One result was a large increase in the number of people trained to interpret the marine environment. Before 1941 there had been about 50 civilian professional oceanographers in the United States; in 1945 there were upwards of 330.

Following World War II, moreover, an Oceanographic Division was established in the U.S. Hydrographic Office while an active program of contract research on oceanography was started in 1946 in the Office of Naval Research, formerly the Office of Research and Inventions. In 1949 the National Academy of Sciences again examined the state of marine sciences in the United States and published *Oceanography, 1951*. But the report contained only twenty-eight pages of text and eight pages of appendices. The nine recommendations of the Committee were quite modest, extremely bland, and without much political attraction. The Committee soon disbanded. For marine science the issue of the report came at a relatively inauspicious time, with the attention of the United

States riveted on the postwar economic recovery of Europe and the June 1950 aggression of North Korea against South Korea involving UN forces.

During the early 1950s the government agencies in Washington continued to seek advice from the ocean science community in view of the changing nature of naval warfare, the plight of the merchant marine, and new problems in fisheries (all of which will be examined in later chapters). They particularly requested help in preparation for the first UN Law of the Sea Conference held in 1958. An Informal Oceanic Discussion Group (IODG) was formed in Washington composed of both scientists and government officials with marine concerns; then in 1956 the Office of Naval Research, the Atomic Energy Commission, and the Bureau of Commercial Fisheries, which had been represented in the IODG, urged the National Academy of Sciences to appoint a group of experts who might be called on for advice on oceanic problems. In 1957, therefore, the Academy chose Harrison Brown, Professor of Geochemistry at the California Institute of Technology (not an oceanographer) as chairman of a new Committee on Oceanography and Athelstan Spilhaus, Dean of the University of Minnesota's Institute of Technology as vice-chairman. Beginning on 15 February 1959 the Committee published a twelve-chapter report, *Oceanography, 1960–1970,* strongly recommending that the federal government assume responsibility for an expanded national program in research, education, training, and construction to be supported by a three-fold increase in expenditures in the following decade.[13]

Meanwhile, the U.S. government itself was increasingly conscious of the need to encourage basic scientific research and to exploit technological developments for the benefit of the nation.[14] The Atomic Energy Commission had been established in 1946; the National Science Foundation in 1950; and the National Aeronautic and Space Administration in 1958. A year later Executive Order 10807 created the Federal Council for Science and Technology "to promote, coordinate, and improve planning and managements in Federal programs in science and technology." Among the first items considered by the Council after it was formed was oceanographic research, just as the National Academy of Science Committee on Oceanography began to publish its report. In the following years the Council worked through a number of interagency committees for atmospheric sciences, natural resources, materials handling, and notably, oceanography. The charge of the Interagency Committee for Oceanography established early in 1960 was "to develop a national oceanographic program."

From 1959 onward the tune of the federal government about oceanography changed and the tempo on interest both in the White House and Congress accelerated. The Chief of Naval Operations, Admiral Arleigh Burke, backed a long-range planning program for U.S. Navy oceanography set forth in a report, *Ten Years in Oceanography,* on 1 January 1959. On 23 February 1961 John F. Kennedy became the first president to use the word "oceanography" in a major message to Congress. Two weeks earlier Congressman George P. Miller had already introduced a bill to create a new National Oceanographic Council to develop long-range plans, coordinate interagency programs, establish a new data and instrumentation center, and improve research in marine affairs. This was the first of several bills, dozens of hearings, and scores of amendments, conferences, and reports by the United States 87th, 88th, and 89th Congresses between 1961 and 1965. They all ultimately led to the Marine Resource and Engineering Development Act of 1966. Finally, under Reorganization Plan 2 of 1962, the Office of Science and Technology (OST) was created. Jerome B. Wiesner, an electrical engineer and former president of the Massachusetts Institute of Technology, headed OST and also acted as special adviser to the President on scientific affairs. Edward Wenk, Jr., an engineer with considerable government experience, was made executive secretary to both OST and the Federal Council for Science and Technology.

The committees and subcommittees of Congress had quickly responded to the appeal for legislation and appropriations for the new interest of the United States in marine affairs. The Senate, through the Armed Services, Commerce, Foreign Relations, Interior-Insular Affairs, and Public Works committees considered several marine and off-shore issues, creating subcommittees on Oceanography (Commerce), Ocean Space (Foreign Relations), and Outer Continental Shelf (Interior and Insular Affairs) that indicated the breadth of national concern about the seas. As early as February 1959 the House Merchant Marine and Fisheries Committee had established a Special Subcommittee on Oceanography and thereafter the Armed Services, Foreign Affairs, Government Operations, and Interior and Insular Affairs committees developed a larger competence in organization and staff to assess the future of marine affairs for America. Spending for federal oceanographic programs, only $10 million in fiscal year 1953, had risen to $62.1 million by FY 1961.[15] Some of the laws from 1961 to 1965 that responded to a revived interest in marine sciences were the removal of geographical limitations on operations of the Coast and Geodetic Survey (15 April 1961); expanded functions of Coast Guard in oceanographic research (5 October 1961); expanded authority of the Secretary of the Interior and Geological Survey beyond the national domain (5 September 1962); new co-operative Federal-State research and development programs in fisheries (20 May 1964); Public Law Land Review Commission to include mineral resources on outer continental shelf (19 September 1964); and exemption of oceanic research vessels from certain inspection taxes (30 July 1965).

On 12 September 1963 Athelstan Spilhaus coined the phrase "sea grant colleges" in an address before the American Fisheries Society. He urged that just as the United States under the Morill Act of 1862 had granted land to the states of the Union, with proceeds from the sale of such lands to endow, support, and maintain colleges related to agriculture and the mechanic arts, so too the United States should make grants of seashore and water up to the territorial limits of the United States for the use of sea grant colleges as "experimental plots." Spilhaus interested Congressman Paul Rogers of Florida to his bold idea. Through

John Knauss, Dean of the Graduate School of Oceanography at the University of Rhode Island, Spilhaus stimulated Senator Claiborne Pell of Rhode Island to introduce S. 2349, a National Sea Grant College and Program Act, in 1965. A House bill, introduced by Congressman Paul G. Rogers in July 1966, somewhat modified the Pell provisions and was substituted for the Senate bill as an amendment to the Marine Resources and Engineering Development Act of 1966. As approved it did not actually make grants of the seashore or sea floor, but rather appropriated Treasury funds for the support of sea-grant colleges and education-research programs on a matching basis, "in the various fields relating to the development of marine resources."[16]

Under the Sea Grant program federal funds could not be used to construct facilities, but were intended to finance educational and research expenses at existing institutions. The emphasis of the Act, enunciated in hearings and public statements, was to be placed on the training of technicians, while research was supposed to be of a "practical" nature, designed to help the United States best exploit its marine resources. The Act, approved as an amendment to the Marine Resources and Engineering Development Act of 1966, had authorized $5 million for FY 1967 and $15 million for FY 1968 to be disbursed through the National Science Foundation, but, in fact, only $1 million was appropriated for FY 1967 and $5 million for FY 1968. Nevertheless, the United States was on its way through a highly imaginative system of grants to American colleges to improve research and training for dealing with contemporary problems of marine resource development, exploitation, and conservation. By FY 1977 more than $25 million federal dollars, with additional millions of matching funds from the states, research organizations, training institutes, and the universities themselves, were being spent under the Sea Grant program.

In line with the growing emphasis on scientific competence in the United States and the renewed attention of the government to ocean affairs, President Lyndon B. Johnson had moved forward with another executive reorganization in May 1965 by combining the Weather Bureau and the Coast and Geodetic Survey, and later the Central Radio Propagation Laboratory of the National Bureau of Standards, into a new Environmental Science Services Administration (ESSA). But a more important event was the favorable report of the Senate Commerce Committee on 29 July 1965 of a bill intended to raise and coordinate all federal oceanographic activities by establishing a Cabinet-level National Council on Marine Resources and Engineering Development. The bill also called for an optional Commission of government officials and private citizens to make recommendations on the most effective future structure for U.S. oceanographic activities. The White House demurred on a Cabinet-level Council, and the House passed another version of the bill. But no action was taken until 1966 when a House-Senate conference reached agreement and Congress sent to the President the Marine Resources and Engineering Development Act, which he signed on 17 June 1966 into PL 89-454.

The Act was designed to establish a comprehensive and coordinated long-range national program in marine sciences through (1) the stimulation of scientific research, (2) the development of engineering capabilities, (3) the improvement of education and training in marine affairs, (4) the enhancement of transportation and national security, (5) the rehabilitation of fisheries, and (6) greater international cooperation on the oceans and seabed. It created a self-liquidating National Council on Marine Resources and Engineering in the Executive Office of the President with the vice-president as chairman, and it mandated a citizens' Advisory Commission on Marine Sciences, Engineering, and Resources to report within eighteen months (extended to two years) recommendations for (1) a national marine science program and (2) a governmental organization plan to achieve the programmatic goals. The Council was to dissolve 120 days after the report of the Commission.

Julius Stratton, a physicist and former President of the Massachusetts Institute of Technology, chaired the advisory Marine Sciences Commission, which was divided into seven working panels, served by fifteen professional staff members, and assisted by the verbal and written observations of hundreds of experts. On 9 January 1969 the Commission presented to the President and Congress a total of 126 recommendations in its report, *Our Nation and the Sea.* In addition to its recommendations for a national programmatic plan to improve U.S. marine capability, the Commission proposed the creation of a National Oceanic and Atmospheric Administration (NOAA) as an independent agency reporting directly to the President. To NOAA the Commission recommended the transfer of the Bureau of Commercial Fisheries (from the Department of Interior), the Coast Guard (from the Department of Transportation), ESSA (from the Department of Commerce) and the U.S. Lake Survey (from the Corps of Engineers), as well as the transfer to NOAA of certain programs, such as the National Oceanographic Data Center and the National Sea Grant Program.[b]

Congressional hearings and an extensive review of the Marine Sciences (Stratton) Commission recommendations followed in 1969 and the early months of 1970. President Richard M. Nixon on 9 July 1970 proposed to Congress two executive reorganization plans (Nos. 3 and 4): the *first* established a new independent Environmental Protection Agency (EPA), with various functions relating to waste management, pollution, and health standards to be transferred from the departments of Interior; Health, Education, and Welfare; Agriculture; Atomic Energy Commission; Council on Environmental Quality; and the Federal

---

[b]At one time the idea of a National Oceanic and Atmospheric Administration was opposed by three Cabinet departments, the Bureau of the Budget, and the Corps of Engineers. The advocates of a bold comprehensive national oceanic program, including members of the Stratton Commission, the staff of the National Marine Resources and Engineering Council, and some Congressmen, had been disappointed that NOAA had not been made an independent agency, but relieved that the agency wound up in the Department of Commerce rather than the Department of the Interior via Presidential Reorganization Plan No. 4, 1970.

Radiation Council to EPA. More will be said about EPA in Chapter 6. The *second* reorganization plan of President Nixon created NOAA within the Department of Commerce, not as an independent agency. Otherwise the President's plan generally followed the Stratton Commission recommendations. However, the Coast Guard, which had been transferred to the Department of Transportation from the Treasury Department in 1967, was left in Transportation, retaining all its functions except data buoy development.

In his message to Congress on the reorganization, Nixon had said, "The global oceans, which constitute nearly three-fourths of the surface of our planet, are today the least-understood, the least-developed, and the least-protected part of our earth." He emphasized that the United States already had the scientific, technical, and administrative resources scattered throughout its federal agencies, but that it was necessary to bring them together for an effective, unified approach to contemporary oceanic and atmospheric problems. Congressional hearings on the two plans were held in July and August. Minor opposition to the reorganization was voted down in both houses. Thus NOAA started its life on 3 October 1970, with ESSA as its largest initial component, which had a personnel strength of 10,000 and a budget of $200 million. On 19 February 1971 Robert W. White, who had been the Administrator of ESSA, became the Administrator of NOAA. Although the National Council on Marine Resources and Engineering Development had been scheduled to self-destruct 120 days after the Stratton Commission Report, it was not liquidated until April 1971.

Since the end of the 1960s a plethora of legislation and agency reorganizations have involved more federal agencies with the problems and issues related to the uses of the oceans, the seabed, and the coastal zone of the United States. Additional details on these changes in responsibilities and organizations will be found in succeeding chapters. But the complexity of articulating national policy for the oceans in the 1970s can be seen in some of the metamorphoses of the federal bureaucracy in recent years.

On 8 April 1942, the U.S. Navy's Hydrographic Office and the Naval Observatory, both direct descendants of Maury's Depot of Charts and Instruments, were transferred from the Bureau of Navigation to the Chief of Naval Operations. After World War II an extensive Office of Naval Research, with far-reaching interests in studies, analyses, and reports that contributed to the more effective role of the Navy, was established in 1946. Moreover, in line with the modernization of missions and titles, the name of the Hydrographic Office was changed to the Naval Oceanographic Office on 10 July 1962. The office of the Oceanographer of the Navy, responsible to the Chief of Naval Operations, was created in the summer of 1966.

In 1960 the National Oceanographic Data Center had also been established at the Naval Hydrographic Office for procuring, storing, and disseminating data for educational, scientific, and commercial purposes. In 1962 the Instrumentation Department became the Navy Oceanographic Instrumentation Center and then, in 1970, the National Oceanographic Instrumentation Center.

The Department of Transportation, meanwhile, had been organized in 1967 as a separate Cabinet Department, incorporating the Federal Highway, Railway, and Aviation administrations as well as the Coast Guard. But, contrary to the President's recommendation, Congress left the Maritime Administration in the Commerce Department. Moreover, the Federal Council on Science and Technology, which had originally established the Interagency Committee on Oceanography in 1960, found eleven different departments and agencies conducting marine science activities and oceanic affairs in 1971. Still aiming to obtain more effective and efficient use of federal resources, the Council in April organized a new Interagency Council on Marine Science and Engineering (ICMSE).

Thereafter Congress itself on 16 August 1971 established the National Advisory Committee on Oceans and Atmosphere (NACOA) to undertake a continuous review on the progress of marine and atmospheric science programs, advise the Secretary of Commerce on the operation of NOAA, and report to both the President and Congress on national marine and atmospheric matters. In its first three reports from 1972 to 1974, NACOA emphasized (1) the necessity of developing a long range approach to international arrangements for the use of the oceans; (2) the need to improve federal management of oceanic and atmospheric programs; and (3) the urgency of utilizing wisely natural resources while developing new sources of food and energy. On 19 February 1974 the Senate unanimously authorized its Committee on Commerce to make a National Ocean Policy Study, with a resolution stating that although the Marine Resources and Engineering Development Act of 1966 had been designed to develop a comprehensive, long-range ocean policy for the United States, the implementation had been incomplete and the goals had not been successfully achieved.

One consequence of the feeling in Washington that better long-range arrangements for the use of the oceans and their resources would have to be worked out internationally was the enactment of PL 93-126. This Act of 1974, coincident with the beginning of the Third UN Law of the Sea Conference in Caracas, Venezuela, mandated to a new Bureau of Oceans and International Environmental and Scientific Affairs in the Department of State responsibility for (1) developing a comprehensive and coherent policy on international issues involving the oceans, science, and the environment; (2) advising the Secretary of State on factors affecting the oceans, science, and the international environment before the formulation of any foreign policy; and (3) coordinating the policy of responsibility between the Department of State and the other departments and agencies of the federal government with respect to the oceans and international scientific-environmental matters.

As will be shown in later chapters, the passage of the Outer Continental Shelf Lands Act in 1953 had vested new responsibilities in the Department of Interior for the leasing and exploitation of submerged lands; the approval of the Federal Water Pollution Control Act Amendments of 1972 had expanded greatly the authority of the Environmental Protection Agency over pollution of the internal waters and the territorial seas, of the United States; and the enactment of the Deepwater Port Act of 1974 had given to the Department of Transportation authority to license tanker terminals anchored or built upon the outer continental shelf for deep water draft vessels. During the same years the coastal states of the United States also took a greater interest in the waters adjacent to their shores, reorganizing their planning and resource conservation agencies, enacting protective statutes, and calling for larger State participation in national legislation that affected the use of the bordering oceans and seabed.

By 1975 twelve different Cabinet departments and major agencies had significant ocean programs, not counting the military-naval commands and operations of the Department of Defense. Their expenditures ran to more than $700 million that year with the Department of Defense, the Department of Commerce, the National Science Foundation, the Department of Interior, and the Department of Transportation accounting for about 90 percent of the total. Programs were classified under titles of international collaboration, national security, living resources, transportation, conservation of the coastal zone, non-living resources, oceanic research, education, environmental observation, ocean exploration, mapping, ocean engineering, and national centers or facilities. In the last category alone, more than $14 million was going to support the National Oceanographic Data Center, the National Climatic Center and the National Oceanographic Instrumentation Center, all in the Department of Commerce; two oceanographic sorting centers in the Smithsonian Institution; and polar ice-breakers of the Department of Transportation. Nautical charts, coastal mapping, and geophysical mapping were being done by the Department of Defense and the Department of Commerce while the National Aeronautics and Space Administration, Commerce, Defense, and the Atomic Energy Agency had general purpose engineering programs for satellite and other sensor systems, data buoy systems, deep ocean and manned underseas technology, and ocean nuclear plant siting. The State Department, the Agency for International Development, and the National Science Foundation loomed large in international cooperation-collaboration programs, while the Department of Health, Education, and Welfare and the Environmental Protection Agency were engaged respectively in oceanographic research and conservation of the coastal zone.

Perhaps one dimension of the proliferation of interest and commitment of the United States to ocean programs can be appreciated from the fact that by 1972 the number of federally supported oceanographic ships for research, fishing and living resources, mapping, charting, surveying, and general oceanographic purposes had mounted to 84 at an annual public cost of $76.5 million. Academic institutions, including the Scripps Institution of Oceanography, the Woods Hole Oceanographic Institution, the University of Miami, and fourteen other institutes or universities were using thirty-three of these vessels; NOAA twenty-four; and the Navy sixteen, with the National Science Foundation, the Coast Guard, and the Geological Survey the rest. Although level funding and obsolescence took their toll in the following years (reducing the operating fleet to 71 by 1975), the effort remained impressive.

Beyond the work of the departments, agencies, bureaus, commissions, ICMSE, and NACOA described above, some fifty other federal interagency committees existed in 1975 to deal with particular or functional problems relating to marine science activities and ocean affairs.[17] The kaleidoscopic nature of U.S. policy for the oceans clearly showed through the shift and shove of bureaucratic politics, while Congress endeavored to be responsive to local constituencies and their marine interests. Continually questioning the national goals of the Administration, Congress seemed less sensitive to the foreign policy implications of marine-related legislation than the White House. Yet no ocean policy in the second half of the twentieth century could ignore the impingement of national interest on international relations, which must be conducted within a framework of international law.

International Law for the Oceans and Seabed

Throughout history maritime states have attempted to impose their will over the bays, coastal waters, and seas adjacent to their shores. At one time the Republic of Venice asserted sovereignty over the entire Adriatic; and the Papal Bull of Alexander VI in 1493 decreed that all lands discovered or that would be discovered 100 leagues west of a line drawn between the Azores and the Cape Verde islands belonged to Spain, and that all lands east of that line, extending around the globe, belonged to Portugal. Soon Spain claimed the exlusive right of navigation in the western Atlantic, the Gulf of Mexico, and the Pacific, vigorously protesting to Queen Elizabeth of England the voyage of Francis Drake through the Strait of Magellan in 1578 into the Pacific Ocean. And Portugal arrogantly assumed the same prerogatives for the south Atlantic and the Indian oceans.

From 1598 onward Dutch companies had sent ships to trade peacefully in the East Indies, but the Portuguese had regarded them as sea rovers, trading illegally with colonies under Portuguese jurisdiction. The maltreatment of the Dutch vessels led to the waging of war by the newly organized Dutch East India Company and the seizure of Portuguese ships on the seas as prize. At this juncture of history an intellectual giant appeared to defend the Dutch cause and write a brilliant chapter of world renown on the law of the sea. Hugo Grotius, born in Delft in 1583, was a genius in letters, theology, and law. Before he was twenty-two years old he wrote a book entitled, *De Jure Praedae* (The Law of Spoils), possibly at the request of the Dutch East Indies Company for which he was counsel. The book itself was not discovered until 1864, but Chapter 12, "Mare Liberum," was published by Elsevier in 1609 anonymously at the author's request. In this chapter, Grotius staunchly defended the right of trade between peoples and argued that the Portuguese had no title to the Indies by Papal decree or to the seas, for the oceans were made for the use of humanity under the Law of Nature. The oceans, therefore, were free for navigation. No one could take title to them since they could not be occupied.

In his classic work, *De Jure Belli ac Pacis,* for which he deservedly acquired the soubriquet of "father of international law," Grotius in 1925 admitted that sovereignty could be acquired over a part of the sea, such as portions shut in by land, like bays or straits, but he maintained that such possession "does not give the right to impede innocent passage." He also suggested that sovereignty could be obtained over that part of the sea along the coast where "those who sail . . . may be constrained no less than if they should be upon the land itself."[18]

Thus, in the early history of international relations, from pure reason arose the notion that a coastal state might exercise jurisdiction over a marginal belt of the sea in the same way as it did over its land territory: namely, to the extent its force permitted. A number of later writers took this view, notably the Dutch jurist, Cornelius van Bynkershoek, who in *De Dominio Maris,* first published in 1702, opined, "Control from the land ends where the power of men's weapons ends."[19] In 1782 it was a short step, therefore, for Ferdinando Galiani, the Italian economist-diplomat, to link the range of cannon at that time, three miles, as the fixed width of the marginal belt of sea over which a state could exercise jurisdiction.

The infant republic of the United States, caught between the mighty rivalries of Great Britain and France in the 1790s was much troubled by the capture of belligerent vessels close to American shores. The arrogant French minister to the United States, Genêt, had actually set up prize courts in Philadelphia and New York for the condemnation of captured British ships, rankling the patience of Thomas Jefferson, the Secretary of State, who otherwise had been favorably disposed to France. Capture was legitimate on the open ocean or high seas: the question was, to what distance from the shore did American jurisdiction and protection extend?

In a letter of 8 November 1793 to Genêt, responding to the French minister's inquiry of 13 September, Jefferson wrote that opinions had been divided as to what distance from their shores states might prohibit the "commitment of hostilities." He noted that the greatest distance to which any respectable assent had been given was upward of 20 miles, "the extent of the human sight," and the smallest distance "the utmost range of the cannonball, usually stated at one sea-league." In his view, therefore, no nation could object to the United States fixing the least distance of one sea league or three geographical miles from the American shore "to which we may ultimately insist on the right of protection," a distance which had already been recognized by treaties between the United States and some powers. On 5 June 1794 Congress approved an Act empowering the federal courts to take cognizance of complaints "in cases of captures made within the waters of the United States, or within a marine league of the coasts or shores thereof." Thus was the extent of the territorial sea of the United States established, and it remained unchanged for more than 183 years, even though Jefferson considered the three-mile limit to be provisional and subject to further review.[20]

Important as the delimitation of the territorial sea by Jefferson had been to the United States, the three-mile rule became the norm of international law in the nineteenth century only because Great Britain, the greatest maritime power of the period, accepted it and, when necessary, enforced it. An Englishman, John Selden, had opposed many of Grotius' views with a learned book entitled *Mare Clausum,* published in 1635, to uphold the right of Charles I to exercise dominion over the English (Channel) sea. But during the eighteenth century London made no claim to a wider territorial jurisdiction over the seas than three miles from shore, except for special purposes. By 1805 Lord Stowell, the eminent British judge of admiralty, could say unequivocally that the rule of law was the same as Bynkershoek's dictum, that is, control from the land ends where the power of men's weapons ends, and "since the introduction of firearms, that distance has usually been recognized to be about three miles from shore."[21] Other states, such as France, Belgium, the Netherlands, and Germany, generally followed a three-mile rule, while the Scandinavian countries tried to maintain a four-mile rule. As early as 1760 Spain had opted for a six-mile territorial sea, and Madrid consistently argued for that limit, although generally unable or unwilling to enforce it. Other states, such as Brazil, Chile, Ecuador, and El Salvador claimed no more than a league from their shores in 1900, while Mexico formally adopted the three-mile limit in 1902, and Japan in 1904.

Although a three-mile territorial sea, an area over which the coastal state could exercise exactly the same rights as it exercised over its land territory, was generally recognized as international law by the turn of the twentieth century, nearly all states at one time or another had exercised or attempted to exercise their authority in contiguous areas beyond three miles for purposes of security, including protection against smuggling, health hazards, or the depletion of adjacent fisheries. For example, as early as 1736 Great Britain had passed a law giving justices of the peace power to issue warrants and cause the arrest of anyone within five miles of the seacoast if suspected of smuggling goods ashore. Prohibited articles found on ships within two leagues could be seized. An Act of 1753, moreover, required vessels coming from plague areas to Britain to make signals to other vessels within four leagues of the coast. Other acts to prevent "hovering" and smuggling were approved in 1763, 1784, and in 1802, the last extending the range of British jurisdiction to eight leagues. The Customs Consolidation Act of 1876, nullifying the previous acts, applied a three-league limit of jurisdiction to all vessels belonging in whole or part to British subjects, or when half the persons on board were British subjects, which could include ships of foreign registry.

The United States had also sought to guard against the smuggling of goods by sea into the country by passage of an Act in 1799 that provided that every ship bound for a port or place in the United States might be boarded anywhere within four leagues of the American coast, searched, and required to show a manifest. After 1807 ships suspected of carrying slaves could also be arrested in this wide belt. A number of cases that questioned the extension of U.S. jurisdiction out to sea were raised in American courts, and it was usually held that a state in peacetime might under international law exercise its authority for reasons of security beyond its territorial sea. On this point, however, under different political circumstances, several writers and some courts disagreed. When the United States in the 1920s attempted to control rum-running into its shores by vessels under a foreign flag within a twelve-mile limit, it circumspectly concluded treaties with foreign nations that allowed the U.S. Coast Guard to stop suspected ships at a distance from shore equal to one-hour's speed by that ship.

A more troublesome extension of control over bodies of water contiguous to the three-mile territorial sea in the nineteenth century arose from the desire of certain coastal states to exclude foreigners from the fisheries close to their shores. By practice and treaty, international law had recognized that sovereign rights extended over the fish in territorial waters as well as over vessels, but to preserve a fishery for their own subjects states frequently sought to prohibit distant fishers from catches beyond three miles from their shores. For example, under pressure from Great Britain, the King of the Netherlands in 1824 had enjoined his subjects from fishing within two leagues of the coast of Scotland. Ceylon, Mexico, and Colombia had all prohibited the intrusion of foreigners into their pearl fisheries that lay well beyond their territorial seas in the nineteenth century. In 1886 the United States seized British vessels from the Pribilof Islands 70, 75, and 115 miles from the nearest land in the Bering Sea, fined and imprisoned their masters, first claiming the sea was "closed," then, special jurisdiction 100 miles from shore, and finally, property rights in the seas themselves. The introduction of steamship trawling led such states as Norway, Spain, Portugal, Italy, Austria, Ireland, and Great Britain (Scotland) to prohibit that form of fishing beyond their four-, six-, or three-mile territorial seas.

Other states undertook the closure of parts of the high seas to suspend the capture of whales. In September 1907 the Minister of Agriculture of Argentina declared that an area 10.5 nautical miles from the shore would be under State control for the regulation of fisheries. Russia first attempted to bar all foreign vessels from approaching within 100 miles of her possessions in Asia and Alaska in 1821, a claim stoutly resisted by other states and never enforced. Then the Tsar set up limits of ten miles against sealers for some coasts and thirty miles for others, and finally asserted a twelve-mile customs zone in 1908 and a twelve-mile fisheries licensing area in 1911.

In sum, the three-mile limit of the territorial sea, although never universally acknowledged, became the standard international rule of the nineteenth century, with a recognition, increasingly by international agreement, that certain contiguous zones might come under the control of the coastal state for special purposes of protection, but not for the exercise of sovereign rights. Yet many officials, jurists, and scholars were not satisfied. As the century closed, the private

Institut de Droit International at Paris in 1895 observed that the three-mile limit "ordinarily adopted" not only was insufficient for the protection of coastal fisheries, but also failed to correspond to the range of cannons placed on the shore. The *Institut* called for a territorial sea of six miles, in which all ships without distinction would have the right of innocent passage. In case of war, a belligerent state might regulate or bar the passage of ships in its territorial sea while a neutral might deny the access of warships to its territorial sea. With respect to bays, the *Institut* urged the width of the territorial sea to follow the contours of the coast, but no claim wider than ten miles should be permitted unless historical usage sanctioned a greater width.

Passage through international straits has also been a troublesome question of international law. For those straits no wider than 12 miles and threading the shores of two opposite states, the *Institut* believed a median line of territorial seas should be drawn between them. But it insisted that straits that passed through the territory of a single state and were indispensable to the marine communications of two or more states other than the coastal state should never be blocked. Moreover, the *Institut* would have allowed a state to exercise jurisdiction over a strait through its territory even wider than twelve miles if the entrance and exit of such a strait were not wider than twelve miles.[22]

None of the articles of the *Institut de Droit International* which, with some amendments, were also adopted by the private International Law Association, ever was incorporated into a multilateral treaty. World War I interrupted further peaceful cooperation of the law of the sea. Indeed, the 1914–1918 holocaust drastically changed the possibilities of implementing the rules of naval warfare that had arisen by custom and various acts or agreements, such as the Declaration of Paris in 1856, the Hague Peace Conference conventions of 1907, and the Declaration of London in 1908, which will be treated in greater detail in Chapter 2.

By the end of the nineteenth century scholars, jurists, and statesmen were pressing to codify international law, that is, to make it more precise and unified, in view of the ever-increasing economic and social relations between the states of the world. Various international conventions had already been reached on private rights, such as marriage status, while the International Telegraphic Union and the Universal Postal Union had brought order to rates, forms, deliveries, payments, and so forth for international communications. In addition, the Hague Peace Conferences of 1899 and 1907 had made extraordinary progress in codifying certain rules of international public law.[23]

In 1920 the jurists whom the Council of the League of Nations had appointed to draw up a statute for a Permanent Court of International Justice in accordance with Article 14 of the Covenant recommended that the League continue the work of codifying international law. But it was not until 1924 that the League acted on the suggestion, when it appointed a Committee of Experts for the Progressive Codification of International Law, with M. Hammarskjold of Sweden as chairman. The Experts narrowed the subjects to be codified to three: (1) the responsibility of states for damages; (2) the laws of nationality; and (3) "territorial waters." After further amendments to the work of the Experts and preparations for conference procedure by another committee selected by the League Assembly, which included the distribution of questionnaires to interested states, the League Council called for the first Codification of International Law conference, which met at The Hague from 13 March to 12 April 1930.

Forty-seven states attended the Conference for the Codification of International Law, of which seven, including the United States, were not members of the League, while the Soviet Union sent observers rather than delegates. With respect to the work of the Conference on the territorial sea, two principles secured unanimous assent: namely, that every coastal state was entitled to exercise sovereignty over a belt of water touching its shores, and that the coastal state should put no obstacles in the way of innocent passage for navigation by the vessels of all states in the territorial sea. But there was no agreement on the width of the territorial sea. Some states felt that no uniform distance from the shore should be fixed for jurisdiction over all matters for all countries, given the different kinds of control required by countries with different geographical, security, or economic conditions; other states sought the definition of a contiguous zone, beyond a fixed territorial sea, up to twelve miles distant from the shore, in which a state might exercise control for customs, sanitation, and so forth. This notion was opposed by the United States, Great Britain, Canada, Australia, South Africa, and India, as well as by Sweden, Japan, and Brazil.

No treaty could be concluded in view of the staunch defense of the three-mile limit by the great maritime powers. A poll taken at the Conference revealed that twenty states favored that distance for the territorial sea and they included the states with the greatest shipping tonnage. But the four Scandinavian states insisted upon a four-mile limit, while twelve other states, notably Spain, Portugal, Brazil, Uruguay, Chile, Italy, Roumania, Turkey, and Yugoslavia, either maintained or desired a six-mile limit. Several states also called for jurisdiction over a contiguous zone beyond the territorial sea for special purposes. Nevertheless, the Conference prepared a draft of thirteen articles on "The Legal Status of the Territorial Sea," which was provisionally approved and included in the Final Act of the Conference. Furthermore, the Conference adopted two recommendations: (1) on the legal status of foreign vessels in inland waters and (2) the protection of fisheries, calling for cooperation in scientific research on marine fauna and the protection of fish fry in coastal areas. Finally, the Conference resolved that the work of codification of the law of the territorial sea ought to go forward. It requested the Council of the League to communicate to governments its draft articles while the Council considered whether the Secretary-General should collect official information about baselines used by states for the territorial sea and whether a new conference to deal with the question of the law of the territorial sea should be convened. Thereafter the League of Nations was paralyzed by wars in Japan and Ethiopia and it took no further action on the law of the sea in the 1930s. World War II led to the death of the League itself.[24]

Meanwhile, despite its insistence on a territorial sea of three miles, the concern of the United States about the depletion of its own coastal fisheries had never waned. The mighty drain on food resources caused by World War II only increased the determination of Washington to do something about fisheries conservation, but action to protect coastal species could scarcely be effective if limited by a legal line only three miles seaward of the shore. Moreover, late in the 1930s the technology for drilling and recovering underwater petroleum resources had improved dramatically. In view of the tremendous consumption of petroleum during World War II, Washington also began to formulate a new policy with respect to the submerged continental shelves of the United States in which vast stores of oil and gas might be located.

On 28 September 1945, a little more than a month after the end of World War II, President Harry S. Truman issued two proclamations. The first asserted the U.S. right to establish fisheries conservation zones in those areas of the high seas contiguous to its coasts "wherein fishing activities have been or in the future may be developed and maintained on a substantial scale." Unilateral means would be used where only American fishers were involved, and agreements would be sought where the nationals of other states used such fisheries. The second proclamation—the "Truman Proclamation"—asserted that the natural resources of the subsoil and the seabed of the continental shelf beneath the high seas, but contiguous to the coasts of the United States, were subject to American jurisdiction and control. Just how far out the continental shelf extended from the shore was unclear, but a press release suggested that the average depth of the end of the continental shelf might be 200 meters under the sea. Other nations of the world quickly followed the American example in asserting their rights to the resources of their continental shelves, thus giving consensus to a new international rule. But some states, like Peru, Chile, and Ecuador, with virtually no continental shelf and a greater concern for their free-floating resources, the fish, than offshore minerals, laid claims to jurisdiction over a belt of sea as wide as 200 miles. Thus many of the old questions about the jurisdiction of a coastal state over its marginal waters and new questions about control over the seabed were dramatically raised to public forums as soon as peace had been restored in Europe and Asia.

Under Article 13, Paragraph 1 (a) of the United Nations Charter of 1945, the General Assembly had created an International Law Commission to develop and codify international law. At its first session in New York in 1949 the Commission decided to undertake the codification of the regime of the high seas (in addition to arbitral procedures and the law of treaties), and at its third session in Geneva in 1951 the Commission agreed that the codification of a regime for the territorial sea was both necessary and feasible. Yet from the first year of its work onward discussions within the Commission had embraced questions about the legal status of the continental shelf as well as the high seas, the territorial sea, and the contiguous zone.[25]

In 1954 ten nations, including the United States and the United Kingdom, sponsored an agenda item for the General Assembly entitled, "Draft articles on the continental shelf," but the Assembly decided not to deal with that item separately. Thereafter the International Law Commission combined its drafts of articles on the high seas, the territorial sea, the contiguous zone, and the continental shelf into one draft of "the law of the sea." By 1956 the Commission was ready to recommend to the General Assembly the convocation of an international conference to examine the law of the sea, taking into account not only the legal, but also the technical, biological, economic, and political aspects of the issues. The Commission urged that such a conference embody its work into one or more international conventions.

Following General Assembly Resolution 1105 (X1) of 21 February 1951, the first U.N. Conference on the Law of the Sea met at Geneva from 24 February to 27 April 1958. During those sixty-two days the representatives of eighty-six countries, working with the articles that had been prepared by the International Law Commission, adopted four conventions. The first convention dealt with the territorial sea and contiguous zone. Again, as in 1930, the states could not agree on the width of the marginal belt of waters in which a state could exercise territorial jurisdiction. Although claims to wider margins of the sea had been pressed over the years by several states, the International Law Commission itself could not reach agreement, giving its own view that "practice was not uniform and international law does not permit an extension of the territorial sea beyond twelve miles." Again the United States and Great Britain, with other maritime powers, were reluctant to go beyond the three-mile limit and subject international navigation to greater coastal control. However, the United States did propose a six-mile territorial sea plus an additional six-mile zone beyond the territorial sea in which a coastal state might exercise control over fisheries. This proposal received the largest vote (45-33) of any proposal on the subject, yet failed to receive the requisite two-thirds majority.

Despite the inability of the Convention on the Territorial Sea and Contiguous Zone to include a definitive territorial sea for all states and settle the question of fisheries zones beyond the territorial sea, its other provisions (1) clarified the drawing of coastal baselines from which the territorial sea could be measured, (2) set forth the right of a State to establish a contiguous zone up to twelve miles from its shore for control over customs, fiscal, immigration, and sanitary regulations, and (3) made a rule that no suspension of the innocent passage of foreign ships should take place through straits that were used "for international navigation between one part of the high seas and another part of the high seas or the territorial sea of a foreign state."

Three other conventions were also adopted at the first UN Law of the Sea Conference under titles of (1) the High Seas; (2) Fisheries and Conservation of the Living Resources; and (3) the Continental Shelf. All of them will be described in more detail in the following chapters that deal with those subjects of marine policy. In addition to the four conventions a number of resolutions touching such subjects as nuclear tests, pollution of the high seas, conservation conventions, coastal fisheries, and historic waters were approved. Still the lack of any universal international agreement on the width of the territorial sea and a fisheries zone beyond it, from which so many other legal consequences might flow, troubled international law.

In 1960 the Second UN Law of the Sea Conference met in Geneva to seek a resolution to these issues. From 17 March to 27 April the representatives of eighty-six nations wrestled with resolutions and articles. Some proposals would have let a state establish a territorial sea anywhere it wished up to twelve miles; some would have allowed a combination of territorial sea and exclusive fisheries zone up to twelve to eighteen miles; a United States–Canadian compromise which would have provided for a six-mile territorial sea and a six-mile fisheries zone in which all the "historic" rights of foreign fishers would be phased out in ten years came close to receiving the stamp of law. But by one vote the Conference failed again to reach an accord.[26]

The 1958 and the 1960 UN conferences on the law of the sea, therefore, did not resolve the question of the limits of the territorial seas for nations and the contiguous fishing zones over which coastal states might exercise their jurisdiction. Moreover, although four conventions had been adopted at the first conference, a remarkable step forward in the progressive development of international law, ratifications of the conventions were slow, not all of them being in force until 1966, and some states of maritime and fisheries significance failed to ratify the conventions. To this lack of a universally agreed-upon law of the sea should be added the consideration that only after 1958 did a large number of African and Asian countries achieve independence and, therefore, had never participated as sovereign states in the discussion and drafting of the conventions.

During the 1960s three problems precipitated anew initiative to reach another agreement on the law of the sea. First, the uncertain line that had been drawn by the Continental Shelf Convention for a state's jurisdiction over the seabed, leaving the criterion to 200 meters or "where the superadjacent water permits of exploitation" of the resources; second, the threat that the deep seabed would be used for the emplacement of nuclear weapons; and third, the ways and means of recovering manganese nodules that could be found on the floor of the deep ocean.

The demand for energy had been rising rapidly throughout the world in the 1960s. With ever-increasing investments coupled to new technologies, the exploration and exploitation of offshore oil and gas advanced inexorably into deeper waters. Offshore crude oil production in the United States rose from 190,000 barrels a day in 1960 to 870,000 barrels by 1967. Latin America and Africa, which had had no true offshore petroleum production in 1960, were together producing about 240,000 barrels a day by 1967; and in the Middle East offshore production multiplied almost ten times in seven years, amounting to over a million barrels a day by 1967. More details on the growth of oil and gas discovered and recovered from submarine areas will be found in

Chapter 5. In brief, during the 1960s the drilling capability of petroleum companies advanced from depths of less than 30 meters under the sea to more than 200 meters, the depth limit specified in the Continental Shelf Convention of 1958. Scholars, jurists, and statesmen began to perceive that national jurisdiction over the ocean floor was creeping further and further out from the coastline over the continental shelf by exploitation of the seabed resources, for the Continental Shelf Convention had permitted states to assert control over the resource lying at a depth of 200 meters or "where the superjacent water permits of exploitation."

At the same time the UN General Assembly had been calling for efforts to reach agreement to prevent the further spread of nuclear weapons. In 1963 a treaty had banned atomic explosions in the atmosphere, outer space, and under territorial waters, but there remained a vast underseas area, not subject to the jurisdiction of any state, which might be used for the emplacement of weapons of mass destruction.[27]

Finally, during the early 1960s the world began to learn more about the presence of vast quantities of manganese nodules lying on the ocean floor that might have great value for their content of manganese, nickel, cobalt, copper, and other elements if they could be recovered and processed. But if such minerals could be recovered, who had title to them? Who owned, if anyone, the bed of the sea beyond national jurisdiction on which lay this potential treasure of minerals?

A number of private individuals and nongovernmental organizations had begun to discuss the encroachment of nation-states into the bed of the sea for mineral resource exploitation and the likelihood of international conflict as rival claims and uses of the ocean floor clashed. (Several private individuals and nongovernmental organizations had the issue of the seabed under study at this time, particularly the Commission to Study the Organization of Peace in 1957 and in 1966.) A full-scale public consideration of the issues, however, was precipitated on 17 August 1967 when the Permanent Representative of Malta to the United Nations, Arvid Pardo, requested the Secretary General of the United Nations to add an item to the agenda of the 22d General Assembly, "Declaration and Treaty Concerning the Reservation Exclusively for Peaceful Purposes of the Sea-bed and of the Ocean Floor, and the Suboil thereof, Underlying the High Seas Beyond the Limits of Present National Jurisdiction and the Use of Their Resources in the Interests of Mankind." What Pardo had in mind was a treaty that would ensure that no additional claims to the seabed and ocean floor would be made by states and that the area beyond national jurisdiction should forever be used exclusively for peaceful purposes. He also wanted to see the resources of the area beyond national jurisdiction exploited for the benefit of mankind, under the aegis of an international agency, with financial returns to be used primarily for the assistance of the developing countries.

On 18 December 1967 the General Assembly decided to establish an ad hoc Committee to study the Pardo proposal. A year later the General Assembly resolved to create a permanent forty-two-member committee on the Peaceful Uses of the Sea-bed and Ocean Floor beyond National Jurisdiction. By 1970 this UN Sea-bed Committee had ready a Declaration of Principles Governing the Sea-bed and the Ocean Floor, and the Suboil thereof, beyond the Limits of National Jurisdiction, which approximately incorporated Pardo's proposals. The General Assembly overwhelmingly adopted the declaration with only fourteen abstentions and no dissenting votes.

At the same time the General Assembly decided to convene a comprehensive conference on the Law of the Sea in 1973 to deal with the host of other legal questions that appeared to be linked to any delimitation of the seabed and the fixing of its juridical status. Enlarged from forty-two to eighty-six (later ninety) members, the UN Seabed Committee was charged with substantive preparations for a conference to reach agreement on a regime for the high seas, the extent of territorial waters, passage through international straits, the limits of the continental shelf, fishing rights, and the prevention of marine pollution.

The UN Seabed Committee first organized itself into legal and technological working groups, then in 1969 established three subcommittees. Subcommittee I dealt exclusively with the international regime for the seabed; Subcommittee II dealt with boundaries, fisheries, navigation, coastal resources, and all other issues connected to these subjects; Subcommittee III was limited to deal with pollution, freedom of scientific research, and transfer of technology. From 1971 to 1973 these subcommittees and the UN Seabed Committee itself received scores of working papers, many draft articles and declarations, and a vareity of principles, observations, and other documents from the member states. In addition, a number of detailed Secretariat studies were made at the request of the UN Seabed Committee on such subjects as the exploitation of manganese nodules on the seabed. The specialized agencies of the United Nations, including the Food and Agriculture Organization and the International Maritime Consultative Organization, also provided appropriate papers dealing with international fisheries, marine transport, and other matters. The final report of the UN Seabed Committee to the General Assembly in the fall of 1973 ran to more than a thousand pages in six volumes.[28]

In that final report Subcommittee I had submitted texts illustrating areas of agreement and disagreement among the member states on (1) the status, scope, and basic provisions of the international regime and (2) the role, functions, and powers of an international "machinery." These texts covered fifty-two possible draft articles, in which a number of variances were included, many of them substantively different. Even the preamble to a treaty on the use of the seabed for peaceful purposes that had been prepared by a working group of the Subcommittee was questioned as being beyond the competence of that group and appearing to prejudge the outcome of certain substantive questions.

Similarly Subcommittee II included in its report a tentative comparative table of proposals, declarations, working papers, and so forth, on those subjects and issues that had been allocated to it. Thus, with respect to the territorial sea, including the delimitation of historic waters, bays, and island, the breadth of the sea, innocent passage, and so forth, the numerous texts that had been submitted by many states and groups of states were placed in juxtaposition. Needless to say, the diversity of draft articles on this item and twenty-one other items was considerable. Although consolidated texts had been prepared for five major items, namely, the territorial sea, straits used for international navigation, the continental shelf, the management and conservation of living resources on the high seas, and archipelagos, there was no consensus on any one set of articles.

Subcommittee III, which did not establish its program of work until 29 March 1972, discussed the elimination and prevention of pollution of the marine environment, scientific research, and the transfer of technology. Two working groups established by the Subcommittee received a number of proposals on these subjects and began considering texts, with alternatives, in 1973. Subcommittee III's work, therefore, was even further behind the very limited achievement of Subcommittee I and Subcommittee II in arriving at a consensus on some draft articles.

Despite the incomplete work of the UN Seabed Committee, many states, sensing the urgency of prescribing international rules of the use of the oceans and the seabed in the light of technological developments that were fast exceeding legal constraints, called for the convening of a UN Law of the Sea Conference as early as possible.

The UN General Assembly on 16 November 1973, therefore, by a vote of 117-0, with ten abstentions, expressed its appreciation for the preliminary work of the UN Seabed Committee and decided to convene a first organization session of the Third UN Conference of the Law of the Sea in New York from 3-14 December 1973 and a second substantive session for a period of ten weeks from 20 June to 29 August 1974 in Caracas, Venezuela. Well aware that no consensus on draft articles had been reached in the UN Seabed Committee and conscious of the long, delicate process of negotiation likely to be required to resolve some critical issues, the General Assembly also approved a subsequent session or sessions that the Conference might decide on. In fact, the first session of the Law of the Sea Conference in December 1973 only managed to elect the officers of the Conference and provide an agenda, failing to set the rules of procedure.

As a general policy, the great maritime states clearly preferred a relatively narrow territorial sea, with unimpeded passage through international straits, in order to give their navigation the widest liberty for defense and trade. But other coastal states sought jurisdiction over a 200-mile belt of the marginal seas which they felt necessary to protect and conserve their natural resources, to be called an exclusive economic zone. States that bordered international straits, moreover, rejected the idea of free transit through such narrows if and when they formed part of a territorial sea. Landlocked states and those not blessed by geography with a wide continental shelf could hardly gain from the steady advance of petroleum rigs further out to sea in order to mine resources that would belong exclusively to those states with wide continental shelves rather than to the international community. Nations with distant-water fishing industries, taking their catch along the coasts of other countries, could scarcely agree with the intention of those coastal countries to take jurisdiction over all the fisheries up to 200 miles from their shores. And it was plain that sharp differences existed over the organization and powers of any international marine authority to be established for the seabed. While some states favored a coordinating, standard-setting, mediating mechanism, other states called for a strong, operating, managerial organization: one that could actually exploit by itself the seabed resources or arrange a joint venture with mineral extracting companies.

From 20 June to 29 August 1974 delegates from 147 states met in Caracas to resolve the issue frustrating a single multilateral convention on the law of the sea. It was probably the largest international conference in modern times involving some 5000 representatives, officials, and advisers in addition to nongovernmental groups and observers. They did not succeed.

Progress was made in developing a comprehensive set of working papers; in recognizing that a consensus existed on establishing a 12-mile territorial sea and a 200-mile exclusive economic zone; in acknowledging that an area of the seabed beyond national jurisdiction should be administered by international "machinery." Finally there was an agreement on the procedural rules for the Conference itself, which stressed the necessity of trying to reach consensus without voting and which, as a last resort, required not only a majority vote in committee, but also a two-thirds vote in plenary sessions that must include at least a majority of the states participating in that session of the Conference. Nevertheless, no agreement was reached on the formulation of the articles for a multilateral convention on the law of the sea.[29]

The second substantive session of the Third United Nations Law of the Sea Conference was held at Geneva from 26 March to 10 May 1975 in a different mood from the great assembly at Caracas. Three years of preparatory work in the UN Seabed Committee and almost another year of informal negotiations followed by the eight weeks of committee and plenary meetings in Venezuela had failed to yield a working text of articles that might be discussed, amended, and approved. The leadership of the Conference, therefore, decided to hold few plenary sessions, eliminate general debate, and recommended to the three main committees that they elaborate a single text that would incorporate articles on all the subjects before the Conference based on discussions and negotiations to date. Such an informal "Single Negotiating Text," of course, was neither agreed-on articles nor statements of consensus, but rather served as a starting point for further negotiations. In fact, only on the last day of the Geneva session of the Third UN Law of the Sea Conference were the single negotiating texts of the three main committees distributed.

Committee I had prepared seventy-five draft articles on the seabed and ocean floor beyond national jurisdiction with an annex on the basic conditions of exploration and exploitation of the resources. Committee II had organized a document of seven parts, including 137 articles that dealt with (1) the territorial sea and the contiguous zone, (2) straits used for international navigation, (3) the exclusive economic zone, (4) the continental shelf, (5) the high seas, (6) land-locked states, (7) archipelagos, (8) the regime of islands, (9) enclosed and semi-enclosed seas, (10) territories under foreign occupation or colonial domination, and (11) the settlement of disputes. And Committee III had delivered three separate texts on the protection and preservation of the marine environment; the conduct and promotion of marine scientific research; and the development and transfer of technology.[30]

When the 147 delegations to the Third UN Law of the Sea Conference met again on 15 March 1976 for eight weeks of negotiations in New York, they had before them the informal single text. But their labors through April and the first week of May brought few compromises on the key political issues dividing them and only a slightly modified "Revised Single Negotiating Text."[31] The fifth session of the Third UN Law of the Sea Conference held in New York from 2 August to 17 September 1976 and attended by 156 states intensified discussions on the mining of the international seabed area, but brought no agreement upon a treaty. However a consensus seemed to have been reached about (1) a 12-mile territorial sea and (2) a 200-mile exclusive economic zone under the jurisdiction of the coastal state except for navigation and overflight, and (3) an international seabed area beyond national jurisdiction and (4) some form of dispute settlement. Opinion was split on the composition and powers of the International Seabed Authority, how landlocked countries and other geographically disadvantaged states might obtain some income from resources placed under coastal state jurisdiction, and several complementary issues.

Some of these issues will be explained in detail in the following chapters. In large measure, however, the dynamics of the Third UN Law of the Sea Conference flowed from the efforts of coastal states from 1945 to 1975 to obtain jurisdiction over a very wide belt of the sea and its fisheries around their shores as well as the resources in the subsoil as far as technological developments might permit. This massive encroachment on the oceans by nations, tantamount to a rapid and unrelenting division of a vast global area once legally free and accessible to all, awakened the resistance of the landlocked and otherwise disadvantaged states, which, because of geography, might not share in the plunder of the free swimming resources or the minerals on the ocean bottom. At the same time most politicians of the coastal countries, badgered by scientists, scholars, and publicists, also recognized that even the widest claims seaward across the continental shelf, slope, or rise still permitted an area of the seabed beyond national jurisdiction that might be regarded as the "common heritage of mankind." Yet how should it be shared?

As the delegates reconvened in New York in May 1977, certainly the customary international law of the sea and the Geneva Conventions of 1958 had been greatly altered by unilateral acts. More than two-thirds of the states of the world had extended their territorial seas beyond three miles and more than thirty-eight states had extended their exclusive jurisdiction over fisheries beyond twelve miles to distances of fifty, one hundred, and two hundred miles from their shores. The leasing of the continental shelf for mineral exploration and exploitation was moving into deeper and deeper water, and at least one state, with a broad continental shelf, had granted leases beyond 200 miles from its shores.

Problems and Issues

In this march seaward the United States had played a prominent role. First, in 1945 Washington had announced that it would take control over the resources of its continental shelf; then, in 1966 the United States had declared a twelve-mile exclusive fisheries zone adjacent to its shores; by 1974 America was ready to sanction an international convention giving coastal states the right to establish two hundred-mile offshore zones in which the economic resources would be under their jurisdiction. Finally, in 1976, impatient with the 2.5 years of dawdling negotiations in the Third UN Law of the Sea Conference, Congress approved and the President signed the Fisheries Conservation and Management Act, which took effect on 1 March 1977 and extended unilaterally a "fishery conservation zone" two hundred miles seaward under the exclusive fishery management authority of the United States.

Yet the gains of the United States in acquiring control over its marginal seas and their resources must be placed against the success of coastal states around the world in seizing jurisdiction over wide belts of the sea, the seabed, and the subsoil. Many of those coastal states have had antagonistic attitudes toward America. For a great maritime power the narrowing of the high seas passages by the outreach of coastal states over waters and resources far from their shores spelled political trouble in the international field. In Washington it required a careful reassessment of national policy. Noting the importance of freedom of the seas to the well-being of nations, the expected quadrupling of seaborne commerce within a few decades, the new resources of food and energy to be found in the marine environment, and the growing threats to the ecology of the oceans, Henry Kissinger, the U.S. Secretary of State, concluded in 1976, that these developments carried with them competitive claims and practices, "which unless they are harmonized threaten an era of unrestrained commercial rivalry, mounting political turmoil, and eventually military conflict."[32]

Despite all the efforts of the American people, the Congress, and the President to focus on a national ocean program, despite the several acts and administrative reorganizations within the federal government, and despite the extraordinary resources channeled to scientific research, surveys, vessel construction, subsidies, and other forms of aid to the marine community (as the following chapters will show) the U.S. General Accounting Office reported late in 1975 that the United States "had no comprehensive national ocean program" and that it was doubtful whether the resources of the eleven departments and agencies closely involved with marine affairs "are being applied to best serve national purpose." What troubled many observers of the development of A-merican policy for the oceans was the fragmentation of the decision-making process into several agencies, often competing or overlapping in their functions. Washington, beset not only by the organized interests of the shipping industry, fishermen, energy producers, environmentalists, and others, but also traumatized by the politics of its bureaucracies, seemed inept in setting priorities and in-capable of implementing a strong, purposeful ocean policy to embrace both domestic and international needs.

The contact of the American people with the seas is phenomenal. For a decade the key to the U.S. strategy of deterrence against nuclear attack and national defense has been the submarine launched ballistic missile. Ninety per-cent of American foreign trade has been moving on water. About 2.5 million tons of commercial fish have been landed by American entrepreneurs each year. This is only a fraction of current U.S. fish consumption, which has trebled in thirty years. Some 30 million Americans each year visit ocean beaches to swim; 11 million come to fish; and 44 million to sail or motor in pleasure boats. The offshore recovery of petroleum in the Gulf of Mexico and California extending further and further out to sea became a billion-dollar-a-year industry. About 17 percent of all the oil and 16 percent of all the natural gas consumed by the energetic American economy has lately come from domestic and foreign under-water wells. All the U.S. supply of magnesium and 75 percent of all American bromine comes from seawater. More than 800,000 factories in the United States use water in their production of goods and services—and they have discharged three or four more times the oxygen-demanding wastes into streams, lakes, and rivers than all the private apartments or homes recently connected to sewers. About fifty million tons of waste, sludges, solids, and debris have been dumped into Atlantic, Pacific, and Gulf waters in a single year by Americans in their pursuit of happiness.[33]

This quick and dramatic catalogue of some of the uses of the seas by the United States indicates the magnitude, diversity, and bold challenge of the problems that lie ahead for responsible leaders. Political choices that make for the most efficient and equitable use of the oceans will not be easy.

No precise figures can be applied to all the public expenditures for marine activities of the United States, but some idea of the magnitude of American interest in the oceans, including the continental shelf, the shoreline, and the estuaries, can be obtained from current budget estimates of the federal govern-ment. The U.S. Navy alone by the mid-1970s was costing about $25 billion a year; the Department of Commerce's marine science activities and oceanic affairs programs run well above three-quarters of a billion dollars a year; and the

Department of Transportation, with the Coast Guard, spends an approximately equal amount. The Department of Interior, the National Science Foundation, the Environmental Protection Agency, the National Aeronautics and Space Administration, the Energy Research and Development Administration, the Department of State, and the Smithsonian Institution all have programs in marine science activities and ocean affairs, which together were taking another $200 million. To show the kaleidoscopic nature of the American interest in the oceans, some of the more rapidly growing elements of the federal program (excluding strictly military activities) have been studies and the development of ocean satellites; renewable sources of energy from the seas; the recovery of natural gas and oil from the continental shelf; coastal zone management; and the enforcement of fisheries regulation.

American private and public interests in the oceans and the seabed are bound to conflict. The enterprising developer of the shoreline proposes the building of roads, apartments, and hotels along the beaches, leaving for the future the problems of erosion and pollution. Marine scientists fret at any governmental restriction of inquiry and press to have channels of research and communication widened at home and abroad for their colleagues, calling for additional public funds to support scientific work. The individual sportsman cannot believe that his small fishing catch could deplete a whole species, while the coastal commercial fisherman resents the encroachment of foreign trawlers on banks where he has been fishing, even though the foreign fishermen may be more efficient and taking their catch from the high seas. The petroleum industry earnestly wants to profit from the savings of transporting oil across the oceans in very large tankers of two, three, or four-hundred thousand tons although sometimes the vessels collide offshore causing disgusting and deadly spills in the water. The oil driller and the exploiter of hard minerals would like to lease the seabed as quickly as technology permits, and they are impatient with the fuss of international claims and the slow determination of title by international law. Shipbuilders and shippers, construction workers and seamen, although often bitterly opposed in wage negotiations, make common cause in calling for a publicly subsidized merchant marine. And every citizen ponders the necessity for multiplying nuclear submarines, new surface warships with fighter aircraft, and a billion-dollar weapons system in view of the contemporary needs of health, education, welfare, and other peaceful concerns of American society.

Inescapably the use of the ocean for the safety, success, and comfort of the American people coincides or collides with other nations that use the seas for their own defense and trade, for the withdrawal of resources, or for the deposit of wastes. Unlike the dry land of the earth, which has been totally divided up among sovereign states and falls under the jurisdiction of one nation or another, the high seas have remained free from appropriation by any flag. Without national jurisdiction and with little international regulation, the oceans have been a facility, commodity, and utility for every state that could launch a ship, haul out water, sand, and fish, or dump its wastes into the deep. As already indicated, the political and economic interests of many nations conflict on the high seas and the ocean floor on such issues as the deployment and tracking of missile-equipped nuclear submarines; the innocent passage of vessels through marginal seas and straits as well as the overflight by airplanes; the harvesting of migratory ocean species of fish and mammals; the exploitation of underwater petroleum resources in the continental shelf; the collection of hard minerals lying on the ocean floor; and the means of reducing ocean pollution due to runoffs and blow-offs from coastal states or by the deliberate or accidental dumping of noxious wastes.

Ocean policy can hardly be narrowed to simplistic slogans that will obscure the complexity of the issues involved. A variety of needs and motivations, affecting different public and private interests, has always produced redundancies and even paradoxes in the making of public policy. Leaders associated with the marine environment will not be immune from that democratic political process. But an analysis and understanding of the elements that must be taken into account in formulating ocean policy can be helpful in considering the options and may prove helpful in making better, if not perfect, public decisions.

The major policy concerns of the United States about the oceans can be categorized as (1) security and national defense, (2) transport and trade, (3) fisheries, (4) mineral resources and energy, and (4) the environment and pollution. The ordering of the list does not necessarily reflect the degree of importance of the subjects, but rather encompasses systematically the major marine interests of the American people in the coming years. The five chapters that lie ahead, therefore, trace the historical background of each of these policy concerns, delineating their political and economic context as well as the laws or treaties that have led to new institutional arrangements for particular issues.

Clearly many problems remain for the American people in determining how to protect their country on the oceans; how to best utilize the seas for merchant shipping; how to catch and conserve fish; how to exploit the bed of the sea and its subsoil for mineral resources; and how to guard against the destruction of the beautiful, beneficial marine environment. It is essential to build on experience and examine rational policy alternatives for the future through which the United States may reach its full potential for wise and effective use of the oceans, the seabed, and the coastal zone.

2

The Navy, the Oceans, and American Security

Since the birth of the United States as a nation, the Atlantic Ocean has been a vast moat providing security for the American people against the great European powers and distance from the political troubles of that continent. In addition, the thousands of miles of waters stretching from the Pacific coast to the far reaches of Japan, China, and the East Indian islands have separated America from the pressing populations and turmoil of Asia. With Canada to the north, a country limited by climate in its growth, and Mexico to the south, a land only freed from colonial exploitation and internal division in the twentieth century, the United States had little to fear from other nations so long as it could control its approaches from the sea.

The Early American Navy

At the time of their revolution from the British crown in 1776, the American colonies had no navy of their own. The provisional Continental Congress mainly relied on the arming of merchant ships, commissioned, sometimes questionably, to attack British commerce or repulse attacks. Of the five war vessels that became available to the Philadelphia government during the hostilities with England from 1777 to 1781, only one, the *Alliance* commanded by Commodore John Barry, actually survived the war. In fact, it was the French fleet, with sixty-three well-fitted warships, that clinched victory at Yorktown in 1781 and moved the British to grant independence to the United States through the Paris Peace Treaty of 1783.[1]

Wearied of war and intent on economic repair and growth, the confederation of American states had no money to spend on a navy; the new federal government in 1789 didn't even create a Cabinet department for a navy. But commerce by sea was important to the thirteen states of the Union. While the depredations of the Barbary pirates on Atlantic and Mediterranean waters on American commerce increased in the 1790s, amounting to some $12 million in 1800, the United States paid tribute. But money to the rulers of Algiers, Tripoli, and Tunis could not buy the protection needed to secure both ships and sailors from violence. In 1794 Congress finally established a small navy for use against the pirates, and in 1797 the first vessel, the *United States,* 1576 tons built at a cost of $300,000, skidded into the Delaware River to be armed for action.[a]

At the same time a larger threat to United States commerce stemmed from the Napoleonic wars and French captures of neutral American merchant vessels. Fortunately three frigates had been launched in 1794 while new legislation in 1798 called for additional war vessels as well as the refitting of other ships for combat. Almost at war with France between 1798 and 1801, the United States naval forces of 45 public ships and 365 private vessels commissioned for armament made a number of spirited attacks on French warships until Paris modified its policies.

Beginning in 1803 France and England were locked in a life or death struggle in which ocean commerce with neutrals was a key factor of survival. President Thomas Jefferson endeavored to secure American shipping rights against capture by the two belligerents and to prevent the impressment of seamen aboard United States vessels by the British. His weapons were economic coercion, nonimportation acts, and an embargo of exports, not the expansion of the American navy. The policy was partly, but not wholly successful. When war with England came in 1812 to the United States, where public opinion was much divided, the government had only nine frigates and eight other armed vessels to command against the mighty British navy of one thousand ships.[2] Fortunately for the United States the British had their hands full, first, in defeating Napoleon, and, second, in negotiating the reconstruction of Europe at Vienna beginning in September 1814. The success of the American naval forces on Lake Erie and Lake Champlain, moreover, ended British hopes to establish an Indian barrier state to American westward expansion. Although the Peace of Ghent on 24 December 1814 essentially returned to the status quo ante bellum, it opened a period of reconciliation between Washington and London. Friendly relations with Great Britain and its uncontested navy enabled the United States to relax on its Atlantic frontier until the American Civil War of 1861.[3] Appropriations for the U.S. Navy were slight as energies were turned toward the development of the interior, the acquisition of the enormous territories of California, Nevada, Utah, New Mexico, Arizona, and parts of Wyoming and Colorado through war with Mexico, and the burning issues of states rights and slavery. By 1850 not one American warship could match the best warship of any of the several European powers.

A modest ship construction program of five steam sidewheelers was started in 1850 and six screw frigates in 1855, ships a little over three thousand tons. But the Navy was hardly prepared for the Civil War in 1861, for fifty out of the ninety vessels available were obsolescent. Of the forty listed steamers, moreover, five

---

[a]The American Continental Congress established a Maritime Committee to supervise naval affairs, which was superseded by a Board of Admiralty. The Board was discontinued in 1781, and although the Congress thereafter provided for an Agent of Marine, no one was appointed to the post. By default Robert Morris, Superintendent of Finances, became responsible for naval affairs—such as they were. Under the Federal Constitution of 1789 a Department of War was created in 1790, but a Department of the Navy was not established until 1798.

were unserviceable, eight laid up, and many of the rest scattered around the world. A large number of officers were ready for retirement and on 10 March 1861 only 207 trained seamen were actually available in all the ports and receiving ships on the Atlantic coast. Large-scale recruitment of personnel and a convulsive mobilization of warships by the Union followed in order to blockade the long coastline of the secessionist South from European imports or exports and to dominate the Mississippi river. During the four-year war between the States, the federal forces raised a fleet of some 700 vessels totalling about 500,000 tons and armed with 5000 guns. It was control of the seacoast that strangled the South, for the Confederacy depended on its agricultural exports to Europe to buy armaments and other manufactured products essential to the war effort.

Once the national emergency had passed, however, U.S. concern and care for a fleet to protect the ocean approaches to its mainland collapsed. Within four years after the end of hostilities at Appomatox in 1865, the Civil War naval force dissolved to some two hundred ships, many of them obsolescent. By 1878 only seventeen war vessels were in service, none of them first-rate. As late as 1880 the United States did not have a single armored sea-going ship.

As the United States continued to move west, exploring, populating, and exploiting vast lands, it seemed to require nothing more than a small navy for coastal patrol and enough armament ashore or afloat to provide a defense for its ports. Any attack by seaborne hostile forces other than British at this time was incredible. And relations between Washington and London between 1812 and 1860 were on the whole amicable. Nevertheless, the United States was on the verge of becoming an imperial overseas power, partly by design and partly by the accidents of history. Three major episodes contributed to the ascendancy of American seapower.

First, the opening of China to European and American trade, in the early nineteenth century, the new whale fisheries off Oregon and Washington, the discovery of California gold, the beginnings of steam navigation, and the increased speed of communication between the Caribbean Sea and the Pacific Ocean across the Panama Isthmus all led to the dispatch of Commodore Matthew Perry to Japan in 1852. Anchoring in Yedo (Tokyo) Bay with four ships in 1853, he not only delivered a virtual ultimatum to grant trading concessions to the United States, but sailed away to take possession of some islands 500 miles south of Japan, obtained a coaling station on Okinawa, and dreamed of laying hold of Taiwan as one of the several links in the American naval chain to East Asia. In 1854 he returned with seven ships to Tokyo Bay and by agreement "opened Japan" to American trade.[4]

Second, the United States had already expressed its dissatisfaction with any power seeking to subvert the Hawaiian government or seize those islands ten years before Perry's arrival in Japan. Although the United States itself was reluctant to annex the Hawaiian islands, it was determined to prevent their control by any other state. Inexorably by missionary advice and coups Hawaii fell under the vital interests of America.

Third, Captain Charles Wilkes in the first U.S. Exploring Expedition to the Pacific had negotiated in 1839 a commercial shipwreck agreement in Samoa, islands lying about midway between Honolulu and Sydney. The United States increased its interest in the Samoan islands, especially in the fine harbor of Pago Pago, after 1869, and in 1878 negotiated a treaty with the local government to prevent the islands from coming completely under the dominance of either Great Britain or Germany.

This physical outreach of the United States to Samoa, Hawaii, Japan, and China precipitated a dramatic, large-scale naval construction program in 1883 that marked historically the United States' debut as one of the world's great powers. The first ship to come off the ways in 1885 was the dispatch boat *Dolphin*, initially commanded by an officer who would soon be a national hero, George Dewey. New war vessels followed the *Dolphin* into the sea year after year, reflecting the vigor, industry, and technological accomplishments of American life during the last quarter of the nineteenth century. At the same time the advocates of a strong American navy found doctrinal support in Alfred Thayer Mahan, whose widely published lectures and writings stressed the importance of seapower for trade and defense as well as the need for a transoceanic canal that would provide American linkage between the Atlantic and Pacific oceans. United States foreign policy, according to Mahan, ought to be based on American political dominance in the Caribbean, political cooperation in the Pacific, and political abstention in Europe. As an Anglophile he assumed that Great Britain would continue to balance power in Europe.[5]

The United States as a Naval Power

On the eve of the Spanish American War in 1898, the United States fleet was formidable. It consisted of four first-class battleships, two second-class battleships, two armored cruisers, ten protected (semiarmored) cruisers, and additional gunboats, monitors, and auxiliary vessels. Seapower decided the battles at Manila Bay in the Philippines and the harbor of Santiago de Cuba, with the modern American navy outmaneuvering and outgunning the decrepit Spanish fleets. The war itself lasted only 109 days; but it brought to the United States a protectorate over Cuba and possession of Puerto Rico, Guam, and the Philippine Islands, enormously extending the commitments of American security across the Pacific Ocean to the South China Sea.[6]

In 1900 the United States commissioned its first regular submarine, the *Holland*.[b] Beginning in 1903 the Navy began constructing two capital ships a year. To demonstrate the new power of the United States on the oceans, President Theodore Roosevelt sent the "great white fleet" of sixteen warships and other vessels from Hampton Roads on a four-month, 46,000-mile voyage around the world, including a call at Yokahama.[7] Nevertheless, when the Germans crossed the Belgian frontier on 4 August 1914 to begin a war that was soon to engage every great power, shatter empires, and change the course of history, the United States still ranked only fourth in the scale of naval strength. World War I changed irrevocably that relationship and altered American strategy in the use of the oceans for the next thirty years.

World War I had started with a massive army invasion by Germany designed to overwhelm France. It was to be followed by a rapid transfer of troops to the east to defeat Russia before any British naval blockade of the Continent could become effective.[8] But the next four years turned into a titanic struggle that ultimately hinged on marine transport and sea-borne supplies. Millions of men died in the land armies, battered to a bloody standstill in the filthy trenches of Europe, but victory for the Allies came from the fresh strength of the United States across the seas, largely carried by the British merchant fleet.

True to its traditional policy of no entangling alliances with Europe, America had first set out to uphold its neutral rights of commerce on the high seas. Again as during the Napoleonic wars, the major belligerents were less than scrupulous in observing neutral sensibilities. The definition of goods that were contraband, that is, aided and assisted the war effort of a belligerent and, therefore, could not be shipped by a neutral to a belligerent without liability of capture and confiscation, was arbitrarily widened and eventually included almost everything. Moreover, even ships with goods shipped by the United States to another neutral, such as Sweden, were stopped, searched, and sometimes captured on suspicion of being trans-shipped to Germany. Great Britain's navy dominated the Atlantic and seized American merchant vessels despite the frequent and sharp protests of President Woodrow Wilson. But as World War I progressed, the Germans, on the verge of vanquishing France, resorted to unrestricted submarine warfare in order to destroy the imports of England whose life depended on the sea.[9]

---

[b]The *Holland* submarine was named for John Philip Holland, an Irish immigrant to New Jersey, who first built a one-man, ten-foot long submarine in 1875. It was small, but more workable than some other underwater devices that had been previously used in naval operations. With financing from the Fenian (Irish independence) Society, he launched the submarine *Fenian Ram* in the Hudson river in 1881 and finally, with the aid of U.S. naval officers, the *Holland* was built, the first submersible with an internal combustion engine for surface sailing and an electric motor for underwater cruising.

International law had required the stopping and searching of merchant vessels to ascertain their flag, their goods, and their destination before their capture by a belligerent. However, the very nature of a small submerged war vessel with a weapons system based on surprise attack precluded these legal niceties. In 1915 Germany had a flotilla of 27 submarines; a year later she had 52, of which 18 could be cruising at one time; and in 1917 the maximum of 140 was reached. Submarine attacks killed 223 neutral Americans, 28 of them on U.S. merchant ships, mounting in intensity after 1 February 1917. These attacks drove the President to ask Congress to declare war on Germany on 2 April 1917.

The essential mission of the U.S. Navy in World War I was to convoy soldiers and supplies to Europe, which it achieved with such success that the tide of battle inexorably swung in favor of the Allies. More than two million American soldiers were transported by sea to England and France, mainly to Liverpool and Brest. Over six million tons of supplies were ferried to France alone. Moreover, the first small destroyers began to arrive in British waters in May 1917, and 120 special sub-chasers, armed with depth charges to kill the German U-boats, were sent from America to Europe in June 1917. The sinking of British and neutral shipping had risen to the alarming total of 875,000 tons in April, ruthlessly severing the supply lines of England and slowly strangling its life. With American assistance in supply, equipment, and patrol, the sinkings by the German submarines were reduced to just under 300,000 tons in November 1917. By May 1918 the Allies were building ships faster than they could be sunk by German submarines. By the autumn of 1918, as Bulgaria, Austria-Hungary, and, finally, Germany collapsed, more ships were coming from American yards than from British.

The giant naval construction program begun in 1916 promised to make the U.S. seapower greater than any in the world. But Allied victory raised as many new domestic and foreign policy issues for the American people as the war had resolved. The Treaty of Versailles, with the League of Nations Covenant, had been rejected by the Senate on 19 November 1919 and President Warren G. Harding, elected a year later, began his administration by denying any American approach to the League of Nations. Japan, not Germany, now loomed as a potential threat to American overseas interests, and Japan was linked to Great Britain by an alliance of 1911, subject to abrogation by either party after 1921 by one year's advance notice. The Harding administration realized that the American people were not likely to fight for the integrity of China against the determination of Japan to assert its hegemony over east Asia. They were even less likely to resist Tokyo's designs on Siberia, which had been occupied by Japanese troops during the Russian civil war. Moreover, the days of lavish U.S. Congressional appropriations for naval construction had passed. This was the backdrop for the American invitation to the Principal Allied and Associated Powers (except Bolshevist Russia) to a naval disarmament conference in

Washington in 1922 and to discuss issues relating to the Pacific Ocean and East Asia. U.S. Secretary of State Charles E. Hughes boldly proposed a treaty that required the sinking or scrapping of certain capital ships and a ten-year holiday in the building of vessels over 35,000 tons. The treaty also set a ratio of permitted battleship tonnage at 500,000 (USA), 500,000 (Great Britain), 300,000 (Japan), and 175,000 (France and Italy each) and aircraft carrier tonnage at 135,000 (USA), 135,000 (Great Britain), 86,000 (Japan), and 60,000 (France and Italy each). But nothing was said about light cruisers, destroyers, or submarines.[10] From 1922 to 1928 American naval construction was slight. By 1927 Japan had far surpassed U.S. tonnage in cruisers either afloat or under construction. The London Naval Conference at 1930, coincident with the worldwide economic depression, postponed the replacement of capital ships until 1936 and additionally set a 10:10:7 ratio for cruisers among the United States, Great Britain, and Japan with parity among them for submarines. A third and final conference in 1935-1936 failed to achieve anything. The clouds of World War II were beginning to gather. In 1937, when the limits on ship construction expired, both the United States and Great Britain still lagged far behind their permitted naval strength under the disarmament treaties.

Meanwhile, the conduct of submarine warfare and the rights of neutral commerce on the high seas, which had propelled the United States into World War I, were undecided. None of the peace treaties or other agreements with the defeated states of World War I had mentioned the subject. In 1922 France failed to ratify a treaty signed by the United States, Great Britain, Italy, Japan, and France that would have prohibited the use of submarines by any of them. However the London Naval treaty of 1930, which was ratified by the United States, Great Britain, and Japan, pledged those states to order their submarines to respect international law for merchant vessels during war and, in particular, to place passengers, the ships' crew, and the ships' papers in a place of safety, before any sinkings. Six years later the signatory powers plus France, Italy, and Germany adhered to a protocol renewing these articles of the London treaty. Russia adhered in 1937.

Nevertheless, the United States had already taken a new position on the law of the sea and its traditional claim to neutral rights by enacting neutrality legislation from 1935 to 1937 in response to the Italo-Ethiopian crisis. American citizens were enjoined from sending arms, ammunition, or implements of war to any belligerent, to any neutral port for shipment to a belligerent, or for any use of a belligerent, and they were forbidden to make loans or extend credits to a belligerent in time of war as defined by the President. Beyond this, the President was empowered to forbid the shipment of any other articles to a belligerent. Americans could not travel under a belligerent flag, except as prescribed by the President, and the arming of American merchant ships trading with belligerents was made illegal. In essence, the United States abandoned the "rights" over which it had agonized and fought from 1915 to 1918. Washington conceded that it was not worth risking war by insisting that American nationals should be able to travel safely on belligerent merchant ships and that American merchants should have a right to trade with belligerents in a large number of noncontraband goods and services.[11]

To stimulate the domestic economy during the catastrophic economic recession of 1933 and 1934, some new cruiser construction and ship replacement programs had been authorized. In 1936 the Maritime Commission was established to help expand the American merchant marine through direct subsidies. President Franklin D. Roosevelt watched the rise of bellicose dictatorships in Italy, Germany, and Spain with apprehension, while a militant Japan continued its assaults on China. No one doubted that the first line of defense for the United States was the Navy: year by year appropriations climbed, reaching almost a billion dollars in 1937. Finally, in 1938 Congress responded to the President's clear alert of potential danger by authorizing a massive 20 percent increase in naval tonnage.

Naval preparation for World War II and the direct attack by Japan on Pearl Harbor left a great deal to be desired. To begin with, the total number of naval officers and enlisted men for all operations and services averaged under 108,000 during the interwar years. Then, battleship and cruiser construction had lagged behind the onrush of perilous international politics. Too little attention had been paid to naval aviation and aircraft carriers; too little heed had been given to the growing role of the submarine in naval warfare; and virtually no thought had been given to amphibious operations. But the greatest dilemma for the Navy lay in strategy. Since the 1920s the major U.S. fleet forces had been committed to the Pacific; only in February 1941, at the express order of the President, were three battleships, three carriers, with several cruisers and destroyers, transferred to the new U.S. Atlantic Fleet. Suddenly the United States was confronted with a two-ocean war, a contingency the naval planners had hardly expected in the 1930s. Moreover, the plan to mobilize giant warships heavily armored with long-range guns that would destroy the enemy's battleships at sea, a plan that had dominated naval thinking since Mahan, was soon proven wrong in the mighty contest for control of the seas and airspace between the Allied and the Axis powers.

On the eve of American entry into World War II, the American navy consisted of 17 battleships in commission and 15 under construction; 7 aircraft carriers and 11 under construction; 37 cruisers and 54 under construction; 171 destroyers and 191 under construction; and 111 submarines with 73 more under construction. But this great force had to be divided between the Atlantic and Pacific oceans. Japan's naval tonnage, which had been only half that of the United States in 1922, was 81 percent of the American total in 1941. The surprise Japanese attack on the naval base at Pearl Harbor cost the United States five battleships. Moreover, German submarines swiftly scurried into the Atlantic waters along the North American coast, and during the first four months of the war they sank 87 vessels totalling 514,366 tons. In the single month of May 1942, German submarines sank 219,867 tons of unescorted merchant ships in the Gulf of Mexico and the Caribbean, about one-half of them oil tankers. Only seven hours after the Pearl Harbor disaster, Washington itself had ordered unrestricted submarine warfare against Japan, contrary to all the principles so diligently espoused by the United States in the past an annulling the provisions of the London naval treaty of 1930. But a new era of naval warfare based on bold inventions and improved engineering capabilities had dawned.

Once again the vast oceans provided the United States with the precious space and time needed to mobilize its labor force and industry for war with virtually no interruption by an enemy. In the Pacific the Japanese failed to follow up their air attack with any landing of troops on Hawaii, which might have served as a forward base for bombing California; in the Atlantic the submarine was a grave menace to merchant shipping, but Berlin never managed to put more than a dozen U-boats in the western Atlantic, never attacked American ports, and by 1943, the United States was producing more tonnage than Germany could sink. American and British warships controlled the north Atlantic, convoying millions of men, and millions of tons of munitions, equipment, and supplies from the United States to overwhelm the Nazi war machine.[12]

In the Pacific the United States quickly recovered from its shocking loss of five battleships at Pearl Harbor, especially since three aircraft carriers had completely escaped the surprise bombardment by Japan. In fact, the contest for control of the vast oceans and the Pacific islands that stretched across thousands of miles from New Guinea and the Solomons to the Marianas and the Philippines was largely decided by air strikes. At the battle in the Coral Sea in May 1942, two opposing fleets fought without seeing each other. Their ship-based aircraft carried the attacks. By the autumn of 1943 the twenty-two aircraft carriers ordered by the Navy in 1941-1942 began to arrive for combat operations. This immense superiority of American naval aircraft, especially at the battle of Leyte Gulf in October 1944, doomed Japanese seapower. About 306,000 tons of Japanese warships were destroyed while the United States suffered a 37,000 ton loss. Moreover, the United States had twenty-three large submarines immediately available in the Pacific in 1941 capable of cruising twelve thousand miles and carrying twenty-four torpedoes with a crew of eight officers and eighty men. New submarines were gradually added to this flotilla. The Japanese completely failed to use effectively their submarines against Allied shipping. They also neglected adequate convoys for their own transport, so that 1113 Japanese merchant vessels totalling 5,320,000 tons, in addition to 201 military ships, were sunk by American submarines.[13]

The United States emerged from the ashes of World War II with the largest and most powerful navy in the world. It then began to question whether America needed a navy at all! The use of strategic power in Germany—and the two devastating atomic bombs that had dramatically ended Japanese resistance—made the American public wonder whether large land armies and naval forces would ever be needed again. From 1945 to 1950 it seemed that air force squadrons armed with atomic bombs, once they were based or ferried within striking range of an enemy, would be irresistible. Naval units could perform an auxiliary role in probing and herding enemy forces for air attacks as well as transporting air force units. But the Strategic Air Command, it was vigorously argued, should henceforth be the first line of American defense with prime attention (and money) given to its organization, equipment, training, and services. Between 1945 and 1950 only the Soviet Union, which had no great navy, could conceivably challenge the might of the United States. Germany and Japan had been crushed, and Western Europe was exhausted. U.S. Naval personnel dropped from 3,380,817 officers and men in 1945 to 381,538 in just five years. U.S. Naval aircraft, which had been about equal in number to the Air Force in 1945, dropped to 9099 planes compared to 12,572 in the Air Force in 1950.

The naivete of the postwar strategic doctrine quickly evaporated after three major events: the explosion of an atomic bomb by the Soviet Union on 23 September 1949; the Korean war from 25 June 1950 to 27 July 1953; and the stunning start of the space age when the Soviet Union launched the first earth satellite on 4 October 1957. The monopoly of the atomic bomb by the United States had ended far sooner than the American experts had anticipated, and military attention quickly shifted to methods for improving the weapons delivery and intercept system; also, the Korean war demonstrated the possibility of a long, bitter war, even in the atomic age, in which conventional weapons, large-scale sea transport, and amphibious operations were still required. The Soviet launching of Sputnik confirmed its power to send ballistic missiles across the oceans—which hitherto had protected the U.S.[14]

The Korean war cost the United States 150,000 casualties, but President Harry S. Truman successfully resisted the call of General Douglas A. MacArthur to escalate the conflict by the strategic bombing of China after Peking had sent two hundred thousand "volunteers" into battle. As soon as an armistice had been reached, American military appropriations started to dcline, but not much. From a peak of $51,830 million in 1953, major national security expenditures declined to $44,414 million in 1957, when the figures began rising again. Any mood of parsimony in the Dwight D. Eisenhower administration soon melted away with the news of the Russian earth satellite and the Soviet development of intercontinental ballistic missiles. In 1958 the civilian National Aeronautics and Space Administration (NASA) was created to forge a new national missile research, production, and operation program as rapidly as possible.

The Korean war, which had virtually doubled the number of Navy ships to about 11,000, followed by the landing operation in Lebanon in 1958 to quell revolution there, as well as the several incidents in the Formosa straits where the interposition of the American fleet between mainland China and Taiwan had been a deterrent to attack, all indicated an important security role for a modern Navy.[15] Strategic air bombing with atomic bombs still attracted support as an ultimate weapon, but not as a single alternative for international security. Indeed, the very development of unmanned missiles capable of delivering larger and larger payloads of atomic bombs discouraged reliance on the prospect of such a horrendous war and made recourse to flexible military responses far more attractive. From 1957 to 1959 the Navy held its own in the battle for appropriations against the Air Force, while the Army lost ground. Then the Navy obtained an entirely new weapon and an entirely new role in the strategic use of the oceans.

New Strategic Uses of the Ocean

Until the 1950s the range and diving powers of submarines had been limited by the need for oxygen in diesel engine propulsion, electric battery ignition, and surface communication systems. On 21 January 1954 the U.S. Navy launched its first nuclear-powered submarine, the *Nautilus*. Concomitant tests were made of a land-based prototype of the thermal reactor to be installed in the submarine, a reactor capable of producing enough power to send the vessel, fully submerged, full speed around the world. When the operational tests of the *Nautilus* were completed in January 1955, a new chapter had been opened not only in underseas warfare but also in the use of nuclear energy by ships of all types. Indeed, 1955 could be marked as the birth date of a new U.S. Navy. From guns to guided missiles, from gunpowder to nuclear weapons, from subsonic to supersonic aircraft speeds, and from petroleum to nuclear fuels, American naval forces began to move toward a dramatically important role in the defense strategy of the United States.[16]

At the same time, however, the Soviet Union began to emerge as a great maritime as well as land power. Before World War II the Soviet Union had ranked seventh among the naval powers of the world. After the defeat of Germany, Italy, and Japan, as well as the decline of France as a world power, the Soviet Union rose to third place. Great Britain still ranked second, but only because of its large reserve fleet. Moreover, the mighty armada of the United States that had been so grandly mobilized for World War II began to suffer obsolescence. In 1954 the United States could still count on 27 attack and light aircraft carriers against none for the Soviet Union and twice the number of destroyers that operated in the Soviet fleet. But the Russians had already gained an advantage in cruisers and far surpassed the Americans with submarines of all types. The major technological breakthrough of installing nuclear power plants, first in submarines and then in surface vessels, profoundly affected both the tactical and logistic aspects of naval warfare and the defense strategy of the two superpowers.

During 1956 the first guided-missile cruiser, the *Boston*, joined the U.S. fleet, and another was commissioned. In 1957 the *Nautilus* cruised 60,000 miles before refueling, and a third atomic-powered submarine was commissioned as a second atomic-powered submarine was launched. By then the Navy had five guided missiles of proven effectiveness that could strike from surface to air, from air to air, from air to surface, or from surface to surface. On 11 April 1957 the keel was laid for the *Halibut,* the first submarine to be designed from the keel up to carry missiles, and another thirteen nuclear-powered submarines were under construction. The Navy's first guided-missile destroyer, the *Gyatt,* was completed in the same year, the Navy also emphasized the importance of ship-based aircraft, armed with appropriate weapons systems, to combat the ever-increasing threat of submarines. With top priority, moreover, Fleet ballistic missile systems became the largest development program in Navy ordnance. In December 1956 the Navy was assigned responsibility for the new, comparatively smaller, solid propellant ballistic missile Polaris. Although the weapon was first designed to reach capability in 1963, its development and testing were so successful that the program was accelerated to reach capability in 1960.

The Navy quickly perceived the importance of the Polaris missile. In the semiannual report of the Secretary of Defense it was described as "a single missile with a single purpose—massive retaliation against an all-out agressor—and on this single-purpose weapon may rest the security of the nation and the peace of the world." But the Navy did not neglect attack aircraft carriers. Six conventional carriers had been authorized after the end of World War II. On 4 February 1958, the keel of the *Enterprise,* the first nuclear-powered aircraft carrier was laid, and the ship was completed on 31 January 1962 as the world's largest aircraft carrier ever constructed: over 1000 feet long with a flight deck 252 feet wide and covering an area of four and one-half acres, the *Enterprise* could accommodate about 100 airplanes and was capable of steaming five years without refueling.

As the Eisenhower administration came to an end in 1960, the first two submarines armed with Polaris missiles were commissioned. On 20 July 1960 the *George Washington* successfully launched two Polaris missiles underwater, thus beginning an entirely new chapter in naval warfare. President John F. Kennedy faced at least five key issues in the development of U.S. defense strategy. How much and at what price should the ballistic missile effort be accelerated? What mix of bombers and guided missiles should obtain in future years? Were American retaliatory forces able to survive a first assault? What would be the best defense against enemy ballistic missiles? What was the minimum requirement for tactical forces and supporting air and sea lift operations in conventional war? Some of these intractable problems have continued to haunt the President and Congress in their annual debates over the best national security policy for the United States within the cost limits dictated by domestic politics.

Kennedy's State of the Union message in 1961 directed the Department of Defense to accelerate the Polaris program and called for a revision of the fiscal year 1962 budget to allow the construction of ten more submarines to be delivered by December 1964, about two years earlier than the former five-submarines-a-year program, in order to reach a total number of twenty-nine Polaris-equipped submarines. In fact, by the end of 1961 five Polaris-equipped submarines were on station with eighty missiles that could be fired within fifteen minutes of a command from the White House.

Clearly the days of the great fleets that circulated about fixed stations of the oceans had passed. The United States planned to have attack carrier air groups and carrier antisubmarine air groups, patrol and warning squadrons, and ultimate deterrence missiles aboard cruising submarines—a mix of forces and squadrons that could deal flexibly with outbreaks of conflicts anywhere in the world. The broad ranges of capability that the Navy called for, with its argument that its forces must include air, sea, and ground strength for its diverse missions, cushioned the impact of technological developments and guaranteed a regular share of the defense appropriations of the nation. The Navy successfully avoided identification with a single mission, but rather insisted that it had a vital role in strategic retaliation, in limited war, in antisubmarine defense, in regional stabilization (whether the area be the East China Sea or the Mediterranean Sea), and in support services for the Air Force and the Army. As a result, although the Army's appropriations varied 18.1 percent and the Air Force appropriations varied 15.3 percent between fiscal years 1950 and 1961, the Navy's share varied only 4.4 percent. The Army's share of total defense appropriations dropped from 39.1 percent in 1951 to 21 percent in 1958. The Air Force share rose from 33.7 percent in 1951 to 48.3 percent in 1958. But the Navy's share of total defense appropriations was essentially stable at 26.2 percent in 1951 and 28.6 percent in 1958.[17]

The opening years of the 1960 decade, therefore, not only witnessed a drive to deliver the twelfth to the twenty-ninth Polaris-equipped submarines at the rate of one a month, but also the delivery of the most modern aircraft carrier *Enterprise* and the first nuclear-powered fighting ship, the *Long Beach*, completed on 1 September 1961. The *Long Beach* was designed and constructed as a cruiser from the keel up, armed with a main battery of guided missiles powered by a nuclear engineering plant. In fiscal year 1963 alone, twenty-five new ships were commissioned, including six guided-missiles destroyers, two guided-missiles destroyer leaders, three nuclear submarines, four ballistic-missile submarines, and a nuclear-powered attack carrier. At the same time the Navy embarked on an extensive fleet rehabilitation and modernization program of the hulls, machinery, weapons, and equipment of scores of ships to offset obsolescence. During the deadly confrontation between the Soviet Union and the United States over the delivery of Russian missiles and bombers to Cuba in 1962, the Commander-in-Chief of the Atlantic was given unified command for the enforcement of the quarantine of Cuba that President Kennedy declared on 22 October. The commander of the Second Fleet assumed operational control for enforcement of the quarantine until, after delicate negotiations between the White House and the Kremlin, forty-two missiles were loaded on eight Soviet ships beginning 2 November, and the quarantine ended 20 November 1962.[18] That year the Secretary took pride in portraying the Navy as a flexible instrument of national policy with an "ability to supply in selective and graduated manner the precise degree of power required by the circumstances, whether it be a show of force, an amphibious landing, or a heavy nuclear strike."

In 1964 the deep and bitter involvement of the United States in Viet Nam began on 2 August with the attack, imagined or real, on the U.S. destroyer *Maddox* and attacks upon two other U.S. destroyers on 4 August.[19] From the carriers *Ticonderoga* and *Constellation* sixty-four air sorties then bombed and sank twenty-five North Vietnamese patrol boats while destroying large petroleum reservoirs. In 1965 air attacks from Navy carriers against North Viet Nam steadily increased, and that summer four attack carriers, one cruiser, and twenty-five destroyers were in place for offensive action supported by service vessels and amphibious ships. Three years later, just before President Lyndon Johnson suspended the bombing of North Viet Nam on 31 March 1968, the Navy was flying 57 percent of all air attack sorties in the high-risk areas with F-4 Phantoms, F-8 Crusaders, A-6 Intruders, and A-4 Skyriders making a tactical fighter and attack aircraft force of some 300 planes.

As the expenditures for the U.S. Defense Department soared from $47,411 million in fiscal year 1956 to $79,542 million in fiscal year 1969, the armed services greatly increased their strength in general purpose forces, in nuclear forces deployed within a war theater, and in strategic forces for deterrence against direct attack by the Soviet Union. America had come a long way from the massive retaliation strategy of the Eisenhower administration in the 1950s that only included 140 heavy and medium strategic bomber squadrons and the first Atlas intercontinental ballistic missiles armed with nuclear warheads. At the end of 1969 the United States had 1054 intercontinental ballistic missile launchers and 581 intercontinental bombers. Early in 1961 the first three Polaris-armed submarines had arrived at their stations. By 1969 all 41 Polaris-armed submarines authorized were operational and capable of launching 656 missiles.

But the armament of the Soviet Union had also increased at a fabulous and frightening rate. The Soviet Union had announced its first successful test of an intercontinental ballistic missile on 26 August 1957. Nine years later it was estimated that the number of launchers under Moscow's command totalled only 250, less than a third of the number that were operational in the United States. Furthermore, the Soviets had no submarine-launched ballistic missiles. By the end of 1968, however, the Soviets were estimated to have 900 intercontinental ballistic-missile launchers and 45 submarine ballistic-missile launchers. A year later Russia had surpassed the United States by 1060 to 1054 in intercontinental ballistic missile launchers and had increased its submarine-launched ballistic missiles to 110 as against the 656 of the United States. Both countries also possessed intercontinental bombers, with the United States maintaining three times as many as the Soviet Union. But the role of the manned vehicle for strategic deterrence seemed to be declining.

In his statement before the House Subcommittee on Department of Defense appropriations during his presentation of the 1969 budget, Secretary of Defense Robert S. McNamara left no doubt about the importance of strategic deterrence in maintaining international peace and security when he said that "Neither the Soviet Union nor the United States can now attack the other, even by complete surprise, without suffering massive damage in retaliation." The Kennedy and the Johnson administrations had both labored, first, for a strategic missile force that would survive any first strike attempt to destroy the United States and leave aggressors no doubt that their own cities would be destroyed in retaliation regardless of the surprise or the strength of first assaults. Second, both presidents, with the experience of Cuba, the Dominican Republic, Viet Nam, and the Middle East, had encouraged the growth of conventional armed forces to provide a graduated level of response to any threat to peace anywhere in the world. Between 1962 and 1968 Congress provided $47 billion in new obligational authority to Kennedy and Johnson for research, development, and testing alone. The Johnson budget for fiscal year 1970 projected $85.6 billion in total obligational authority for the Department of Defense—the highest in two decades.

The use of the ocean for the strategic deterrence policy of the United States continued with the strengthening of the forty-one submarines armed with Polaris missiles in 1969 when it was announced that thirty-one of them would be refitted with the new Poseidon missile system. Two years later the Secretary of Defense could say that "We believe our Polaris and Poseidon submarines at sea can be considered virtually invulnerable today," as he recommended study be given to a new underseas long-range missile system. Moreover, although in 1971 the United States had not increased its number of launchers of missiles, maintaining 1000 for the Minuteman, 54 for the Titan, and 656 for Polaris and Poseidon, it had clearly extended its reach of strategic deterrence from the seas and was installing multiple independent reentry vehicles (MIRV) in the warheads, thus multiplying the number of its strikes from the same launchers and making it far more difficult for enemy defenses against missile penetration.

The conversion and modernization of the Navy both to provide a strategic deterrence and to offer flexible responses to conflict in any area of the world had tremendous impacts on the American budget. By fiscal year 1968 defense spending equalled almost 10 percent of the gross national product of the United States. The results could be seen not only in the Polaris- and Poseidon-equipped submarines but also in the 15 attack carriers, with 72 squadrons of fighter-attack aircraft, 4 antisubmarine warfare carriers, 52 nuclear and 52 conventional attack submarines, 500 antisubmarine warfare aircraft and the 242 escort ships.

Accompanying the development of the new American navy was the recognition of oceanography as a discipline essential to the military uses of the sea. Naval personnel, of course, had always made outstanding contributions to the science of the oceans through expeditions, inventions, and study. In 1896, for example, Commander C. D. Sigsbee was the first man to use an electrical system for processing meteorological data, and in 1921 a civilian scientist at the United States Naval Academy, Dr. Harvey C. Hayes, made an enormous contribution to oceanography when he developed the sonic depth-finder. After the recommendations of the Schofield board in 1929 that the Navy expand its work in oceanography, research and equipment support from Washington began flowing in large sums to the Scripps Institution of Oceanography and to the new Woods Hole Oceanographic Institution. On contracts or grants scientists not only helped to develop sonar operators' manuals for the Fleet and studied optimum maintenance of the trim of submarines, but they engaged also in improving oceanographic instruments and in making bottom sediment charts. In 1933 a separate section on oceanography was established in the Hydrographic Office of the Navy, and in 1946 the Office of Naval Research was established.

During the 1950s the Navy was engaged in such programs as sea ice forecasting, a continuous airborne geomagnetic survey of the world, and a polar oceanographic program. Furthermore, it established a tower off Cape Cod to gather data on the temperature, the salinity, and wave patterns for its environmental prediction system and released a ten-year program plan in oceanography that encompassed a three-fold increase in research, the construction of 34 new research and survey ships, instrumentation development, and a major increase in data collection. In 1962 the U.S. Navy Hydrographic Office was renamed the Oceanographic Office and in the summer of 1966, the Secretary of the Navy established the Office of the Oceanographer directly under the operational control of the Chief of Naval Operations.

Scientific and engineering support are essential to every water-borne weapon and surveillance system in the oceans today, whether to protect shipping, to survey the movements of foreign naval forces, to maintain optimum strategic deterrence through submarines, or to mount and support amphibious assault. Oceanography, in the words of the Secretary of the Navy, had become "an essential element in maintenance of American seapower."

The 1960s were filled with dramatic developments in the history of oceanography. At the opening of the decade, the nuclear submarine *Triton* made the first submerged navigation of the world, and in the same year the *Trieste* descended 35,800 feet in the abyssal Mariana trench, where startling evidence of animal life was found in the deepest ocean known to humans. Between 1961 and 1965 the Navy participated in the Indian Ocean Expedition, a cooperative venture of scientists from thirteen nations loosely coordinated by the National Science Foundation. They also participated in the Tropical Atlantic Sounding and Mapping Program under the auspices of the International Oceanographic Commission of UNESCO. Meanwhile, important experiments to test man's ability to live and work for long periods on the ocean floor began in 1964 while a deep ocean technology program was initiated in 1967. A year later the Navy had three oceanographic research ships in operation with twelve more being built; four surveying ships in operation, with three being built; and it had under construction the first vessel ever specifically built for hydrographic survey, a ship that held four 36-foot sounding boats and two helicopters. During these years, moreover, 10 oceanographic buoys had been moored in the seas to support the antisubmarine warfare environmental prediction service, while a fixed ocean station, 40 feet in diameter, had been emplaced on the sea floor to measure 100 oceanic factors and to report the data to a collecting station 2500 miles away. As the 1970s began the U.S. Navy had fewer than 100 oceanographers and about a dozen hydrographic subspecialists on active duty, but it was the largest employer of oceanographers through its support of private research. Such support had averaged little more than $1 million annually from 1946 to 1949, but by 1969 it had risen to about $20 million a year.

By the mid-1970s, of the $200 million or more annually spent through the entire Navy ocean science program, about a third was going directly to ocean sciences, which included underwater acoustics, marine geology, geophysics, and biology. Underwater sound has been the only practical means for transmitting or receiving information beyond a few hundred feet. Patterns of refraction, dispersion, and reflection of sound in various depths, salt solutions, and temperatures of water, therefore, must be known to detect and track vessels. The texture of the sea bottom must be recorded to calculate the bounce of sound reflected from the sediment and to determine optimum conditions for the construction of emplacement of instruments. Because magnetic sensors have been used, the Navy has needed data on the spatial and temporal values of the earth's magnetic field. Information has had to be gathered continuously about the variability of water temperature, salinity, and circulation from the surface to the depths to make quick estimates of sound, speed, and direction. Finally, a knowledge of the marine biota not only has helped in identifying static or interference with sound transmission, but has been valuable for the prevention of fouling or corrosion of vessels and instrumentation.

Ocean engineering had already placed men in the sea itself for exploration and experimental work at depths below a thousand feet with prospects of two thousand feet in the near future. By the mid-1970s vehicles were being tested at depths from 2000 to 20,000 feet in order to improve reconnaissance and salvage operations in the deep ocean. Moreover, the oceanographic operations division of the Navy ocean science program, which included environmental prediction services, led to physical and topographic surveys, many in conjunction with other friendly nations, and a continuous flow of data on the weather, state of the sea, the formation and drift of ice, and optimum environmental factors for shipping.

Finally, of the more than eighty oceanographic research vessels that were federally supported in the mid-1970s, the Navy operated more than a dozen and leased others to universities or oceanographic institutions. The close cooperation among the leading university marine science programs, private oceanographic institutions and the Navy is illustrated by the large percentage of their operating budgets that depend on Navy contracts or grants. Other major sources of support are the National Science Foundation and the Atomic Energy Commission. At the same time the Soviet Union had about 160 vessels engaged in oceanographic efforts with about 55 large enough to conduct worldwide operations. Although the Russians and Japanese were probably far ahead of the United States in financial support of oceanography to complement their large and distant fishing industries, and although the Russians probably had a larger number of ships engaged in oceanographic research itself, the United States seemed better equipped to gather data and analyse the naval applications of oceanography.[20]

U.S. Defense Policy

The nternational system has undergone a fundamental transition from the post-World War II period, when two superpowers had dominated almost all international conflict situations. But since 1945 there has been only one immediate and realistic threat to the national security of the United States: the Soviet Union. As indicated earlier, between 1957 and 1969 Russia had leaped ahead of the United States in the number of intercontinental ballistic missiles in place. In addition Moscow had pushed forward the production of naval vessels to match America both on the surface and under the seas.

Among the major powers engaged in World War I from 1914 to 1918 the Russian navy had ranked last. The Stalin government had shifted to a shipbuilding program during the 1930s, with considerable foreign technical assistance. When Russia faced Germany and Japan in 1941 during World War II, its fleet included 218 submarines. But only some 33 new destroyers, two modern cruisers, and no modern battleships were available to the Soviet forces. In the war itself only the submarine fleet was really engaged in battles—and it was not very effective. During the 1950s the Soviet Union, gaining in part from the transfer of German designs, undertook a herculean shipbuilding program. For example, between 1950 and 1958 the Russians constructed close to three hundred submarines of three advanced types. Moreover, as new ship building yards came into being, two new series of cruisers, the *Skoryi* and the *Sverdlov* classes skidded down the ways, ready for deep ocean patrols, while almost a hundred destroyers were in service at the beginning of the 1960s. The Soviet Union had also built an increasingly powerful nuclear-fueled ballistic-missile fleet. About 1959 the Russians sent their first nuclear-powered submarine out to sea. In the 1960s they started building the Y-class submarine, which mounted 16 tubes for launching missiles, roughly comparable to the American Polaris system. Although Moscow only had four submarines of this class operational in January 1967, there were twenty-five in operation by January 1972.

In brief, in the early 1970s the Soviet Union had achieved the world's largest fleet of surface and submarine vessels. Moreover, between 1945 and 1958 the Russian merchant marine tonnage doubled—and it doubled again in the next decade! By 1973 the Soviet Union ranked third in the number of merchant vessels (led by Japan and Liberia) and sixth in total carrying capacity, because its vessels tended to be smaller in size, although very modern in design and operation. To this formidable capacity for using the seas, the Russians, never in history a distant-water fishing people, added a stupendous fishing fleet. From 1960 onward they began to fish from the western Atlantic to the waters off Alaska, in the Indian ocean, off the west coast of Africa, and elsewhere, so that by the 1970s some 4000 ocean-going vessels and perhaps another 15,000 coastal ships were bound to make the Soviet Union one of the greatest, if not the greatest, harvester of fish in the world.[21]

The United States, on the other hand, had decided to decommission many of its aging World War II vessels, while its shipbuilding program lagged, with only seven ships built in 1968 and five in 1969, rising to ten in 1970 and fifteen in 1971. Thus there was a sharp decline in the total number of combat ships available to the Navy. Nevertheless, in addition to its land-based Minute Man and sea-based Polaris-Poseidon missile systems, the United States had continued to support more than 500 heavy bombers, the third element of its strategy of deterrence. Through dispersion, constant alert, and continuous air patrols, the survival of these planes from a first strike to the Soviet Union was expected to ensure the destruction of Soviet cities in retaliation.

The stark and dreadful truth in the early 1970s was that both the United States and the Soviet Union possessed a sufficient number of intercontinental ballistic missiles adequately dispersed or protected so that each state was confident that it could survive a first strike of the other and could retaliate with enough force to destroy all the major population centers of the other. Under these circumstances thirty months of negotiation lead to the Strategic Arms Limitation Agreement (SALT) between the United States and the Soviet Union on 26 May 1972. Under the agreement the number of intercontinental ballistic missiles were limited for both states to those either under construction or deployed at the time of the signing of the treaty of 1 July 1972, which was about 1618 for the USSR and 1054 for the United States. Moreover, construction of submarine-launched ballistic missiles on all nuclear submarines was frozen at the July 1972 levels. New construction of submarine-launched ballistic missiles was only permitted by simultaneously dismantling an equal number of older intercontinental or submarine launchers.

Both the Soviet Union and the United States were committed to negotiating a more permanent and comprehensive agreement, but the interim understanding was to last for five years. At the same time an actual treaty was drawn up that limited each power to only one antiballistic missile (ABM) site for defense of its national capital and to one ABM site for defense of an intercontinental ballistic-missile field, with a total of one hundred ABM interceptors at each site.

It was further provided that the number of radars at such sites were to be limited and that the Soviet site would be at least 1300 kilometers from Moscow while the United States site would be at Grand Forks, North Dakota. The Anti-Ballistic Missile Treaty was of unlimited duration, with the right to withdraw permitted on six months' notice only "if supreme interests are jeopardized."[22]

The dramatic rivalry between the United States and the Soviet Union over the creation, magnification, and deployment of strategic nuclear deterrents did not obviate the continuing reliance of both superpowers on general purpose forces. Such forces, with either nuclear or conventional armaments, were required both to attack strategic forces and to be used in restricted conflicts. In 1974 the Soviet Union had launched ten nuclear attack submarines and another nine in 1975, and Moscow expected to have more than thirty of these vessels in operation by 1978 in addition to some two hundred other submarines. Moreover, the number of Russian major operational combat surface ships surpassed the United States by 1974 as a new American shipbuilding program got underway. To its several hundred medium bombers, the Soviet Union gradually added a capability in naval aviation, first with ships that could carry and receive helicopters, then by launching its first aircraft carrier, the *Kiev* in December 1972 with angled flight deck of 550 feet suitable for both helicopters and vertical/short takeoff and landing planes.

An important element in the procurement of new Navy vessels has been their staggering costs. Under Title VII of the Defense Appropriation Act of 1975, all future aircraft carriers, major surface combat vessels, and strategic or attack submarines were required to be nuclear powered. With America's growing dependence on foreign oil, the new shipbuilding policy sought to make U.S. national defense at sea less dependent on the vicissitudes of international oil supplies. Conventionally powered vessels, moreover, often required foreign bases for refueling. But the arrangements for foreign bases in the third quarter of the twentieth century were politically hazardous, running against the grain of the spirit of independence so fiercely proclaimed by the developing nations of the world in Asia, Africa, and Latin America. Vice-Admiral Hyman G. Rickover, one of the staunch advocates of a nuclear-powered Navy, had convincingly argued before Congress that conventionally powered ships would be inescapably vulnerable to Russian attack, especially if the Soviet submarine fleet should ruthlessly destroy tankers, tenders, and other supply ships as well as interdict foreign bases. Nevertheless nuclear-powered vessels had drained the U.S. defense budget.

In 1975 Secretary of the Navy J. William Mittendorf, III, stated before Congress that the cost of nuclear-powered ships could be, according to their type, as much as 30 to 50 percent higher than conventionally powered ships. While a majority of Congress and Navy leaders believed that the sharply higher costs provided greater benefits for the national security of the United States, not all analysts concurred. As the critics worked from different scenarios of international relations, a different estimate of Soviet intentions and capabilities and a different evaluation of American national needs emerged.

In any case, both the Polaris and the Poseidon submarines were beginning to obsolesce by the 1970s, and the Navy pushed its plans forward for a new Trident submarine to be equipped with a Trident I missile. The Polaris/Poseidon missiles in use in 1977 were able to strike targets up to 2500 miles from the submarine. The Trident I, however, had a range of 4000 miles. Moreover, the patrol capability of the Polaris/Poseidon submarines was limited to sixty days compared to the seventy days in which a Trident might be kept continuously submerged on its mission. Nevertheless, Navy officials continued to worry about the number of vessels in the combat fleet. Although the delivery of new ships had averaged about nineteen per year between 1957 and 1977, with new calls for more construction in the 1970s, Navy leaders expressed fears about reaching the goal of 600 ships set for the 1980s. In fact, by the summer of 1976 only about 480 ships were available, albeit of far greater efficiency than the World War II vessels they had replaced.

Yet a comparison of the number of ships between the United States and the Soviet Union has often seemed pointless. Not only have the technical capabilities of the different vessels been difficult to relate to each other, but much has depended on the national purpose for which each navy is being built. In the mid-1870s, for example, the United States regarded its navy's chief function as coastal defense; in the mid-1970s the United States seemed to expect a navy that could not only (1) provide strategic deterrence against a nuclear-armed aggressor, but also (2) maintain a naval presence in many areas of the world to support political changes, (3) exert power to control the seas, especially the vital lanes of supplies to allies, and (4) project power ashore by coastal and amphibious operations. On the other side of the equation, the Soviet Union until the early 1970s sought (1) strategic deterrence and (2) the denial of sea control through its great attack submarine fleet. In recent years it has been able to assert a naval presence, as in the Indian ocean and the Mediterranean sea, and it has developed a very limited amphibious capability.[23]

A strong defense for any country under conditions of modern warfare has been frightfully expensive. By 1977 the U.S. Defense budget was approaching $110 billion, or about 25 percent of the entire federal budget of the nation. Of this amount the Navy was scheduled to receive close to 40 percent as it urged the construction of twenty-five new ships and particularly two new Trident submarines, while it dropped its plans for another nuclear aircraft carrier to add to the four already in commission. Intent on modernizing and expanding its strategic forces to deter nuclear attacks, nevertheless the Navy urged the launching of about 157 ships by 1983, with many of these oil powered rather than nuclear powered. And a new weapon in its arsenal would be the cruise missile to be launched from surface and submarine ships, as well as from air bombers, which was heralded as remarkably accurate, though of shorter range than ballistic missiles, and able to fly a low, flat trajectory below the observation of the enemy's radar. With more than 700,000 men and women in its forces, including the Marines; with its mixture of strategic submarines, aircraft carriers, attack submarines, cruisers with nuclear missiles, and destroyers; and supported by patrol frigates, hydrofoils, and amphibious assault vessels, the Navy had a mighty armada in the mid-1970s. President James Earl Carter had to consider very seriously the uses and the costs of this powerful force within the framework of his disarmament policy. The impending SALT talks with the Soviet Union, whose navy was in some ways superior and in other ways less effective than the American fleet, were of crucial importance.

International Relations

As the navigation of the oceans acquired a new importance after 1960 for the deployment of both underwater and surface naval forces, vital international legal questions were raised (1) about the width of the territorial sea over which a coastal state held sovereign rights; (2) the role of a contiguous zone beyond the territorial sea in which the coastal state could exercise jurisdiction for customs, sanitation, immigration, and other purposes; and (3) the status of an economic zone in which the coastal state might have exclusive control over marine resources, both in the water column and the seabed, with the exclusive right to use that area for artificial islands, deepwater ports, and other installations.

During the late nineteenth and early twentieth century, it was generally regarded as international law that the territorial jurisdiction of a state extended beyond its shoreline to a distance of three miles out to sea. Through the territorial sea, ships—both private and public—could make an "innocent passage," that is, so long as it was not prejudicial to the peace, good order, and security of the coastal state. Beyond that narrow territorial sea, however, navigation was completely free to all ships under the flag of any nation of the world without interference by any other nation in time of peace and only subject to arrest in time of war by a belligerent under certain restricted circumstances. While some states had claimed a territorial sea wider than three miles, the great maritime powers of the early twentieth century—Great Britain, France, Japan, and the United States— were constantly alert to any encroachment on their freedom to navigate the high seas.

At the beginning of World War II, there was still no international convention to which the nations of the world had agreed, setting forth the width of the territorial sea, and as late as 1960 at the Second UN Conference on the Law of the Sea in Geneva no limits had been fixed by multilateral convention. Nevertheless, as explained earlier, there had been a move toward claiming wider areas of jurisdiction over the seabed, followed by expanded claims of control over adjacent coastal waters, especially in Latin America. Indeed, by 1971 most states had claimed more than a three-mile territorial sea. However, the United States, Japan, France, and Great Britain, among others, continued to resist such claims. And the Soviet Union drew a line at twelve miles.[24]

Closely connected to the navigation of the high seas, moreover, was passage through straits used for international navigation, for the ability of the great maritime states to traverse or overfly without interruption such narrows as the Strait of Gibraltar, the Strait of Malacca, the Strait of Dover, and the Strait of Bab el-Mandeb was considered vital to their international interests. In the very first case to be decided by the International Court of Justice in 1949, the *Corfu Channel Case,* the issue turned on whether British warships could exercise a right of passage that was innocent through the strait, although the strait lay within Albanian territorial waters. The Court found the decisive criteria were that the channel connected two parts of the high seas and that it was used for international navigation, conditions that had customarily allowed the innocent passage of both merchant and war vessels. But the decision of the Court was far from unanimous and reflected attitudes of the pre–World War II period better than the challenge to western maritime power in later years.[25]

When the UN International Law Commission in 1956 drafted its articles on international straits for the First UN Law of the Sea Conference, it provided that there must be "no suspension of the innocent passage of foreign ships through straits normally used for international navigation between two parts of the high seas," but in the final Geneva Convention on the Territorial Sea and the Contiguous Zone in 1958 not only was the word *normally* dropped out, but a strait was also defined as connecting "one part of the high seas and . . . the territorial sea of a foreign state." This amendment, supported by the United States, had been primarily designed for the Strait of Tiran, which connects the Red Sea and the Gulf of Aqaba leading to Israel. Although the innocent passage of foreign vessels through the territorial seas of a state had long been recognized and permitted by customary international law, and although it was given positive form in Article 14 of the 1958 Geneva Convention, legally the right of innocent passage remained only an abatement or an easement, very carefully circumscribed, of the sovereign's territorial jurisdiction. Passage was innocent so long as it was not prejudicial to the peace, good order, or security of a coastal state, and states could require notification or authorization of war vessels traversing their territorial waters, while submarines were required to navigate on the surface and to show their flag.

Article 17 of the 1958 Geneva Convention on the Territorial Sea and the Contiguous Zone forbade the suspension of innocent passage of foreign ships through straits that were used for international navigation between one part of the high seas and another part of the high sea or the territorial sea of a foreign state. But this article carried in committee at Geneva in 1958 by only one vote. Moreover, some states had put reservations to the article on straits, and many others had never ratified the Convention as a whole. Finally, the innocent passage rules for vessels through territorial seas did not apply to airplanes flying over such waters. While the scheduled commercial airlines of states have enjoyed free transit in flying over states without landing, military aircraft have only had the right of free transit over the high seas.

Upon the establishment of the standing UN Committee on the Peaceful Uses of the Seabed and the Ocean Floor beyond National Jurisdiction in 1968, the United States and the Soviet Union, which were determinedly developing their surface and submarine navies, had to examine the implications of proposals to extend the jurisdiction of coastal states further out to sea around the world, with the evident possibilities of interference with merchant vessels and political protests over the passage of warships through "national" waters. Any contraction in the free ocean space would clearly limit the tactical and strategic maneuvers of both great navies. The remarkable mobility of the submarine, the difficulty of detecting its movements in the vast volume of the oceans, and the absolute impossibility in the 1970s of eliminating all missile-carrying submarines by one surprise attack were excellent arguments in the United States for keeping the high seas as large as possible. For its defense America sought maximum freedom both in the oceans and on the seabed for various tracking and sensing devices that could be set for any Soviet submarines, which might furtively use the broad territorial waters of a third state.

Steadfastly clinging to the three-mile limit of the territorial sea established by Thomas Jefferson in 1793 and among the last states still maintaining that rule in 1977, the United States recognized the universal movement toward enlarged sea boundaries. But Washington retained its concern that any widening of the territorial sea would also threaten passage through international straits wider than six miles, for such straits, once regarded as part of the territorial sea of coastal states, might be subjected to a regime of innocent passage despite the Geneva Convention of 1958. The United States estimated in 1970 that 116 straits connecting high seas would fall completely under the national jurisdiction of states as a result of an expansion of sovereign rights over the ocean.

On 3 August 1971 the American delegation to the UN Committee on the Seabed specified that its support of a twelve-mile territorial sea at a new Law of the Sea Conference depended on an agreement to designate corridors in international straits that would permit the free transit of ships and the free overflight of planes. The draft articles proposed by the United States prescribed that "all ships and aircraft in transit (through straits used for international navigation) shall enjoy the same freedom of navigation and overflight as they have on the high seas." As the U.S. Representative to the UN Seabed Committee, John R. Stevenson, put it, ". . . the United States believes that straits wider than six miles currently have high seas within them, where states may exercise the freedom of the high seas." The United States, he suggested, would be willing to give up this freedom in such straits in exchange for a limited but vital right of "free transit" through such straits.

The great shipping companies and, above all, the U.S. Navy argued the necessity of a positive international guarantee of free transit corridors through international straits, while a chorus of other interests in America and other developed countries emphasized the importance of free overflight. Yet the upsurge of marine traffic and the character of the vessels passing through straits raised grave fears in the coastal states that their peace, good order, and security could be assured. As the tonnage of oil tankers multiplied, both in number and individual size, carrying cargoes that could by accident spoil the water and coasts of the states adjacent to straits, countries like Indonesia, Malaysia, and Spain became more concerned about marine traffic safety and pollution regulations. Their concern was shared by many developing countries, which also recognized that the passage of nuclear-powered submarines carrying ultradeadly weapons through straits might pose serious hazards for the coastal states.

To allay such fears in the meetings of the UN Seabed Committee in 1972, the United States proposed that the International Maritime Consultative Organization (IMCO) be given authority by a Law of the Sea treaty to establish separation schemes in all areas of heavy shipping traffic and to make those rules binding on the parties to the treaty. Power to enforce the traffic separation schemes would be vested in the coastal state, which also could insist on observance of its own laws by ships navigating through the free transit corridors. With respect to aircraft, the United States urged that the Law of the Sea treaty provide that state aircraft exercising the right of free transit over international straits or other land corridors provided by coastal states would normally respect International Civil Aviation Organization (ICAO) standards and its recommended procedures or practices as they were applied to civil aircraft over the high seas.

On the question of free transit of international straits, the United States and the Soviet Union were in almost complete accord. The Russian position, clearly stated in the draft articles that it presented to the UN Seabed Committee on 25 July 1972, was that in straits used for international navigation between one part of the high seas and another part of the high seas, "all ships in transit shall enjoy the same freedom of navigation, for the purpose of transit through such straits, as they have on the high seas." While the Soviet Union recognized that all ships should avoid any threat to the security of the coastal state and comply with international regulations to prevent accidents or pollution, the draft articles also forbade any interference, interruption, or stopping of transiting vessels by the coastal state.

The very communion of the United States and the Soviet Union on international straits hardly mollified the irritation of several states bordering international straits. As negotiations at the Third UN Law of the Sea Conference proceeded from 1974 onward some reconciliation was required. Under the Revised Single Negotiating Text of 1976, a document that reflected the main views and consensus of many delegates, but to which no state had indicated full agreement, (1) straits used for international navigation between one part of the high seas (or an exclusive economic zone) and another part of the high seas (or an exclusive economic zone) were carefully differentiated from (2) straits that linked the high seas (or exclusive economic zone) to the territorial sea of a foreign state and (3) straits lying between the island of a state and its mainland where another high seas (or exclusive economic zone) route existed seaward of the island and that offered similar navigational convenience.

In category (1) straits, all states were expected to enjoy the "right of transit passage" for navigation and overflight while making a continuous and expeditious crossing from one part of the high seas to the other. Coastal states were enjoined from hampering or suspending transit passage. But they could make laws and regulations for the safety of marine traffic, such as safety lanes, subject to adoption by "the competent international organization" and conforming to international regulations. They could also make pollution laws for the straits to give effect to international conventions. In category (2) and (3) straits, however, only a right of innocent passage, rather than a right of transit passage, was allowed. Nevertheless the draft text stated, "there shall be no suspension of innocent passage."[26]

When the Third UN Law of the Sea Conference resumed its sessions on 23 May 1977, some of the language and intent of the articles on international straits still remained unclear. Yet the larger problem was not a lack of consensus about the legal position of straits, but the suspicion nettling the policy of both maritime powers and developing states about the right uses of the territorial sea, the economic zone, and, parenthetically, straits. The argument that a twelve-mile territorial sea radically limited the availability of water and air transit passages around the globe seemed exaggerated, for the strait of Malacca had technically been "closed," that is, within the territorial waters of one or more states, at the Singaport Strait under the three-mile limit. The same was true of the Danish Straits. The Dardanelles have had their own international regime established by the Montreux Convention of 1936. Gibraltar was closed under a six-mile rule, to which the United States had been ready to accede in 1958 without special transit provisions. Although the Dover Strait, the Bering Sea, and the Strait of Hormuz were only closed under a twelve-mile territorial sea rule, submerged nuclear submarines could find ample and convenient passages around the British isles. In the Bering Sea the two major powers were themselves the littoral states. And since the Persian Gulf is a very shallow sea, no part of which is deeper than one hundred meters, submerged entrances through the Gulf of Hormuz seemed somewhat pointless.[27]

In the Caribbean, the Indonesian and Philippine archipelagoes, the Kuriles Island chain, and elsewhere, a large number of passageways were closed under a twelve-mile territorial sea, yet only a few of them had been of significant importance to commercial surface or air transit and probably even fewer to penetration by submerged ships. While it cannot be denied that a twelve-mile territorial sea has some effect on the flexibility of worldwide air and sea passage, history demonstrates that the key issue has been the political relationship between a coastal state and the flag state of traversing vessels or aircraft, rather than the specific number of miles of a marginal sea over which a coastal state has exercised jurisdiction.

No law-of-the-sea treaty in the long run will be able to deny to the United States or the Soviet Union the utilization of the oceans for their vital security needs. As a medium for the maintenance of strategic deterrence and the posting of multipurpose naval forces as sentries for national defense, the seas have been indispensable to the superpowers. For the United States, in particular, sea control to support its allies and to protect international trade, including crucial petroleum supplies, would not be abandoned for legal articles only approved by the developing nations of Africa, Asia, and Latin America. Yet accommodations of naval interests have been made in the past to respect the sensitivities of coastal states and to acknowledge their paramount interest in their marginal seas. While a law-of-the-sea treaty could not in itself change the balance of naval power, it could require new tactics based on geographical constraints and a reallocation of effort by Washington to realize a navy suitable for a world in which many coastal nations have asserted greater control over the seas than ever before in modern history.

Problems and Issues

Following World War I the great battleship, bristling with long-barrelled guns of mighty firepower and heavily armored against attack, had been regarded as the prize ship of the U.S. Navy. After World War II the aircraft carrier, a vast, floating deck for launching fighter planes and bombers, electronically monitored, cleverly compartmentalized, and lately nuclear powered, was regarded as the essential ship of the U.S. Navy. To be sure the ultimate weapons at sea were Polaris, Poseidon, and Trident deployed around the oceans of the world to guard the United States against first-strike nuclear attack by the Soviet Union. But submarine-launched ballistic missiles had not been suitable for wars in Korea, Viet Nam, the Middle East, or in any area where a U.S. naval presence might have made a difference in the outcome between smaller rival forces in civil or international conflicts. As always the American people were confronted with conflicting arguments over the value of their naval forces, such as the giant aircraft carrier, and the right mixture of surface and submarine vessels of various types in a modern navy. And as always such questions led back to the fundamental problem of defining the foreign policy objectives of the United States with an assessment of the most effective U.S. Navy, at the least cost, to obtain those objectives.

In the late 1970s the trumpets of Congress, with notes furnished by the Pentagon and military contractors at one extreme and by the peace groups with pure faith in disarmament at the other extreme, resoundingly debated in its chambers and in the press the huge appropriations for American defense. Studies showed that the Soviet Union had almost three times the number of submarines as the United States, more missile cruisers, destroyers, amphibious attack ships, and frigates. But other studies revealed that U.S. submarines and missiles were more technically advanced; that America with its NATO allies had about 2.5 times the naval tonnage of the Soviet Union with its East European allies; and that the United States had thirteen aircraft carriers that could launch over two thousand planes compared to an almost negligible capability of the Russians for this style of combat.

Still the arguments raged over the rates of growth and the comparative change in naval power between the Soviet Union and the United States. After Admiral Sergei Gorshkov took command of the Soviet Navy in 1956 and particularly after the humiliating Russian experience in Cuba in 1962, when Moscow had to yield to the demand of Washington for the removal of missiles from Castro's island, the Soviet Fleet rapidly expanded to a formidable first-rank force able to meet, if not match, American seapower. Never in history had Russian ships appeared in such strength in so many distant seas of the world. In 1975, for example, to the dismay of the United States and its NATO allies, some 200 Russian surface ships and 100 submarines participated in maneuvers on the Mediterranean sea while many other Red Flag warships were sailing in the Indian ocean as well as in the Pacific near Japanese and Philippine waters.[28]

A comparison of the number and types of ships between the Russian and the American navies was far less relevant in the late 1970s than a definition of the purposes for which the United States maintained a navy, which involved indispensable commitments to national security both at home and abroad. Thus, only enough American submarines with ballistic missiles to assure certain retaliation on the Soviet homeland in the event of a surprise missile attack was required, not an ever-increasing number of such submarines. In the assertion of sea control, too, the problem for the United States was misstated as reaching the same total of ships by types or by tonnage as the Soviet Union, whose mission of sea denial was quite different. Only enough ships of certain types to guarantee survival against Russian attack submarines and attack aircraft with their missiles, only enough to clear and guard the seas from enemy warships that might endanger vital shipping between the United States and its allies were required. Finally, in the projection of power ashore or maintaining political presence in remote areas, the Washington issue was not a matter of exceeding the number or designs of ships produced by Moscow, but rather determining when and where in the world the United States considered naval appearance or intervention as vital to its own security interests and then creating mixtures of forces to achieve such limited goals.

Just how much defense is enough for the American people? No one can possibly have an exact answer to that question. Buying insurance for the future must always be paid for with current premiums out of current income that could be spent for health, education, housing, and a hundred other demands for a peacetime economy in a democratic society. Logical calculations can be made about the potential force of an enemy. But prognostications about political intentions, domestic constraints, leadership, timing, and all other variables that make up a political estimate are bound to be uncertain. Moreover, the preparation of the U.S. budget, like other national budgets, is an exercise in competing claims. And those claims, when amalgamated, cannot exceed the expected government revenues, from taxes or borrowing, without subjecting the President to serious political risks.[29]

Because it is impossible to calculate the optimum size of the defense budget and because nearly every military commander tends to urge newer, larger, and stronger forces against distant contingencies, presidents Truman, Eisenhower, Kennedy, Johnson, Nixon, Ford, and Carter had to place rather arbitrary ceilings, whether they acknowledged them or not, on the national defense budgets.

When Senator George McGovern in 1972 proposed reducing military spending to a $54.8 billion level by fiscal year 1975, he was making merely another judgment, not a technical estimate, on the relative importance of security to the United States in the contemporary international environment. Similarly when presidential candidate Jimmy Carter was campaigning in 1976, vague suggestions that the U.S. defense budget might be cut by $5 to $15 billion were premised on some conceptions of wasteful management within the armed forces and some hypotheses, which hardly could be proved, about the defense needs of America over the next decade. Bearing in mind that more than 50 percent of costs in U.S. national security had been going for personnel alone during the mid-1970s and that budgetary decisions taken in one year by any president affect a stream of construction whose usability only becomes apparent five or more years hence, the challenge to rationalize outlays for the U.S. Navy can be fierce, if not futile. For example, obsolesence keeps putting ships out of commission almost as fast as they are built. During the first year of the Carter administration, the President found more than sixty ships waiting for major repairs or overhaul. Contracts had also been let for the construction of about 115 new vessels, some of which would not slip into the water until 1980.

Thus, apart from pruning outright waste and inefficiency, often with severe political consequences, as in closing shipyards or bases, a president's instant decision on revising the mission and, therefore, the number and types of ships for the U.S. Navy, may take years to become effective, if at all. This is especially true because, given obvious strategic and tactical requirements and the dire domestic consequences of changing the direction of federal funds, the margin of budgetary cut or reallocation will tend to be marginal. And not too much zeal can be expected from Congress in trimming U.S. Navy priorities or proposals, despite the euphoria for renewing the power of the House and Senate in the dismal wake of the Nixon administration. Figures on Department of

Defense budgetary proposals from 1971 to 1977, with the Navy's share least affected by review on Capitol Hill, indicated that Congress tended to whittle little from the administration requests and never truly blunted the long-range plans of the Chief of Naval Operations as approved by the Joint Chiefs of Staff and the Secretary of Defense.[30]

Heated debates of the late 1970s centered about (1) the extension of nuclear-powered aircraft carriers, very costly ships open to high risk, and their diverse escort armadas; (2) new nuclear strike cruisers, priced at about a billion dollars each, alleged to be capable of independent sea operations; and (3) more 7000-ton nuclear-attack submarines, whose cost might run to slightly less than half-a-billion dollars each. Some critics felt that all major warship construction should be halted pending a reassessment of American foreign policy and the needs for a U.S. Navy in the world environment of 1980–1990.

Yet so much of the fodder that stuffs the debates over American naval development must be culled from assessments of the future conduct of the Soviet Union in the world. The evidence of rising Russian seapower in the late 1970s did not seem to point to any intention of Moscow to defend any distant lines of communication over the oceans or to mass forces that would be capable of amphibious action far from the motherland. On the contrary the enormous attacking strength of the Soviet cruisers and submarines could be recognized as powerful threats to American efforts to safeguard vital U.S. sea lanes and as menaces against any projection of American power abroad, especially at the perimeter of the Soviet sphere of interests, including the Baltic, the eastern Mediterranean, and the western Pacific oceans. Moreover, although boldly deployed across the seas around the world and showing the flag more frequently, for the moral and material encouragement of favored political factions, as in Cuban or Angolan waters, the Russian ships hardly seemed capable of resisting mobilized American fleets in distant seas.

Would Moscow require its own sea lanes to its future allies and commensurate sea control? Would the Kremlin endeavor to project its naval power further abroad, with foreign bases and aircraft carrier forces? Would the Soviet fleet acquire a technological gain in antisubmarine warfare that tilted the balance of underwater strike and kill in its favor? These were questions that gave qualms to U.S. policymakers and static to a national consensus on the role of the American fleet in the future.

The legal uses of the oceans for navigation by the United States, the Soviet Union, and other maritime powers remained unclear throughout the negotiations of the Third UN Law of the Sea Conference from 1974 to 1977. For the United States there could be no compromise on the right of vessels to sail through or the right of airplanes to fly over straits used for international navigation, yet adjustments of policy could be made to take account of the coastal states' suspicion and fear of the transit of warships and merchant carriers loaded with hazardous cargoes.

An equal or greater concern existed in Washington, looking forward to the 1980s, that national claims to exclusive economic zones stretching seaward 200 miles from coastal states, national claims to waters located between the island outposts of archipelagoes, and claims to the seabed as "the common heritage" of humankind, which encompass all the remaining area of the world beyond national jurisdiction, might delay, impede, or frustrate navigation. To avoid misunderstanding the United States continued to insist that the "high seas" legal status of the area beyond national jurisdiction not be altered. Washington was willing to concede certain rights to coastal states and perhaps an international authority for their resource conservation and management responsibilities.

The U.S. Navy, in sum, will operate in a radically different legal, political, and economic environment in the next decades. Not only will Soviet naval power tend to match American strength, although with different capabilities, but other coastal states may complicate, if not resist, flexibility in the management and movement of fleets through the narrow waterways and broad expanses of the seas. In such a world the President and Congress, more than ever, will be compelled to examine the plans of the admirals. And they will continue to be troubled by inadequate information further complicated by conflicting technical opinions. The wise statesman, harassed by domestic pressures either to spend generously or economize on the preparation for war, will strive to resist both the intimidation of the hawks, who shout about an impending catastrophe, and the doves, who endlessly preach world peace through idyllic persuasion and prompt disarmament.

3 The American Merchant Marine

The United States was formed from seafaring peoples. During the sixteenth century intrepid fishers from Britain, France, Portugal, and Spain had sailed their fragile boats every year to the Newfoundland Banks, to Nova Scotia, and to the waters off Cape Cod to make their catch of cod, halibut, and mackerel. In 1577 about 350 vessels were fishing in the oceans adjacent to the continent of North America. The Plymouth Company failed in its first attempt to settle a colony in America in 1607 at the mouth of the Kennebec River in Maine. But the pioneers managed to build a fort, fifty houses, a church, and a storehouse. They built also the first British oceangoing vessel built in America, "a pretty pinnace of some thirty tonnes, which they called the Virginia." The next and permanent Plymouth settlement in Massachusetts, carried by the *Mayflower* across the stormy Atlantic, brought some 101 men, women, and children who were remarkably ill-equipped for their frontier life in New England. Among their first disconsolate appeals to their British managers was an urgent request to send shipwrights to the desperate colony.

The Boston settlers to the northwest of Plymouth fared better. By 1631 the Massachusetts Bay colony had already launched its first seagoing vessel, a ship of thirty tons owned by Governor John Winthrop. By 1638 the first American shipyard, employing sixty men had been established near Portland, Maine. In 1641 the tiny village of Salem, Massachusetts, was making such profit from fish that it launched an enormous ship of over 300 tons, a monster for its time, considering that of the 1232 ships owned in Britain, only a handful exceeded 200 tons. Shipbuilding boomed all along the New England coast, but the Massachusetts Bay area excelled with such feats as two 200-ton vessels in 1644, a 400-ton vessel in 1645, and a 300-ton vessel in 1646.[1]

The Early American Merchant Marine

From New Hampshire to the Carolinas, the ocean was the highway to commerce and the indispensable medium for the developing economy of the feeble English colonies strung along the coast of America. While Boston prospered from the trade of fish and raw materials from the Massachusetts hinterlands, Rhode Island increased its manufacture of rum. Soon Newport led the colonies in the lucrative swap of rum for Africans to be worked on the growing plantations of the West Indies, South America, and the southern American colonies. Just before the

American revolution from England, some 150 Rhode Island ships were engaged in the slave trade. In 1771 the colonies imported (officially) over 4 million gallons of molasses from the West Indies, about half of which was used to distill rum; they also imported over 2 million gallons of West Indian rum and more than 200,000 gallons of heavy wine. Part of the rum went to the slave trade, but most was guzzled by hard-working Americans.

Cattle, dairy products, and iron manufactures were shipped out of Connecticut towns on Long Island Sound while New York, with its incomparable harbor, grew from a village of 8622 in 1730 to about 25,000 in 1775. The largest port city in America was Philadelphia, with a population of 40,000, and the town experienced a threefold growth in tonnage exports between 1730 and 1774. In 1770 more than 330,000 tons "entered" from overseas and more than 340,000 tons "cleared" the ports of the twelve colonies for overseas—this was in addition to all the coastal shipping. Further south the Chesapeake Bay was dotted with ships and Charleston thrived on the export of rice, turpentine, silk, and tobacco.

With virgin forests to provide excellent oak and pine at low cost and with their creative response to the challenge of the marine environment, the American colonies became great shipbuilders. The line, trim, and speed of Salem sailing ships, for example, became famous in America and around the world. Boston and Philadelphia were great shipbuilding centers, but the construction of vessels stretched from towns in Maine to the shores of the Chesapeake Bay. The whaling industry also contributed enormously to the development of shipbuilding and seamanship along the eastern seaboard of America. In the eighteenth century Nantucket led the world in the profitable harvest of whale oil and whale bone. That small, stark island alone off Cape Cod had 125 deep-water whaling ships in 1770, averaging 93 tons each and cruising the widest reaches of the Atlantic Ocean. Just before the Revolutionary War the colonies probably had about 360 vessels totaling 33,000 tons in whale fisheries with 4850 tough, resourceful, and bold sailors for crews.

The shipbuilding energy of the American colonies was stupendous. In the single year of 1769 the twelve colonies combined built 389 ships, about 70 percent of them constructed in New England. At the time of the Revolution, one-third of all ships flying the British flag had been constructed in America. Moreover, during the eighteenth century the flag of the United States bearing Yankee products sailed to some of the farthest ports in the world. Exactly thirty-nine days after Congress proclaimed the Paris Treaty of Peace with England and the independence of the United States, the first American vessel, the *Empress of China,* had sailed from New York to Macao and Canton to begin the vastly profitable China trade. Robert Morris, friend of George Washington and banker of the American Revolution, invested $120,000 in the enterprise. Carrying a cargo of ginseng herb to the "East Indies," as all Asia was then known to

Americans, the ship returned in 1785 with $50,000 worth of tea as well as chinaware, silks, and muslins. The profit on this single voyage was $30,727. Fifteen ships flying the Stars and Stripes' banner dropped anchor in Macao and Canton in 1788. By the end of the eighteenth century, Elias Hesket Derby, a great ship owner and merchant of Salem, had started trade routes to such distant places as St. Petersburg, Russia, and Capetown, South Africa.[2]

The feats of Yankee merchantmen were phenomenal. Salem exemplified the prodigious energy and enterprise of a very small seaport town. By the end of the eighteenth century, with Baltic, West Indian, and African commerce, and the monopolized pepper trade of Sumatra, Salem contended against Philadelphia, New York, and Boston for fabulous shipping profits. Derby, whose net worth was one million dollars, may have been the first American to study systematically ship models to increase the speed of the oceangoing merchant vessels and, with his own funds, he established a school of navigation for young seamen. One of his ships sailed from Salem to the Irish coast in 11 days and another, in 1783, sailed from Salem to France in eighteen days.

Year by year the ocean trade of America grew, increasing the wealth of the young nation. In 1789 the new federal United States had an aggregate of 123,893 tons in its merchant marine. By 1800 despite the French spoliations, which almost led to war, the aggregate American tonnage was 667,107; and by 1810, after the failure of the Jeffersonian embargo on trade, it was 981,019 tons.[3] Although the United States hardly had a Navy, merchant shipping flourished. Enterprising ship owners, usually handling their own goods and sharing profits with the officers and seamen aboard their vessels, drove the American flag around the world in fine wooden ships with a daring display of sails to obtain highly lucrative returns. Inevitably their competition for trade stimulated envy and hostility in the older maritime nations as well as the greed of pirates. It was the despolitation of American merchant commerce by British, French, and Algerian forces, under a thin veneer of official captures or ill-concealed robberies which amounted to a loss of more than 600 ships and about $20,000,000 before 1800, that finally stimulated Congress to raise the first American Navy under the federal constitution.

The American merchant marine was in that early period of history a formidable fighting force capable, when armed, of capturing and destroying enemy commerce. Indeed, privateers or armed merchantmen were an indispensable part of the seapower of the Americans in both the Revolutionary War and the War of 1812. In 1776 the rebellious United States of America had only thirty-one public vessels. The *Alliance* was the only effective public warship that actually survived the Revolution. By contrast in 1781 there were 449 privateers, managed by private ship owners, which mounted 6735 guns. No fewer than 800 British vessels, evaluated at about $24 million as prizes of war, were captured by American ships in the first two years of the conflict, with privateers accounting for three-quarters of the total. During the War of 1812, about 120 privateers sailed from New York and a total fleet of 515 American armed merchantmen took 1345 British ships as prizes.

United States commerce also suffered heavily in both the Revolutionary War and the War of 1812. During the Revolutionary War, in the port of Halifax, Nova Scotia alone the British libeled 201 American vessels and reported the recapture of 90 British craft. Many privateers were sunk or captured. From Newburyport, Massachusetts twenty-two American vessels with a thousand men were said to have left and never to have returned. The vigorous whaling industry was temporarily destroyed. In the War of 1812, despite dramatic American victories at sea and a bold harassment of British commerce by privateers, 1328 merchant vessels flying the United States flag were lost as prizes. On the whole the American commercial losses during the two wars were probably greater than the British, but considering the relative size of the navies the surprise lay in the effectiveness of the United States armed merchant marine.[4]

With the restoration of peace American commerce revived rapidly. Coastal and river shipping of passengers and cargo flourished. Then, in 1817, five businessmen offered to the public regularly scheduled transatlantic crossings in packet vessels between New York and Liverpool. The four ships, about 400 tons each, all built in New York, offered eastward departures on the fifth of each month and westward departures on the first of each month. During its first ten years of operation the packets of the new Black Ball Line averaged a twenty-three day eastward and forty-day westward crossing of the Atlantic twice a month. In 1821 the Red Star Line was organized and other passenger-cargo lines were started between Philadelphia and London and between New York and LeHavre. Although the packets carried little tonnage, they were scheduled and speedy, greatly facilitating transatlantic communications. They also started the trend of cargo owners contracting for line shipments rather than owning and operating their own boats. Gradually the New York to Europe packet service dominated the transatlantic route. In 1830 there were thirty-six American liners in service, in 1855 there were fifty-six; no foreign lines were able to match the speed, efficiency, or safety of the American vessels. Not until 1847 did the German Hamburg-American line, with four 700-ton ships, attempt to compete with the United States for the transatlantic sailing route.[5]

The American whaling industry, after its eclipse from 1776 to 1815, also grew phenomenally. The tonnage of vessels engaged in whaling more than tripled between 1820 and 1840, when 5 million gallons of whale plus sperm oil and 2 million pounds of whalebone were exported in one year by the United States. In 1854 there were 668 American vessels engaged in hunting, killing, and butchering whales. But the most remarkable development in the merchant marine took place in cargo transport. Until the 1840s, large American ships had been designed for strength to carry heavy cargo, ploughing slowly through the water like beasts of burden. Other vessels—whether caravels, cutters, schooners, sloops, or packets—had been designed for speed, but they were small ships. In 1832 a very different type of ship, the *Ann McKim,* following the design of earlier brigs and schooners, was launched in Baltimore. It was a 493-ton vessel with rather long and convex water lines. The stern, stem-post, and masts were raked. Although not of great carrying capacity, the *Ann McKim* was fast and heralded the great American clipper ships that soon followed, such as the 750-ton *Rainbow* in 1845, with a radical design of a curved forward stern, long hollow water lines, and other architectural innovations. The discovery of gold in California in 1848 led to a great rush for ocean passage to the Pacific while the shipment of Canadian–New England fish cargos to South America, the lucrative China tea trade, and the American carriage of Australia-England trade all stimulated the building of hundreds of swift Yankee clippers that raced in full sail across the oceans of the world. This was, indeed, the greatest era of the American merchant marine.

The growth of the early, vigorous American merchant marine had been achieved entirely by private initiative and enterprise. But there had been some indirect public assistance to favor American shipping. The first business of the first meeting of the House of Representatives under the new United States Constitution of 1789 was a bill to lay a duty on imports. By two laws that year Congress applied lower tariff rates to imports on American vessels and levied higher tonnage and port charges against foreign ships. Such legislation, however, was largely defensive against Great Britain, which discriminated against the Americans and which refused to open the important West Indian trade to U.S. vessels until 1830. The discriminating American tariffs were gradually mitigated by reciprocal trade agreements with foreign nations, and the Tariff Act of 30 July 1846 ended general discrimination. By 1854 the United States led the world in marine architecture, in shipyards, and in seamanship, with a splendid merchant marine nearly equal in tonnage to that of Great Britain and superior to the old mistress of the seas with respect to the average size of the vessels, their speed, management, and profitability. On the eve of the Civil War in 1860, the ocean-borne trade of the United States amounted to more than $687 million of which two-thirds was carried on American vessels totaling 2,379,396 tons, a high-water mark in the history of the merchant marine.[6]

The technological change from sail to steam spelled the decline of the U.S. eminence on the oceans. Despite the familiarity of Americans with steam propulsion, they failed to exploit its advantages. Although Great Britain had made the first steamship able to carry goods and passengers the *Charlotte Dundas*—in 1802, Robert Fulton's 133-foot long *Claremont,* steaming from New York to Albany on the Hudson River in thirty-two hours in the autumn of 1807 was the first vessel propelled by steam successfully placed on a long-distance service. About 48 steamships had been built on the Clyde River in Scotland by 1822, but in America no fewer than 300 steamers were already being used in river and lake services. In 1819 the 300-ton *Savannah,* built in America, was the first sailing vessel to cross the Atlantic by using steam for auxiliary power. Nevertheless, wedded to the excellence of its wooden sailing ships, the United States responded slowly to steam and iron vessels, and builders were especially laggard in abandoning the paddle wheel for the screw propeller after 1844.

In 1838 the British effectively demonstrated the practicality of transatlantic steamship crossings when, in a single year, the *Sirius, Great Western, Liverpool,* and *Royal Williams* crossed the Atlantic powered by burning wood and coal. The 1340-ton *Great Western,* with 440-horsepower engines, made the eastward crossing in 15 days and the westward crossing in 14 days, marking the end of the American packet supremacy. In the same year Samual Cunard arrived in England from Halifax, Nova Scotia and proceeded to organize the British and North American Royal Mail Steam Packet Company, obtaining a mail subsidy of £55,000 a year from the British government, later raised to £81,000 a year. Service from Liverpool to London via Halifax was inaugurated in July 1840. Additional subsidies of £240,000 a year went to the Cunard Company for service to Mexico, Cuba, and southern ports of the United States.

By contrast, the first attempt to capitalize an oceanic steam navigation company in New York in 1838 was abandoned for lack of subscriptions. The U.S. Congress defeated an Act to authorize the Postmaster General to contract with American vessels for mail carriage until 1845. One contract provided $100,000 a year for each ship of the Oceanic Steam Navigation Company that would make bimonthly round-trip voyages between New York and Bremen and $75,000 a year for such services between New York and Le Havre. Another contract went to the E. K. Collins Line in an effort to wrest the important New York to Liverpool service from the British. The Collins Line obtained four new, very fast, 3000-ton steamers, mounted with 800-horsepower engines. It beat the British speed records and forced a reduction in transatlantic rates. However, the cost of constructing the American steamships required for these crossings and their maintenance of tight schedules throughout their round trips far exceeded the estimates of the promotors. Mail subsidies to the Collins Line for the New York to Liverpool run, for example, had originally been set by Congress at $19,250 per voyage for the liners when they made two voyages a month for eight months of a year. Later Congress not only had to advance money to construct the vessels, but by 1854 its subsidy amounted to $33,000 per voyage. In the first 28 voyages the average cost was $65,215; the average income, including the subsidy, was only $42,286. Mail subsidies went to more steamship services between the Isthmus of Panama, New York, and Oregon, particularly after the gold rush in California. But in 1858, after having paid over $14,400,000 in subventions to liners, Congress ended the practice and in the following years paid only for the actual costs of mail carriage on American vessels.

Serious problems for the American merchant marine were already emerging before the Civil War whittled away the early lead of the United States in shipbuilding and sea commerce. During the protracted conflict between the American states the merchant marine declined precipitously. Many of the old wooden ships had been destroyed, but the industry as a whole was slow in utilizing iron, steam, and modern machinery for ocean transport. In fact, the United States in the nineteenth century was among the slowest of the mercantile nations to utilize the advanced technology of iron, steam, and machinery for shipping. The first large British iron steamship for Atlantic services, 3270 tons with screw propulsion, had been the *Great Britain* launched in 1843. By comparison, in the United States the Harlan and Hollingsworth Co. of Wilmington, Delaware built the first iron deep-sea coasting vessel of 450 tons, the propeller-driven steamship *Bangor,* in 1843–1844. Not until 1870 did the American foundries develop heavy machinery and adequate rolling mills for the construction of large iron ships. Between 1872 and 1882 American steamship tonnage grew from 842,000 to only 1,360,000. By 1885 Europe was leading the United States in the use of twin screw propellers, quadruple expansion engines, higher boiler pressures, and steam turbines.

In large measure the decline of the U.S. ocean transport was a result of American concentration on the development of the great wealth of the U.S. interior. Lavish government subsidies to the railroads and a completely protected coastal trade that barred all foreign vessels hardly helped the development of the merchant marine. The sailor's career, with its arbitrary and harsh discipline, appealed less and less to young Americans attracted to the prospering industries in the cities, while the declining efficiency of American ships brought higher insurance rates and other disadvantages in the face of foreign competition. In the halls of Congress calls for government assistance to American shipbuilders and shippers began to grow louder.

Near the end of the Civil War some new government subventions had been granted to American lines, under the guise of mail rates, to develop shipping routes. Subsidies had gone to a Philadelphia and Rio de Janeiro line between 1865 and 1876 and other lines between China, Japan, and San Francisco via Honolulu between 1867 and 1877. But after 1877 the only direct payments to American liners were for sea postage under an act of 1872, revised as a postal aid act in 1891, with conditions on the structure, ownership, and manning of the vessels. Total subventions in this post–Civil War period ran something over $25,000,000. Foreign merchant marines meanwhile received far more generous government assistance. France and Italy, for example, paid general bounties to all their merchant ships on the basis of tonnage, mileage, or some common denominator. From 1850 to 1876 the bounties or subsidies paid by the Crown to British ships ranged from $4 million to $6 million a year; they continued in somewhat smaller amounts to the end of the nineteenth century. But the opponents of shipping subventions in Congress argued that public subsidies had not and would not increase the efficiency of the merchant marine, indeed, that they would thwart competition, innovation, and development, all at a high cost to the taxpayers.

In any case, by 1890 only 928,062 tons of American shipping were engaged in foreign trade and by 1910 only 782,517 tons, although 6,668,966 tons of ships were being used in the monopolized U.S. coastal trade. Only one transatlantic U.S. shipping line remained in operation in the closing years of the nineteenth century. Although the United States had carried 35.6 percent of all American exports and imports by sea in 1870, by 1910 only 8.7 percent of this trade was carried under the American flag. Partly to remedy the dearth of shipping subject to U.S. jurisdiction, the Panama Canal Act of 1912 had provided that foreign ships, less than five-years-old and purchased by American citizens, could be registered in the United States. In 1914 the five-year limit was removed, but the timing was late. In June 1914 Great Britain owned 47.7 percent of all the world's seagoing iron and steel steamers; Germany owned 12 percent, Scandinavia owned 8.7 percent, France owned 4.5 percent, the United States owned 4.3 percent, and Japan owned 3.9 percent. It hardly helped to note that some 100 to 200 million dollars of American capital had been invested in ships with foreign flags by owners who had found greater profit in not registering the ships in the United States.

World War I and the U.S. Shipping Act of 1916

The decline of the American merchant marine was undeniable. But the major policy issue turned on the means of revival. One group, which largely included Democrats and ship operators, had wanted a revision of the navigation laws to permit the purchase of cheaper foreign ships by American citizens for registry in the United States. The other group—mostly Republicans and shipbuilders with their suppliers—had sought protective tariffs and direct subsidies in mail and/or bounties to the shipbuilding industry. Neither party was able to prevail completely. Although the pressure for general subsidies and bounties had failed, a few special subsidies were given to U.S. shipping services to Brazil, Hawaii, China, and Japan as well as for mail services. But all subsidies had been curtailed by 1890 for want of success, the smell of scandal, and political impasse. A very modest shipping subsidy act had passed in 1891, but agitation for greater public assistance continued furiously. As labor costs rose, the shipowners tended to join the position of the shipbuilders in requesting public subsidies, but the agrarian West opposed favors to the industrial-commercial magnates of the eastern seaboard.

In 1903 President Theodore Roosevelt called for the creation of a Merchant Marine Commission to study how the United States might resume its former position in the ocean carrying trade. The Commission, composed of senators, such as Henry Cabot Lodge of Massachusetts, and representatives of Congress, refused to consider the idea of purchasing foreign ships for the American merchant marine, but opted for bounties to all U.S. ships in foreign trade, the establishment of new subsidized ocean lines, and a naval reserve fleet substantially supported by public funds. Legislation to enact these recommendations and other Congressional attempts to provide direct payments to American shipowners and shipbuilders all failed to win a majority vote, but the divisions were close and bitter right up to World War I.

World War I found the United States dreadfully short of merchant tonnage. With British, German, French, and other vessels drafted into their own war services and with additional strains placed on the neutral European commerce by the belligerents, America faced a disastrous shortage of ships for handling its foreign trade, then worth $3785 million. As the nations of Europe committed more and more forces to the widening conflict, demands on worldwide shipping grew. Some 12 million tons of shipping were constantly afloat on the high seas during the war years.

At the same time that concern was being expressed about the decline of the American merchant marine, the public had begun to question the growth of rings, combinations, or cartels of shipping lines in the form of "conferences" that set rates for ocean transport. The rapid increase in ocean tonnage in the nineteenth century, because of the introduction of the steamship with its opportunity for regular, rapid, dependable, and less expensive commerce, had raised the spectre of ruthless competition between lines, which could drive prices down, not only eliminating marginal competitors, but reducing profits to the point of inhibiting investment and innovation in the industry. From 1860 to 1880, for example, British registered steamship tonnage had increased from 450,000 to 2,720,000 tons. The opening of the Suez Canal in 1869 and the frenzied competition for the Indian trade led to the first successful steamship conference, the Calcutta Shipping Conference of 1875, an agreement by the liners that they would all apply the same rates between Calcutta and a number of British ports of departure. Two years later, in response to protests from shippers who had enjoyed more favorable rates, the Conference agreed to permit rebates to shippers who patronized a Conference liner exclusively over a period of years. Unique in this agreement was the rule that rebates would be deferred until the shipper had not only given all business to the conference line for an initial contract period, but also for a number of subsequent years.

Uniform price-fixing agreements of voluntarily associated liner companies and dual-rate schedules for preferred or "loyal" shippers were the essential characteristics of the shipping conference system. The rapid growth of the conference or steamship "ring" system in the closing years of the nineteenth century, with its obvious monopolistic practices as private cartels, prompted two major public inquiries: the British Royal Commission on Shipping Rings in 1906, which issued a five-volume report in 1909, and the U.S. House of Reppresentatives Committee on Merchant Marine and Fisheries investigation in 1912, which led to a four-volume report in 1914.

The findings of the majority of the British Commission were tolerant of the conference system, noting that unrestricted competition in shipping lines would be disastrous to all concerned and that self-regulation by the industry, if not abused, provided the best means of achieving stable rates, regular sailings, and other reasonable expectations of a sound import-export trade. Deferred rebates, it found, also fit the system, but the Commission's majority suggested that shippers might organize to exercise leverage on the lines and that the Board of Trade should receive copies of all conference agreements and assist in arbitration between lines and shippers.

The American approach to the shipping conference system was, first, to recognize, like the British, the value of more numerous and dependable dates of sailing, the stability and uniformity of freight rates, over-time, and certain other advantages of the conference system of ocean transport. But, second, being sensitive to the public clamor against trusts and other combinations to restrain trade at that time, the U.S. Congress wanted to insure open information and fair business practices in the conduct of the industry. The Merchant Marine and Fisheries (Alexander) Committee Report, therefore, maintained that ending the conference system would not ensure free competition, and indeed, would penalize the United States insofar as foreign countries would continue their combinations or rings. It recommended, however, that agreements and rates charged by ocean carriers should be under the supervision of the Interstate Commerce Commission.[7]

The Alexander Committee's recommendations were not enacted exactly into legislation, but its general philosophy was acceptable. Instead, after decades of debate and vacillating support of the American merchant marine, Congress passed on 6 September 1916, a decisive U.S. Shipping Act. The Act essentially recognized the legality of shipping conferences, exempting them from antitrust legislation, but subject to regulation by a Shipping Board composed of five commissioners appointed by the President with the advice and consent of the Senate. Deferred rebates were prohibited, and various forms of retaliatory, discriminatory, or unfair practices against shippers were barred, including the use of "fighting" ships, which conferences, without regard for losses, sometimes used to duplicate services and undercut the prices of a competitive newcomer to their routes.

The Shipping Board was expected to inquire into rates, regulate conditions, and otherwise deal with problems of merchant shipping due to the emergency conditions of the great war in Europe. With the entry of the United States into World War I, however, the national crisis in shipping required instant attention and direct government intervention to expand and to develop the merchant marine. The promotional aspects of the Shipping Act of 1916, therefore, took priority over the regulatory aspects—and this has been the pattern of all later merchant marine acts.

The following pages *first* will deal with the government's efforts to increase the size and efficiency of the American merchant fleet and *second* with the activities to regulate ocean transport—although both aspects of merchant marine policy have been complementary and coterminous.

On 16 April 1917 the Shipping Board, under its statutory powers, organized the U.S. Shipping Board Emergency Fleet Corporation, capitalized at $50 million, and appointed Major General George W. Goethels, builder of the Panama Canal, as General Manager. The division of authority between the Chairman of the parent Shipping Board and the General Manager of the Fleet Corporation, however, led to the resignations of Goethels and two successors in 1917. Finally the appointment of one man, Charles Piez, as both Chairman of the Shipping Board and General Manager of the Fleet Corporation solved that organizational dilemma.

From the beginning, the Fleet Corporation worked heroically to get ships constructed and to build "a bridge of ships" across the Atlantic to the beleagured Allies in Europe. This involved not only contracting for the construction of wooden, prefabricated, and steel vessels, but requisitioning and completing for service American ships under construction or seized enemy vessels, and, beyond that, the building of shipyard plants. The expenditures, ultimately more than 3.3 billion dollars of public money, were enormous, and huge profits were made by private contractors through lump-sum contracts or cost-plus contracts paying a percentage of labor and materials costs to the contractor for overhead and profits. Many of the contractors had little or no experience in shipbuilding. Everything, of course, had to be done in an atmosphere of emergency, almost regardless of cost, and the statistics on shipbuilding were impressive. In 1917 there had been 61 shipyards (24 of them for wooden vessels) operating in the United States, but by 1918 there were 341 shipyards with 1284 launching ways, double the total of all other nations. In fiscal year 1918 American shipbuilding doubled the production of 1917, tripled that of 1916, and was four times greater than in 1915. On 30 June 1918 the United States had 9,924,518 tons of merchant shipping under its flag, of which 4,292,405 were ocean-going vessels over 1000 tons.

Juxtaposed to these figures, however, is the fact that over half-a-million tons of shipping came from the seizure of German vessels. Neutral Dutch ships were also commandeered. Before the end of the war the regular Shipping Board construction program had delivered less than one million tons of shipping. After the Armistice the Board had permitted the laying of keels for 5 million tons of shipping, although most of the contracts were later cancelled. Then, under political pressure from labor and shipbuilders, who had become used to the income and profits from the huge shipyards that public money had created, the Board continued to let contracts in 1919. One-third of the whole fleet built for the Shipping Board was started after World War I had ended.

At the end of World War I, Congress, returning to "normalcy," sought to foster and develop a sound American merchant marine that would be able to carry the greater portion of American commerce in time of peace and to serve as a military or naval auxiliary in time of national emergency. Under the guidance of Senator Wesley Jones and the Senate Committee on Commerce, a far-reaching Merchant Marine Act was passed on 5 June 1920.

The highly nationalistic Act was intended not only to give preferential rail rates to American shippers over foreign competitors, but to restrict the coastal trade of Samoa, Guam, and the Philippines to American vessels. It also directed the President to give notice to foreign nations of the United States' intention to abrogate treaties that restricted foreign trade discrimination. President Woodrow Wilson, President Warren Harding, and their successors simply refused to denounce the reciprocal trade treaties. Second thoughts about railroad preferences and the plea of the Philippines for competitive coastal trade, coupled with deliberate inaction by the Chief Executive, vitiated some of the mercantilist objectives of the 1920 Merchant Marine Act. The Act also provided for generous mail subsidies to U.S. vessels. The Shipping Board membership was expanded to seven members, who retained all the regulatory authority conferred by the Act of 1916. They were given additional power to operate and to sell the government fleet that had been acquired under the emergency legislation to private operators.

Having been frustrated in obtaining discriminatory tariffs against foreign competitors, the shipping interests next sought direct subsidies from the U.S. government. In 1922 President Harding asserted that the United States was losing $16 million a month on its publicly owned fleet, which was being operated under generous contracts by private managers. The President favored quick sale and low prices to private companies and the Shipping Board sweetened an attractive bill by recommending a large merchant marine fund from which all American vessels in foreign trade would receive bounties per mile-ton with additional sums for fast vessels. Opponents of the bill objected that, first, the government intended to sell its ships, which had cost more than $3 billion, for $200 million, and, second, pay subsidies of about $750 million on these same ships and others to the new private owners over the next ten years. The bill narrowly passed the house, but the Senate blocked any vote on it. Nevertheless, between 1921 and 1928 the Shipping Board sold 1164 ships at an average price of $14-$18 a ton. Some of these transport vessels had cost $300-$400 a ton to build. Other cargo vessels were sold for scrap at $8 a ton and still other vessels were withdrawn from service. Despite President Calvin Coolidge's recommendation to restrict the Shipping Board to regulatory functions, Congress did nothing. Later a Congressional investigation of the tremendous losses of the Fleet Corporation scathingly blamed the lobbying of the shipping interests for obtaining inordinate profits and denounced their sympathetic treatment by the Corporation.

The Jones Act of 1920 failed to revive the American merchant marine. A surplus of aging ships, a decline in international trade, and the extravagant management of public shipping discouraged the construction of new vessels. In 1925 Germany built twice the tonnage of the United States and Great Britain eight times as much. In 1927 the U.S. Shipping Board reported that since 1921 Great Britain had launched forty-one first-class merchant vessels for every one sliding down the ways of the United States. Four years after the great economic depression began in 1929, international trade amounted to only 64 percent of its monetary value in 1913, but the world merchant marine had increased by 50 percent and it was far more efficient than prewar sea transport. Technological changes, moreover, were rapidly making the American fleet obsolete. In 1913 about 90 percent of all the steamships in the world burned coal; by 1928 only 60 percent were burning coal. Diesel motor engines were rapidly replacing steam engines; very few vessels had oil-fueled motor engines before World War I, but by 1928 about 5 million tons of shipping were propelled by oil.

In 1926 the Shipping Board had pointed out to Congress the necessity of a replacement program for American vessels, whether under public or private ownership, and had made certain legislative recommendations. A new Merchant Marine Act in 1928 provided for mail contracts up to ten years for American vessels on routes certified by the Postmaster General and allowed graduated and more valuable subsidies for faster and heavier ships. The Act also granted new authority to the Shipping Board, enabling it to recommend a ship replacement program and to undertake construction in American shipyards with Congressional appropriations. The Act permitted the Board to establish an insurance fund for ships in which the United States had an interest and to increase its revolving construction fund to $250 million. Loans by the Board could be extended to twenty years, up to three-quarters of the construction cost of vessels, and at low interest rates for ships operated in foreign trade. The Shipping Board, still empowered to dispose of the publicly owned fleet, which was managed mainly under generous contracts, continued to sell its vessels at greatly marked-down prices and often without competitive bidding. By the 1928 Act, the managing operators of the government vessels were lured to further exorbitant profits in buying cheaply the government-owned ships and then obtaining bountiful mail contracts for them. From fiscal 1929 to 1934 the cost of mail contracts rose from $9 million to $39 million. First limited by the intervention of the director of the Budget, they were finally cancelled in 1937.[8]

The Merchant Marine Act of 1936 and World War II

For some years Congressional criticism of marine subsidies that had plainly enriched many shipowners and operators had been mounting. The election of President Franklin D. Roosevelt and a Democratic Congress, in the depth of national economic disaster, spurred a thorough reexamination of American marine policy. To begin with, the President was authorized to modify or cancel any existing mail contract he found not serving the public interest. Then in 1933 the Shipping Board, independent since 1916, was reduced in size and made a Bureau within the Commerce Department. Next an investigation by a Select Committee of Congress revealed great waste and inefficiency in the private ownership of merchant (and air) transportation under government subsidies and called for the complete end of such public assistance. But the administration, stressing the importance of the merchant marine to the United States, urged Congress to put an end to disguised subsidies and to provide instead direct payments for differentials between United States and foreign construction and operating costs of the merchant marine under proper administrative safeguards.

After numerous drafts, fifteen models, and many compromises, Congress finally adopted the great Merchant Marine Act of 1936. The Act started from the old premise that the United States had to maintain an "adequate" merchant marine for carrying a substantial part of American trade over essential routes and be convertible to national defense needs in time of emergency. To achieve that objective the Act provided for "parity" between U.S. and foreign trade lines through direct public construction and operating subsidies to compensate the American shipping industry for its higher costs in materials and manpower. Moreover, the old construction loan revolving fund was continued at a 3.5 percent interest rate on all new loans. In a period of massive unemployment Congress also made every effort to protect the jobs of American seamen by severely limiting the number of aliens that could be employed on U.S. flag vessels and by regulating the hours, the conditions of work, and the minimum wages of the crews. It also legislated the practice that all American exports financed in whole or part by any instrumentality of the government should be carried by U.S. flag vessels. Finally, as a national defense measure, special compensation went to shipbuilders incorporating Navy-recommended design features on any subsidized vessel, while—in case of emergency—all vessels constructed with subsidy aid were subject to repurchase by the United States at cost less depreciation.[9]

Whatever its faults, the 1936 Merchant Marine Act was the first comprehensive formulation of the U.S. maritime shipping policy through direct subsidies and other forms of government assistance. In some ways the Act reorganized and improved the past maritime subsidy programs; in other ways it became a model and source for all subsequent merchant marine acts. The Act took special care of American sailors. Congress, moreover, had insisted on the creation of a new independent five-member U.S. Maritime Commission, with commissioners to be appointed by the president for terms of six years on a nonpartisan basis. The Commission was given authority to investigate, regulate, and help operate the American merchant marine and further provided with ample financial resources as well as wide latitude in recruiting staff.

The new U.S. Maritime Commission set to work vigorously in April 1937, under the chairmanship of Joseph P. Kennedy. Within two months a settlement was reached on thirty-two of the forty-three outstanding mail contracts, for less than $750,000. The Commission also started to pay operating subsidies, sold 33 of the government's 189 moored vessels, announced plans for 95 ships to be built within three years, and endeavored to bring about efficiency by reducing the number of routes and operators that would receive subsidies so that lines would merge.[10] Admiral Emory Land succeeded Kennedy, who became U.S. Ambassador to Great Britain in 1938, but the Commission, despite its resources in money and professional staff, faced the perennial and intractable difficulties of the American shipping industry. A recommendation for new legislation to permit construction of ships abroad, if the subsidies required for American construction should exceed the legal maximum, failed. Many small lines, moreover, chose to operate without government subsidies rather than consolidate with other companies. And a revised Commission program to construct fifty ships a year had barely gotten under way by 1939 when World War II began to devastate Europe.

In 1920 the United States had registered some 16 million tons of merchant marine, about 28 percent of the world's total; by 1939, despite all the efforts of the government to bolster the shipping industries, the tonnage had decreased to 12 million, about 17 percent of the world's total. Moreover, in 1921 about 52 percent of the 82 million tons of cargo of U.S. foreign trade sailed on the American merchant marine, whereas in 1939 only 22 percent of 93 million tons was transported under an American flag. Some critics of prevailing policies had argued that the very premises of the American merchant marine acts were wrong—that it was not necessary for either economic or national security reasons to develop artificially a large U.S. flag merchant marine. They further argued that the best merchant marine for the public interest would not be provided by a system of subsidies to private entrepreneurs but rather by direct government construction and operation of the required vessels. Such criticism, however, had failed to penetrate Congressional legislation prior to 1939 and was, of course, buried in the emergency war years from 1941 to 1945.

During World War II an emergency shipbuilding program again galvanized the tremendous resources of the American people, who, once more, were granted continental security from immediate attack from Europe or Asia by the oceans. At the end of 1938, under its construction program, the U.S. Maritime Commission had contracted for fifty-two new ships. In 1939, as Germany struck at Poland, bringing war to Great Britain and France, the Commission contracted for an additional eighty-nine ships. Then, in 1940 President Roosevelt ordered an emergency fleet of 200 vessels, followed by another directive to add 112 more ships to the imperative schedule.[11]

The Neutrality Act of 1934 and a Presidential proclamation had essentially prohibited American vessels from entering the waters of the European belligerents and, until the Lend-Lease Act of March 1941, the Act had denied credits for the purchase of badly needed supplies to the very states, notably Great Britain, to whom the American people were sympathetic. To circumvent the neutrality laws, up to 200 U.S. ships, with Washington's encouragement, had transferred their registry by November 1941 to "flags of convenience," such as Panama, Liberia, and Honduras, in order to transport fuel and material directly to Great Britain. Faced with a crushing necessity for mass production, moreover, the U.S. Maritime Commission adopted the design of a British 10,000-ton vessel, a clumsy, but serviceable and easily built ship to be known as the Liberty ship, and ordered construction. The Commission received the first ship of this type, the *Patrick Henry*, about the same time as the Japanese attacked the United States at Pearl Harbor, Hawaii, on 7 December 1941.

After the outbreak of war with Japan and Germany, the construction of ships in the United States was phenomenal: during the four years from 1942 through 1945 about 4070 cargo vessels, 720 tankers, and 125 passenger and passenger-cargo vessels were built, apart from some 1500 warships. The aggregate of this fantastic four-year outpouring of people, money, and materials into merchant vessels was 36,960,592 tons of merchant shipping.

Following the precedent of World War I, an independent agency, directed by the Chairman of the U.S. Maritime Commission, was created by Executive Order on 7 February 1942 to be responsible for wartime ship operations and the administration of shipping practices. But the U.S. Maritime Commission itself continued to manage the shipping construction program. Early in 1941 the Commission had found that existing private shipyards could not possibly handle the extraordinary demand for vessels, so it began the construction of government-owned shipyards, first for the production of Liberty ships, then for other types of ships. Some 4,000,000 American men, women, and children were employed in shipyards and in factories for supplying shipyards during the peak of the crisis. The ocean logistics of World War II were staggering. Millions of U.S. troops were convoyed across the Atlantic and to the farthest reaches of the Pacific, all of whom had to be supported with food, fuel, equipment, weapons, and ammunition. The invasion of Normandy in June 1944 alone had kept 1.5 million tons of shipping busy. Estimates of World War II logistics concluded that 6 tons of cargo space per man were required for establishing beachheads and thereafter 1 ton per man per month was required for maintenance.

From 1936 to the end of World War II the U.S. merchant marine had quadrupled in number of ships to 5529 and quintupled in capacity to 40 million tons. The greater part of these vessels were the prefabricated Liberty and Victory ships. The British merchant fleet, which had been roughly double the United States in number of ships and tonnage in 1939, emerged from its ordeal only slightly reduced in size. But by 1945 the British had only half the number of vessels and 37 percent of the tonnage of the United States. Norway, the Netherlands, France, and Sweden were the only other states left with more than a million tons afloat, all greatly reduced from 1939, except for neutral Sweden. In addition to the enormous American tonnage built by the emergency program and still intact in 1945, some 604 U.S. merchant ships had been lost by direct enemy action and another 139 sunk through marine hazards due to war conditions.

Even before the war ended the United States had recognized that without a reconstruction of the economics of western Europe, leading to increased trade and full employment, there could be no world-wide prosperity. Specifically the 1946 Merchant Ship Sales Act, therefore, was designed not only to rescue the U.S. government-owned vessels by sales at fixed prices with cut-off dates to American citizens, but, if no offers were received from American citizens, to sell them to foreign purchasers. In fact, by 1948 the U.S. Maritime Commission had sold over 1000 ships for foreign registry, bringing the American percentage of the world merchant marine tonnage down to 36.4 percent while augmenting the British, Norwegian, French, Danish, and other fleets.

Maritime Board, Maritime Commission, and Maritime Administration

The following decade was marked by the 1951-1953 Korean War years and the Suez crisis of 1956-1957. Heavy demands were placed on world shipping during both these emergencies, which resulted in the development of large oil tankers and a highly profitable ocean carriage. But this period also saw rapidly escalating wages in the United States, which increased the difficulty of matching the high construction and operating costs of American vessels against foreign competition by some "parity" formula. Furthermore, a slowing of economic growth at the end of the decade and an abundance of worldwide shipping hardly helped the situation of U.S. flag ships, particularly the tramp steamers, which did not enjoy the direct operating subsidies of line operators on essential routes. Despite the government subsidies extended to the construction of ships and despite the subsidies paid for the operation of some 300 line ships of passenger and/or general dry cargo on "essential" routes, the total amount of tonnage in foreign trade under the American flag barely increased in twelve years, from 9.14 million in 1950 to 10.2 million in 1962.[12] During the same period, moreover, the share of U.S. foreign trade carried on American ships steadily declined to only 9 percent in 1962 for all cargoes combined. Although the subsidized liners had fared rather well in obtaining a large share of U.S. foreign trade, tramp vessels, generally contracted for single voyage bulk cargo delivery, were hard hit. Without the legal requirement that at least 50 percent of all U.S. foreign assistance commodities had to sail under an American flag (cargo preference), the liners would not have done so well and the tramp steamers would have disappeared completely. By 1962 about 20 percent of all outbound cargo from the United States fell under the cargo preference rule; half of all the revenues to liners and virtually all the revenues to tramp steamers were then derived from government orders. (Categorization of ships by purpose and service is complex. Passenger lines are clearly advertised, but also carry cargo; so-called combination passenger-cargo vessels have accommodations for more than 12 persons; "reefers" carry chilled cargo and "refrigerators" carry frozen or chilled cargoes. Tankers usually carry petroleum products, but could carry creosote or molasses. Liners are distinguished from tramp vessels by their regular scheduled service under one management between designated ports and by their offering to carry all cargo and passengers offered on a space-available basis before a fixed sailing time.)

A major shift in tanker shipping occurred after World War II. During the war about 500 tankers had been built in the United States, and American-flag tankers had led the world in numbers. From 1955 to 1963, however, only about sixty tankers were built in the United States. By 1964 only 381 of 3000 tankers in the world were registered in the United States—and 62 of the American tankers, owned by the government, were actually tied up. The United Kingdom and Norway had more tankers in service than the United States while Japan and the Soviet Union were rapidly increasing their fleets. Many ships owned by foreign affiliates of U.S. companies, however, as in the past, had been placed in foreign registries—Liberian, United Kingdom, Panama, Netherlands, France, Honduras, and so forth—to avoid the costs of purchasing American-built vessels, the high wages of American crews, and U.S. taxation.

In 1950 the President's Reorganization Plan 21 had created a new three-member Federal Maritime Board located administratively within the Department of Commerce. The Board retained, however, both its independent regulatory powers under the 1916 Shipping Act and its authority to promote a sound merchant marine so long as they were in harmony with the policies of the Secretary of Commerce. The administrative functions of the former U.S. Maritime Commission were simultaneously transferred to a new Maritime Administration within the Department of Commerce, although until 1961 the Chairman of the Federal Maritime Board also headed ex officio the Maritime Administration.

During its eleven-year existence from 1950 to 1961 the Federal Maritime Board pursued the mandate of the 1936 Merchant Marine Act to provide an American merchant marine that would be sufficient: (1) to carry a substantial portion of U.S. waterborne foreign commerce; (2) to maintain essential international shipping routes; (3) to serve as a military auxiliary in national emergency; (4) to be owned and operated under the U.S. flag by U.S. citizens as may be practicable; and (5) to be composed of the best equipped, safest, and most suitable vessels constructed in the United States and manned by trained citizen personnel. To achieve these goals, the Board continued to approve direct subsidies for merchant vessel construction and operation; however, with new legislation by Congress, drummed up by the pressure of the shipping interests, the Board not only augmented the direct subsidies, but also added various indirect subsidies.

These practices were continued after August 1961 when Congress approved the President's Reorganization Plan #7 creating a new five-member Federal Maritime Commission, separate from the Commerce Department, to handle regulation of the merchant marine, and delegating all promotional and administrative responsibilities to the Secretary of Commerce and a Maritime Administration in the Commerce Department. Then, by a Departmental order, a three-member Maritime Subsidy Board, chaired by the Maritime Administrator, was established to award, terminate, or amend subsidy agreements.

The maximum ship construction subsidy paid by the government to achieve parity with foreign builders had originally been fixed at 50 percent of cost in the 1936 Merchant Marine Act. In 1960 the maximum subsidy to ship construction had been raised to 55 percent for a two-year period; in 1962 that authority had been extended for two more years, but Congress also raised the maximum subsidy on passenger ship construction to 60 percent; in 1964 the subsidies had been extended by Congress for another year, in 1965 again for a year; in 1966 the construction subsidies were extended another two years, only to be extended again in 1968 to June 1969. In fiscal year 1960 the ship construction differential subsidies had amounted to $69.1 million; from 1965 through 1969 they averaged over $137 million a year.

Operating differential subsidies to liners, meanwhile, had also risen from $152.7 million in fiscal year 1960 to an average of almost $190 million annually in the second half of the decade. The subsidies were paid to fourteen companies in order to maintain thirty-three essential trade routes and six services. In addition, the Federal Maritime Board had steadily expanded the benefits of the government-paid insurance of the unpaid balance (75 percent) of loans and mortgages covering the construction costs of vessels. In 1938 the benefit had applied only to ships in domestic and "contiguous" foreign trade; in 1953 the vessel loan-mortgage insurance, covering 90 percent of the unpaid (75 percent) balance, was extended to subsidized vessels in the foreign trade; then, in 1954, the insurance was extended to 90 percent of the unpaid (87.5 percent) balance of unsubsidized vessels; and, finally, in 1956 the Board was authorized to cover 100 percent of the unpaid (90 percent or 87.5 percent) balance. By 1968 the government-paid insurance on American shipping had a value of $651 million and covered 129 vessels.

To this gross public assistance to the merchant marine there also had been added in 1960 by Public Law 86-575 a program of exchanging old operating vessels owned by private unsubsidized companies for better ships of the U.S. reserve fleet. From 30 June 1960 to 30 June 1969 eighty-one government-owned vessels were exchanged for eighty-five private ships. The Maritime Administration received $11.4 million from the shipowners for the differential in value, but the Fleet vessels were a good bargain for the private entrepreneurs. Finally, the shipping industry received additional government aid through special payments for incorporating national defense design features in vessels, for wage differentials between American and foreign seamen, for training merchant seamen, and for navigational research and experimentation programs.

Whether the American fleet had met or still could meet the standards expressed in the Merchant Marine Act of 1936 nevertheless remained in doubt. In fact, the available vessels had grown larger in tonnage and more modern in design, while "essential" routes had been maintained. And the U.S. reserve fleet had an appreciable value for national emergencies. In 1965, for example, the Department of Defense called on ships in the National Defense Reserve Fleet, then totaling 1959 vessels, to assist in carrying military supplies to Vietnam. From 30 June 1965 through 30 June 1969 more than 160 ships were withdrawn from the fleet, repaired, and assigned to private shipping companies under a General Agency Agreement for operation under direction of the Military Sea Transportation Service. Of 33.2 million tons of cargo carried by U.S. ships to Vietnam in this period, 26 percent was carried by Maritime Administration ships, 67 percent by privately owned ships, and the balance by vessels of the Military Sea Transportation Service.

The costs of the U.S. Merchant Marine to the public, however, were very high. Moreover, the American merchant fleet was older than the world average, and the share of U.S. foreign trade sailing under the American flag had steadily declined. In 1956 more than 20 percent of U.S. foreign trade had still been carried in U.S. flag ships; by 1959 the figure had dropped to 9.7 percent, by 1965 it had gone down to 7.5 percent, and by 1969 only 5.6 percent of U.S. foreign trade sailed under an American flag.

In 1965 President Lyndon B. Johnson had promised new proposals for revitalizing the American merchant marine, but a comprehensive program was not presented to Congress until 1968—only to be met with disappointment and dismay by the interested legislative committees, vessel builders, shippers, and maritime labor. The administration had earnestly sought an overhaul of the ship-operating differential subsidies, including the termination of assistance to passenger ships; it proposed the continuation of ship construction subsidies, but at levels determined by the new Department of Transportation and the Department of Defense; and it recommended the end of discrimination against the purchase of vessels abroad by American ship operators. Basically the Johnson Administration had wanted to transfer the Maritime Administration from the Commerce Department to the new Department of Transportation and only to extend annually and temporarily the merchant marine subsidies until Congress approved alternatives. Congress, on the other hand, wanted to strengthen the Maritime Administration by making it an independent agency and to move forward with a big, bold new ship construction program of thirty-five to forty vessels a year rather than the twelve to thirteen annual rate in the late sixties. The result was a stand-off between the White House and Capitol Hill. The Maritime Administration remained in the Commerce Department. But a bill to create an independent Federal Maritime Administration was pocket-vetoed by the

President in 1968. A thorough revision of the President's proposals by the Merchant Marine and Fisheries Committee was in turn blocked by the Rules Committee in the House of Representatives.[13]

Regulation of Shipping

The U.S. Shipping Act of 1916, although enacted in the spirit of regulating the shipping industry, had become more notorious for its promotion and development of the U.S. Merchant Marine. Indeed, the regulatory aspects of the 1916 Shipping Act had hardly been approached until the end of World War I—and in the 1920s the Shipping Board, through its Emergency Fleet Corporation, had itself been an active member of most of the important shipping conferences that were handling American foreign trade. The acts of 1920, 1928, and 1936 had also been primarily concerned with the growth and efficiency of the American merchant fleet, seeking to maintain a substantial portion of U.S. foreign commerce aboard American flagships and to ensure the merchant fleet's availability as a naval auxiliary. The regulatory functions of the Shipping Board, somewhat expanded by the Merchant Marine acts of 1920 and 1936, had been transferred to the U.S. Shipping Board Bureau of the Department of Commerce in 1933, then to a new independent agency, the U.S. Maritime Commission, in 1936, then to the Department of Commerce again in 1950 with its new Federal Maritime Board, then once more to an independent, bipartisan agency, the Federal Maritime Commission in 1961.

At issue through the several agency reorganizations was whether to associate or to disassociate: (1) the regulation of shipping routes, services, and agreements; (2) the quasi-judicial functions of interpreting, amending, or terminating the ship construction and operating subsidies; and (3) the administration of the subsidy contracts and ship construction laws, the maintenance of the reserve fleet, and other administrative requirements of the laws relating to the merchant marine. Put another way, the question was whether to juxtapose the promotion of a modern American merchant marine, which could transport larger portions of U.S. trade and serve as an auxiliary in national defense, with the need to ensure fair competition for all ship operators and reasonable charges to all shippers at minimum public cost.

When Congress has been presented with a choice between regulation of the shipping industry to maintain aggressive competition and the promotion of a larger, U.S. trade-bearing merchant marine, owned and operated by Americans, the promotional interests have clearly had more political weight. In 1961, for example, Congress faced the question of regulating dual-rate contracts in the shipping industry. This was another form of the deferred-rate or the loyalty rebates given by past shipping conferences, which were originally outlawed by the 1916 Shipping Act. After three years of investigation, a bill emerged from the House of Representatives that would have allowed the dual-rate system but strongly subjected it to specific conditions to prevent abuses. A Senate bill on the same matter not only watered down the conditions for dual rates, but also stoutly affirmed the need to protect the shipping conference system, even with dual-rates contracts, in the interest of maintaining a strong U.S. merchant marine. In 1961 the Senate bill was enacted into Public Law 87-346.[14]

No simple answer to questions of promotion versus regulation of the American merchant marine has been available in the past; nor is there likely to be an easy resolution of the issues in the future, because ocean shipping is an international enterprise. It functions under the laws, administration, and economic interests of two or more nations, with buyers, sellers, and transport companies of diverse nationalities. It makes use of the high seas, which are not subject to the jurisdiction of any state, and, under international law, it passes innocently through all territorial waters or enters peacefully the harbors and ports of the world. Subject to the observance of public rules for navigation, safety, health, and other legal requirements, moreover, shipping companies, with large capital investments in vessels, must make profits in their carriage of trade unless operated completely at public expense. Moreover, a unilateral attempt by the United States in peacetime to regulate both ends of its foreign ocean trade by prescribing the freight prices and the shipping practices for all vessels entering its harbors is fraught with perils of confusion, resentment, and retaliation by other nations that could seriously damage American commerce.

Since ancient times ocean transport has been international in character. With the great revival of water-borne trade in the Middle Ages, special agreements between private individuals concerned with the security and success of their hazardous overseas enterprise were required. Over the centuries a large body of public law, commonly known as admiralty, was developed to apply to the operation of vessels, the shipment of cargo, and the conduct of seamen. Customary international law—the common, although not always universal, practice of nations—had by the nineteenth century recognized the right of all registered ships of coastal states to navigate the high seas without interruption in peace and had acknowledged other maritime rules relating to war and neutrality.

The first major public international conference dealing exclusively with the problems of safety of life and property at sea was held in Washington from 16 October 1889 to 23 December 1889. The conference adopted a number of resolutions and made recommendations for national legislation to prescribe lights, signals, speeds, and the markings of vessels as well as rules for saving life in event of shipwreck, qualifications for seamen, designation of lanes on frequent routes, and the removal of dangers to navigation. The delegates in Washington also considered the establishment of a permanent international maritime commission, but then resolved that it would not be expedient to create such an organization at that time. Eight years later the omnipresent dangers of navigation on the seas and the multiplication of technical questions affecting the secure, rapid, and equitable shipment of goods from one foreign port to another stimulated the formation of the International Maritime Committee. The Committee was a private group pledged to study and recommend improvements in law for international shipping. Between 1897 and 1937 it held 19 conferences and it was instrumental in drafting conventions on collisions, salvage and safety at sea, uniform documentation for the transport of goods, and other maritime matters.

On 23 September 1910, with the assistance of the International Maritime Committee, two conventions were signed at Brussels at the third international conference on maritime law. The convention provided for the unification of rules of assistance and salvage at sea, and for collisions at sea. Two years later the fateful disaster of the *Titanic,* which sank with great loss of life after hitting an iceberg, led to the 1914 Convention on Safety of Life at Sea, signed in London on 20 January 1914. Partly due to the outbreak of World War I the Convention did not completely come into force, but the United States, even though it had not ratified the convention, undertook through its Coast Guard an ice patrol of the North Atlantic with the expenses of the patrol shared by other nations of the world.[15]

As early as 1884 the chief draughtsman of a U.S. hydrographic surveying expedition, E. R. Knorr, had suggested the advantages of common bathymetric and other ocean charts. He had with great imagination called for a permanent international hydrographic institution that might serve as a clearing house for coordinating the activities of the several national hydrographic services created in the 19th century. In 1912 an international maritime conference in St. Petersburg, dealing with various navigation and shipping problems, acknowledged the need for more accurate ocean charts, a need that was greatly dramatized by World War I. The heads of the hydrographic services of Great Britain and France then took the lead in discussions that led to convening the International Hydrographic Conference in London in 1918. The twenty-four states represented at the conference between 24 June and 16 July, including Prince Albert of Monaco, an oceanographer of great renown, adopted a number of resolutions on navigation but, above all, agreed to establish an International Hydrographic Bureau, which came into being on 21 June 1921 and was located in Monte Carlo. The Bureau, whose task has been to make worldwide navigation safer and easier through advancements in the science of hydrography and by obtaining a uniformity in hydrographic documents, has held several general conferences since its establishment. Although the resolutions of the Bureau have had no legal force, they serve to improve the coordination of the more than forty-member hydrographic services, including the United States. Publication of the *International Hydrographic Review* twice a year as well as the *International Hydrographic Bulletin* monthly has provided statistics and studies of value to ocean navigation and transport.[16]

The outbreak of World War I, as indicated earlier, raised critical problems of ocean shipping for the Allied Powers. Early in 1917 an Inter-Allied Shipping Council was formed to coordinate allocations of tonnage for the war emergency, but its work was only partially successful. After the Americans entered the war, however, the Allied Maritime Transport Council was established in December 1917, which greatly assisted the Allied war effort by analyzing tonnage data and elaborating shipping requirements with recommendations for the best allocations of the Allied merchant fleets. But its functions were limited to the war emergency.

The Peace Treaty of Versailles, signed on 28 June 1919 and embodying the new League of Nations, looked forward to securing and maintaining freedom of communications and transit. Under the auspices of the League of Nations, four general conferences on communications and transportation were held: in Barcelona (1921), where a declaration of the rights of inland states to possess a merchant fleet on the high seas was approved; in Geneva (1923); in Geneva (1927), where a permanent Committee for Communications and Transit was approved; and, finally, in Geneva (1931), where draft conventions on the equality of treatment of vessels in ports and uniform tonnage measurements were considered. Then, in 1938, a completely new statute for the Committee for Communications and Transit was approved by the League. It provided great autonomy for the Committee and authorized it to hold general conferences, to establish special committees on air navigation, rail transport, maritime ports, navigation, and other subjects, and to appoint its own secretariat. Unfortunately World War II began in Europe in 1939, suspending the work of the Committee for Communications and Transit and leaving the League's secretariat to carry out its functions as feasible under wartime conditions until 1946.[17]

To meet the marine tonnage and routing crisis of World War II a Combined Shipping Adjustment Board had been formed in 1942, essentially to coordinate the national shipping authorities of the United States and the United Kingdom that had been established for the war emergency. Some consultations with the Soviet Union and China occurred, but it was not until July–August 1944 that eight allied countries met to establish the United Maritime Council. By the end of World War II the Council through intergovernmental agreements, regulated routes, sailings, cargoes, and freighter charter rates, included eighteen governments, and controlled 90 percent of the tonnage under Allied and neutral flags.

With the surrender of Japan in August 1945, World War II came to an end. The final meeting of the United Maritime Council's Executive Board in London in February 1946 agreed that when the authority of the Council terminated in March there was still need for some provisional or international shipping organizations to provide an orderly reallocation of postwar tonnage and to support the extraordinary relief and rehabilitation activities then taking place. The Board decided, therefore, that there should be a voluntary pool of merchant tonnage and a provisional United Maritime Consultative Council to serve as a forum on shipping problems pending the full restoration of peace and normal economic life.

Meanwhile the United Nations Charter, signed on 26 June 1946, had set forth in Article 1, among its purposes, "To achieve international cooperation in solving international problems of an economic, social, cultural, or humanitarian character . . ." The UN Preparatory Commission, meeting in London in December 1945, suggested the creation of a Temporary Transportation and Communications Commission, which was established by resolution on 16 February 1946. Three months later the Commission reported to the Economic and Social Council that only the International Hydrographic Bureau, the International Commission for the Maintenance of the Cape Spartel Lighthouse, and the Provisional United Maritime Consultative Council were functioning for problems of maritime transportation and communications. The Commission then invited the views of the United Maritime Consultative Council on the establishment of a worldwide organization for shipping to deal with technical matters. At its second and final meeting in Washington from 24 October to 30 October 1946, the Provisional United Maritime Consultative Council agreed that international machinery was needed to permit governmental cooperation in the field of public regulation and practices on technical matters affecting shipping engaged in international trade; to encourage adoption of the highest practicable standards of maritime safety and efficiency in navigation; to help remove all forms of discrimination and unnecessary restrictions by governments affecting overseas shipping; and to provide for consideration of any shipping problem of an international character that might be referred to it by the United Nations. The Council then recommended that a new Intergovernmental Maritime Consultative Organization, consultative and advisory in function, be created as a specialized agency of the United Nations. After preliminary work by the UN Transportation and Communications Commission in 1946, a provisional Intergovernmental Maritime Consultative Organization met in Paris in May 1947. Then, at the invitation of the Economic and Social Council, thirty-two governments met in Geneva from 19 February 1948 to 6 March 1948, and twenty-one approved the establishment of the Intergovernmental Maritime Consultative Organization with functions almost identical to those outlined by the United Maritime Consultative Council in 1946.

The Intergovernmental Maritime Consultative Organization (IMCO) became effective as a permanent specialized agency of the United Nations on 17 March 1958 after twenty-one states, including seven with at least one million gross tons of shipping, had ratified the convention. IMCO's structure has consisted of (1) an Assembly with about one hundred members by 1977, which has met every two years; (2) a Council as the governing body, which originally consisted of the leading maritime countries, but in the mid-1970s included some developing countries; and (3) a number of committees, the most important of which was the Maritime Safety Committee, once with limited membership but later opened to all member states. IMCO has had administrative responsibilities for certain conventions, prepared codes, and engaged in studies that lead to new international agreements or regulations, such as the subdivision and stability of ships, oil pollution, tonnage measurements, codes of safety for fishing vessels, fire test procedures on vessels, safety measures for tankers, and so forth. With the assistance of IMCO, for example, the International Code of Signals drawn up in 1931 was revised and prepared in nine languages; the Code of Safe Practice for Bulk Cargoes was published in 1966; the International Convention for the Safety of Life at Sea was revised in 1960 at a conference organized by IMCO and the amendments put in force on 26 May 1965; the International Maritime Dangerous Goods Code was approved by the fourth IMCO Assembly in 1965 with recommendations for adoption by national governments; and the International Convention on Load Lines in 1966 was drafted and approved with IMCO assistance. In the late 1960s and 1970s IMCO took a special interest in ocean pollution. The various conventions concluded under the auspices of IMCO to reduce oil and other hazardous pollution of the seas will be examined more fully in Chapter 6. In fact, by the mid-1970s IMCO had become the depository for more than a dozen multilateral conventions on safety at sea and pollution and, from the point of view of the United States, had become a valuable instrumentality in gaining international cooperation in setting higher maritime standards.[18]

The interest of the UN system in ocean transportation and shipping has not been limited to safety, unification of legal documents and procedures, or marine pollution. The developing countries have expressed increasing concern over shipping rates under the liner conference system. In the early 1970s, for example, a working Group on International Shipping Legislation of the UN Conference on Trade and Development (UNCTAD) discussed a Draft Code of Conduct for Liner Conference Systems, which had been submitted by the European National Shipowners' Association. The Third UNCTAD session in Santiago, Chile in 1972 requested the UN General Assembly to call a conference of plenipotentiaries to elaborate and sign such a code. But the elaboration of this code revealed the division between the many poor nations that have sought resolutions to assist their own limited merchant marine or to obtain more favorable shipping rates for their commodities in international trade and the fewer mercantile nations that essentially dominate the shipping industry, whether through public regulation or private international cartels.[19] In the mid-1970s, moreover, the UN Commission on International Trade Law also had under consideration international legislation on shipping, especially the liability of carriers at sea, to supplement the International Convention for the Unification of Certain Rules Relating to Bills of Lading, adopted in 1924, with a protocol in 1968. Thus, increasingly, the merchant marines of the world were bound to take greater account of international rules.

The Merchant Marine Act of 1970

Despite all the legislative remedies and the billions of dollars of appropriations to support U.S. shipping from 1916 onward, when President Richard M. Nixon assumed office in 1969 doubt and wonder about the true state, real costs, and desirable goals of the American merchant marine continued. While one-quarter of the world's shipping was twenty years or older, three-quarters of U.S. shipping was twenty years or older. Only 6.3 percent of all ocean-borne tonnage in U.S. foreign commerce was being moved under American flags. In his first appearance before the Committee on Merchant Marine and Fisheries on 15 April 1969, the Maritime Administrator, when asked for his assessment of the American merchant marine, replied bluntly, "I think it is in very bad shape."

The need for a new merchant marine act had been well recognized in the 1960s. But the President and the Congress had been divided on its objectives while the maritime industry had failed to pull its dissident elements of shipbuilders, ship operators, sailors, oil interests, unsubsidized operators, and other groups into one cohesive lobbying block. In 1938 an American Merchant Marine Institute had been incorporated to advance the interests of the shippers, replacing the old American Steamship Owners' Association. One month after the 1968 presidential election the American Merchant Marine Institute had merged with other trade and labor interests to form a new American Institute of Merchant Shipping (AIMS), which included 39 companies that owned and operated 539 flagships or 62 percent of all active merchant tonnage. The lobbying of AIMS, a Labor-Management Maritime Committee, and other shipping interests was welcomed by congress members, especially those from coastal states who had strongly favored public support of the American merchant marine. All that was needed was a lead from the White House.

President Nixon had appointed Rocco Siciliano, a former executive vice-president of the Pacific Maritime Association, as Under-Secretary of Commerce and Andrew E. Gibson, former senior vice-president of Grace Lines, as Maritime Administrator. On 23 October 1969 the President called for a new maritime subsidy program to "replace the drift and neglect of recent years and restore this country to a proud position in the shipping lanes of the world." A month later a bill to amend the 1936 Merchant Marine Act was introduced. Brief hearings in 1969 and extensive hearings the next year before the House Merchant Marine and Fisheries Committee and the Senate Foreign and Interstate Commerce Committee led to reports and amendments, which were agreed to by a conference committee. Congress cleared the way for Public Law 91-469 on 7 October 1970, and it was hailed as "the most sweeping overhaul of the nation's maritime policy in more than three decades."

Essentially the Merchant Marine Act of 1970 was a substantial amendment of the Merchant Marine Act of 1936. It authorized a ten-year government-financed program to revitalize the U.S. merchant marine by providing for the construction of 300 new ships over the next decade and authorizing 22 ships for 1972. From the current 55 percent public subsidy to the cost of vessel construction in 1970, the Act established a 45 percent rate for 1971 to be reduced by 2 percent thereafter to reach a permanent 35 percent level in 1976. Payments were to be made directly to the shipyard rather than to the owner or operator as in the past. Moreover, construction differential subsidies were extended for the first time to bulk carriers, both dry and liquid, not merely liners or other vessels scheduled for essential routes. The calculation of operating differential subsidies under the Act was significantly amended by allowing only for wage or insurance costs that exceeded comparable foreign operations, thus ending the difficult calculus of material, repair, and other differential costs. A new Commission on American Shipbuilding was established to review regularly the state of the American merchant marine and to report within three years whether the 35 percent construction subsidy figure could be reached or recommend alternatives.

Other provisions, very generous to the shipping industry, were approved under the pressures of concerted labor, industry, and congressional favor: the authority of the government to insure ship mortgages was greatly increased; direct subsidies for bulk carriers were approved in principle; and tax deferment, previously extended to the subsidized ship operators by allowance of a fund into which nontaxed profits could be funneled for future ship construction or rehabilitation, was extended to all qualified ship operators. Finally, under special pressure of the Great Lakes shipping industry and their congressional representatives, the definition of ocean foreign commerce was extended to vessels plying between American and Canadian ports on the lakes, giving them all the benefits of the Merchant Marine acts. To top the Christmas tree $23 million dollars of interest due to the U.S. Treasury from the St. Lawrence Seaway Corporation, which had been designed to promote ocean commerce to the Great Lakes by developing, operating, and maintaining the St. Lawrence Seaway System in the United States, was cancelled.[20]

Following the Merchant Marine Act of 1970, a new Assistant Secretary for Maritime Affairs, to serve also ex officio as Maritime Administrator, was established in the Department of Commerce in 1971. The first report of the Maritime Administration (MARAD) for fiscal year 1971 indicated that $423.6 million had been spent on subsidy construction for fifty-one ships, an average rate of 41 percent of costs. The first new operating differential subsidies were signed to cover two 85,000-ton ore bulk-carry vessels and eight break-bulk vessels. Old ships of the National Defense Reserve Fleet were sold netting the Treasury about $74,000 per ship; and a National Maritime Research Center was created at the U.S. Merchant Marine Academy, Kings Point, New York, a constant beneficiary of merchant marine appropriations.

Congress kept plunging straight ahead in refurbishing the American merchant marine fleet from 1972 to 1976, aiding the construction of cargo ships, granting subsidies to cargo carriers and passenger liners, purchasing vessels for the reserve fleet, and generously appropriating funds for research and training. At times the Congress appropriated more money than the administration requested and MARAD budget rose to about one-quarter of the entire Department of Commerce budget, exceeded only slightly by the whole National

Oceanographic and Atmospheric Administration.[21] For 1977 Congress appropriated $403.7 million for ship operating differentials to enable American carriers to charge rates competitive with foreign merchant vessels; over $22 million went for research and development, $13 million for marine training at Kings Point, and $4.5 million for the National Defense Reserve Fleet. But for the first time in twenty-five years not a dollar was authorized to subsidize American shipbuilders, with funds still being available from previous authorizations.

In all appropriations during the 1970s for the merchant marine, research and development have been emphasized. Rapid and fundamental changes in the technology of the shipping industry, involving both ocean transportation and cargo handling, have raised new political, economic, and legal policy issues for the United States both at home and abroad. The most dramatic change in ocean carriage between 1950 and the 1970s was the increase in bulk cargoes, liquid or dry, reflecting not only a universal demand for oil and agricultural commodities, but the economices of transporting a single cargo by sea and its rapid handling in port. Tankers had usually carried 12 to 20 thousand tons of oil in the years following World War II, but by 1970 the *average* tanker on order around the world was scheduled to carry more than 70,000 tons. Dramatizing the rapid growth in the size of tankers the world's largest ship, the 477,000-ton *Globtik Tokyo* was launched in October 1972, a vessel designed to carry 130 million gallons of crude oil on each voyage between the Middle East and Japanese refineries.[22]

The total tonnage of freighters had increased at a 20 to 25 percent annual growth rate. Moreover, transportation companies sought new types of vessels, such as liquified natural gas carriers or roll-on & roll-off ships that could receive and discharge automotive trucks with their complete cargo.

A dramatic shift had also taken place from breakbulk cargo to containerized cargo in ocean transport. Pressure for more rapid, efficient, and economical handling of cargoes in port had grown during the 1950s and 1960s because of soaring labor costs of longshoremen under union leadership and an inordinate number of work stoppages that penalized the shipping industry. Other rising costs of materials handling, including insurance against breakage, theft, and turn-around expenses had brought total port charges to more than half the costs of ocean commerce. Paperwork alone was estimated by the American transportation industry at $6.5 billion a year in the mid-1970s. More and more goods began to be shipped in uniform boxes, generally 8 feet wide, 8 or 8.5 feet high, and anywhere from 17 to 35 feet long. Such containers could be easily hauled by truck or freight train to ports for direct loading on "containerized" ships with minimum handling. By the beginning of 1970 the United States led the world with seventeen new container-designed ships and sixty-seven vessels that had been converted to full containerships, while the introduction of computers streamlined and simplified the complex documentation required for synthesizing truck, railroad, and ship operations into a rationalized import and export trade.

Hope for a more efficient merchant marine also stemmed from development of the nuclear-powered ship. The improved designs of ship hulls and more efficient screw propellors, particularly with new metal alloys, had accounted for much of the development of larger and faster American ships from 1920 onward. In 1956 the first atomic-powered cargo ship, the 12,000 ton *N.S. Savannah,* had been authorized at an estimated cost of $37 million. Launched in 1959, the ship went into operation in 1962 at greatly increased costs. By 1968 the Savannah, under bareboat charter, had already traveled 331,680 miles using only 122.4 lbs. of uranium. The Administration was ready to lay up the expensive, experimental vessel. But the intervention of Congress with new appropriations kept the ship running until 1970.

The physical, if not the economic feasibility of an atomic-powered merchant marine had been demonstrated. In the early 1970s Japan had the *Mutsu* running under atomic power, but with no commercial success. In 1976 the shipping magnate, Ravi Tikkoo, owner of the British Globtik Tankers, signed a letter of intent with the Newport News Shipbuilding and Dry Dock Co., a subsidiary of Tenneco, Inc., to obtain up to three 600,000-ton tankers powered by nuclear energy. Realization of the project depended on many factors, such as suitable insurance, financing, U.S. government indemnities, and guarantees of American-bound oil cargoes.[23]

The tremendous technological changes in the shipping industry, which has developed larger, faster, and more economical vessels with giant carrying capacities, have also led to further hazards for the shoreline and the oceans from pollutants. These problems will be treated in Chapter 6. For the mammoth vessels of the mid-1970s, however, which required sixty to seventy feet of water to navigate, the Gulf and Atlantic ports of the United States no longer had adequate channels to permit the close-in discharge of cargoes. In the Delaware River estuary, for example, through which about 2000 tankers have passed a year to reach six refineries, it became necessary to off-load the very large crude oil carriers into smaller boats before proceeding up the river.

Even with extensive and costly dredging to permit the entry of mammoth carriers to ports, the dangers of collision, spillage, or other discharge raised serious hazards to life, property, and the marine environments. Oil importers and big shippers urged the construction of deepwater ports off the coasts of the United States, which might handle tankers of more than 200,000 tons, and stressed the energy dependence of the country on seaborne petroleum, while groups concerned about the concentration of oil depots and giant ships that might exacerbate pollution problems for the shores and their adjacent waters balked at permissive legislation. After extensive, and often, passionate discussion in 1973 and 1974, Congress finally cleared on 17 December the Deepwater Port Act of 1974.[24]

The Secretary of Transportation was given primary responsibility for licensing and regulating American deepwater ports for receiving oil that might be built beyond the three-mile territorial sea. It became the Secretary's duty to consult with the Federal Trade Commission and the Attorney General for any antitrust implications of such a construction, and to receive the certification from the Environmental Protection Agency that such a port would conform to the Federal Water Pollution Control Act and the Marine Protection, Research, and Sanctuaries Act, which are discussed in Chapter 6. Finally, any "adjacent" state, meaning a state linked by pipeline to such a port, or within fifteen miles of such a port, which might suffer adverse environmental consequences similar to a state linked by pipeline could veto the application for construction. In December 1976 the Secretary of Transportation, William Coleman, approved the license applications for the construction of the first two offshore oil terminals of the United States near Grand Isle, Louisiana and Freeport, Texas.

Problems and Issues

The Merchant Marine Act of 1970 definitely propelled the United States into a decade of vigorous shipbuilding. By the mid-1970s well over two billion dollars in new contracts for the construction or rehabilitation of vessels had been signed, including public subsidies of about one billion dollars. But it was apparent that the new American merchant marine would remain smaller than the fleets of other maritime nations, that it had become highly specialized in design, and that it tended to consist mainly of breakbulk, container, and tanker ships.

By the mid-1970s the United States, with about 14 million tons of merchant shipping, had dropped to seventh place on the list of major maritime nations, both in number of ships and deadweight tonnage, far behind countries like Liberia (which had more than 41 million tons of registered tanker shipping alone in 1977), Japan, the United Kingdom, Norway, the Soviet Union, and Greece. Roughly 3 percent of the total number of merchant vessels and total deadweight tonnage in the world were registered in the United States. Moreover, the projections of the American merchant fleet for 1980 only indicated about 274 ships carrying dry cargo, of which about 139 would be breakbulk, and about 94 container vessels plus barge carriers, roll-on/roll-off ships, and a handful of dry bulk vessels. About 277 tankers, including liquid natural gas carriers, were also projected for 1980. Yet the tonnage available under U.S. registry was expected to rise from about 14 million deadweight tons in 1975 to about 22 million tons in 1980.

For the future, one issue will be the use of the merchant marine for national defense. The days when the merchant fleet could be converted into privateers and fierce men-of-war, of course, have long since gone. By the mid-1970s the value of a large merchant fleet for troop transport was also in question. Yet no one can be sure what role the "fourth branch" of the defense services might play in another major war. In the 1970s new support was given to tankers and bulkers by subsidies, an act undoubtedly responsive to commercial needs. But these and other specialized ships of the American merchant marine may have a limited national defense value. A laid-up national reserve fleet has its uses, demonstrated in both the Korean and the Vietnam wars of the 1950s and 1960s. But under the best of circumstances such a fleet is obsolescent, and the mere transfer of highly specialized craft to such a pool may be useless.

Whatever the form of the American merchant marine, national defense interests must be considered under the assumption that soldiers and/or cargoes will have to be moved massively and quickly by sea. Some strategists foresee no significant role for ocean shipping in future wars, but common sense dictates that the eventualities of blockades, pacific support of allies, and limited conflicts, which would not involve nuclear weapons or a confrontation of the major powers, ought to be considered in maintaining the American merchant marine. Other analysts have pointed out the flexibility of certain dry carriers and especially container ships for receiving "modules" of weaponry and communications, rapidly transforming such merchant vessels to auxiliary warships ready for surveillance or combat support. The weight of these considerations will be arguable but worth considering.

A second issue of the American merchant marine will be the further solicitation by the shipping industry of construction and operating subsidies, which have been systematically reduced. Certainly shipping interests will be quick to defend their privileges of publicly guaranteed mortgages and tax deferrals or exemptions. Their powerful lobbies, well received by many members of Congress from coastal constituencies, will continue to be a factor in U.S. merchant marine policy. Most governments of the world, in fact, continue to consider their merchant marine as essential to their national security and economy, and they offer a number of subsidies, direct and indirect, to their fleets, including construction and operational costs, tax advantages, loan guarantees, schools and medical care for seamen, and so forth. By and large they tend to "protect" their merchant marine against foreign competition as the need arises rather than on the basis of long-term economic logic. Should the United States be less responsive or more rational in the allocation of its public resources? In this connection, the fears of rate-fixing by private shipping cartels have not been laid at rest, either among Americans—who suspect the leverages of large combined firms over smaller, independent, struggling companies—or among less developed countries, which view rate-fixing as extensions of discriminatory policies by the richer mercantile nations. No one can disguise the increasing concentration and conglomeration of the U.S. shipping industry or the windfalls of profit that have occurred from construction, operation, sales, insurance, and tax benefits under public legislation. A U.S. Treasury study of the advantage of tax deferral for shipping corporations over a twelve-year period estimated that 60 percent of the benefits were received by the four largest subsidized firms. Of the thirteen major shipbuilders in the United States in 1970, only two were not part of a corporate conglomeration.[25]

A third issue related to national security but more pertinent to embittered labor interests has been the registration of American-owned ships under foreign flags—called "flags of convenience" or "flags of necessity" or even "runaway flags," depending on one's point of view. In the mid-1970s more than 400 vessels, totalling more than 20 million tons, fell into this category. Tankers accounted for about four-fifths of all such tonnage and bulk cargo carriers nearly all the rest. Exxon, for example, has sailed about a third of its world fleet of 150 tankers under the Liberian flag. As noted earlier, the practice of registering American-owned vessels under foreign flags, especially in states like Liberia, Panama, and Honduras, has depended on the allegations of the owners, most often oil companies, that only such savings in taxes, insurance, and labor costs make certain shipping operations feasible, that their transfer to an American flag would produce deficits and either require public subsidies for the vessels involved at great cost to the taxpayer or loss of the business to cheaper foreign competitors. On the contrary, labor interests have argued that American seamen have been deprived of work by the greed of U.S. firms that pay low foreign wages, maintain substandard vessels, and avoid taxation. The issue is complex and hardly one-sided. Both the Congress and the public will hear more about it.[26]

A fourth issue has been cargo preference legislation, strongly supported by maritime labor and probably more expeditious to achieving its objectives than restrictions against flags of convenience. By various statutes and administrative rules at least 50 percent of public goods, such as defense supplies or agricultural commodities sent abroad as foreign aid, have been required to be shipped on U.S. flag vessels. Escape clauses, which have permitted some administrative discretion on comparative costs, sometimes have let the federal bureaucracy avoid the requirement, much to the chagrin of labor. Cargo preference has been pressed to ensure business for U.S. carriers and jobs for American seamen—regardless of disparate costs between a foreign shipper and a U.S. shipper. In the mid-1970s proposals to reserve a portion of all U.S. oil imports to American flag ships came close to enactment, and labor will undoubtedly continue to seek such legislation.

Direct assurance that U.S. trade will be carried in large part by American flag vessels can also be obtained through bilateral transactions that specify not only the terms of trade but also the details of delivery. The potential of this line of policy was dramatized in 1972 when the United States agreed to sell to the Soviet Union 17 million tons of grain with the understanding that at least one-third of the tonnage would be delivered by U.S. ships, one-third by Russian vessels, and the balance by other flagships. This agreement, applauded by American labor interests, was estimated to involve 59 U.S. ships and required extended negotiations over the costs of the U.S. marine carriage. Such arrangements build the costs of ocean carriage into the terms of trade. They subsidize the carriers to the extent that their rates are higher than freely competitive rates, and they reduce to some degree opportunities for the cheaper and possibly more efficient ships of third countries. They almost certainly restrict the opportunities for any infant merchant marine of a developing country. Ultimately, of course, a rigid system of bilateral trade agreements tied to flag ships would be a regression to mercantilism, narrow, complicated bureaucratic trade blocs, and woeful world economic inequities.[27]

Finally, because ocean shipping is international in character, the national policies of the United States toward its own merchant marine will have to be examined within an international framework. National public regulation of ocean shipping rates and services, as already indicated, faces the hazard of foreign retaliation against American vessels and trade as well as domestic resistance to government control. Public subsidies for the merchant marine must not only bear in mind reasonable profits for an industry that affords employment opportunities for thousands of Americans, but also they must remember the ability of that merchant marine to match foreign economic competition and to assist the national defense effort in the event of war. Safety at sea, standardization of shipping forms, procedure, and law, or efforts to reduce pollution of the marine environment by vessels—all require a concert of private interests, a dozen federal government agencies, and international organizations.

Among international organizations, the UN Conference on Trade and Development has taken a great interest in ocean shipping rates. The great maritime states, including the United States, will have to argue their policies in UNCTAD's forum with a minority of votes. IMCO is the international shipping forum more favored by Washington, but it is by no means a mere echo chamber for American interests. Under the auspices of IMCO, however, the United States has worked for greater progress toward worldwide agreements on maritime affairs to provide universal standards and shipping security. As indicated in Chapter 2, the Third UN Law of the Sea Conference heard the United States reiterate its policy to gain free transit through international straits, with a willingness to abide by traffic pattern regulations to be established by IMCO. Any new international convention regulating the limits of territorial seas, the width of the contiguous zone, and an exclusive economic zone 200 miles out to sea will affect the merchant marine of all nations. By advocating narrow territorial seas and the retention of the legal status of the ocean beyond that limit as "high seas," the United States has sought to preserve the widest freedom of movement for international oceanic trade. But the issue has hardly been resolved, and the likelihood that many coastal states will exercise jurisdiction over wider portions of the sea may raise a distress signal for several maritime countries.

Whatever the American public may decide about the support of the U.S. merchant marine for real or imagined benefits; whatever degree of private combination and private pricefixing the citizen may permit the shipping interests; and whatever controls the U.S. government may exercise over the maritime industry for traffic safety or preservation of the environment, they will all have to be formulated and legislated with a sensible regard for their international consequences.

4 Fisheries and Foreign Policy

Under a patent from Henry VII of England, John Cabot sailed, with one ship and eighteen men, from Bristol and sighted the New World in 1497. The Italian-born and English-commissioned navigator rushed back across the Atlantic with exciting news about the abundance of codfish near Newfoundland. Within only a few years after Cabot's return to England scores of European vessels began making annual trips to the teeming fisheries of America, taking their catch by line, often curing and drying their harvest in rude places along the New England, Nova Scotia, and Newfoundland coasts, and sailing back to Europe for their profits. In his "Description of New England," published in 1618, Captain John Smith predicted that its fish would be a greater treasure than the gold found by the Spaniards in southern America. Long before the Pilgrims arrived in Plymouth in 1620 many tons of fish had been transported from American waters to Europe. None of the early settlers of New England would have survived without fish, and by 1641 the infant Massachusetts Bay Colony was bringing thousands of pounds of dry fish to market.

American Fisheries before 1940

By the end of the seventeenth century Massachusetts was exporting about 11,000 tons of dried codfish a year, worth approximately $400,000, taken from its coastal waters and the Nova Scotia-Newfoundland fisheries.[1] As early as 1652 regulations against killing codfish, haddock, hake, and pollack in December-January had been promulgated to conserve those species. Before George Washington was born in Virginia in 1732, Marblehead, Massachusetts had at least 120 fishing schooners of more than 50 tons each. The total New England fisheries by then employed more than 5000 workers, and about 25,000 tons of cod and other species were being exported to Europe annually for an estimated price of $700,000. From the profits of New England fish sales the first free schools were often established as well as various charitable funds for widows and orphans.

By the Paris Peace Treaty of 1763 ending the French-British struggle for dominion over Asia and America, France had lost its entire empire in the New World to Great Britain, except for the islands of St. Pierre and Miquelon.[2] The right of French or British nationals to fish in American waters had been one of the sore points. The English colonists had expected that with the final removal of France from all of Canada, Nova Scotia, and Cape Breton (the French retained some fishing rights off the banks of Newfoundland), the growth of their New England fishing trade would, without molestation, rapidly increase. But the expansion of the British empire in America had also required larger revenues for imperial defense and Indian administration. Enactment of the Sugar Act by London in the year following the settlement with France required the colonies to pay high duties on the import of sugar, rum, and molasses from the non-British islands in the West Indies. Although the earlier Molasses Act of 1733 had also placed prohibitive duties on molasses, it had not been enforced. The Sugar Act of 1764 realistically lowered the duties on molasses, and, after protests, the three-pence-per-gallon levy was reduced to one pence per gallon. New Englanders had generally exported the better-eating fish directly to Europe and the worse fish to the West Indies in exchange for sugar, molasses, and tropical products. The rum manufactured in New England could then be used for barter with the Indians as well as for the purchase of slaves in Africa, and the whole trade with the West Indies was very profitable to the colonies.

Bearing in mind that in 1763 Massachusetts and Rhode Island together imported 29,000 hogsheads of molasses, of which only 3000 came from the British sugar islands and that such molasses was paid for by the fish and timber of New England, enforcement of the Sugar Act spelled economic ruin for many merchants. British policies for the collection of revenue from America went from bad to worse, stirring up more and more resentment. On 21 March 1775, in severe retaliation against the covert rebellion by the Americans and to isolate the northern colonies, London moved to cut the mainstay of the New England economy by forbidding the Americans to fish the banks of Newfoundland and Nova Scotia, the coasts of Labrador, and the Gulf of St. Lawrence after 1 July 1775. But it was too late; the battle of Lexington and Concord started the Revolution on 19 April 1775.

Up to the eve of the Revolution the American fisheries had prospered. No fewer than 9000 people, both on land and sea, and 600 vessels were then employed annually in the New England fish industry, mostly for cod and mostly in Massachusetts, with a total catch value estimated at well over a million dollars. London, moreover, had encouraged the delivery of whalebone to England from America by lowering the duties, and the importation of whalebone directly from colonies to England multiplied fifty times between 1761 and 1764. The Revolution, however, devastated the New England fishing industry as ships turned from trade to raiding British commerce, with the fishers providing the resources for the armed merchant marine or navy. Rotting hulks at the wharves of Marblehead, Gloucester, Plymouth, and Salem as well as the mourning of thousands of widows and orphans attested to the suffering the American Revolution inflicted on New England fishers.

Revival of the fishing industry took place slowly despite the Paris Peace Treaty of 1783, which had generously allowed the Americans to continue to take fish of every kind on the banks of Newfoundland, in the Gulf of St.

Lawrence, and "at all other places in the sea" where they had ever fished before. The suspension of fishing activity leading to ship and wharf depreciation, and the lack of seasoned fishers, as well as trade discrimination by Britain against her former subjects, all had weakened the industry.[3] On 4 July 1789, Congress responded to the distress by its second act under the new Federal Constitution, which authorized a bounty of 5¢ for every 220 lbs. of dried fish and 5¢ for every barrel of pickled fish exported. The bounty was increased to 10¢ in 1790, raised again in 1797, and later bounties were based on both barrels and the tonnage of the exporting ships. With only one interruption between 1807 and 1813, bounties were paid to the export trade until 1854.

The early years of the nineteenth century saw expanding and profitable exports of cod to France, Spain, and the West Indies. In the ten years up to 1808, an average of 96,000,000 lbs. of dried fish were exported annually, but the Embargo Act of 1807 cut the industry in half within two years. The war (1812–1814) with Great Britain, which was highly unpopular in New England, reduced the fishing trade even further.

After the restoration of peace in 1815, the recovery of the American fishing industry was rapid. The catch of cod and of mackerel, combined with the whaling industry, were outstanding factors in America's commercial development from 1815 to 1860. Mackerel, which until 1817 had been used chiefly for bait, became an important fish for both domestic and foreign consumption. Only 2000 barrels of mackerel had been inspected in 1818 in the village of Gloucester. This figure soared to 154,938 by 1864. At the time of the Civil War Gloucester alone accounted for nearly half the value of the Massachusetts' fishing industry. By 1860 cod and mackerel fishing required more than 200,000 tons of shipping, and the total annual catch of these two fish in Maine and Massachusetts alone was valued at about 3.5 million dollars.

Whales had been caught in Atlantic waters since colonial days, but in 1791 the first Nantucket ships sailed around Cape Horn into the Pacific in search of sperm whales, and by 1835 most deep-sea whaling took place in the Pacific Ocean from the coasts of Asia to the coasts of America. The largest part of the whale products was consumed in the United States, but from 1840 to 1860 more than 700,000 gallons of sperm oil and over 1,600,000 pounds of whalebone were exported annually. In 1857 New Bedford, the leading port for whalers, had a fleet of 329 vessels worth more than $12,000,000 and employing over 10,000 seamen. Herring, halibut, and shad were also caught in large quantities, while menhaden, first used only for fertilizer, became more valuable when the practice of extracting oil from the fish began. About 1830 the lobster catch from Maine began to experience greater demand, and in 1843 the first canning of lobsters assured a growing industry. About 1840 oyster beds were laid in the shore waters of Rhode Island and Connecticut from seeds imported from New Jersey and then Virginia. These fin and shell fish were mainly consumed by the appetite of the rapidly growing American population, but the gross export of fish and whale products continued to increase, although their share of total American exports diminished in comparison with the shipments of Southern cotton, Eastern manufactures, and Western grain. After the Civil War, the development of inshore fisheries of the Atlantic and Gulf coasts, the Great Lake fisheries, and the Pacific coast fisheries tended to reduce the importance of deep-sea fishing.[4]

Early statistics on American fisheries are largely estimates. Comprehensive official data were first sought in 1850, and the 1870 census valued the American fisheries at only $11 million. But errors still probably ranged from 15 to 20 percent, and possibly more. Not until 1880, following the establishment of the U.S. Fish and Fisheries Commission, were approximate figures obtained. At that time 131,426 persons including 101,684 fishers and 29,742 auxiliary handlers, helpers, and others connected with the trade, were counted as being employed in the industry. The value of the products was estimated at $43,046,053, with oysters accounting for $13,403,852 of that total, whales and seals $5,525,756, menhaden $2,116,787, and "general" fish $22,405,018.

Although the quantity and value of fishery products continued to grow between 1870 and the eve of World War I, the change in the importance of species, the shift in the regional importance of fisheries, and the displacement of fish and whales from the export trade were significant. Cod, mackerel, and whale had dominated the flourishing early 19th Century American fishing industry, but after 1860 the wreckage of ships by the Civil War or weather combined with economic march of the United States inland changed the value of fisheries. Whaling was almost completely eclipsed by refining of petroleum for fuel. The tonnage of ships engaged in catching cod and mackerel diminished from 204,197 tons in 1862 to 47,291 tons in 1910. Although early settlers had found the streams, rivers, and inshore waters of the mid-Atlantic region of America abundant with fish and oysters, the commercial development of these resources had been slow until the mid-nineteenth century when the oyster production of New York, New Jersey, Maryland, and Virginia reached an annual value of about one million dollars. Shad, clams, squeteague, and mullet also gained in value in these states as well as in the Carolinas, Georgia, and the Atlantic coast of Florida. By the end of the nineteenth century the middle and southern Atlantic states accounted for almost 40 percent of the total value of United States fisheries. Far ahead of all fisheries in value in the early years of the twentieth century were the oysters, followed by salmon and cod. In 1905 the fishing industry employed 219,534 people, and the value of the total catch was estimated at $61,047,909. Of this amount oysters accounted for over 30 percent and salmon over 20 percent, followed by cod, shad, menhaden, clams, lobsters, haddock, squeteagues, haddock, mackerel, and trout.

Not only had there been a shift in the magnitude of the catch in species of fin fish and shell fish but also in the regional importance of American fisheries. The Gulf states by the turn of the century accounted for 10 percent of all the value of the U.S. fisheries, but the greatest growth in fisheries occurred on the

Pacific coast, which, except for fur seals, had hardly existed before 1850. Commercial salmon fisheries had begun in 1852 at a settlement that became Seattle, Washington. The industry boomed when some enterprising New Englanders on the Sacramento River started a cannery there in 1864. Transfer of the early industry to the Columbia River and an increasing consumer demand, both in the United States and abroad, as well as the opening of new canneries in Alaska in 1878 and on the coast of Puget Sound soon made salmon the most valuable seafood catch of the United States after the oyster. In 1864 about 2000 cases of 48 one-pound cans were packaged at Sacramento; in 1909, including Puget Sound, Columbia River, and Alaskan canneries, 4,322,513 cases were packed. Halibut also became an important Pacific fish product while some cod was caught. Finally, whaling from the Pacific coast obtained commercial importance, reaching one million dollars in value of products with about thirty vessels operating in San Francisco in 1891. But the whaling industry as a whole kept declining thereafter.

World War I, like the other wars fought by the United States, dealt harshly with American fisheries. In the first years after the hostilities, the industry was faced with a general decline in consumption, an overexpansion of operations, and price increases due to war inflation that made competition with foreign imports more difficult. As the 1920s advanced, however, the American fishing industry stabilized. The salmon fisheries of Alaska maintained their vigor, accounting for 4,429,463 cases of 48 one-pound cans in 1920, worth about $35 million—or almost three times as much as in 1905. The catch of certain other species also showed a marked improvement. By 1928 the Gulf fisheries, with their shrimp, oysters, and mullet were more productive than any year since 1880. In the same year Boston, Gloucester, and Portland fish landings amounted to 277,981,691 pounds, over 50 percent of which was haddock. And California had surged ahead as a fishing state, with a record of landing 371,648,275 pounds of fin and shell fish between 1920 and 1925. Of this amount, about 8 percent were being taken from Mexican waters and with almost 80 percent of the yellow tuna already coming from foreign waters, international complications were on the horizon.

Some grave warnings about the deterioration of the American fisheries were broadcast, and there were already earnest attempts to grapple with the problems of depletion that still haunt the fishing industry today. In the 1921 report of the U.S. Bureau of Fisheries one can read, "The well-known decline of some of the most valuable fisheries should be an effective warning that in the past proper consideration has not been given to the vital matter of conservation and should encourage the more direct and extensive application of scientific studies in the future." The same report mentioned the rapidly increasing pollution of both fresh and salt waters from the development of industry, especially from petroleum and its products, and the wastes that were known to be harmful or suspected of being so. In the same vein, the report called for more experimental data, a plea that was met by a miniscule appropriation of $7500 that year for a scientific investigation of the problem.

The dour outlook for some species in the American fisheries continued throughout the decade. For example, the smelts of Casco Bay, Maine were seriously depleted; the catch of cod in the northeast Atlantic showed no increase in thirty years while the catch of blue fish, scup, and squeteague dropped by a third or more; little by little the oysters of New York were being extinguished and those of New Jersey, Maryland, Delaware, and Virginia declining; halibut landings on the Pacific dropped to 7,805,000 pounds after averaging 12,104,000 pounds in the previous years. Sockeye salmon was less and less available in the old fishing grounds. In the Great Lakes from 1918 to 1925 the total catch of fish dropped from 150 million pounds to 100 million pounds. Whitefish declined from 21 million to 4 million pounds and sturgeon was reduced from 7.5 million to barely 100,000 pounds in less than half a century.

As the 1930s began there were 191,000 people engaged in the fishing industry, of which 123,000 were actually commercial fishermen. The 1929 total American catch amounted to 3,567 million pounds, worth about $123,054,000 to the fishermen. At the same time, sports fishing, very little regulated and an additional assault on the natural regeneration of the stocks, was attracting about 8.5 million anglers in the United States whose gear or tackle alone was worth about $25 million. Moreover, the fishing industry suffered severe blows from the great economic depression that brought misery to farmers and factory workers everywhere, with numbing unemployment and depressed prices. By 1934 the total catch had decreased by more than half a billion pounds from 1929, and the value to the fishers was less than half of what it had been five years earlier. In 1937, when the worst of the depression was over, the total catch had recovered somewhat to 4,840 million pounds, but the number of fishers employed was no greater than in 1929, and the value of that catch was still far less than in 1929.

Major technological changes were also underway in the fishing industry. The canning of fish in the nineteenth century had opened a wider and more flexible market to the industry for certain species. By 1924 canned fish in the United States was valued at $72 million. At the low point in the economic depression of 1934 their value was reduced to $60 million, but by 1938 the figure had risen to $105 million for 749,197,000 pounds. Early in the twentieth century, moreover, foreign fishers had begun the commercial practice of freezing fresh catches and in 1920 the U.S. Department of Commerce introduced the first brine freezing plant. On the eve of World War II in 1938 some 200 million pounds of fresh and frozen packaged fish and shellfish were already worth more than $27 million to the industry. However, neither the increases of the American catch nor the technological improvements to make fin fish and shell fish more attractive and convenient for the consuming public could overcome the price differential of foreign fish in an industry where a large part of costs were labor. In 1925 the United States imported more than twice as much fish, in value, as it exported; in 1937 more than three times as much as it exported.

The world's annual commercial catch of fish just before the year in which Germany attacked Poland was 33.6 billion pounds worth about $740 million. Only Japan harvested more fish than the United States, but the value of the American catch was still larger than any other single nation. Nevertheless, the industry was hardly thriving and the warnings against the depletion of species taken by the American fishers solemnly continued. The Bureau of Fisheries in 1935 reported that one of the most serious limitations to their program of maintaining adequate levels of food and game fish in interior waters through their extensive program of hatcheries and restocking of species was "pollution from domestic and industrial sources" and cautioned that the destruction of fish was rapidly growing throughout the more industrialized sections of the country. For example, the cisco had virtually disappeared from Lake Erie after 1926, whereas the decline of shellfish and other species in the intensively used estuaries of New York, Delaware, and the Chesapeake seemed inexorable.

In retrospect from 1920 to 1939, there were some bright spots in the fishing industry, some stagnation, and some serious declines. In the Gulf of Mexico the harvest of crabs, for example, rose from 1.5 million pounds in 1923 to 33.9 million pounds in 1940 while the shrimp industry thrived; on the Pacific coast mackerel catches multiplied from 3 million pounds in 1920 to more than 120 million pounds in 1940 while the catch of pilchard (sardines) soared from 118 million pounds to over a billion pounds before World War II. Meanwhile the rising demand for Pacific tuna was unexcelled, and the landings of the fish increased from 45.7 million pounds in 1920 to 210.2 million pounds in 1940. However, the landings of cod in New England remained about 100 million pounds annually, while there was no increase in mackerel landings and a decline in haddock. Little or no growth was registered in the oyster industry of the Middle Atlantic region. More and more effort was going into the catch of the same or fewer salmon. The valuable Pacific halibut had been overfished by both Canadians and Americans. The number of sets of gear, for example, had risen from about 200,000 to more than a million, but the halibut catch per gear had declined from 260 pounds to 36.5 pounds. Sea otters, seaks, and whales, pursued in an unregulated hunt for ocean mammals, had all been killed in numbers exceeding their natural annual regeneration, and some species were threatened with extinction.[5]

As the United States entered World War II in 1941, attention to the living resources of the sea virtually stopped in the crisis of national survival, but the same issues raised for American fisheries by population growth, economic development, technological change, and cultural modification were bound to emerge again as soon as worldwide hostilities ceased.

Early Policies and International Cooperation

The transfer of British sovereignty over the American colonies by the Treaty of Paris of 1783 to the thirteen United States of America had also conveyed to them jurisdiction over their coastal and inland waters, including the beds of streams, rivers, lakes, and bays. In 1789 the Constitution had delegated powers to the federal government to regulate both foreign and interstate commerce and had also given to the federal courts jurisdiction over admiralty and other maritime matters, thus conferring on Congress a broad sweep of powers over navigation. At the same time the federal government, acting for the sovereign United States, set the limits to its territorial seas and obtained those rights and responsibilities common to all nations on the high seas under international law. Basically the state and federal governments have concurrent jurisdiction over the internal and territorial waters of the United States. The federal government is able to enact all necessary and proper laws respecting navigable waters under its commerce and admiralty powers while the states have all reserved "police" powers over their territorial waters, including the fish therein.[6]

Despite the importance of the American fisheries to the United States economy in its early history their regulation had been left exclusively in the hands of the states of the Union—except as affected by a few international agreements. Alarmed by the apparent depletion of certain stocks of fish, however, the Congress jointly resolved to establish the Commission on Fish and Fisheries, an Act that was approved on 9 February 1871. The initial mandate of the Commission, headed by Spencer F. Baird, Assistant Secretary of the Smithsonian Institution, was to investigate the conditions of the American fisheries, for which Congress appropriated $5000. But a year later the Commission was further charged with the increase of fish stocks by artificial propagation. The beginnings of the present National Marine Fisheries Service can be traced back to the Joint Resolution of the U.S. Congress on 9 February 1871 which directed the President to appoint a Federal Commissioner of Fisheries in order to settle the question of whether "the food fisheries of the eastern coast of the United States have been decreasing in number." The Resolution also called upon the Commissioner to ascertain the cause and, if possible, to suggest a practical remedy.

In 1870 only eleven states actually had state fish commissions—and these had few personnel with very limited budgets. By 1877 there were twenty-six state commissions, in large measure on account of the federal government's interest in the conservation of fishing stocks. The U.S. Fish Commission not only embarked on a large number of studies of fish and the fishing industry, both in the United States and abroad, but also, with the cooperation of other public agencies and private interests, obtained millions of eggs from hatcheries, which were transferred or introduced to brooks, rivers, lakes, and bays all over the United States. Special effort was put into trout, salmon, shad, carp, cod, and rockfish. Many millions of eggs, moreover, were sent to France, the Netherlands, Germany, and other countries for experimental purposes and to promote international comity. At the International Fisheries Exhibition in Berlin in 1880, Commissioner Baird received a grand prize as the "first fish culturalist of the world." Nevertheless, the concern of the Commission of Fish and Fisheries over the feeble regulation of fisheries by states was intimated in its 1877 report that "The question as to who possesses jurisdiction over the fisheries proper along the coast of the United States and in navigable waters is yet unsettled. At present the United States does not exercise any, but leaves to the State enactment of laws on the subject."

During its life from 1871 to 1903 the U.S. Fish and Fisheries Commission distributed billions of fish eggs, fingerlings, and adults to replenish the American stocks that were under the increasing assaults of men and their industries. Despite the tremendous gains that accrued from the hatcheries and propagation of fish, however, there were ominous signs for some species, such as the shad in the Atlantic states. Replenishment simply could not overcome rapacious catches, traps, or industrial blockages of spawning streams, and pollution. Worse was the failure of the states to enact protective legislation for their fish and their inability to take concerted action with neighboring states. Legislatures balked at the reaction of their constituents to fisheries regulation, whereas the Fish Commission, which could only make scientific studies and cultivate fish for distribution, had no power.

On 1 July 1903 the independent Fish Commission was transferred to the new Department of Commerce and Labor and named the Bureau of Fisheries. The final appropriations for the Commission had been $474,000, about half of which went for salaries, $175,000 for the propagation of food fish, $36,000 for the maintenance of vessels, and $22,000 for inquiries respecting food fish. None of the old problems of American fisheries in the states had been solved by the change of name and the bureaucratic relocation of the Fish Commission in the U.S. government. In 1903, however, the U.S. Congress passed the Alaska Fisheries Act, the Salmon Fisheries Act, and the Alaska Fur Seal Act, which consolidated and codified earlier laws for these fisheries. Congress then entrusted the Bureau of Fisheries with the administration of these acts in the Territory of Alaska giving to the Bureau a great, new responsibility and its first real authority.

From 1903 to 1913, when the Department of Labor was separated from the Department of Commerce, leaving the Bureau of Fisheries in Commerce, vigorous efforts were made in Alaska to protect the salmon and the fur seal fisheries through both internal regulations and international agreements. The Bureau not only served as the chief adviser to the government on fishing accords with foreign nations, but as the agent for the United States (1) in observing the *modus vivendi* with Great Britain for American vessels in Newfoundland waters in 1905, (2) in efforts to establish the International Commission for the waters contiguous to and forming a boundary between the United States and Canada in 1908, and (3) in assuming control over the fur seal fisheries of the Pribilof Islands in 1910. Nevertheless, the influence of the Bureau of Fisheries on the American fisheries in the states, off their coasts, and on the high seas was minimal. While the propagation of fish and biological studies increased with greater resources and skill, the annual reports of the Bureau were filled with plaintive notes of the failure of the states to take corrective action to conserve their stocks and with pleas to the federal government to consider control over migratory fish in interstate commerce. For the Bureau the problem of pollution was already alarming in 1911, and it reported that the "Effects of industrial wastes upon fishes . . . has received considerable attention in the investigation of several fish epidemics . . ."

Not until an Appropriations Act of 1915, however, did the Bureau gain some leverage over the disregard of the states for the maintenance of their fisheries resources. Under the Act, Congress required states to have adequate laws for the protection of fish before receiving the benefits of species propagation offered by the federal government through the Bureau. A year later, the Bureau cut off its hatcheries aid to Havre de Grace, Maryland, and Saint Marcos, Texas, noting, in the case of Maryland, that annual reports, communications to the governor, cautions to the fishermen and the public, and general appeals had all indicated the necessity for a radical change of policy to arrest the depletion of once-valuable species. But "nothing has been done to improve the situation." The withholding of stock replenishment by the Bureau, nevertheless, was a weak instrument for the reform of the state fisheries laws, given the political interest of many members of Congress to placate fishermen in the states. And by 1923 the Bureau not only conceded that some federal hatcheries had already reached their desirable maximum in the production of game and food fish for internal waters, but also suggested that the states themselves should assume species propagation activities.

In Alaska, where the investment in fisheries amounted to almost $74 million by 1919 and yielded a product, over 85 percent salmon, worth about $59 million, the Bureau was influential, although complaining that regulations by law even there were inadequate and obsolete, with bills pending in Congress for eight years. In the Pribilof Islands the fur seals recovered in numbers during the five-year moratorium on the commercial taking of the animals, so that the Secretary of Commerce, on the advice of the Bureau, authorized a catch of 25,000 in 1918. The catch later was increased to 35,000, and the United States began a well-regulated, profitable business, under contract to a St. Louis firm, that no longer saw the pelts exported to London for dressing, dyeing, and re-importing to America.

During the 1920s and the 1930s, which was marked by the great economic depression that gravely affected the fishing industry, the Bureau continued its customary distribution of fish and eggs, amounting to over 7 billion in 1927–1928 falling to only 3.2 billion in 1933-1934, and then stabilizing at about 8 billion from 1936 to 1939. In addition to its scientific studies, the Bureau began to enlarge its technical assistance to states and industry for the handling, merchandising, and manufacturing of fisheries products. On 6 May 1935 the first citizen's Fishery Advisory Committee appointed by the Secretary of Commerce met (briefly under the chairmanship of Bernard MacFadden) to consider fishery problems "from a national standpoint." The committee was composed of representatives from science, transportation, and medicine as well as members of the fishing industry. In Alaska the powers of the Bureau over the territorial fisheries had been strengthened by Congress in 1924 while the Pribilof fur seals, which seemed on the verge of extinction in 1910, increased mightily to 1,872,000 animals in 1938 under a program of controlled annual harvesting.

Of great import to U.S. policy for fisheries, however, was the shift of American consumption, albeit low, from domestic to imported fish. Also important was the new approach of foreign vessels to the coasts of the United States for their catch. Beginning with his report of 1927, the Commissioner of the Bureau of Fisheries placed "international relations" in the first section. It was in this area, which involved the depletion of species due to both overfishing and pollution and which affected the livelihood of the American fisher, that some of the most interesting policy issues were emerging.

Some idea of the capacity of the Bureau of Fisheries in the early twentieth century within the federal government can be gleaned from its appropriations: the old independent Fish Commission had received, as noted earlier, a total of $474,000 in its final year of 1903. Fourteen years later the Bureau of Fisheries appropriation was a mere $1.1 million. In fiscal year 1939, one world war and twenty-two years later, Congress provided only $2.2 million for the Bureau. For such a small investment the American people received a prodigious return in scientific studies and a spectacular distribution of eggs, fry, and adult fish, the administration of the Alaskan fisheries, a voice against the malpractice of states in their poor regulation of catch and in their apathy toward pollution, and reasonable participation in a number of international conferences and commissions that dealt with the conservation of marine resources.

Since the early American fisheries extended far beyond the coastal waters of the United States, international controversies were almost bound to arise. Two major, acrimonious, and long-standing issues clouded the nineteenth century, both of which were finally settled through arbitration and appropriate international conventions.

First, under the 1783 peace treaty with Great Britain, Americans had continued to enjoy unmolested the right of fishing on the Newfoundland banks, in the Gulf of St. Lawrence, and all other places in the sea where they had customarily fished; they also had the liberty to take fish on such parts of the coast of Newfoundland as British fishers used and all other coasts, bays, and creeks of the British dominions (essentially Nova Scotia–Canada) in America. During the negotiations for the Peace of Ghent in 1814 the United States took the position that nothing in the Treaty of 1783 with respect to fishing rights had been changed by the War of 1812. The British strongly disagreed—and prolonged, complex arguments led to the deletion of an article on the subject. Seizure of American fishing vessels in Canadian coastal waters, however, led to strong protests from Washington to London and finally the signature of the Convention of 1818. Among other articles settling certain issues unresolved by the Peace of Ghent, the United States obtained "forever" the liberty to fish, dry, and cure on the southern coast of Newfoundland and Labrador, to fish the west coast of Newfoundland, and to enter for shelter, repair, or wood and water supplies other bays and harbors. Excepting these provisions, the United States renounced any right to take, dry, or cure fish within three marine miles of the British North American dominions. Nevertheless, different interpretations of the agreement by both parties led to thirty-six years of further quarrels, seizures, and claims.

In 1854 a new Reciprocity Treaty essentially restored the rights of American fishermen that had existed under the 1783 treaty in exchange for allowing Canadian fish to enter the United States without duty. But this treaty was abrogated in 1866. Another treaty, somewhat similar to the 1854 convention was concluded in 1871, but it was terminated in 1885. Relations between American fishermen and both the Canadian and Newfoundland governments, therefore, had been rough during these years as the British sought to limit U.S. fishing along the Canadian Newfoundland coasts and in the bays but at the same time wanted to export their own catch duty-free to the American market.

In 1909 after almost a century of controversy, the parties finally referred seven questions, including whether American fishers had to submit to Canadian and Newfoundland regulations, how bays should be defined, and what methods should be used for territorial waters, to the Permanent Court of Arbitration. The entire matter was based on diverse interpretations of the 1818 Convention, but a decision was reached by the Court on 7 September 1910, which was amicably accepted by the United States and Great Britain.[7]

The second major international fishing controversy involving the United States in the nineteenth century was the fur seal dispute with Great Britain. Since the seventeenth century the Russians had hunted the North Pacific sea otter for its fur and, upon the virtual extinction of that animal in the eighteenth century, the fur seals. In 1786 a Russian named Pribilof discovered a group of islands in the middle of the Bering Sea that were visited by millions of seals annually. Under a Russian-American company, chartered by the Tsar, the problem of conserving the herds, especially the females, against gross and wanton killing was discussed and occasionally regulated from 1799 onwards. Rational exploitation of the animals during the 1850s and 1860s had checked their precipitate decline in numbers and was beginning to restore the herds to their former vigor. However, the sale of the islands with Alaska in 1867 to the United States was followed by an instant and incredible slaughter of 300,000 seals by California and New England interests. In 1870 Congress enacted conservation laws and provided for leasing the seal industry under the Secretary of Treasury. But the kill quotas had been set too high and too indiscriminately. Moreover, after 1879 vessels from Japan, Russia, Canada, and the United States itself, began hunting the seals on the high seas, guaranteeing the eventual extinction of the species by their slaughter of females. In March 1869 the Pribilof Islands had been proclaimed a U.S. government reservation and the killing of fur seals was restricted to 86,000 animals and 23,000 in 1870. Under the first twenty-year lease (1870–1890) of the fur seal industry by the U.S. Secretary of Treasury, 100,000 animals were allowed to be killed annually; during the second lease from 1890 to 1910, the herds were on their way to extinction, and the North American Commercial Company, except for one year, never was able to kill more than 30,000 seals. For several years the Company took fewer than 10,000 animals. In 1911 the Alaska Fisheries Service of the Bureau of Fisheries was entrusted with all matters relating to the fur seals, including the killing of the seals and the sale of their pelts.

To stop pelagic sealing, the U.S. government had attempted to claim the Bering Sea as closed, from rights acquired from Russia in the purchase of Alaska, and to claim that the United States had property rights in the seals, but in 1893 the Paris Arbitration Panel denied the U.S. claims. The Panel suggested, however, a sixty-mile protective belt around the Pribilof Islands. The United States and Great Britain reached a *modus vivendi* incorporating a closed season and a sixty-mile protective zone in 1894. But the zone was too small and the closed season too short, whereas the Japanese continued to hunt the seals on the high seas. Between 1890 and 1909 about 342,000 seals were taken on land while 622,000 were taken on the high seas. In 1897, at the International Fur Seal Conference, Russia, Japan, the United States, and Great Britain agreed to suspend all pelagic sealing in 1898, but then Canada balked.

Only after more years of irritable relations, protests, diplomacy, an arbitration in 1893, and finally a convention in 1911 that bound Great Britain (Canada), Russia, Japan, and the United States to prohibit their citizens from pelagic sealing in the North Pacific, Bering, Kamchatka, Okhotsk, and Japan seas was the matter settled. The fur seal herds quickly began to revive. In the history of international fisheries, moreover, the fur seal convention was extraordinary in providing that (1) in addition to a cash settlement in advance for their rights to future harvests, the Canadians and the Japanese would receive from the United States 15 percent of the seal skins taken annually on its Pribilof Islands; (2) Russia would also give to Canada and to Japan 15 percent of its harvest of the Commander Islands; and (3) Japan would give to the United States, to Russia, and to Canada 10 percent of its harvest from its Robben Islands and other shores under its jurisdiction.[8] Nothing prevented the United States from suspending the seal-killing in the interests of conservation, but payments had to be made to the other parties as advances against their shares when harvests were resumed. Although the Pribilof herds nearly doubled in two years after 1910, Congress, against the advice of the President, passed an Act in 1912 suspending for five years the harvesting of the seals, not discriminating between the need to maintain a female population and the utility of thinning out the polygamous males in the herds. With the resumption of rational exploitation of the animals after 1917, the herds continued to increase after 1918 reaching a total of 1,872,438 in 1938 despite a kill of 58,364 that year.

After the agreement on sea otters and fur seals, the first U.S. treaty that actually regulated a high seas fishery through an international commission was the American-Canadian Pacific halibut treaty for the North Pacific Ocean, including the Bering Sea. New England fishers had begun to fish halibut on a commercial scale as early as 1888 near Cape Flattery in the state of Washington. By the early twentieth century the fishery extended all along the coast of British Columbia and southeastern Alaska, becoming by the 1920s the world's principal source of halibut. From 1914 to 1916, however, a number of scientific studies for the British Columbia Commissioner of Fisheries had indicated a decline in the productivity of the old halibut fishing grounds and diminishing returns on the units of catch.

The American-Canadian Fisheries Conference that met in Washington in January 1918 to discuss certain problems associated with the Fraser River sockeye salmon, U.S. lobster fishing off the Canadian shores, the protection of sturgeon, the protection of whales, and other matters also dealt with the Pacific Halibut fishery. A first draft treaty, providing for a closed season for the fishery and the elimination of nets in certain fresh waters, failed to receive the consent of the U.S. Senate because it also provided for reciprocal port privileges with Canadian vessels and no duty on halibut imports for fifteen years. But on 2 March 1923 a new treaty was signed, which became effective in October 1924, with agreement on (1) a closed season from 16 November to 15 February and (2) the creation of an International Fisheries Commission to make studies and recommendations to preserve and develop the halibut fishery.

The International Fisheries Commission had no regulatory power, other than observing the closed season, which proved almost negligible as a conservation measure, but it vigorously launched scientific investigations of the halibut fishery. In 1928 it recommended to Canada and the United States that the Commission be given additional powers, which were incorporated in a new treaty signed in Ottawa in 1930. Under the treaty, effective 14 May 1931 for five years, the four-member Commission was empowered to divide the fishing grounds into areas, to regulate the total halibut catch annually in such areas, to fix the size and character of equipment to be used in the halibut catch, to collect statistics, including the licensing and clearance of vessels to determine the condition and trend of the fishery, and to close areas to all fishing where the halibut population was small and immature. A new treaty, effective 28 July 1937, virtually duplicated the 1930 treaty, and remained in force for five years, continuing thereafter unless denounced by either contracting party, in which case the treaty would terminate in two years.

Not only did the total catch of halibut increase significantly under the Commission's regulation between 1932 and 1940, but more importantly the amount of catch per fishing effort increased with a larger proportion of adult, mature fish. The result was more efficient investment and better prices for the industry. The industry itself, divided into Canadian and American interests, also played an important role in self-regulation to obtain a better distribution of landings throughout the season by splitting the fleets, by laying up fishing vessels between trips, and by prescribing per-person per-trip quotas for the fishing vessels. Not all policy issues between Canada and the United States—or within the industry—were resolved, of course, but there was general agreement that this first public international effort to conserve and restore a depleted deep-sea fishery had happily succeeded.

Another fishery that called for international cooperation prior to World War II was the Canadian Fraser River sockeye salmon between the State of Washington and British Columbia, extending to the Gulf of Georgia, Puget Sound, and the Strait of Juan de Fuca. Until 1891 Canadians alone had harvested this fishery, and until 1897 the Canadian pack of this species had been much greater than than of the United States. During the following decade, however, the salmon pack of the two countries was equal. After 1906 the American share became larger, exceeding the Canadian pack until 1934. Up to 1906 in some years and from 1907 to 1913 sockeye salmon provided the largest share of the total North American salmon pack, including Alaska, the Columbia River, and the Puget Sound areas. However, a disastrous rock slide in Hell Gate's canyon in the Fraser River coupled to other blockages in the streams, mining and industrial pollution, and overfishing throughout the gulfs, sounds, and straits greatly depleted this anadromous fish.

Regulation of the fishery independently by the state of Washington and by the province of British Columbia had occurred from the 1870s onward. Nevertheless, most controls had been based on inadequate scientific investigation, tempered by the private pressures to exploit the fishery, with a lack of reckoning on the effects of overfishing, obstruction, and pollution. The local fishermen, moreover, stubbornly opposed joint action under an international treaty. In fact, the first discussions of an international convention to conserve and regulate the Fraser River sockeye salmon began in 1892, but it then took forty-five years before an agreement was ratified by both the United States and Canada.

As the condition of the fishery had worsened, regulation of the salmon catch by both the state of Washington and British Columbia, including closed seasons, escapement provisions, and prescriptions of gear, became stricter, so that during the 1930s there was some improvement in the size of packs from the system. Nevertheless, congruent action in the area through an international commission seemed to many observers like a far more rational and effective approach to the development of the fishery. In 1908 a new British-American agreement had created an International Fisheries Commission to investigate the conditions of fish contiguous to the boundaries of the United States and Canada, and to recommend regulations for the protection and improvement of the stock. Among other recommendations, the Commission proposed that there be a closed season for sockeye salmon, modification of traps, and a uniform licensing system for both American and Canadian vessels in the fishery. Canada ratified the treaty, but the United States, owing to the protests of the state of Washington, did not. The American-Canadian Fisheries Conference of 1918 drafted another agreement with regulations for sockeye salmon. Again Canada accepted the agreement, but Americans and resident aliens in the state of Washington objected particularly to the licensing system and the restraints on purse seine fishing. No treaty was concluded. In 1921 and 1922 new efforts to secure international regulation of the species also failed. Finally, with the catch of the sockeye salmon clearly declining, negotiations led to the signature in 1930 of a convention for the protection, preservation, and extension of the Fraser River sockeye salmon. This convention covered not only the territorial waters of the two states, but certain extraterritorial waters as well; it provided for a six-member International Pacific Salmon Fisheries Commission, with both investigative and regulatory powers; and it sought to realize a fifty-fifty share of the catch for each state. Protests from the state of Washington once more delayed ratification of the treaty for seven years. When it was ratified in 1937, it forbade the Commission from undertaking any regulation until scientific investigations covering two runs of the salmon, that is, eight years, had been completed.[9]

In addition to participating in the international regulations of the fur seal, the halibut, and the salmon, the United States joined other states to conserve the whale. Although the whaling industry of Europe dated back to the eleventh century in the Bay of Biscay and was of major importance to New England ports until the American Civil War in 1860, the greatest threat to the extinction of these mammoth ocean mammals did not emerge until the late nineteenth and early twentieth century. This was because of three technical innovations: a Norwegian patent on the shell harpoon fired from a cannon in 1870 and 1873 that made the kill more swift and more certain than the old, hand-thrown harpoon, thereby extending the whale hunt to faster, hardier species; second, the use of the floating factory ship after 1906 to which the catcher boats dragged the whale's carcass for disembowelment and dissection, then to be hoisted aboard piecemeal; and, third, the provision of slip-ways after 1920 in the stern of floating factories that made it feasible for the entire whale to be drawn aboard at sea where blubber, meat, and bones were processed, thus bringing the industry to great efficiency.

The early primitive whale hunts had started the depletion of the North Atlantic waters, driving the whalers of New England and Europe to the South Atlantic and parts of the Pacific and Indian Oceans even before the great stocks of whales in the Antarctic were first exploited in the twentieth century. As early as 1881 a Norweigian newspaper, *Fredning af Hval* (Christiania), in supporting a royal decree to protect whales, had written, "It is to be hoped that it will be more generally recognized that we owe it to the coming generations to protect the useful and interesting animal life of the Arctic and Antarctic regions." But little or nothing was done of international significance for another half-century, although in 1918 one of the items on the agenda of the American-Canadian Fisheries Conference was the international protection of whales. In 1923, however, both Norway and Great Britain, the two states that dominated the whaling industry at that time, established commissions that collaborated in investigating whaling in the North Atlantic and the Antarctic oceans. These commissions also provided valuable data for the League of Nations, which was interested in the protection of marine resources through international law. In 1929 and in 1930 Norway approved laws for her own nationals that regulated the catch of certain species of whales, prohibited the kill of nursing cows, calves, and undersized animals, and also established, in collaboration with the International Council for the Exploration of the Sea, the International Bureau of Whaling Statistics at Oslo. Meanwhile, the League of Nations had opened for signature an International Convention for the Regulation of Whales, containing many of the provisions of the Norwegian law, but applicable to all oceans and to the nationals of all states adhering to the Convention. The Convention became effective only in 1935, and even then Russia, Japan, Chile, and Argentina did not ratify it. Cartel arrangements between the British and the Norwegian companies, coupled to the worldwide economic depression of prices, had served somewhat to limit the worst ravages of whales, but the Japanese and the Germans in the 1930s had begun to expand their whaling operations. Another international convention with stricter standards was plainly needed to save the whales from extinction.[10]

In 1937 a new International Agreement for the Regulation of Whaling, further amended in 1938, was achieved by nine states, including the United States. The killing of certain species was completely prohibited and the killing of other species was limited, depending on their size. Provisions were made for a closed season, a whale sanctuary, and some limitations on the use of factory ships. It was a step forward, but hardly enough to assure the conservation of the giant mammals, especially since Japan, Russia, and Chile failed to sign the Convention. Except for a brief revival in San Francisco at the end of the nineteenth century, the United States whaling industry had steadily trailed down to slight significance before World War II. Nevertheless, the United States adhered to the international whaling regulations, supported even stronger international controls, and several times prosecuted American vessels that had taken undersized whales on the high seas.

Elsewhere and for other marine species, the U.S. pace on marine conservation policy was plodding. In the Northwest Atlantic, despite the long history of intensive fishing by Americans and Europeans in this area since the sixteenth century, no international regulation for the development and conservation of the resources had been reached prior to World War II. The Europeans around the North Sea had moved a little faster. In fact, the first multilateral convention on fisheries had been signed in 1882 and became effective for Belgium, Denmark, France, Germany, and Great Britain in 1884. But the agreement essentially regulated the conduct of fishing, that is, the marking of vessels, rules to avoid collisions, prohibition of net-cutting tools, and so forth, not the conservation of the marine resources. All the states, however, were alarmed by the increasing signs of depletion of the heavily fished stocks, and a Select Committee of the British Parliament in 1892 heard extensive evidence on the need for more scientific information before devising any regulations to conserve the resources. Preparatory international conferences were held in Stockholm in 1899 and in Christiania in 1901 leading to the formation and first meeting of the International Council for the Exploration of the Sea (ICES) in 1902 in Copenhagen, basically an organization to encourage and coordinate scientific fisheries investigations. In 1920 this model of inquiry, research, and comparative study was followed by the North Atlantic Council on Fishery Investigations created by Canada, Newfoundland, and the United States, later joined by France, which held twenty-four meetings up to 1937 but was discontinued in 1938.

On the Great Lakes, despite some fifty years of conferences and the formation of an International Fisheries Conservation Council of the Great Lakes among the American states and Canadian provinces and despite the frequent alarms over the depletion or extinction of such species as whitefish, sturgeon, and cisco, no international treaty was brought forth to regulate the resources. Controls were left to the individual states or provinces, with rather poor results for the fish.

American Fisheries since 1946

American fisheries after 1946 were characterized by the following new and significant features: (1) the weight of the total commercial catch varied very little from year to year; (2) the value of the total commercial catch, adjusted for inflation of prices, grew slightly, although some species gained greatly in value; (3) the menhaden completely dominated the fin fish catch in weight, but the tunas and the salmon were the big money fish; (4) shellfish accounted for more than half of the total value of the harvest of the seas—and among these the shrimp was worth more than any other fin or shellfish; (5) the per capita consumption of edible fish in the United States was almost unchanged, although total consumption increased with larger and larger portions from frozen packages and cans; (6) the imports of fishery products into the United States greatly increased while exports remained static; (7) fishing fleet concentration and modernization proceeded slowly, except for a few sectors like the tuna industry; (8) foreign fishing fleets, especially the Japanese and the Russians, increasingly entered and exploited the fisheries in the oceans contiguous to waters under the jurisdiction of the United States.

Following World War II the total consumption of fish in the United States, including industrial and animal feed uses, increased rapidly, but the total landings remained almost constant. Indeed, the American catch of both edible and industrial fish hovered between 4.6 billion pounds and 5.4 billion pounds in the twenty-five year period from 1945 to 1970. The value of the total harvest at dockside, moreover, hardly increased between 1950, when estimated at $347 million, and 1960, when estimated at $354 million. A real rise in value did occur between 1960-1971 when the harvest was figured at about $640 million. Discounted for price inflation, therefore, the gains for the fishing industry as a whole may have amounted to 4 percent per annum for the decade. The gains in value, however, for some species, such as the tunas, shrimp, and lobster, were substantial, while other species appreciated rather little.

Surveying the quarter-century of American fishing after World War II, it is apparent that the landings of manhaden, a fish used almost entirely for the oil and meal industry, came close to outweighing all the other commercial fin fish put together. In 1950 more than 1026 million pounds of menhaden were landed; in 1960 more than 2018; and in 1971, something about 2190 million pounds. Landings on the Atlantic shores generally declined, but the catch in the Gulf of Mexico increased. The two most important fin fish that followed menhaden in weight of landings, but far exceeded menhaden in value, were the tunas, mainly yellowfin and skipjack, and the salmon. In 1950 these two species alone accounted for more than 14 percent of the total value of the catch of U.S. fisheries; in 1960 and in 1971 they accounted for approximately 23 percent of the total value of the American commercial harvest of fish.

Salmon was already an important stock in American fishing by the end of the nineteenth century, but the great demand for tuna did not begin until after World War II. In 1920 about 500,000 standard cases of canned tuna were consumed in the United States; in 1930, about 1,750,000; and in 1940, about 4,000,000, a phenomenal growth rate reaching some 23,000,000 cases by 1965. The landings of tuna by U.S. fishermen totaled 182.0 million pounds in 1939, skyrocketing to 392.2 million pounds in 1950, and maintaining a more moderate annual catch around 300 to 350 million pounds in the following decades. The American tuna industry had started in Southern California with the canning of albacore. Gradually the fishing fleet had moved south to the eastern Pacific ocean contiguous to Mexico and Costa Rica, then Ecuador and Peru. During the 1960s the United States and Japan, which had introduced large tuna fleets into the Pacific, the Indian, and the Atlantic oceans, took between them more than three-quarters of the total world catch of tuna.

Shellfish remained immensely popular in the United States after World War II, especially with the introduction of new methods of cutting, cleaning, and packaging. But the production of oysters, once the great delicacy common to seashore and rivertown tables, continued a century of decline from only 60 million pounds in 1960 to barely 55 million lbs. in 1971, worth less than either shrimp or lobsters or crab in that year. From the early 1950s onward shrimp was worth more each year than any other species of fin or shell fish landed in the United States. In 1971 alone shrimp accounted for about 26 percent of the value of the entire American catch. The great demand for shellfish by Americans almost tripled the value of lobsters between 1960 and 1971 while crabs went up in value from $9.7 million in 1954 to $51.4 million in 1971.

Although the total weight of landings of fish in the United States remained almost constant over a twenty-five-year period, shifts in the catch of some fish were considerable. The availability of the stock from the sea, consumer demand, and price all influenced the amount of landings by species. One phenomenon was the virtual disappearance of the Pacific sardine (pilchard) which amounted to 715 million pounds in 1950 but only 120 thousand lbs. in 1965; the sea herring in the same period dropped from a catch of 364 to 110 million pounds; the amount of haddock landed hardly increased while halibut, with international regulation, had its ups and downs in the late 1960's. Atlantic cod, once the king of American fisheries, was far down the list of leading fish, worth two or three million dollars per year from 1950 to 1965. By contrast, flounders were popular and plentiful. Fish like snappers, jack mackerels, whiting, and catfish had a generally good demand and rising catch while scallops enjoyed a good market.

By and large California, particularly with its landings of tuna in San Pedro, had become the leading state of the nation in the value of fish landed. Louisiana, with its catch of shell and fin fish from the Gulf, led the country in volume. Alaska followed California in value of landings while the rich shrimp harvest put Louisiana in third place in the late 1960s and early 1970s. A lot of fin and shell fish were still caught in New England, but Boston, which had led the nation in landings by volume in 1932, dropped to 11th place in 1965. And Gloucester, a port that once was first in its wealth of fish ranked only 13th by value in 1971.[11]

One of the remarkable features of the total consumption of fish in the United States, which increased dramatically from 1940 to 1970, was the transformation of the product to fishmeal and other undifferentiated protein products. As late as 1938 only 8.1 percent of the world production of fish was used this way, but by 1968 more than 35 percent of the fish harvest was being converted into fishmeal and other feed or oil products. The old ways of preserving fish by drying, smoking, or salting steadily declined. Frozen fish and shellfish, which had been virtually unknown to the American table in the 1930s, became more and more important as a consumer product between 1950 and 1970. Although the per capita consumption of fish, by edible weight, remained almost the same in the United States during this period, ranging around ten or eleven pounds, increases in total consumption came from the substantial increases in the American population and the greater transformation of fish to feed or industrial products. In 1971 about 2.4 billion pounds of the American fish catch went to human consumption and about 2.6 billion pounds for feed and industry. To meet the demand of the American market the United States had to rely more and more on imports of fish. Thus, in 1946 the imports from abroad for human consumption amounted to 474 million pounds; in 1956, some 802 million; in 1966 about 1594 million; and in 1970 more than 1843 million pounds. A large part of these imports came from Canada and Mexico, but additional sources were Japan, Korea, and a few South American and European states. At the same time the value of nonedible fish imports into the United States rose from about $40 million in 1946 to $227 million in 1970. Whereas the exports of edible fish from the United States accounted for almost half the weight and half the value of American imports in 1946 and 1947, in 1969 and 1970 the exports accounted for only 8 percent of the imported edible fish by weight and less than 12 percent by value.[12]

The general disadvantages of the American fishermen in competing for the domestic market, let alone the foreign markets that had been the mainstay of the early U.S. economy, stemmed from high wage costs coupled to the over-capitalization of low-yielding fishing efforts, or, put another way, a reluctance to consolidate and rationalize the fishing effort on an economic basis. Closed seasons and quotas in some fisheries often served only to intensify the fishing efforts within the permissible period or amount of catch. Thus the stock was barely conserved while the economic yield was reduced. Moreover, the large government subsidies for the fishing industries of such states as Japan and Russia during these years hardly helped the American fisherman in competition off the Atlantic or the Alaskan-Pacific banks, especially when he remained wedded to traditional fishing habit, smaller ships, less efficient gear, and individual competition for limited marine resources.

Remarkably the number of commercial fishermen in the United States remained almost constant for thirty years: 131,325 in 1939; 130,431 in 1960; and 132,448 in 1969, for instance. Even more remarkable the ratio of fishermen on vessels to those on small boats and on shore also remained almost constant over thirty years; roughly 1:2. What did change markedly in the decades following World War II was the average net tonnage of fishing vessels. Whereas in 1939 the 5413 American fishing vessels averaged about twenty tons, by 1960 not only had the number of vessels more than doubled, but their average tonnage had increased to more than thirty-three tons. By 1969 the average had reached more than forty tons for 13,187 vessels. These figures do not include motor boats, which numbered 31,809 in 1939 and 68,197 in 1969. The average growth of tonnage per fishing vessel, however, did not mean an equal growth in all regions and all fisheries. Menhaden and tuna fleets were leaders in the industry. Until 1951 the menhaden vessels had never exceeded 150 feet in length, but by the 1960s vessels longer than 200 feet came into the fleets. In 1958 purse seines had been introduced into Atlantic menhaden fishing, which, with nylon nets and power machinery, greatly increased the catch with smaller crews, while refrigeration on the larger vessels insured a more marketable product. Indicative of the refinement of fishing techniques in this industry was the use of spotter planes after World War II, nine being employed in 1960 and seventeen by 1965. The tuna industry, moreover, with U.S. government subsidies, had by 1970 one of the finest fishing fleets in the world with a total of 182 vessels, some of which could carry two and three thousand tons of fish in their holds.[13] Nevertheless, the concentration and modernization in other fisheries was sluggish, beset not only by competition between individuals and between coastal states of the United States, but also threatened by the distant water fishing fleets of foreign nations close to American shores.

The Japanese had long been a great fishing nation in Asian seas. In 1930, however, Alaska became alarmed at the appearance of Japanese vessels scarcely more than three miles from the American shore in search of crabs. In the next years the Japanese began to challenge the whalers of Norway and Britain and began expanding into other fisheries as part of the policy of an aggressive government. World War II eclipsed the Japanese fishing effort until 1952, but by 1954 Japanese fishermen were already sailing to the Indian Ocean as well as to the south and central Pacific oceans. By 1962 the Japanese had 1590 fishing vessels of over 50 gross tons and a total fishing fleet exceeding 340,000 tons stretched around the world in the equatorial zone—probably the greatest high seas fishing fleet in history up to that date. Ironically, the contamination of the central Pacific by the U.S. nuclear blasts in the Trust Territory of the Pacific (Micronesia) in 1954 had also forced the Japanese to seek more distant waters, so that their first tuna vessel entered the Atlantic in 1955 while other Japanese vessels shifted to the eastern Pacific.

A completely new threat to fisheries that had been exploited by Americans emerged in the 1960s as the Russians entered eastern Pacific and western Atlantic waters. Russia had not been a great distant-water fishing state, but Soviet planning in the post–World War II period called for a greater consumption of fish with appropriate government support of the state fishing industries. In 1920 the Russian catch had been only 1,760 million pounds, but by 1961 the catch had risen to more than double that amount and was still increasing. Moreover, about 75 percent of the Russian catch was taken from the open seas. Between 1950 and 1960 the number of Russian fishing vessels increased 2.8 times and their motor power increased 2.7 times, moving further out to sea in larger, more efficient factory vessels to harvest waters long exploited by Alaskan, Seattle, and New England fishermen. Norwegian, Portuguese, Korean, and a few other foreign fishing vessels also began to appear closer to American waters in the competition for the free resources of the sea.

A final element to be noted about the fisheries of the United States after World War II was the sports fisherman. Satisfaction of this large constituency in the country became an important concern of politically sensitive legislators as well as a real pressure on the exploitation of stocks of interest to both sportsmen and commercial fishermen. Sport fishing in the United States had gained great popular favor in this period of domestic peace and affluence that permitted more time for recreation. In 1954 more than 18 million angling licenses were sold in the states of the United States, about 2.5 times the number sold in any year before 1946. By 1970 the Bureau of Sports Fisheries and Wildlife estimated that there were some 33 million Americans who fished substantially for sport and spent some $4.9 billion dollars for equipment, bait, guides, food, lodging, licenses, and fees. Of these, some 29.3 million were primarily fresh water fishers whose licenses, tags, and permits alone cost over 100 million dollars. The fish hatcheries and propagation programs begun by the Fish Commission in the 1880s was continued after 1956 by the Bureau of Sports Fisheries and Wildlife with about 100 national stations in the 1960s. Over a billion eggs, fry, fingerlings, and fish were distributed annually, first, to stock waters on lands under federal ownership, especially with trout, second, to assist states in their public waters, notably salmon for Oregon and Washington, and, third, for the replacement or for the initial stocking of private farm and ranch waters. The effect of the sport-fishing on marine species, however, was somewhat less than on fresh-water species, since sports fishers fished rather little beyond the three-mile territorial seas where the federal and the state governments exercised concurrent jurisdiction.[14] It was on the oceans beyond the territorial seas that the major U.S. national and international policies on fisheries were shaped in the 1950s and 1960s.

U.S. Policy in Fisheries

The independent U.S. Fish Commission of 1871 became the Bureau of Fisheries situated in the combined Department of Commerce and Labor in 1903, and remained in the separated Department of Commerce after 1913 for twenty-six years until a general reorganization of the administration took place. Under Reorganization Plan 2, effective 1 July 1939, the Bureau of Fisheries was transferred intact to the Department of the Interior. A year later the Bureau of Biological Survey, which had also been transferred to the Department of the Interior from the Department of Agriculture as another "natural resource" agency, was combined with the Bureau of Fisheries to form the new Fish and Wildlife Service. Meanwhile the Department of State had become increasingly involved with international fisheries commissions and foreign negotiations over American rights on the high seas and in waters contiguous to other nations. In 1949, under industry and Congressional pressure, the Department appointed Wilbert M. Chapman as Special Assistant for Wildlife and Fisheries, to head a small group in the Office of the Under Secretary of State.[15]

The shape of the new Fisheries and Wildlife Service in the Department of the Interior lasted only ten years after World War II. As early as 1954 the Secretary had appointed a study team to consider a reorganization of the Service. Commercial fishing interests still felt that their concerns were not reflected strongly enough at an important level of government in the Fish and Wildlife Service and that the growing importance of international negotiations required fisheries officials of higher rank. Some fifty or sixty bills on fisheries administration were introduced into Congress between 3 January and 17 May 1956, some calling for the establishment of another independent Fish Commission, others for the transfer of fishery functions from Interior to Commerce, and still others proposing various reforms and reorganization. Finally, by Public Law 84-1024, the Fish and Wildlife Act of 8 August 1956, the U.S. Fish and Wildlife Service was established with an Assistant Secretary for Fish and Wildlife, a Commissioner for Fish and Wildlife, and two separate bureaus: the Bureau of Sport Fisheries and Wildlife and the Bureau of Commercial Fisheries.[16]

Under the 1956 Act, the Bureau of Sport Fisheries and Wildlife retained control over the large national fish hatcheries and propagation program, with its appropriate research as well as wildlife activities. But the basic reorganization of the Service achieved by the Act had been prompted by commercial fishing interests, alarmed at the plight of their industry in the face of efficient foreign competition. National attention and legislation was thus focused on the need for a "strong, prosperous, and thriving fishery and fish processing industry." Two years earlier the Saltonstall-Kennedy Act had already provided that 30 percent of the U.S. customs (up to 3 million dollars a year) that was collected on fishery products imports should be transferred to the Department of Interior for research and marketing assistance to promote the use of domestic fish. In 1956 the 3-million-dollar limit was eliminated. In 1958 another Act, which was implemented two years later, transferred, from the Department of Commerce to the Department of Interior, the fishing ship mortgage insurance program, which provided a revolving fund of $10 million to assist in the building and purchasing of fishing vessels. Then, in 1960, Congress approved a fishing vessel subsidy by which $2.5 million per year for three years was made available to pay up to one-third of the costs of fishing vessels constructed in the United States and used in fisheries threatened by foreign imports. In effect the new subsidy was only enjoyed by those vessels built for the catch of New England ground fish. But in 1964 Congress went further in its support for commercial fisheries by permitting one-half, rather than one-third, of the costs of new construction to be subsidized (requiring only that the design be modern!) and by entirely eliminating the proviso that the vessel be employed in fisheries threatened by foreign imports. Moreover, up to $10 million a year, rather than $2.5 million, was authorized for such subsidies.

These measures to support U.S. commercial fisheries by economic incentives were complemented by acts to deter or eliminate foreign competition for fish in American territorial waters and the contiguous zones of the high seas. The appearance of an increasing number of Russian and Japanese fishing vessels in the Northwest Atlantic, the Northeast Pacific, and the Bering seas close to American shores angered the fishers of New England, Alaska, Washington, and Oregon, who regarded their own industry as "depressed" and now subject to foreign competition. Although fishing by foreign vessels in U.S. territorial waters had long been prohibited, violations had increased and were hardly punished. Fishermen were especially irked when, in 1964, eight Japanese factory ships entered U.S. territorial waters not only to purchase raw salmon, but to process it on board. Several other incidents within U.S. territorial waters contributed to pressure on Congress to act. By Public Law 88-308 of 20 May 1964, therefore, the same day in which the Commercial Fisheries Research and Development bill was enacted, foreign vessels were expressly forbidden from fishing in U.S. territorial waters or in waters where the U.S. had the same fishing rights as in its territorial waters, unless permitted by treaty, with penalties up to a fine of $10,000 and one year in prison.[17] By the same legislation foreign fishermen were also enjoined from taking "living organisms belonging to sedentary species" on the U.S. continental shelf, "that is to say, organisms which, at the harvestable stage, either are immobile on or under the seabed or the subsoil of the Continental Shelf."[18] Such measures, however, did not satisfy the fishermen of northeast and northwest America, who urged the extension of exclusive fisheries jurisdiction for the United States up to twelve miles from the shore or even beyond, regardless of the three-mile territorial sea.

The U.S. government faced a serious dilemma. It wanted simultaneously (1) to protect and develop its marine resources in the New England, Alaska, and Northwest contiguous zones of the high seas, (2) to maintain its own distant water fisheries in tuna and in shrimp off Latin America and (3) to prevent any extension of jurisdiction by coastal states into the high seas that might hamper the passage of American ships or provide haven for belligerent submarines. Some of the difficulties in reconciling these policy goals had been apparent in the discussions at Geneva during the two conferences on the Law of the Sea in 1958 and 1960.

The UN Internatinal Law Commission, which had prepared draft articles for the Geneva Conference of 1958 on the Law of the Sea, had recommended that in a zone of the high seas, not to exceed 12 miles from the baseline from which the breadth of the territorial sea was measured, a coastal state might exercise the controls necessary to prevent infringement of its customs, fiscal, or sanitary regulations. Nothing was mentioned about jurisdiction over fisheries in the contiguous zone, and this became a highly contentious issue of the 1958 conference as well as the succeeding 1960 conference to resolve that issue. The question necessarily involved agreement on the breadth of the territorial sea itself. Some states opted for a twelve-mile territorial sea; others wanted a narrower territorial sea, but with exclusive fisheries jurisdiction for the coastal state extending out to twelve miles from shore; still others sought different limits and conditions of jurisdiction.[19]

The United States in 1958 had first hoped for an international agreement on a three-mile territorial sea. But seeing the futility of that position it had proposed a six-mile territorial sea and a six-mile contiguous zone in which the coastal state would have the same rights over fishing as in its territorial sea, providing that states which had fished regularly in the contiguous zone for five years previous to the signing of the proposed convention would continue to have the right to fish there if they observed internationally agreed conservation measures. This American proposal in a plenary session of the conference in 1958 received a majority of votes, but fell far short of the necessary two-thirds required for acceptance as a treaty article. In addition to the opposition of some Latin American and Afro-Asian states, as well as the Soviet Bloc, Iceland and Canada would not accept any "historical" fishing rights in the proposed contiguous zone. No agreement on this issue was reached in 1958. The UN then convened another conference in 1960 specifically to resolve the question of limits to the territorial sea. Compromising, the United States and Canada jointly proposed a six-mile territorial sea with a six-mile contiguous zone in which the coastal state would exercise exclusive fishing jurisdiction, except that any other state that had regularly fished in that zone for five years immediately preceding 1 January 1958 would continue to have the right to do so for a period of ten years from 31 October 1960. Although slightly amended to recognize the preferential fishing rights of a coastal state beyond the territorial sea and the exclusive fishing zone where special conditions prevailed, the Canadian-American proposal failed, by one vote, to receive the two-thirds majority required. Thus, the international legal situation on the breadth of the territorial sea and any contiguous zone for fisheries jurisdiction reverted to its status in 1958 before the Law of the Sea Conference.

The lack of a universal international agreement on the limits of territorial waters and contiguous fishery zones, however, could not forestall national governments from asserting claims to conserve and develop marine resources adjacent to their coasts. On 18 August 1952 Chile, Ecuador, Peru, and Costa Rica had boldly asserted exclusive sovereignty and jurisdiction over 200 miles of the high seas from their shores for the avowed purpose of conserving, developing, and utilizing marine fauna and flora in that area. The effect on the U.S. distant water fishers was immediate. Between 15 September 1951 and 28 June 1963 half a dozen Latin American countries, primarily Peru and Ecuador, seized about seventy American tuna vessels from four to thirty-five miles off their coasts. While the Department of State protested to the Latin American governments, the Congress, through Public Law 88-308 of 20 May 1964, provided reimbursement to the owners of fishing vessels for the fines imposed on them and authorized the Secretary of State to take steps to collect from the foreign governments the costs of the seizures. Nothing was collected—and Congress threatened to cut off foreign economic assistance in retaliation, again with little result. Other states, without going so far as the extreme Latin American claims, had also extended their exclusive fisheries zone jurisdiction in the high seas contiguous to their territorial waters after the 1960 failure in Geneva to reach a universal convention. In fact, by 1 July 1966 apart from the seventeen states that had asserted fisheries jurisdiction beyond twelve miles, forty-nine coastal states claimed a twelve-mile jurisdiction over fisheries from their shores. Of the great maritime powers only Japan and the United States still retained the three-mile limit; however, Japan had already recognized by treaty with Korea the right of either state to establish twelve-mile fishery zones.

In the summer of 1964 bills were introduced into both the Senate and the House of Representatives to extend the fishery jurisdiction of the United States into the high seas. In commenting on the Senate bill the Department of Interior first observed that it had little significance for conservation of American commercial fisheries, but it later admitted that the presence of Soviet vessels within twelve miles of the Pacific coast added weight to the argument for its passage. The Department of State, which, after the failure of the 1960 Geneva conference to reach agreement on territorial waters and contiguous fishing zones, had maintained for five years that there was no legal basis for the assertion of an exclusive fisheries jurisdiction twelve miles out to sea, turned about and held that recent developments in international practice now sanctioned the passage of the legislation. Thus Public Law 89-458 of 14 October 1966 established an exclusive fishery zone for the United States nine miles beyond American territorial waters, "subject to the continuation of traditional fishing by foreign states within this zone as may be recognized by the United States." Furthermore, on 26 July 1968, foreign vessels in U.S. territorial waters or in contiguous fishing zones were enjoined by Public Law 90-427 from any activities that would support a foreign fishing fleet on the high seas.[20]

As early as 1959, through the Tuna Conventions Act, and again in 1962, through the Trade Expansion Act, the President had been authorized to impose economic sanctions on nations that violated fish conservation agreements. In 1971, through amendments to the Fishermen's Protective Act of 1967, the President was further authorized to prohibit the importation of fish products from nations that conducted fishing operations detrimental to international conservation programs, a measure that was clearly aimed at the Japanese and Russian fleets. Although armed with such powers, the Chief Executive, acting on the advice of the Department of State, hesitated to resort to international retaliation, preferring patient negotiations on specific species and fisheries as problems arose, a tactic not much to the liking of members of Congress with fishing constituencies.

In 1964 the Soviet Union first agreed not to use mobile gear during certain months near Kodiak, Alaska; in 1965 it accepted a quota for the catch of king crab in the east Bering seas; and in 1967 it agreed to refrain from fishing in certain areas of the high seas off Oregon and Washington in order to enable American fishers to take ocean perch there. These agreements were all extended on 12 February 1971 with further constraints on mobile gear that harmed American stationary gear; with a reduction of the crab quota; and with a broadening of the area on the high seas in which the American ocean perch catch would be unimpeded. In return, the Soviet Union obtained the right to fish in the 3-12-mile U.S. contiguous fishing zone in the Aleutian Islands, the use of certain contiguous zones for loading and transfer operations, and permission for vessels of their fleet to make four calls a month at Seattle and Portland. In another protocol with the United States the Soviet Union agreed that its vessels would not take more than 4000 tons of herring per year between 1971 and 1973 in the Middle Atlantic in exchange for the right of Soviet vessels to make four calls per month to Philadelphia and Baltimore.

On 21 February 1973, moreover, the United States and the Soviet Union agreed to establish fisheries claims commissions in Moscow and in Washington to which fishermen whose vessels or gear were damaged by other fishermen might apply. Rules for the lighting of ships, and lines, as well as for the marking of buoys over pots, were established as part of the agreement. On the same day the USSR further agreed to refrain from fishing, from trawling, and from the use of certain gear and nets in various parts and at various times in the Pacific Ocean contiguous to U.S. waters. In exchange Russia received some fishing and loading rights in the 3–12-mile contiguous U.S. fishing zone as well as the right of their vessels, under proper arrangements, to enter Seattle, Portland, and Honolulu for water, ship stores, bunkers, or crew rests. Other protocols signed the same day were designed to prevent damage to fishing gear in the northeastern Pacific by forbidding mobile gear at certain times and places, and to allow the USSR to take 260,000 king and 4.2 million tanner crabs in 1973 and in 1974, while the Soviet Union acknowledged the crabs to be a continental shelf resource of the United States.

In addition to the regulations of the High Seas Fisheries Convention of the North Pacific Ocean, which is discussed in the next section, Japan and the United States had also been bound by a number of bilateral agreements on fisheries, such as the agreement of 20 December 1972, which was a renegotiation of earlier protocols, that further reduced the Japanese quota of king and tanner crabs for 1973 and 1974 and limited the fishing of Japanese vessels off Alaska on the high seas. The Japanese maintained that the crabs were high-seas resources. In exchange the United States conceded fishing, loading, and transfer operations to the Japanese in certain contiguous fishing zones of the United States. On 24 November 1972 the United States and Korea also reached a new bilateral agreement that permitted Korea somewhat similar activities in the U.S. contiguous zone for fishing in exchange for Seoul's agreement to abstain from the catch of salmon or halibut east of 175° west longitude.

These efforts to limit the foreign distant water fleets off American shores were complemented by a variety of subsidies by the government to the domestic fishing industry. The Anadromous Fish Conservation Acts of 1965 and 1970 permitted the federal government to initiate programs in the states for the conservation, development, and enhancement of the nation's anadromous species and the Great Lakes fisheries by making grants from 50 to 60 percent of costs providing that the states cooperated with standards of the Bureau of Sports Fisheries and Wildlife. In 1964 the U.S. Fishing Fleet Improvement Act of 1960 was extended for five years to provide additional fishing vessel construction subsidies. In 1965 the Bureau of Commercial Fisheries' loan program to fishing vessels was also extended for five years, and the earlier requirement that a new vessel had to replace an existing ship was abandoned. Finally in 1972, the Commercial Fisheries and Research Development Act of 1964 was extended to 1977, with more than 6 million dollars a year authorized for cooperative federal-state grants to study, improve, and maintain commercial fisheries. Back in 1966 puffy political rhetoric had also attended a grandiose plan to develop fish protein concentrate "to feed a hungry world," but rather little had come of it by 1971. The overblown expectations of invigorating the American fishery industry while assisting the developing nations of the world were thwarted by the initial high costs of manufacture, wrangling within industry and government, bureaucratic inertia, and weak responses in the undernourished countries. Least helpful was the conservative attitude of the U.S. Food and Drug Administration, which first regarded the crushed fishmeat and bones as "filthy" and then as possibly dangerous with their residues of lead and fluoride. Despite this setback, support for American commercial fisheries by the U.S. government was substantial in the 1960s. Further growth of the fishing industry through the development of concentrates and flours still seemed possible. However, whether the total investment of public revenues into fisheries had justified the return to the economy of the nation was debatable.

As described earlier in the first chapter of this book, major oceanographic policy changes were taking place in the United States government during the 1960s. It will be recollected that the President had first formed the Interagency Committee on Oceanography in 1959 under the Federal Council on Science and Technology to point up the importance of the oceans to the nation. Then a host of bills had been introduced into Congress between 1960 and 1965 to go further and fix responsibility for all civilian oceanographic activities in one responsible executive agency. Although the Senate had wanted to create immediately a permanent Cabinet-level National Council on Marine Resources and Engineering Development, it compromised in 1966 with the House in agreeing to a temporary Council and the formation of an independent commission. The outcome was Public Law 89-454 of 17 June 1966, the Marine Science, Resource, and Engineering Development Act. The Marine Sciences Commission provided for in the Act, under the chairmanship of Julius Stratton, set to work vigorously and after two years of study, hearings, and monthly meetings brought forth 122 major and 52 detailed recommendations.[21]

Among its findings and recommendations on fisheries the Commission emphasized the importance of managing these valuable marine resources to obtain the largest net economic gain consistent with the biological capabilities of the exploited stocks. The Commission pointed out, among other things, that excess fishing effort had to be reduced in order to improve economic returns; that the U.S. fishing fleet, although the second largest in the world, was in many sectors technically outmoded, especially since 60 percent of the vessels were over sixteen years old and 29 percent were over twenty-six years old; and that the welter of conflicting, overlapping, and restrictive laws or regulations that were applied to fishing operations in the United States, with ill-defined relations between the federal government and the states, seriously impeded the rational exploitation of fisheries. In fact, it was "unable to identify a single instance of systematic programs being prepared jointly by two or more states for the management or development of their fisheries resources."

In evaluating the fisheries effort of the federal government the panel of experts for the Commission noted that the Bureau of Commercial Fisheries budget had risen sharply since 1950, indeed, more than doubling in one 7-year period in the 1960s but that during this period fish landings had not increased at all. The panel sharply criticized the absence of an integrated plan drawn to specific objectives for fisheries; the inflexibility of the Bureau's budget, which was subjected to constraints by specific legislation to favor specific interest groups; the lack of adequate statistical data on location, distribution, and yield potential of many stocks; and the failure to deal with economic problems of the industry while conducting biological research. In sum, said the Commission, the management of marine fisheries, "in the sense of manipulating the resource to enhance or redirect its beneficial contributions to mankind, is still in a primitive condition."

The Commission frankly stated that there was no reason why the United States should be completely self-sufficient in fishery products, citing the logic of purchasing products at the lowest cost at home or abroad in this or any other industry. But it felt that important segments of the U.S. fishing industry could be restored to competitive and profitable operations. To achieve this end the Report recommended to the President and Congress that they provide the Bureau of Commercial Fisheries with authority (1) to establish national priorities for the development and utilization of migratory marine species, through federal and state cooperation; (2) to assume jurisdiction over and regulate species that migrated between states or entered interstate commerce when they were "endangered" and no action was being taken by the states for their conservation; and (3) to analyze major fisheries, make better assessments of stocks, improve statistical analyses, develop a fisheries extension service, and improve research into fishing technology while maintaining its basic studies of habitats, population dynamics, and environmental effects. Legislation either to remove the prohibition of foreign-built vessels being registered for the domestic fisheries of the United States or to expand the subsidy to American fishing vessels was also suggested.

They key questions about the Stratton Commission report, however, were whether or not a new National Oceanographic and Atmospheric Administration (NOAA) should be created, whether it should be an independent agency or within a Cabinet Department, and what offices it should contain as the lead civilian agency in oceanography matters. In the end, after months of political maneuvering in both Congress and the federal bureaucracy, the President transmitted to Congress on 9 July 1970 Reorganization Plan 4, which established a new agency, combining several existing bureaus and programs for the oceans and atmosphere, in the Department of Commerce. With only minor opposition, Congress accepted the Plan and NOAA was born on 3 October 1970. Moved into NOAA from the Department of the Interior, among other programs and projects, were the Bureau of Commercial Fisheries (except for one commission, one laboratory, and two research projects) and the marine sports fishery program of the Bureau of Sports Fisheries and Wildlife, which were then combined into the new National Marine Fisheries Service.[22]

International Organization and Fisheries

By the twentieth century it was amply clear that the living resources of the sea were no longer inexhaustible and that only international regulation, reached by agreements among states, could protect ocean fish and mammals from the rapaciousness of man. Consequently a substantial part of the recommendations of the Stratton Commission for U.S. policy with regard to fisheries had dealt with problems of international law and organization for marine resources.

As early as 1839 France and Great Britain, seeking to avoid collisions among their fishers, had signed an agreement to entrust to a mixed commission the drafting of regulations regarding the use of long lines and trawling for fish, as well as the taking of oysters, in the waters lying between their shores. The subsequent Anglo-French Declaration of 23 June 1843 sanctioned eighty-nine articles that regulated fishing tackle, gave some protection to fish on the high seas in the area, and restricted the taking of oysters. As noted earlier in this chapter, the multilateral North Sea Convention of 1882 had also attempted to resolve conflicts that had arisen in the conduct of fishing operations by the fishers of different nationalities. The first public international organization to study the oceans, however, particularly the living resources of the sea, was the International Council for the Exploration of the Sea (ICES) formed in 1902. The United States joined ICES in 1912, but dropped out of the organization during World War I. Loosely organized to encourage, draw upon, and coordinate the scientific studies of its member states, ICES became a model for other international fisheries research organizations. Through the revision of its statutes in 1950 and the signing of a new convention on 12 September 1964, a more formal organization was created, which became effective 22 July 1968. Although the Council was called "international," all its member states have been European, except for Canada. Special attention has been given to the North Atlantic ocean through a structure of committees that promote and publish research as well as through a secretariat that collects hydrographic and fisheries data.

Following the success of ICES the International Commission for the Scientific Exploration of the Mediterranean, was established in Madrid in 1919. A year later Canada, Newfoundland, and the United States also attempted to match the success of ICES by forming the North American Council on Fishery Invest-igation. But neither the Mediterranean Commission nor the North American Council worked as well as ICES—and the North American Council was dissolved in 1938. ICES, the Mediterranean Commission, and the North American Council were essentially research organizations. But they pointed the way to the need for fisheries conservation. On 17 December 1929 Denmark, Germany, Poland, Danzig, and Sweden signed the first conservation treaty under ICES auspices, a convention covering plaice and flounder in the Baltic Sea with a closed season, size limits to fish caught, and a general prohibition of trawling in territorial waters. Another convention was signed in 1932 by Sweden, Denmark, and Nor-way covering plaice in the Skagerrak, Kattegat, and Sojnd of the North Atlantic. Still another agreement on net sizes and catch limits for certain species in the North Atlantic was reached in 1937 by Belgium, Denmark, Germany, the United Kingdom, Iceland, the Irish Free State, the Netherlands, Norway, Poland, and Sweden. Each state was represented on a permanent commission to review the implementation of the agreement. Prior to World War II, therefore, a number of progressive fisheries conventions were in force in Europe, including regulations by Sweden and Finland for the Baltic and by the Soviet Union and Finland for Lake Ladoga.[23]

A new and important thrust of international organization into the problems of fisheries came with the creation of the UN Food and Agriculture Organization (FAO) in 1944. Dedicated to raising the levels of nutrition and to improving both the production and distribution of food and agricultural products, in-cluding marine products, FAO first established a Fisheries Division in its secre-tariat and then, on 1 January 1966, upgraded the Division to a Department of Fisheries. At the same time a Committee on Fisheries, representing members of FAO, was created in which senior fishery officials could review the programs of the Organization, discuss worldwide problems of fisheries, and evaluate the effectiveness of international regulations. In the constitution of FAO, moreover, Article 14 had provided that the Council and the Conference of the Organization might submit draft conventions to member states. Under this provision, FAO helped to create the Indo-Pacific Fisheries Council through an international convention signed 25 February 1948 and the General Fisheries Council for the Mediterranean through another convention signed on 24 September 1949. Both councils have been advisory in character, working through data collection and study groups. An effort to create a Latin American Fisheries Council of the same type, however, failed for want of ratifications of the agreement that was signed 22 September 1951. FAO also established fishery commissions or committees within the Organization itself for the Southwest Atlantic, the Indian, and the Eastern Central Atlantic oceans. Again these were advisory bodies to encourage, promote, assist, and coordinate fishery development in their regions and to make recommendations to the Conference of FAO.[24]

After World War II, a number of international agreements, to which the United States was not a party, were reached for the conservation and development of fisheries. In Europe the pre-World War II cooperation in Atlantic fisheries was revived through the Convention for the Regulation of the Meshes of Fishing Nets and the Size Limits of Fish signed on 5 April 1946 with a permanent commission to give effect to the agreement. Dissatisfaction with this agreement led to a new Northeast Atlantic Fisheries Convention signed in London on 24 January 1959, again chiefly concerned with net meshes and minimum fish sizes in catches but with a commission to administer the provisions and to make recommendations for improving the rational exploitation of any of the stocks in the area. In 1952 Norway, Sweden, and Denmark reached an understanding on the protection of the shellfish taken by their nationals, and the Soviet Union and Japan signed the Convention on the High Seas Fisheries of the Northwest Pacific Ocean on 14 May 1956 in Moscow, through which a Japanese-Soviet commission could review conservation measures, determine the annual catch of some stocks (notably salmon), and coordinate the research programs of the two countries.

Other notable fishery conventions not including the United States were the accord between the People's Republic of China, North Vietnam, North Korea, and the Soviet Union in 1956 to establish a commission to promote joint research as well as make recommendations for the conservation and improvement of fishery resources in the western Pacific; the 1957 agreement of Norway and the Soviet Union to conserve seals in the northeastern Atlantic; the 1959 agreement between Bulgaria, Roumania, and the Soviet Union to prescribe the minimum fish sizes for certain species caught in the Black Sea; the 1965 agreement of Japan and Korea, reached after a long controversy, to establish a Joint Fisheries Commission to regulate the high-seas fisheries between their coasts; and the 1969 convention establishing the International Commission for the Southeast Atlantic, a step initiated by the Committee of Fisheries of FAO, in order to conserve the living resources of that area.

As the 1970s began the United States was participating in nine independent international fisheries commissions outside the FAO system. Only two of them had been actually established prior to World War II. The International Fisheries Commission for the halibut, agreed to by the United States and Canada in 1923, and the International Pacific Salmon Fisheries Commission for the Fraser River system, agreed to by the United States and Canada in 1930, had continued their work through the 1940s. On 2 March 1953 the Convention for the Preservation of the Halibut Fishery of the Northern Pacific Ocean and Bering Sea was signed in Ottawa and changed the name of the International Fisheries Commission to the International Pacific Halibut Commission. The Commission, composed of six members, three appointed by each party, was empowered to make decisions by the concurring vote of at least two of the commissioners of each party and was charged, as in the past, with the division of Convention waters into fishing areas, limiting the fish size and quantity of the catch, regulating fishing appliances, collecting statistics, and so forth, all to develop the stocks of halibut in the territorial seas and waters contiguous to the western coasts of the United States and Canada. The Commission has been ably assisted by a small independent international staff of scientists that has made proposals for regulations that resulted in the stocks of halibut increasing dramatically at first and then being more or less sustained. The catch of 68 million pounds in 1972 can be compared to the 44 million pounds caught before international management of the fishery began.

The other pre-World War II international fisheries commission joined by the United States, the International Pacific Salmon Commission, came into existence with the ratification of the Convention for the Protection, Preservation, and Extension of the Sockeye Salmon Fishery of the Fraser River system in 1937. But the Commission exercised no regulatory powers until 1946. Since then, with the same number of members and voting procedure as in the Halibut Commission, it has been assisted by as many as fifty scientists in its independent staff and, since 1957, it has taken responsibility for pink as well as sockeye salmon. With power to ensure an adequate escapement for the species in their runs from river to ocean to river and with authority to divide the catch between U.S. and Canadian fishers, the Commission greatly succeeded in restoring the stock from its previous depletion.[25]

The United States had led the way with Great Britain, Japan, and Russia in designing the first treaty specifically intended to save a marine animal from extinction: namely, the North Pacific Sealing Convention of 7 July 1911, which was described earlier in this chapter. But the Convention left all the implementation of the articles to the contracting states and created no international commission. In October 1940, as World War II approached, Japan gave notice of its intention to withdraw from the treaty and did so a year later. From 1942 through World War II and up to 1956 the United States and Canada continued a provisional agreement for the conservation of the species by the prohibition of pelagic sealing to their nationals and by the United States sharing 20 percent of its annual harvest of the Pribilof Island herds with Canada. On 9 February 1957 an Interim Convention on Conservation of North Pacific Fur Seals was signed by the United States, Canada, Japan, and Russia, which essentially restored and strengthened the 1911 Convention. Each state pledged to prohibit all persons and vessels under its jurisdiction from the killing or taking in any way the fur seals north of the 30th parallel, in the north Pacific Ocean, including the Bering, Okhotsk, and Japan seas. In return for their abstention from sealing, Canada and Japan received, under the new Convention, 15 percent of the sealskins taken commercially each season by Russia in the Commander and Robben Islands and 15 percent taken by the United States in the Pribilof Islands. Moreover, the 1957 Convention created the North Pacific Fur Seal Commission, which was composed of one member from each contracting state and required a unanimous vote for any action. The Commission was charged with the formulation and coordination of research programs that could lead to appropriate recommendations on the fur seal fisheries to the contracting parties.

A new Convention for the Conservation of Antarctic Seals was approved by a conference of eleven states in London from 3 to 11 February 1972 and signed by the United States on 28 June 1972. Although the Antarctic Treaty of 1959 had given protection to seals on land and on ice shelves, its provisions had not covered the animals on sea ice or in the water. Under the 1972 convention the taking or killing of crabeater, leopard, and Weddell seals was limited to 175,000, 12,000, and 5000 animals respectively. The Convention also prohibited the catch of Ross, southern elephant, and arctocephalus seals, while, in other articles, it provided for sanctuaries and banned pelagic sealing.

International concern about the decline of certain species of whales, as indicated earlier in this chapter, had been expressed through the League of Nations and an International Convention for the Regulation of Whaling signed in Geneva in 1931, which had entered into force for the United States in 1935. That convention was followed by the International Agreement for the Regulation of Whaling signed in London in 1937 as well as a protocol amending and extending the 1931 Convention with respect to a sanctuary and a closed season for whales in the Antarctic. But none of these acts was effectual, especially with the coming war, and they failed to stop the violent depletion of the whales in Antarctic waters from which 85 percent of the world's catch was taken in the late 1930s. More than 29,000 blue whales were caught and killed south of the 40th latitude in 1931 alone. Just before the outbreak of World War II, a record 55,000 whales were swept from the oceans of the world in one year.

In 1944, looking forward to normal postwar fishing operations, Australia, Canada, Great Britain, New Zealand, Norway, South Africa, and the United States, subsequently joined by Argentina, Denmark, and Mexico, signed a protocol to limit the 1945–1946 whale catch to 16,000 blue whale units (one blue whale = 3 humpbacks = 5 sei or, later, one blue whale = 2 fin = 2.5 humpbacks = 6 sei). Articles of agreement by international conferences and protocols, however, were a clumsy way to regulate a fishery, with its fluctuating needs and demands. In 1946, therefore, the representatives of nineteen countries and observers from the FAO met in Washington to sign on 2 December a new International Convention for the Regulation of Whaling, which became effective on 10 November 1948 and established an International Whaling Commission. In 1972 there were fourteen states represented on the Commission. In addition to its functions of study, collecting data, making appraisals, and disseminating information to maintain and increase the population of whale stocks, the Commission was empowered to amend the Schedule, which stipulated among other things, protected species, length of hunting seasons, size limits for each species, methods of whaling, types of gear, and statistical requirements, as well as (since

1956) methods of inspection. Amendments to the Schedule, however, required a three-quarters vote of the Commission members, whereas any member state lodging an objection to an amendment within ninety days of its adoption by the Commission was not considered bound by that amendment.

Unfortunately the Commission did not amend the 16,000 blue whale units (BWU) quota for the Antarctic that it inherited in 1948, a number patently too high and too broad in its application to the species for sustaining the whale population. And that quota, applied to pelagic whaling, did not include the land stations in the Antarctic. Only in the 1953–1954 season was the quota dropped to 15,500 BWU and not until 1956–1957 did it fall to 14,500. This quota was further divided by agreement among the Antarctic whaling countries themselves into national quotas. Failing to agree on their national shares the Netherlands and Norway withdrew from the Convention in 1959. Only voluntary catch limits, therefore, were in effect for three years, but the depletion of the stocks became increasingly evident to the whalers themselves, who were unable to take their own declared catch limits totalling more than 17,000 BWU. By 1964 both the United Kingdom and the Netherlands had dopped out of the competition for whales in Antarctica, leaving only Japan, Norway, and the USSR to divide a fishery that was close to economic disaster, if not biological extinction. Light finally broke through when the Commission agreed in 1965 to set 4500 BWU for the season, and subsequently the Antarctic quotas were dropped year after year, reasonably adjusted to the best scientific estimates of the maximum sustainable yield of the stock.[26]

As the Antarctic whale fishery became depleted, the hunters, especially from Japan and the Soviet Union, increased their pursuit of the great sea mammals in the North Pacific ocean, where pelagic whaling was virtually unrestricted. By 1967, however, a ban on killing of blue and humpback whales was agreed to by the whaling nations, and specific quotas were placed on the catches of fin, sei, and sperm whales in the North Pacific, rather than using the Antarctic blue whale units. Despite these gains in meshing the scientific assessments of stocks of whales with economic demand, the enforcement of catch regulations remained a worrisome problem. The placing of international observers from the member states of the Commission on board the factory ships had been approved in principle in 1959, but not until 1972, under further pressures for the curtailment of the catch of whales expressed at the UN Conference on the Environment, was the practice accepted. Internationally the round-up of the huge mammals seemed to be abating in the mid-1970s, with Japan and the Soviet Union as the chief hunters. In 1975, for example, the Soviet Union further reduced its whaling fleet in the Antarctic to only four motherships and 80 catcher boats, while domestic environmental groups in Japan took strong stands against the killing of whales.

Whaling in the United States continued to decline after World War II. With public interest aroused to protect the environment and especially awakened to the threats to marine life posed by modern industry, the catch of Leviathan, once the greatest adventure of American seafarers, came to an end. By 1969 the number of whales landed in the United States totaled only 183, of which 111 were brought in by special scientific permits; in 1970 the total was 73, and in 1971, only 53. More than two dozen bills for the protection of marine animals were introduced into Congress in 1971 and in the following year, the Secretary of Commerce, pursuant to the Marine Mammal Protection Act of 21 October 1972, permanently halted the taking or processing of all blue, bowhead, finback, gray, humpback, right, sei, and sperm whales by all U.S. nationals, while forbidding the importation of whales or any of their products into the United States.

The international halibut, salmon, seal, and whale commissions owed their existence to conventions that were primarily concerned with the depletion of one stock of fish or mammal. A different type of agreement, however, was reached on 8 February 1949 when the United States signed the International Convention for the Northwest Atlantic Fisheries in Washington (ICNAF). This was the first multilateral regional fishery regulation in which the United States participated, covering an area from Greenland in the east to the North American shore in the west and extending southward to the 39th degree north latitude. Earlier in this chapter the effort of Canada, Newfoundland, and the United States from 1920 onward to cooperate in research on the northwest Atlantic fisheries had been noted through the North American Council on Fishery Investigations, an endeavor that ended in 1938. ICNAF, established by the 1949 convention, was designed to investigate, protect, and conserve the fisheries of the Northwest Atlantic by (1) receiving recommendations from panels established for five sub-areas of the total convention area and (2) by making proposals to the contracting states on fishing seasons, size limits for species, spawning sanctuaries, fishing gear, and catch limits, as may be appropriate on the basis of panel recommendations and scientific evidence. Ratified by the United States, the United Kingdom, Iceland, Canada, Denmark, Spain, Norway, Portugal, and Italy between 1949 and 1952, the Convention has also been adhered to by West Germany, France, Japan, Poland, Roumania, Bulgaria, and the Soviet Union.

Scientific research for ICNAF has been carried out entirely by member countries under the coordination of a standing Research and Statistics Committee, which has also established various ad hoc committees on statistics, gear, environment, and so forth. Primarily to prepare statistics and carry on the general administration of ICNAF an executive secretary and a small staff have been the only permanent employees. During the first twenty years of its existence ICNAF was handicapped by an awkward procedure requiring that proposals by the Commission for the management of the fishery start with a recommendation from the panel of the subarea, then be submitted for review to the panel after elaboration by the Commission, and then not take effect for any member until four months after acceptance by all the member states of the panel. Beginning in 1970, however, the recommendations of ICNAF became binding on all the member states except for those states that formally object to the provisions.

Cod, haddock, halibut, herring and other fish have come under special study by ICNAF, with attention given to the assessments of stocks, modes of fishing, and rules on minimum mesh sizes to prevent overfishing. But such regulations, slow in being adopted, uneven in administration and control, and hardly addressing the rational exploitation of the fishery for equitable economic yield in conjunction with maintaining the stocks, did not go far enough. Haddock, for example, visibly declined in the face of exhaustive fishing by the Soviet Union on Georges Bank, much to the irritation of the United States and Canada. Only in 1969 was an overall quota for haddock finally reached. In 1970 ICNAF recommended a ban on high-seas fishing for salmon that had spawned in North America, but a few states fishing that species were reluctant to abandon their catch. By 1973 regional quotas had been also set for yellowtail flounder, salmon, silver hake, ocean perch, and red hake as well as regulations on the minimum sizes for scallops. In 1976 ICNAF recommended the reduction of the overall catch of herring on Georges Bank from 150,000 to 60,000 tons—and no major fishing of that species for six months. Nevertheless, where quotas were established by ICNAF, a fair distribution of the total quota among competing fishers from different nations, some of them better capitalized and more advanced technologically than others, still remained a political and economic issue.

In the history of American fisheries tuna had a late start and only became an important harvest in the 1930s. The demand for tuna continued to grow in the 1940s and the Inter-American Tropical Tuna Commission (IATTC) was established by the United States and Costa Rica under a convention signed on 31 May 1949 at Washington at a time when ever-larger catches of tuna were needed to satisfy the voracious American market. No one was concerned about the exhaustion of the stock itself, so essentially the Commission was charged with the study of the species in an area extending from southern California to northern Peru and several hundred miles seaward into the Pacific Ocean.

In the following decades Ecuador, Panama, Mexico, Canada, and Japan adhered to the Convention for the Establishment of IATTC, although Ecuador remained as a member only from 1961 to 1967. Each contracting party has been entitled to send one to four delegates to a national section of the Commission, but all decisions of the Commission have been taken by the unanimous vote of the national sections. Central to the work of the Commission has been the Director of Investigations, chosen by the Commission for his technical competence and responsible for drafting the research program, preparing budget estimates, supervising technical staff, appointing internationally recruited scientific staff, and preparing reports under the Commission's guidance.

In the Convention the Commission was charged with the investigation of the "abundance, biology, biometry, and ecology of the yellowfin and skipjack tuna in the waters of the eastern Pacific Ocean" fished by the High Contracting Parties designed to keep the population of fishes covered by this Convention at those levels of abundance which will permit the maximum sustained catch." Collecting statistics and publishing reports has been amply and ably performed by the Commission, in large part through the some thirty internationally recruited scientific personnel. The task of sustaining yield through limited catches, however, has proved more difficult. As the depletion of stocks became evident, the Commission first proposed to limit the total take to 83,000 tons of yellowfin tuna in 1962. But it was not until 1967 that any catch quota became effective. Subsequent total catch limitations, again without fixing national quotas, intensified competitive effort at the opening of the season and shortened the period in which the allowed quota of the yellowfin has been filled.

One of the problems faced by the Commission was the limited resources available to it, for the United States alone had to pay upward of 90 percent of the annual costs; another was incidental mixtures of yellowfin tuna into skipjack catches, since skipjack landings have been greatly encouraged; and a third was the lack of adequate evaluations of optimum economic and equitable returns from the fishery. In the early 1970s the arrests of American tuna boats by Ecuador and Peru within two hundred miles of their shores hardly helped the management of this important fishery. Nevertheless, the Coordinator of Ocean Affairs in the State Department and former Director of the Bureau of Commercial Fisheries stated in 1972 that the IATTC was the only organization of its kind in the world which had "a clear record of success in the conservation of a migratory resource of the ocean through international cooperation."[27]

Until the twentieth century the United States and Canada did not compete for the valuable stocks of fish and crustacea along their north Pacific ocean coasts from Alaska to California. As noted earlier, both halibut and salmon were just beginning to be placed under conservation measures by these two states when in 1930 the first Japanese floating crab factories appeared in the Bristol Bay of Alaska. In the following years the approach of Japanese salmon fishers to these waters caused consternation. Two bills to extend American fisheries jurisdiction beyond the three-mile territorial waters were introduced into the U.S. Congress, but in 1938 firm diplomatic pressure from Washington brought forth a declaration from the Japanese government that it would henceforth restrain its nationals from fishing in Bristol Bay. War between the United States and Japan broke out only three years later. With victory American fishing interests in the postwar years of 1946 to 1950 had first hoped to force Japan into an abnegation of fishing rights in the North Pacific as part of the Treaty of Peace. However, Article 9 of the 1951 treaty did not go so far, but rather required Japan to "enter into negotiations for the regulation or limitation of fishing and conservation and development of fisheries of the high seas."

To implement Article 9, a Tripartite (United States–Canada–Japan) Fisheries Conference was held in Tokyo between 9 November and 14 December 1951, which drafted the International Convention for the High Seas Fisheries of the North Pacific Ocean, signed on 9 May 1952 and in force 12 June 1953. The most important and novel element of the Convention was the principle of abstention: (1) when fishing stocks were being fully utilized and more intensive fishing would not lead to a greater sustainable yield; and (2) when such stocks were subject to a conservation program accompanied by extensive research, then states not participating in fishing those stocks were required to abstain. Under the Convention, therefore, Japan agreed to abstain from halibut on the high seas along the coasts of the United States and Canada, from herring in the same area, except for the Bering Sea and west of a meridian at the extremity of the Alaskan peninsula, and from salmon in an area generally encompassing Bristol Bay. Both Canada and Japan agreed to abstain from salmon that spawned in U.S. rivers, excepting the area west of the 168th line of west longitude. The Canadians were satisfied with protective articles for their halibut and salmon catch in the North Pacific, which provided that abstention would not apply where a state had substantially exploited the stock in the last twenty-five years, or where there had been an historic intermingling of fishing operations, or a history of joint conservation measures.

In force for an initial period of ten years, with options of annual renewal, the Convention also established the North Pacific Fisheries Commission. The most important responsibility of the Commission lay in determining whether abstention should be continued or modified for those stocks of species described in the Convention and whether new stocks should be placed under the abstention principle by one of two of the member states, all on the basis of scientific information. Action was taken by unanimous vote. The Commission also had the responsibility to investigate, on the request of any one of the three members, those stocks fished by at least two of the members that have not been placed under any conservation regulations and to find whether there was need for a joint conservation arrangement of such stocks.

Some of the problems of the Commission stemmed from the discontent of the Japanese with the abstention "principle," which was agreed to by Tokyo during its postwar political weakness. Indeed, some stocks were removed from abstention, but none was added. Given the responsibility to determine the western meridian that divides American salmon from Asian salmon, moreover, the Commission found "intermingling" that inevitably led to political disputes over the correct legal demarcation. The Commission has depended on national programs for scientific research, rather than its own independent staff. Despite the intrinsic value of these studies, they prompted no new conservation measures for such important species as the king crab. Unable to reach a better agreement, the parties to the Convention continued it by annual renewals. Neither Russia, whose fleets vigorously entered these waters in the 1960s, nor Korea, a more recent fishing state in this area, joined the Convention for the High Seas Fisheries of the North Pacific Ocean. Thus many arrangements for conservation were left to a series of bilateral agreements and protocols that had to be frequently negotiated among the interested states.

Efforts to establish an international fisheries commission for the Great Lakes between Canada and the United States had a long, tedious, and tangled web of discussions during the 1920s, 1930s, and 1940s that did not end until 10 September 1954 when the two states finally agreed in Washington to a convention. In force beginning 11 October 1955, the Convention on the Great

Lakes Fisheries was designed to coordinate the efforts of the two countries in determining the need for and the type of measures required to make possible "the maximum sustained productivity" in the Great Lakes fishery and "particularly to eradicate or minimize populations of the sea lamprey."[28]

Not only had overfishing and industrial pollution long been causes of declining yeilds of fish in the Great Lakes, described briefly earlier in this chapter, but in the 1940s the sea lamprey spread from Lake Ontario through the canals all the way to Lake Superior. It ravaged and decimated lake trout, steelheads, and whitefish, a fearful fact that gave final impetus to the international agreement that established the Great Lakes Commission. Composed of two national sections, with not more than four members in each, the Commission proposes and coordinates research programs, publishes or authorizes publication of scientific and other data, and recommends measures to the contracting parties for achieving the objectives of the Convention. The Great Lakes Fisheries Commission alone received 58 percent of the total appropriations of $3.1 million for the nine international fisheries commissions in which the United States participated in fiscal year 1973. Much of the Commission's effort has been centered on the reduction, if not the elimination, of the sea lamprey from the Great Lakes, with success in some areas and only moderate achievements in others. At the same time the Commission has advised and achieved the stocking of some of the species attacked by the sea lamprey as well as the introduction of the Pacific salmon into the lakes.

Chronologically the next major development in international organization for fisheries was the Convention on Fishing and Conservation of Living Resources of the High Seas signed at Geneva on 29 April 1958. This Convention, one of the four concluded at the Geneva 1958 Law of the Sea Conference, imposed an obligation on each contracting party to adopt conservation measures in any area of the high seas fished exclusively by its own nationals. Moreover, where two or more contracting parties fished in the same waters of the high seas the Convention required them to enter into the negotiation of conservation agreements at the request of any of the other contracting parties. Should no conservation agreement be reached between these states within twelve months, then a special five-member commission, either designated by the parties to the dispute, or, if they could not agree, by the Secretary General of the United States, would, by majority vote, render a decision.

Under the Convention new entrants into a fishery that had been placed under an international conservation agreement were also required to abide by that agreement or else, in case of dispute, accept the decision of a special commission. A coastal state was also given the right to adopt unilateral measures for conservation of the living resources of the oceans adjacent to its territorial seas, (1) if there were need for the urgent application of such measures, (2) if such measures were based on scientific findings, and (3) if such measures did not discriminate against foreign fishers. Finally, a coastal state, even if not itself fishing in waters contiguous to its territorial seas, could request the state or states whose nationals were fishing there to adopt conservation measures. In all instances where a dispute arose the contracting parties agreed to make use of a special commission for a final decision.

The laudable purposes of the 1958 Convention to avoid the overexploitation of marine resources by international cooperation and to utilize a five-member commission to resolve disputes have only been realized in rather small ways. It took eight years for the Convention to come into force, waiting until the Netherlands became the twenty-second state to ratify it on 20 March 1966. Moreover, a number of nations, including Japan and the Soviet Union, with two of the world's greatest fishing fleets, never ratified the Convention. The five-member special commission procedure remained virtually dead in practice. The Convention, however, had considerable influence in expressing the need for conservation measures on the high seas and in shaping several bilateral agreements according to its principles.

Another international organization that the United States has joined for fishery conservation and development has been the International Commission for the Conservation of Atlantic Tuna. The west Africans in particular had called for the establishment of a tuna conservation commission analagous to the Inter-American Tropical Tuna Commission. The FAO set up a working party in 1963, which led to a conference of seventeen states, convened by FAO, in Rio de Janeiro from 2 to 14 May 1966. The International Convention for the Conservation of Atlantic Tuna, approved at the Rio conference, was ratified by the United States on 18 May 1967 and came into force on 21 March 1969 when Spain deposited the seventh national instrument of ratification.

The Convention covered tuna and tunalike fish in "all waters of the Atlantic Ocean, including the adjacent Seas." It provided for a Commission, made up of the delegates of each contracting party, and panels, which could make recommendations based on scientific studies, designed to maintain the population of tuna. By the appointment and at the pleasure of the Commission, an Executive Secretary was given authority to coordinate the program of investigations, prepare the budget estimates, collect and analyze data. The purpose was to achieve the maximum sustainable yield of the species. Recommendations for conservation may be adopted (1) by a two-thirds vote of the Commission on its own initiative, whether or not an appropriate specialized panel had been established, or (2) by a simple majority of the Commission when adopting a proposal from one or more panels. Recommendations become binding on all member states six months from the date of their notification. If a majority of the parties should express formal objections to a recommendation, then no state would be bound by its provisions.

The International Commission for the Conservation of Tuna held its first meeting in December 1969, and it illustrated some of the fundamental strengths and weaknesses of all the international fisheries "regulatory" organizations in which the United States has participated and which have been described in this section. *First,* except for the International Whaling Commission, which has had responsibility for a species on a world-wide basis, the activities of the commissions have been generally limited to "convention" areas and a few species. *Second,* the chief activity of all the commissions has been data collection and research, as a base for recommending measures for conservation and development. But only the halibut, salmon, and tropical tuna commissions have had their own international staff, with fairly modest budgets. And in these three instances the budgets were almost entirely supported by the United States and Canada. *Third,* closed seasons, gear requirements, and catch quotas have been the most significant forms of regulation recommended by the several commissions.[29] The apportionment of the total catch quota has been rather successfully resolved in the North Pacific Fur Seal Commission and in both the halibut and salmon commissions, in which only Canada and the United States have participated. But it is a difficult political issue in the other commissions, particularly at the point of allocating national catch quotas.

All the commissions have been criticized at one time or another not only for the quotas that they have set, but for concentrating on the maximum sustainable yield of a species rather than the most efficient and economic use of a fishery. Ultimately, however, the "regulatory" power of the commissions has depended on the acceptance of their recommendations by the states which are parties to the convention on the fishery. In rare instances, as in the salmon commission, changes of regulations have been at the discretion of the commission, but generally recommendations for new rules or the modification of old arrangements have had to be accepted by each contracting member state to be effective. On balance, the mounting concern of the world over the depletion of the living resources of the seas and willingness to seek solutions based on scientific evidence and economic efficiency through international commissions gave some hope for rational and pacific procedures in the management of these resources. But with the extension of exclusive jurisdiction over fisheries by coastal states up to 200 miles from their shores in the mid-1970s, a whole host of questions will be raised about the role of international fisheries commissions.

Problems and Issues

Some thirty-five nations of the world have a substantial interest in fisheries, but of these only about six, including the United States, had a catch worth more than $300 million in the mid-1970s. Only two, Japan and the Soviet Union, were landing fin and shell fish worth more than a billion dollars annually. Peru, which had led the world in weight of landings for a decade up to 1971, for example, had a harvest valued at less than $75 million a year.

In 1975 the United States landed 4.8 billion pounds of fin and shell fish worth about $970 million, with shrimp, tuna, and salmon providing most of the value. The American per capita consumption of fish remained fairly stable over the years while the total landings of fish rose very slightly. Because of an increasing population and a greater demand for nonedible fish used for industry and animal feed, imports of fish into the United States steadily increased. Between 1960 and 1975 the value of edible and nonedible fish bought from other countries rose from $363.2 million to $1.6 billion. The United States also exported fish, and in 1975 some $304 million worth of fish, a jump of 16 percent in value over 1974, were shipped to foreign countries. The value of all processed fisheries products in the United States, including domestic and foreign stocks, climbed to more than two billion dollars in the mid 1970s.[30]

Considerable publicity has been given to the problems and issues of high-seas fisheries, but progress in improving the management of stocks in the inland waters of America and in the seas under the jurisdiction of the United States has been slow despite calls for reform for almost a hundred years. While the sight of Russian and Japanese trawlers often triggered waves of anger among American fishers concerned about their share of fish in the high seas contiguous to the United States, it should not be forgotten that in the early 1970s about 58 percent of all the landings of fin fish by weight and 44 percent by value also were taken within the three miles of the United States. This is an area where the states have exercised—or failed to exercise—jurisdiction over fisheries.

Throughout the twentieth century critics of American fisheries have pointed out that states in the United States, which can manage the living resources of their inland and territorial waters, have failed to do so. Only in the last phases of depletion, or else, under local political pressures, have the states acted and then to take restrictive measures to favor their own constituents rather than analyzing the need both to sustain the stocks and to provide equitable economic returns for the catch. The most common regulations for closed seasons and types of gear have simply not addressed the problem of open access to a limited resource. Restricting access of making allocations by law can lead to political pain, so palliatives for the problem have been prescribed rather than a cure. Moreover, individual state regulations have often been framed without regard to the movement of fish across state boundaries and the urgent need for interstate or regional standards to be enforced uniformly throughout the fishery. Conflicts between the American fishers of one state and another have been frequent, particularly in the 3-12-mile contiguous zone under federal jurisdiction; while disputes between American fishers using different gear or between commercial harvesters and sportsfishers have also agitated the state legislatures.

A major effort to overcome the historically narrow state regulations of fisheries was the creation of the Pacific Marine Fisheries Commission in 1947 followed by the Atlantic States Marine Fisheries Commission, and the Gulf States Marine Fisheries Commission in the 1950s through interstate compacts approved by Congress. Designed to promote the better utilization of marine, shell, and anadramous fish in the region by joint programs, the compacts provided for a Commission which could study and make recommendations to the states for legislation and the coordination of their police powers in order to protect fisheries from overfishing, waste, depletion, or other abuses. Some good has clearly resulted from this focus on the regional interrelationship of fisheries, but nothing in the compacts can be construed to limit the powers of any state, which ultimately determines fisheries policy for its own jurisdiction with its own constituents in mind. To mention only a few examples, anchovy, salmon, king crab, scallops, and oysters have all been poorly managed in the past by states of both the east and west coasts of the United States, guided by the temper of local politics rather than the evidence of scientific fisheries research.[31]

In 1972 the National Marine Fisheries Service launched a program described by its director as the "most significant new step" of the Service to develop cooperative management programs for fisheries under shared federal-state jurisdiction. "Until now," said the Director, "the approach of the federal government seems to have been one of accepting the institutional setting as it existed and working within these constraints. This approach has not worked, especially in commercial fisheries, and we are convinced that it never will work."[32] Among the intentions of the National Marine Fisheries Service were (1) legislation to strengthen the authority of the federal government to promulgate and enforce regulations in the 3-12-mile contiguous fishing zone, (2) legislation to provide up to 100 percent of the costs from the federal government to the states, individually or regionally, for the planning and implementation of fisheries management, and (3) legislation at some time in the future to limit the entry of American fishers to certain stocks. Both fishers and politicians in the states, nevertheless, looked warily at this thrust of federal influence or control into the fisheries along their shores. They remained doubtful about limiting the entry of their own citizens to any fishery as they pointed with alarm to the depletion of some fisheries near the American shores by foreign vessels.

In the 1960s and early 1970s, however, the biggest American fishing news was the approach of foreign fishing ships up to the territorial sea and contiguous zone of the United States. Modern, mechanized fleets of the Soviet Union, Japan, and West Germany swept huge harvests from New England and Alaskan shores. As already noted, the United States extended its exclusive fisheries jurisdiction out to twelve miles from shore in 1966, but this hardly satisfied the local fishermen. In 1970, for example, the Soviet Union took 836 million pounds of fish from "New England waters," an area which until 1969 had been entirely exploited by New England fishermen. By 1975 Russia had the world's largest fishing fleet with more than 4000 ships equipped for crossing high seas and carrying out distant water operations. Angry coastal fishers, with a clout in Congress, sought a unilateral 200-mile extension of U.S. jurisdiction for fisheries over adjacent waters, but other fishermen, like the tuna operators of southern California and the shrimpers who fished in the waters adjacent to Latin American states, feared retaliation. The State Department, sensitive to the international ramifications of unilateral American legislation, preferred to proceed through negotiation in the Third UN Law of the Sea Conference, which began its substantive session in Caracas in 1974.

No line dividing the territorial sea from the high seas had received general international consent at the Geneva Conference on the Law of the Sea in 1958 or in 1960. In a contiguous zone, not extending "beyond twelve miles from the baseline from which the breadth of the territorial sea is measured" a state could exercise control necessary to prevent fringement of its customs, fiscal, immigration, or sanitary regulations. Some states, like the United States, extended their jurisdiction over fisheries out to twelve miles from the shore; others, however, went beyond that point to 50, 100, and 200 miles into the high seas, warning that no living resources could be taken from these areas without permission of the coastal state. Clearly the situation was unsatisfactory, lacking positive international law to satisfy the interests of (1) the coastal nations that feared the depletion of stocks which they fished near their shores; (2) the coastal nations that wished to conserve the resources and share in the gains from stocks in the high seas contiguous to their shores even if they could not fish the resources themselves; (3) the distant-water fishing nations that made investments in their fleets, developed an advanced technology, and regularly fished for a common resource on the high seas lying off the coast of other states; and (4) the maritime nations that insisted on freedom to navigate the ocean highways for commerce and defense without any interruption by a coastal state that claimed a right of surveillance, inspection, or arrest on the high seas.

From 1971 to 1973 the UN Sea-Bed Committee had dealt with the management and conservation of fisheries, exclusive fishery zones, and the preferential rights of coastal states in preparation for the Third UN Law of the Sea Conference. But one trend affecting fisheries had become clear: states were extending their jurisdiction further and further from their shores over the oceans. At first the claims of such countries as Chile, Ecuador, and Peru to an economic resource zone in which the coastal state possessed sovereign rights to all marine, soil, and subsoil resources out to a distance of 200 miles from their shores were regarded as extravagant. Yet by 1973 not only had most Latin American states acknowledged the right of states to such claims, but a number of African and Asian states were fully persuaded that coastal states could establish an economic resource zone extending up to 200 miles from shore and could exercise sovereign rights to protect and conserve the renewable resources in that zone, including exclusive or preferential exploitation. Moreover, by 1973 such states as Malta, Iceland, Canada, and Australia were also ready to support an international convention that would provide for the extension of fisheries jurisdiction by a coastal state as far out as 200 miles from the baselines from which it measured its territorial sea. In advancing their various proposals for a "patrimonial" or "economic resource zone," these states generally maintained that jurisdiction over the resources in the area would be exercised without prejudice to the traditional freedom of all nations under international law to navigate or fly over the high seas and to lay submarine cables and pipelines.

The United States had introduced its first draft articles on fisheries to the UN Sea-Bed Committee in August 1971 with a bold emphasis on international organization. It had proposed that fisheries and other living resources of the high seas be regulated "by appropriate international (including regional) fisheries organizations established or to be established." No discrimination in form or fact would be permitted between the fishers of coastal states and other states, whereas the percentage of the allowable catch traditionally taken by other states would not be allocated to the coastal states by the international organization regulating the fishery. In the event that the interested states in a fishery could not come to an agreement on an international organization or felt that none was necessary, the U.S. proposal fell back to the general principles of the 1958 Geneva Convention on Fishing and Conservation of Living Resources on the High Seas: that is, the coastal state could proceed to establish regulations, with sufficient notification to other states of its procedures and rules, and, in the event of disputes, the interested states would make use of a special commission for the settlement of issues.

The rather generous proposal of the United States (1) to respect traditional foreign fishing interests on the high seas adjacent to its coasts, (2) to proceed to a rational exploitation of the fisheries through international organizations, and (3) failing that procedure, to put disputes with foreign states over any fisheries regulations promulgated by the coastal state before a special commission was greeted with disdain and rancor by most American fishing interests. Complaints that the fishing industry had not been adequately consulted in preparing the position of the United States and pressures from Congress, notably from the House Committee on Merchant Marine and Fisheries, led to a radical change in the U.S. posture before the UN Sea-Bed Committee in 1972. On 4 August before Subcommittee II, the Alternate United States Representative to the UN Sea-Bed Committee confessed

our views on this vital and perhaps pivotal element of the negotiations before us have changed since we introduced our original draft one year ago . . . We have . . . been persuaded . . . that the coastal state should have the right to regulate the fish stocks inhabiting the coastal waters off its shores as well as its anadromous resources.[33]

In its new draft fisheries article the United States about-faced its policy, giving the coastal state the power to regulate and maintain preferential rights to all coastal living resources off its coast beyond its territorial sea to the limits of the migratory range of the specied, including anadromous fish (e.g. salmon) spawned in its waters throughout their migratory range on the high seas. In principle the coastal state would reserve to its own flag vessels only the allowable annual catch that they could harvest, then make allocations, first, to states in the region, and, finally, to all other states.

This complete capitulation to the trend of coastal states to arrogate to themselves greater and greater control over offshore resources beyond their territorial seas was mitigated in only two ways: first, with an eye to American tuna interests, the U.S. draft placed the regulation of "highly migratory ocean resources" under the regulation of an appropriate international fishery organization, giving both coastal states or other states harvesting or intending to harvest such resources an equal right to participate in such organizations; second, disputes that might arise between states under the article would be submitted, at the request of any party, to a special five-member commission.

The Single Negotiating Text that emerged from the 1975 Geneva session of the Third Law of the Sea Conference and the Revised Single Negotiating Text of the 1976 New York sessions left no doubt that in the new "exclusive economic zone," measured 200 miles seaward from the baselines of the coastal states, the coastal state alone would determine the allowable catch of the living resources in that area and would itself judge its capacity to harvest such resources. It might allow access to its exclusive economic zone to foreign fishermen at its own discretion, with licensing, fee payment, and other forms of remuneration as regulatory and rental devices. Coastal states were exhorted to take into account the goals of maintaining or restoring the stocks while seeking maximum sustainable yields and endeavoring to meet the economic needs of coastal communities, developing countries, fishing patterns, and regional or global standards. In the case of highly migratory species (tuna, pomfrets, marlins, swordfish, etc.) the text read, "The coastal State and other States . . . shall cooperate directly or through appropriate international organizations . . . to ensure optimum utilization both within and beyond the exclusive economic zone," surely a troublesome provision.

The coastal state was also given primary conservation responsibility for anadromous species (e.g. salmon) that spawned in its fresh water lakes or streams and swam far out to sea, with the enforcement of regulations effective beyond the exclusive economic zone to be agreed on with other states concerned. Where anadromous or catadromous (which spawn in salt water and migrate to fresh water) fish swam across the zonal boundaries of two or more states, their governments were expected to reach agreement on the conservation and management of the stocks.[34]

Despite a growing consensus by the coastal states of the world on the establishment of an exclusive economic zone by multilateral agreement, a position not entirely shared by the land-locked countries or those juxtaposed to other states whose sea boundaries could not be much enlarged, the UN Law of the Sea Conference made slow progress in 1976. The prospects for a single convention, adopted, ratified, and in force before 1980 seemed uncertain. In view of the prevailing political tendencies and the promptings of many coastal fishermen, therefore, several states began to extend their exclusive jurisdiction over fisheries beyond their territorial seas and contiguous zones unilaterally. In 1974 and 1975 the U.S. House of Representatives Merchant Marine and Fisheries Committee held extensive hearings on fisheries jurisdiction, and the following year Congress passed the Fisheries Conservation and Management Act (PL94-265), which President Gerald Ford signed on 13 April 1976 to take effect on 1 March 1977.

Under the Act, the most sweeping change in the legislative history of American fisheries, the United States has assumed exclusive jurisdiction over the management of fisheries in a zone contiguous to the territorial sea and extending 200 miles seaward from its shores. It also has assumed for the United States authority over anadromous species of American origin and continental shelf species seaward of that zone. To the extent that any surplus of fish beyond the harvesting capacity of U.S. fishermen might be available, as determined by the regional councils established under the Act and by the Secretary of Commerce, foreign fishing can be permitted under license and with allocation of the catch to foreign countries by the United States. The U.S. Fisheries and Conservation Management Act of 1976 particularly affected the Soviet Union, Japan, and West Germany. Japan estimated in March 1976 that the extension of exclusive jurisdiction to 200 miles by all states of the world might mean a loss to her of 4.5 million metric tons of fish.

Eight regional councils, New England, Mid-Atlantic, and so forth, were created under the Fisheries Conservation and Management Act of 1976, composed of voting members to include the principal state official with fisheries management responsibility, the regional director of the National Marine Fisheries Service of NOAA, and other qualified individuals appointed by the Secretary of Commerce from nominations by the state governors. Nonvoting members on the councils consist of officials from the U.S. Fish and Wildlife Service, the Coast Guard, the Marine Fisheries Commissions, and the Department of State. Responsibility for drawing up fishery management plans was given to the regional councils. They were required to seek "optimum yields" in their conservation and management efforts, manage each stock as a unit over its range, promote efficient use of resources, and seek to minimize costs. The councils were expected not only to describe the fishery, but assess its present use and future condition, with its maximum sustainable yield and optimum yield, and to judge to what extent American fishermen might harvest the fishery and what portion of the optimum yield might be left for foreign fishermen. The Secretary of Commerce was given the ultimate authority to approve or disapprove fishery management plans as well as the right to accept or reject the application of a

Governing International Fishery Agreement submitted by a foreign nation through the Department of State in order to obtain permits for its vessels to fish within the 200-mile zone.

Some of the problems and issues attached to these momentous changes in extended fisheries jurisdiction lie in the definition of "optimal sustainable yield," which can be interpreted as maximum sustainable yield tempered by economic, social, and ecological factors. First, the maximum sustainable yield of a fishery depends on scientific analysis, often weak and debatable. Then, relevant economic, social, and ecological factors can become bogged down in a miasma of subjective interpretations, all to be voted on by regional councils. As a complement to the first problem, moreover, the foreign fishermen are assigned the difference between the "harvesting capacity" of the American fisherman and the balance of the optimum sustainable yield, which may again provoke highly subjective feelings about the harvesting capacity (efficient or inefficient?) of American fishermen. And no less a dilemma is the issue of managing a stock as a unit, for fish swim in mixed schools, often compete for the same food and water space or against the same predators, which means the management of one stock impinges ipso facto on the condition of another.[35]

Nothing in the Act affected fishing in the U.S. three-mile territorial sea, where regulations have been made by states, and nothing in the Act intends to tax or limit the entry of Americans to the exclusive economic zone except within the broad parameters of conservation and management set by the councils and approved by the Secretary of Commerce. Obviously the Act cannot improve the situation of the U.S. distant-water fishers, who will face restrictions in other countries at least as narrow as the U.S. Fisheries Conservation and Management Act. Both the east and west coasts of South America had exclusive fisheries zones, which Washington branded as illegal before its own action, and in 1976 both Canada and Mexico proclaimed their exclusive jurisdiction over fisheries up to 200 miles from shore. Finally, the U.S. Fisheries Conservation and Management Act has required an enforcement mechanism to make the Act viable. In 1977–1978 the costs of Coast Guard control alone were estimated at about $35 million.

The fishing industry continues to provide a livelihood for about a quarter of a million Americans engaged in the harvesting and processing of fish products as well as to servicing industries and the public that needs nutritious food. Despite the fact that about one-fifth of the world's fishery resources can be found in or near American waters, the U.S. has not captured this precious bounty. Distant-water fishers in the past took a large part of it. However, the American coastal fishing industry, characterized by small capitalization, inefficient catch, cramped storage, uneconomical marketing units, and sluggish technological innovation, as well as a generally poor history of public management of coastal fisheries due to divided jurisdiction and inadequate scientific information, should also be blamed.[36]

The extended jurisdiction of the United States could bring more rational conservation and management to the coastal fisheries in the 1980s, still providing opportunities for highly efficient foreign fishermen in joint ventures, but the burden of improvement may rest on further U.S. legislative efforts to create incentives for pruning the industry of waste and rewarding the ambitious, well-managed, modern fishing units that will aggressively compete for the optimum sustainable yield.

5 Mineral Resources of the Sea

Until the twentieth century man obtained little of value, except salt, from inorganic resources of the oceans and the bed of the sea. Some placer deposits of minerals, like gold; some diamonds or pearls; and some coal and tin from mines drilled out from land under water in the shallows of the ocean—these were all that nineteenth-century technology permitted entrepreneurs to recover. Today, however, the states of the world are engaged in a relentless conquest of the ocean floor—by scientific study of its contours and composition, by an intensive search of its surface and bowels for gaseous, liquid, and hard mineral resources, and, finally, by commercial exploitation that is rapidly advancing rigs, wells, and dredges from the near shore to the abyss of the ocean.

The political division of the dry surface of this planet among the states of the world and their exercise of jurisdiction within their territorial borders is obvious. Over the centuries sovereigns have conquered, annexed, or purchased lands from other peoples, or occupied vacant territories to the exclusion of other flags. Transfers and titles to such possessions have been legalized in modern times by treaties. But the claim of any state to own or exploit, to the exclusion of others, the nonorganic resources that lie on or within the bed of the sea beyond national jurisdiction is different, because the high seas and the soil beneath them have long been regarded as free, open, and available to all the nations of the world.

The potential wealth of the seabed that lies beyond national jurisdiction is incalculable. Vast reservoirs of petroleum and gas, millions of tons of ferro-manganese nodules containing copper, nickel, and cobalt, and unknown quantities of rich mineral-bearing rock lie under the oceans of the world. Technological problems, of course, must be solved to reach the recesses of such wealth; moreover, the economics of production will be a determinant of the rate of progress toward the exploitation of such minerals since they can also be obtained through dry land. But, above all, political decisions on legal guidelines for the exploitation of the seabed must be taken in concert by the states of the world. Without international agreement there will be no assurance of orderly and equitable procedures in recovering an enormous wealth from many millions of square miles that have been regarded as either belonging to no one or belonging to everyone.

The United States has a profound stake in the petroleum, natural gas, and hard minerals under the oceans of the world. Its interest in the seas for national security, trade, and fish, as indicated in the previous chapters, have taken on a

161

new dimension in the twentieth century when extensive drilling for offshore oil began. Moreover, American enterprise is on the verge of commercial recovery of hard minerals from the floor of the deep ocean. In order to widen the historical perspective of United States dependence upon the seas, some words about salt, until recent times the most valuable inorganic substance recovered from the oceans, should preface the contemporary issues of seabed exploitation. Note should also be taken of other minerals drawn from seawater and the extraction of shells, sand, and stones from the near shore.

Salt, Shells, Sand, and Stone

The modern American pays little heed to the salt he spills on his food for incidental seasoning. It is a cheap and readily available commodity. But salt historically has been one of the precious resources of a people, a key to nutrition, a provider of strength, a vital supply of war, a base of civilization. The cave dwellers of Europe used salt, preserving their fresh kills of meat and thereby freeing themselves of the deadly need for a daily hunt. Written records of the manufacture of salt by the ancient Chinese can be found in the treaties of Peng-Tsao-Kau-Mu on pharmacology written about 2700 B.C. The Egyptians used salt bricks as money, while the Roman troops were paid in salt rations or "salaries." Even today hundreds of expressions in our speech still persist, like "the salt of the earth" and "worth his salt" that recall the great value of this commodity throughout history. In medieval times salt was one of the very few known chemicals. It was used to prepare leather, solder junctions of pipes, help manufacture wine, and included in a number of worthless prescriptions for the cure of toothaches, acidity, and droopy spirits. But the greatest value of salt by far was in the preservation of meat, fish, cheese, butter, and many other foods. Before the age of canning and refrigeration, any community deprived of salt became enfeebled, not only because of the inherent importance of salt to the human diet, but because its food supply would be quickly limited. As a vital commodity of everyday use salt was historically taxed, monopolized, and regulated by the sovereigns of Europe. The salt tax (gabelle) in France, for example, was notorious as one grievance of the great 1789 Revolution. During the 1780s in England some 10,000 people a year were seized for smuggling salt and tobacco, with about 300 winding up on the gallows for dealing in such black markets.

In America, as early as 1614, Captain John Smith had commented on the excellent opportunities for making salt as he mapped the coast of New England. Almost immediately after their settlement the Virginia and the Massachusetts colonies began making salt from the ocean with improvised wooden flats on the sandy beaches in which brine was evaporated or else they boiled brines in pans hung over fires. In fact, the first patent issued by the General Court of

Massachusetts went to Samuel Winslow in 1641, granting to him the sole right to make salt by his process for ten years. In the same year John Jenny received a twenty-one year patent for salt-making in Plymouth. Connecticut granted to John and Stephen Ford in 1746 for a period of fourteen years "the sole liberty of making salt . . . by boiling seawater." Saltworks were established at Salem, Gloucester, Salisbury, and throughout Cape Cod. By 1820 there were 442 saltworks on Cape Cod representing an investment of two million dollars and yielding 500,000 bushels per year from seawater let into canals or drawn from the marsh waters.

Salt was in great demand in the young colonies to preserve their fish, meat, and skins of animals. American ships, laden with lumber and seafood, sailed to Portugal and Spain, returning with salt and wines from the Azores and Canary Island. On 29 December 1775 the Continental Congress urged all the colonial assemblies and conventions to promote the manufacture of salt. Among other early state programs to manufacture salt, Pennsylvania contracted for and protected a saltworks at Toms River in New Jersey, and Virginia undertook a comprehensive program of building saltworks at public expense south of the James River, in Gloucester, Elizabeth County, and between the Potomac and Rappahannock rivers.

The trials of both the Revolutionary War and the War of 1812 emphasized the need of the growing United States to have supplies of inland salt, which were both more secure and cheaper when taken from the brines of salt springs. Commercial inland salt was first produced in the United States from the springs of Lake Onondaga (Syracuse), New York in 1790. Under the direction of the state of New York, which owned 15,000 acres of salt lands, 157 boiling kettles were producing sixty-two thousand bushels of salt a year by 1801, one million bushels by 1828, and more than three million bushels by 1841. The Kanawha Valley of (West) Virginia was not far behind Syracuse in salt production. Several fierce battles of the Civil War were fought that finally deprived the South of this vital supply source and gravely affected the Confederate war effort.

In the West, almost from the moment of their arrival in 1847, the Mormons had begun the production of salt from the Great Salt Lake, whereas several solar evaporation plants had been established on the eastern shores near San Francisco by 1868. Twenty years later salt fields stretched out for almost twenty miles along the shores of the San Francisco Bay. By 1950 the Leslie Salt Company had the world's largest solar evaporation plant, occupying forty square miles of the Bay's shorefront, drawing seawater into shallow ponds, some of which were 800 acres in area.[1]

Of great importance to the future of obtaining mineral resources from the seas, however, in the eighteenth and early nineteenth centuries was the intensive drilling for water and for brine, with a constantly improving technology that was to prove of inestimable value in the recovery of rock oil or petroleum. Today public attention has turned to drilling for natural gas and oil beneath hundreds of feet of water, but in ancient history man had already discovered how to tap an underground spring, under hydrostatic or gaseous pressure, and bring the spout to the surface. By the nineteenth century drilling had reached such an art that on 26 February 1841, after almost seven years of work, the boring rods of a well sunk to 1798 feet in Grenelle, near Paris, suddenly dropped a few yards and within a few hours water gushed forth at the rate of 600 gallons per minute. Between 1857 and 1858 on the very eve of the petroleum revolution in America, a three-inch bore in Louisville, Kentucky, reached a depth of 2086 feet, releasing a stream of water that flowed at 264 gallons a minute and arched 150 feet into the air at the surface of the well. The universal search for such artesian wells and the need for thousands of common water wells with mechanical pumping facilities greatly facilitated the technological recovery of brine and, later, hard rock salt, which was drilled and flushed to the surface. The first modern oil well in the United States was drilled with salt water drilling equipment in 1859. Only ten years later Thomas F. Rowland obtained a patent for a primitive submarine drilling apparatus with a platform to be anchored in water and tended by a boat.

Although Americans have no problems with their needs for table salt today, the history of that commodity in the past was marked by political controversy and capped with remarkable technological innovations that prepared the way for modern gas and oil recoveries. In recent years less than 40 percent of the salt (sodium chloride) produced from seawater, brines, and rock salt (halite) has been consumed as salt in the United States: it is mostly used as sodium carbonate (soda ash) for the paper, rayon, glass, or soap industries, as well as for ice control, or as sodium hydroxide in electrolytic processing. A rapid growth in products using chlorine, such as plastics, solvents, pesticides, antibacterial agents, and various chemical or metallurgical reagents, has also benefited from the plentitude of salt available to the United States.

The oceans can also provide magnesium, the third most abundant element in seawater, and bromine for commercial use. Michael Faraday had first demonstrated in 1833 the formation of metallic magnesium by the electrolysis of molten magnesium chloride. Significant commercial production of the metal began in Germany in the early twentieth century. Essentially seawater, which contains 0.13 percent magnesium, can be pumped into settling tanks, mixed with lime, and precipitated as insoluble magnesium hydroxide. By electrolysis the magnesium hydroxide can be separated into chlorine gas and metal magnesium. The metal can be alloyed with aluminum, zinc, or manganese for a variety of structural products, especially for vehicles requiring light strong materials. The rise of the aircraft industry in the United States after 1910 and particularly the demand for giant bombing planes after 1942 called for larger supplies of magnesium metal alloys. By 1970 almost the entire American supply of about 100,000 tons of primary magnesium came from two plants using the electrolytic process. Magnesite, magnesia, magnesium carbonate, magnesium bromide, and other compounds find use in the American paper, pulp, rayon, rubber, fertilizer, and chemical industries.

Bromine was first isolated as an element by Antoine J. Balard of France in 1826 from the evaporation of Mediterranean seawater. In nature bromine occurs in combination with metallic elements and must be chemically separated. Brines with high calcium chloride are a rich source of bromine and contain anywhere from 0.02 to 0.5 percent of the element, while the ocean, which holds the largest amount of the element in the world, averages about 0.0065 percent bromine. Brines in Pennsylvania had been worked for bromine as early as 1846, but until the twentieth century, the major commercial production of bromine was located in Germany from the salt deposits near Stassfurt. After 1928 the major use of bromine was in ethylene bromide, a compound in anti-knock gasoline. In 1934 the first commercial processing of bromine directly from seawater occurred near Wilmington, North Carolina. By 1970 there were twelve plants in four states, with Michigan as leader producing 393 million pounds of bromine. Eleven of these plants processed well-brines, and one plant, in Texas, used seawater to obtain bromine worth about 88 million dollars. Compounds of bromine are now used for soil sterilizers, fumigants, fire extinguishers, medicines, and photography.

Because of their abundance in the seemingly limitless and open oceans, the minerals suspended in solutions of the seas thus far have raised no political difficulties. Shells, sands, and gravel of the American shores, however, which have greatly gained in commercial value during the last fifty years, must be dredged from fixed sites along the seaboard. Their removal from the shores has raised public concerns about the environment that are a new constraint upon production. Millions of tons of oyster and clam shells have been used to make lime, which is the major ingredient, with silica and alumina, of Portland cement. Beach sands, moreover, contain many minerals of value, notably the gem stones, and in the United States zirconium, titanium, and other stream of beach deposits have been dredged for commercial purposes.

Of greater value to the United States, however, has been the sand and gravel industry. In the late nineteenth century small roadside pits and holes in the backyards of farms were sufficient to supply all gravel and sand required for roads, dams, buildings, and other construction work. Indeed, in 1902, only two million tons of sand and gravel, worth about $1.5 million dollars were mined in the United States, but by 1923 this figure had soared to 140 million tons worth $90 million. Twenty years later, mixing the figures of land excavation and sea dredging, more than 250 million tons of sand and gravel worth $110 million were processed.[2] By 1970 the United States was obtaining from land quarries, river beds, lakes, bays, and the seashores, almost two billion tons of crushed stone, gravel, and sand worth about two and one-half billion dollars. While sand is used in abrasives, filtering media, and glass industries, more than 90 percent of the demand for crushed stone, gravel, and sand, which has risen over 5 percent per year since 1949 has been for building materials.[3] Recently all the coastal states have taken some action to protect their shores against environmental degradation due to the economic development of recreation and industry seaside. Increasingly both state and local legislation has either narrowed the areas for excavating or dredging the abundant resources of gravel and sand or else imposed higher costs for their production by requiring new environmental safeguards. Whether these acts will lead to larger political-economic conflicts cannot be determined yet, but in any event the issues are likely to be more local than national or international.

The extraction of salt, magnesium, bromine, shell, gravel, and sand from the seas and surface of the near shore of the United States, however, is almost trivial in value by comparison with the wealth of petroleum and natural gas now being pumped out of the seabed. Offshore oil and gas production is a dramatic story barely more than twenty-five years old, and its scenario continues to unfold with worldwide political and economic consequences. But the prelude to the petroleum age lay in the great leap forward that mankind took in the exploitation of new energy sources in the early nineteenth century. From this splendid inventive effort came the liberation of millions of people from the drudgery of hand labor.

The Exploitation of Petroleum

It may seem incredible, but between the time of the ancient Roman Empire and 1750 there had been little change in either the manufacture of lamps or the strength of artificial illumination in Europe. A few refinements of lamps had led to greater convenience in handling the wicks and a better diffusion of the flame that was nourished by vegetable or animal oil. But the early eighteenth century lamps gave little more than the one candlepower that had lighted ancient Athens and Alexandria. When in 1784 a Swiss chemist named Ami Argand rolled a flat wick into a cylinder and enclosed it in two brass tubes, he revolutionized artificial illumination, causing Thomas Jefferson, in France, to write of the phenomenon to Charles Thompson, Secretary of the U.S. Continental Congress, that the light from this lamp was "equal to six or eight candles." Other lamps quickly followed and improved on the Argand model. Just about the same time in the marvellous, rapid advance of Europe toward industrialization at the end of the eighteenth century, gas illumination from the distillation of coal became practical.

Coal, often called "burning stones" or "burning rocks," had been known from the most ancient times. In 1275 Marco Polo had informed the Europeans that all over China the people dug out a kind of black stone and burned it like firewood. In England records show twelve cartloads of pit-coal delivered to the Abbey of Petersboro in 852 A.D. and the books of the Bishop of Durham contain the first known western records of coal mining in 1180. Coal, then called "secole" from the pebbles and rocks collected by women and children as the North Sea scoured the east coast of Northumberland, was sent to London in 1240. Both Edward I and Edward II banned the burning of coal because of the smoke, but its use gradually widened, and by 1379 it was being taxed.

In the seventeenth century England began to run out of wood, particularly firewood. To conserve energy the Crown, among other things, required builders to use brick and iron in houses while demanding that exporters of beer have the wooden barrels returned from abroad to England. As the energy crisis sharpened, the substitution of coal for wood increased, but the major impediment to the mining of coal was the flooding of the underground passages. Better pumps were required and during the Elizabethan-Stuart period scores of patents for pumping water were secured. In 1602 about 190,000 tons of coal had been shipped out of Newcastle. By 1750 about one million tons were being shipped out of Newcastle and Sunderland combined.

The contribution of coal to the English industrial revolution in the making of iron and in the use of steam is well known. But of parallel importance was the discovery of coal-gas and coal-oil. J. B. Van Helmont had coined the word "gas" in his *Ortus Medicinae*, published posthumously in 1648, for the spirits or emanations (carbon dioxide) given off by the heating of charcoal. Before 1691, John Clayton, the Dean of Kildare, filled some animal bladders with gas obtained by the distillation of coal, pricked holes into the skins, and lighted the openings. In 1785 Professor Jean Paul Minckelers of the University of Louvain had demonstrated in a laboratory illuminating gas from coal distillation. Five years later, Philippe Le Bon, still considered the father of gas illumination in France, obtained the first patent for a process using wood. But in 1792 William Murdoch at Redruth, Cornwall was the first man actually to light his house and office with gas, a feat with proven commercial possibilities when he lighted the Boulton and Watts engine works near Birmingham, England, in 1802. F. A. Winsor, a German who had followed Le Bon and then independently learned the distillation process helped organize, over the protests of Murdoch, the 1812 Gas Light and Coke Company that first lighted Westminster bridge in 1813 and the streets in 1814.[4]

In the United States coal gas for illumination had been demonstrated to Philadelphia as part of a show by M. Abroise and Co. as early as 1796. Ten years later David Melville of Newport, Rhode Island, like William Murdoch in England, successfully lighted his house and the nearby street with gas made on his premises. The first gas company in America was chartered in Baltimore in 1816; in Boston in 1822; and in New York in 1823. The commercial use of coal was far slower in America than in England. "Sea-coall" was shown on a map near Wilkes Barre in 1762 and coal was imported to New York, Philadelphia, and other ports in the eighteenth century. Not until 1812 was the first anthracite coal burned successfully in large-scale commercial use in Philadelphia.

Bituminous coal was also known and it was generally used in the early production of illuminating gas.

These remarkable innovations in lighting, however, scarcely helped the ordinary person at home in the United States. During the first forty years of the nineteenth century the average dweller in Boston, New York, Philadelphia, or Baltimore still used only candles or sperm oil for illumination. Coal gas lighting for individual houses was somewhat dangerous, generally unpleasant, and far too expensive. Even candles and sperm oil had to be used sparingly, for tallow candles by 1850 sold at fifteen cents a pound, with only six candles to the pound. Sperm oil, which had averaged about 80 cents a gallon until 1845, soared to about $1.77 a gallon on the average between 1845 and 1855.

As industrialization advanced in the nineteenth century it led to more urban life, a greater use of evening hours, and more demands for artificial illumination. The animal-vegetable oils for lighting were inadequate, and gas, limited by piping and the high costs of production, challenged man's ingenuity to produce cheaper, more efficient, artificial illumination for city homes and country farms. Essentially the problem was to find better fuels for the technically improved lamps.

James Young, a Scotsman and an industrial chemist, had made use of a small petroleum spring in Derbyshire in 1847 to obtain both lubricating and burning oils. In 1850 he patented a process for distilling naphtha, lubricating oils, and paraffin oil, making use of various bituminous substances, including boghead coal and shales. In 1854 Abraham Gesner, who had received his medical degree in London in 1827 and then emigrated to Canada where he became a distinguished geologist, patented a distilling process to produce coal oil. He called it "kerosene" and sold his patent and registered title to a company at Newton Creek, New York, to manufacture this new fuel. By 1859 there were more than fifty small coal oil or kerosene plants in the United States distilling lamp oil from soft coal, shale, or natural asphalt, producing about 23,000 gallons a year. The proof that fossil fuels or hydrocarbons could be efficiently burned for illumination after distillation or "cracking" set the stage for the petroleum revolution that so substantially changed human history.

Petroleum or "rock oil" seeping from the gound had been well known and used for countless centuries before the Industrial Revolution. Descriptions of the distillation of "naft," an Arabic word from the classical "naptha," date back to the ninth century. Several early Arabic records contained observations about oil springs and the combustion of mineral oil for lighting before Marco Polo, travelling through Persia in 1271, reported to Europe his observation of Baku, which had so much "oil not good for eating, but good for burning" that a hundred ships at a time could be loaded with it. About the same time an Arab, Hamdu'llah Mustaufi, wrote that the Baku springs were the most abundant in Iran and that the natives had dug a number of wells to get down to the "naphtha," which rose on the surface of the water.

In Europe oil seepages, in tar sands and from springs, were surely known and used from the Middle Ages onward, primarily for their adhesive pitch and their alleged medicinal or healing qualities. The intrepid sixteenth century Spanish captains who crossed the Atlantic and reached the Pacific ocean caulked their ships with residues of crude oil seeping from the water-edge or sands in Cuba, Texas, California, and Peru. The North American Indians used petroleum for paint and medicinal purposes while many tribes were well aware of its combustible qualities when they observed flaming creeks and springs. The drillers of salt wells in the early nineteenth century in New York and Pennsylvania often were annoyed by the black, smelly oils, as well as the gas, that often gushed up with the brine. But it was ultimately the desire to improve fuels for lamps, precipitated by the demonstrated distillation of hydrocarbons by such men as Young and Gesner, that turned the attention of businessmen to petroleum in earnest.

Among those plagued by the nuisance oil from salt wells was Samuel M. Keir of Pittsburgh who, among other things, operated a group of 400-foot brine wells near Tarentum, Pennsylvania. Keir had tried to dispose of the oil by bottling it for medicinal purposes, but without success. On the advice of J. C. Booth, a chemist, Keir first set up a small still in 1850 in Pittsburgh to process the petroleum for burning. This was the first petroleum refinery in the United States. Keir called his product "carbon oil." Seven years later one of the largest dealers in lamp oil in New York, A. C. Ferris, who was searching for better fuels, tried some carbon oil distilled by Mackeowan and Finley. In 1858 Ferris also purchased some of Keir's output and by further refining of the product as well as making lamp adjustments produced a tolerable illuminating fuel from carbon oil. Thus, over one thousand barrels of petroleum (42 gallons to a barrel) were traded in 1858, almost all of them handled by Ferris. The price per gallon began to rise, going from 50 cents to $1.50 to $2.00, creating new incentives for the production of petroleum. Ferris himself sent out agents to investigate seeps in California, Europe, and the East Indies, but the main problem was to increase supplies at lower costs, to improve the technology of collecting oil from the surface of springs by hand.

Meanwhile, Dartmouth College was indirectly responsible for the organization of the first petroleum company in America. Francis B. Brewer, an alumnus of the College, was a physician who had used petroleum rather extensively for medicinal purposes in his practice. He visited western Pennsylvania, then entered the lumber business, and observed the petroleum springs on the company's property. Brewer brought a sample of the petroleum to Professors O. E. Hubbard and Dixi Crosby for examination on a visit to Dartmouth. Soon after George H. Bissell, another alumnus of Dartmouth and a New York lawyer, visited his former tutor, Professor Crosby, and became interested in the sample of petroleum for its commercial possibilities. After paying for Professor Crosby's son to come inspect the Brewer Lumber Company property on Oil Creek, which flows into the Allegheny Rover, Bissell and his partner, Jonathan G. Eveleth, organized the Petroleum Rock Oil Company on 30 December 1854. Capitalized at $250,000, the Company obtained from Brewer title to one parcel of land and oil rights to several adjacent parcels in exchange for Brewer's right to one-fifth of the capital share.

But in 1855 it was no easy task to interest investors in petroleum. The refinery of Samuel Keir was virtually unknown, and no one could predict the market that would be created shortly by the lamp oil dealer, A. C. Ferris. To gain investor confidence an extensive analysis of a sample of the petroleum from the Company's property was sought from Professor Benjamin B. Silliman, Jr., of Yale. When Silliman's report was finally obtained (delayed because the Company didn't have the cash to pay him $526.08 for his apparatus) it concluded, ". . . there is much ground for encouragement in the belief that your Company have in possession a raw material from which, by simple and not very expensive processes, they may manufacture very valuable products."

In 1857 the Company, still in financial straits and making little headway under the New York lawyers, was abandoned as Bissell sought the support of a number of prominent New Haven investors, including James M. Townsend, President of the City Savings Bank. With several secret manipulations of stock transfers and sales, the new Seneca Oil Creek Co. was formed. Nevertheless, in the following year little came of the enterprise, which still depended on skimming the springs by hand for petroleum. One day Bissell happened to see Keir's advertisement in a Broadway store showing how his product surged up from the 400-foot brine wells. Bissell then hit upon the idea of drilling for oil. This idea was adopted by Townsend, who had become President of the Company, and happened to meet an adventurous jack of several trades, Edwin L. Drake, in his boarding hotel in New Haven. The Company hired Drake to visit their property near Titusville and attempt better recoveries of the oil. With pluck and imagination Drake brought in salt water drilling equipment, a steam engine, and some drillers. On 27 August 1859, after the drill had penetrated thirty feet of rock and reached a depth of 69.5 feet, oil rose to the surface. In a day Drake's rig alone brought out 25 barrels; in a year, 2000 barrels. By 1860 there were two dozen producing wells along Oil Creek and 650,000 barrels of crude oil were sold. The demand for whale oil disappeared overnight and every refinery that had been processing coal oil either switched to petroleum or went out of business. In 1862 about three million barrels of crude oil were produced and in 1865 the first short pipelines, five miles of 2-inch wrought-iron pipe with screw couplings buried two feet underground, were in use.

Another fuel, associated with petroleum deposits, had been, like the "burning rocks" of coal, known since ancient times: natural gas. Many "eternal flames" burned mysteriously in Persian, Greek, and Roman temples or shrines, undoubtedly from jets of natural gas, and it is recorded that during the Han dynasty the Chinese conducted natural gas through bamboo tubes whose ends were lighted.

In America "pillars of fire" had been described by missionaries in the Ohio Valley as early as 1775. William Aron Hart tapped a natural gas well 27-feet deep near Fredonia, New York, which was piped and which lighted Westfield, New York in 1826. In 1865 the first company for natural gas in the United States had been formed and in 1872 the first long-distance pipe line brought natural gas twenty-five miles in wooden pipes to Rochester, New York. Coal gas burners for the streets and for homes, however, were increasingly refined and the introduction of the incandescent lamp of electricity after 1880 somewhat stunted the growth of natural gas production. The key problem was the transmission of the gas. As early as 1815 screwed steel gun barrels had been used to convey coal gas, but it was not until 1891, in a line between Greentown, Indiana, and Chicago utilizing high-pressure 8-inch wrought iron pipes, that the horizon for long-distance transmission widened. In the mid-1920s the achievement of steel pipe that could be welded in the fields gave the natural gas industry a major impetus to growth, and the first all-welded line between Lousiana and Beaumont, Texas, extended 214 miles. By the 1960s more than 600,000 miles of gas pipelines were in service around the world, some of them conveying gas for more than 2000 miles from the well-head to consumers.

The use of petroleum for lamp oil started the oil energy revolution of the nineteenth century. Although the United States brought in the first drilled well, other states of the world had also realized the potential of petroleum distillation for fuel. In 1870 a great leap forward in the practical conversion of hydrocarbon energy to industry took place in Russia when the heavy fuel left from the distillation of kerosene was sprayed or atomized, greatly improving its combustibility and making oil heat economically feasible. Demand for petroleum rapidly increased and the search for new sources of the "black gold" soon covered the earth.[5]

At first virtually all the petroleum output in the United States came from Pennsylvania, where the fields were admirably suited to good railway transportation and a large eastern urban market. Oil was then found in West Virginia, Ohio, Kentucky, Tennessee, and Illinois. California production rose from 12,000 barrels in 1876 to 1,000,000 barrels in 1895. Texas oil began to flow in the 1890s, and in 1901 an astounding strike was made near Beaumont while drilling salt domes for sulphur, which proved that oil existed under plains as well as near creeks and mountains. Spindletop (Beaumont) alone flowed at a rate equal to half the entire United States production that year.

In 1882 the United States was producing 82 percent of all the crude oil in the world, about two-thirds of which was exported, but drilling in other nations brought forth rich new sources. Russia had invited foreign entrepreneurs in 1872 to develop its Caspian Sea sources, which had been chronicled for almost a thousand years, and the first vessel used as an oil tanker sailed on the Caspian in 1877. At the end of the nineteenth century Russia accounted for almost half the total crude oil production in the world, even surpassing the United States in 1901. New American wells in Oklahoma, Texas, and California, however, greatly increased U.S. production. Furthermore, British and American interests developed Mexican wells to make that country the third leading source of oil in 1911 and the second-largest producer in the world in 1918 while Russia was ravaged by civil war.

Still the demand for petroleum continued to soar. In the beginning it had been sought for illumination, then for heating, and, finally, for the internal combustion engine that was to completely revolutionize transportation and fundamentally alter the work and play habits of all mankind through its use in the automobile.

The first working road locomotive, a three-wheeled vehicle with a front oiler and steam engine, was designed by Nicholas Joseph Cugnot in 1769. Other steam locomotives ran on highways in Leeds in 1769 and in London in 1784. In the United States Oliver Evans built the first steam-propelled vehicle in 1805. The London and Paddington Steam Carriage Co. was started in 1832, and the most famous designer of steam-driven coaches was Walter Hancock (1799–1852). Some of the vehicles allegedly achieved twenty-five miles per hour in 1840, but there were innumerable problems connected to the regular commercial usage of such coaches, which usually carried eight to eighteen passengers, and they were generally abandoned after 1836. Smaller "steamers" were built in the 1880s and the 1890s, but the gasoline engine equickly proved to be more efficient and economical for cars.

The automobile itself was not the invention of any single person either in Europe or America. As soon as the steam engine had become feasible, inventive minds applied its propulsive power to carriages, beginning in 1769. By the close of the nineteenth century many horseless carriages that could move under steam had been tried. The development of electric power seemed to offer an even greater opportunity to build self-propelled carriages and in 1891 the first electric motor car was built in the United States. But the process of making heat to make steam to move pistons or carrying batteries to turn a motor to move rods were both clumsy and costly. What was needed was a light, maneuverable vehicle that could bear one to six persons without exorbitant costs.

As early as 1784 Robert Street had obtained an English patent for an engine in which an explosion could be caused by vaporizing spirits of turpentine on a heated metal surface. By mixing vapor with air in a cylinder and then firing the mixture, he showed, but never proved, that a piston could be driven by the explosion. Indeed, up to 1859 no engine, other than a steam engine, could work continuously and successfully in factories, commerce, or transport. In 1860 the first noncompression engine driven by piped gas was developed by Jean Lenoir. In 1862 Alphonse Beau de Rochas had described a four-cycle intake, compression, explosion, and exhaust engine, but Nicolaus Otto actually invented one, utilizing atmospheric pressure to move the piston on one cycle. The birth of the internal combustion machine, however, may be dated from Otto's diagram of 9 May 1876 in which he finally solved the problem of a vaporized fuel intake, compression, then explosion through a thick and lean mixture of the fuel to give a smooth power drive with the exhaust cycle. The Otto engine was enormously successful and widely used in industry, but it was large, heavy, and comparatively slow. Gottlieb Daimler, who earlier had worked with Otto in the Deutz Gas Motor Works as chief engineer, patented on 3 April 1885 a light, high-speed, four-stroke engine with a surface vaporizer, carburetor, and electric ignition, which he applied seven months later to a bicycle.

Meanwhile, Karl Benz at the Rhine Gas Motor Works of Mannheim had also been working on internal combustion engines. Benz comes as close as anyone to deserving the accolade of "father of the motor car" since he conceived of the engine and the car as a totality, rather than, as in the case of Daimler, designing an engine that could be applied to bikes, boats, and even balloons. On 29 January 1886 Benz secured a patent for "a vehicle with gas-engine drive" and on 3 July 1886 drove his first car, a three-wheeled motor carriage, on the Ringstrasse. A second Benz model was driven on the streets of Munich in 1888. In the same year Daimler patented a double-inclined cylinder engine, known as the "V" type, and from the first it was applied to carriages, cars, or in modern terms, automobiles. Benz meanwhile built other car models leading to the four-wheeled "Viktoria" in 1893 and the first mass-produced automobile in the world, the "Velo" in 1894. He delivered 67 cars in 1894 and 135 cars in 1895, most of which were Velos. Hundreds of automobiles began to roll on the streets of Europe from the Panhard and Levassor Daimler Motor Carriage Company, the Peugeot Company, and the Benz Company.[6]

In the United States George B. Selden of Rochester had first applied for a gasoline motor patent to be used in an automobile in 1879. But Selden did not obtain that patent until 5 November 1895, partly because he kept revising his designs, partly because there was little likelihood of interesting investors in the production of such a vehicle as long as steam and electricity seemed to offer more immediate prospects of success on the highways. The Benz three-wheeled car had been patented in the United States on 26 June 1888, and in the same year, William Steinway, the piano manufacturer, obtained the rights to the Daimler motor in the United States. The first gas-propelled automobile was not built in the United States, however, until 1892, when George Duryea achieved that honor. The second automobile was built by Henry Ford in 1893 and the third by Ellwood Hayes in 1894.

Nevertheless, the first use of automobiles for public transport was a fleet of a dozen electric battery-powered cabs that rolled at speeds of six to ten miles per hour in New York in January 1897. The early gasoline American cars still had to prove their speed and durability, but with new demonstrations and highly publicized races they began to gain commercial acceptance. On 29 March 1898 the first American gasoline-powered automobile actually sold in the United States went to Robert Allison of Port Carbon, Pennsylvania. Within twenty years about three million gasoline-powered automobiles were bumping along the city streets and narrow, largely unpaved roads of the United States. The petroleum industry again surged with new demands, and in 1911 the sales of gasoline surpassed the sales of kerosene for the first time in American history.[7]

In 1910 U.S. oil production had just reached 0.57 million barrels a day. By 1920 it had more than doubled to 1.21 million barrels a day with another 0.33 million barrels a day from American-owned companies abroad. By 1929 domestic U.S. production had almost doubled again to 2.15 million barrels a day. When World War II began in 1941 production had almost doubled again as 3.84 million barrels a day of petroleum were brought forth at home and 0.61 million barrels a day from American companies abroad.

Geologists, mining engineers, and oil-gas entrepreneurs fanned out across the earth in search of petroleum. Oil was increasingly sought for heat, for power, for engines, in industry, commerce, and private uses. Rumania, the first large-scale oil producer, had dug shallow wells by hand as early as 1857 to obtain about 13 barrels a day, reached a peak of 177,953 barrels a day in 1936. Indonesia began producing oil in 1893. Iran (Persia) began producing oil in 1908 and by 1938 ranked fourth in total output behind the United States, the U.S.S.R., and Venezuela. But the greatest world reserves of petroleum were still to be found—in the Arab countries where the description of the use of "naft" dated back more than a thousand years. In 1928 United States oil companies began their wells in Iraq, in 1935 in Saudi Arabia, and 1938 in Kuwait. Only on the eve of World War II did Middle Eastern crude oil begin to flow in any quantity to European and American refineries and as late as 1945 still accounted for only 10 percent of world production.

From 1901 to 1940 the United States itself accounted for 64 percent of the entire production of crude oil in the world. Dire predictions of oil depletion had hit the news almost from the moment the petroleum industry started. In February 1882 Samuel Wingley, before the Institute of Mining Engineers, estimated that the total remaining petroleum reserve of the United States was 96 million barrels and that with yearly production running at 25 million barrels "the cheque will come back indorsed 'no funds;' and we are approaching that day very fast."[8] Nevertheless many new fields were discovered both at home and abroad to meet the ever-increasing demand for petroleum products. But the demand for petroleum products during World War II was, indeed, phenomenal— literally a matter of victory or defeat, life or death. Consumption by the United States during the war years alone amounted to one-fifth of all the American consumption of petroleum from 1859 to 1941. Petroleum products shipped out of the United States was double the tonnage of all other shipments—arms, equipment, food, medicine, men—combined. The United States supplied about 90 percent of all the petroleum requirements of the nations allied against Germany and Japan. At the end of World War II the United States had 40 percent of all the world's proven petroleum resources within its own territorial jurisdiction while American nationals owned or leased another 25 percent of the proven resources abroad. Yet at the rate of consumption reached by 1945, there were only fifteen years of proven resources left. The Middle East, which was supplying only about 10 percent of the world's oil that year, was bound to be more intensively exploited while the quest for new reservoirs of petroleum was intensified. The United States naturally looked to the potentially large reserves lying underwater off its shores that might be tapped quickly and economically to meet the postwar needs. All that was lacking was a claim to title to the continental shelf of the United States to place those rich resources under the secure control of Americans.

As early as 1869 Thomas F. Rowland had obtained a U.S. patent for a submarine drilling apparatus, with a working platform, hydraulically telescoped legs for support, and a boat tender, never dreaming that within one hundred years people would be drilling the seabed many miles from shore in hundreds of feet of water. At the same time Samuel Lewis of Brooklyn had patented a jack-up drill ship, not greatly different in concept from the rigs that were to offer new opportunities for the recovery of offshore oil in the twentieth century. Neither the Rowland nor the Lewis patents were tested. The first actual recovery of undersea petroleum came from drills on dry land and then from piers built out from the shore.

H. L. Williams had bought the Ortega Rancho near Santa Barbara, California, in 1883 as a retreat and community, to be known as Summerland, for Spiritualists. But the oozes of petroleum from the sands and shorelines, which had been known since Spanish times, opened to him and others a great, new petroleum field. In 1886 a drill from a cliff 250-feet above the Pacific ocean punctured a reservoir of petroleum underlying the Summerland beach. Other drillings quickly followed, right down to the water's edge. In 1895 there were twenty-five wells at Summerland and in 1897 Williams probably built the first pier, five or six hundred feet out to sea, for the emplacement of drilling rigs. By 1918 the Summerland beach was dense with derricks set upon a dozen piers, one of which, Elwood, was 1200-feet long and stood in thirty feet of water. But the field had petered out. Soon the waves rotted and smashed the wharves, ending the first major effort at American offshore oil recovery.

Meanwhile, in Caddo Lake, Louisiana in 1911 the first inland water drilling from wooden piers driven into the lake bottom had been successful. Then in 1924 in Lake Maracaibo, Venezuela a prodigious effort went into underwater petroleum recovery, first from timber piles and later from concrete piles to thwart the terrible wood-boring teredos. In 1932 drilling platforms detached from the land were also tried off the shore of California and in the Gulf of Mexico. A great technological advance occurred with the drilling barge of Louis Galiasso, which could be lowered and raised and floated to another location. It worked successfully on 17 November 1933 in Lake Pelto, Louisiana in fifteen feet of water as its drills reached 6000 feet into the earth. The barge ended the limitations on the mobility of drilling platforms, which were expensive to build and dismantle for each new petroleum field.

In the summer of 1937, however, the first truly offshore recovery of petroleum occurred when the Pure and the Superior Oil Co. built a large 100-foot by 300-foot platform in fourteen feet of water about one mile out from the coast of Louisiana in the Gulf of Mexico. Without radio and accommodations for the crew, some thirteen miles by water from the supply and communications base in the town of Cameron, the operations were always difficult and sometimes hazardous. But after drilling 9394 feet, then returning the bits to a new channel, oil was struck at 5640 feet. Ultimately eleven wells were spudded from this find, producing four million barrels in twenty-five years. The significance of the platform in 1937 was the opening of the Gulf of Mexico to petroleum exploitation on a grand scale. Finally, in 1941, just as the United States was girding for World War II, the British-American Oil Co. struck oil from a platform in seventeen feet of water in the Gulf two miles from the coastline of Louisiana and only one mile from the limit of the territorial jurisdiction of the United States over the seas under contemporary international law.

The Continental Shelf[9]

Roman law had settled for Europe the principle that rivers and their banks were open to public use, not subject to private appropriation, and under sovereign control.[10] In modern times this doctrine was further advanced in England by such men as Thomas Digges who wrote in 1569 that the Crown also had an interest and property in the "great salt river" surrounding the English isles, including the shores and the bottom. That legal opinion, sometimes denied over the next two hundred years, put no limit seaward on the property right of the Crown to the ocean bottom. It must be remembered, however, that the limits of state jurisdiction over marginal waters had not as yet gained any international consensus.

By the nineteenth century some states claimed exclusive rights to sedentary shell fish lying off their shores and in 1858 the Cornwall Submarine Mines Act in England had provided that all mines and minerals lying below the low-water mark under the adjacent sea, which were not part of Cornwall county, were vested in the Crown. Thus, even before the three-mile territorial sea became general international law in the late nineteenth century, sovereigns had customarily exercised some dominion over the seabed and its subsoil adjacent to their coasts.

As the territorial sea obtained definition under customary international law, therefore, few questions arose about the sovereign's right to the submerged land and its resources within national waters. In his international law text of 1910 John Westlake wrote unequivocally, "Within that extent, the water and its bed are territorial and the wealth of both is the property of the territorial sovereign." In 1924 the American Institute of International Law declared that the American republics exercise the right of sovereignty not only over the water, but over the bottom and subsoil of their territorial sea, and "By virtue of that right, each of the said Republics alone can exploit or permit others to exploit all the rights existing within that zone." In the draft convention first drawn up by the Committee of Experts for the 1930 Hague Codification of International Law Conference, Article 1 stated that the State possesses sovereign rights over the zone which washes its coast, including "rights over the air above the said sea and the soil and subsoil beneath it." The final draft, provisionally approved by the Conference, minced no words in declaring "the territory of a Coastal State includes also the air space above the territorial sea, as well as the bed of the sea, and the subsoil."[11] But what about the seabed and subsoil with their incumbent resources, that extends far out from a coastal state under the ocean beyond the limits of the territorial sea?

In France as early as 1803 Gérard de Rayneval had noted that the bottom of the sea, along the coast, could be considered, geologically speaking, as having been formed as part of the continent and still a part of it. Apparently in 1887 Hugh Robert Mill first began to apply the term "continental shelf" in a geographical sense to the rims or margins of the continents. As early as 1916 at the National Fishery Congress in Madrid, Odon de Buen y del Cos, later Director-General of Fisheries in Spain, had urged the necessity of extending the territorial sea of a state to include the whole of the continental shelf, since the shelf was a continuation of the coastal state and more influenced by the contiguous land than by the seas.[12]

The continental shelf, of course, is made up of both the bed of the sea itself and its subsoil. Under customary international law, the subsoil had a less controversial status than the seabed, for it could be occupied by tunnelling without posing difficulties for navigation, fishing, and other international uses of the waters above. Early in the twentieth century international law experts, such as L. Oppenheim, had stated categorically that the subsoil outside the marginal belt of territorial waters belonged to no one, and, therefore, could be acquired as property by the littoral state by occupation. In fact, as early as 1802 the idea of a tunnel connecting Great Britain and France under the English channel of the North Sea had been discussed by the two states. Further negotiations in 1874 led to a Joint Commission report of 1876 in which there was little doubt about the legal right of the states to tunnel beyond their territorial seas. This opinion was strongly reinforced in 1930 by another government committee when the idea of the Channel tunnel was revived. Legal experts of the 1940s and 1950s continued to hold the view that the subsoil could be effectively occupied by a coastal state that tunnelled seaward from its shores.

The bed of the sea was another matter. Access to the subsoil through the bed of the sea posed a problem different from tunnelling. In 1923 Sir Cecil B. Hurst had argued that whenever it could be shown that sedentary fisheries had always been kept in occupation by the sovereign of the adjacent land, even beyond the three-mile limit of territorial waters, ownership of the soil of the bed of the sea where the fishery was situated would be presumed, with the right to legislate for the soil so owned and for the protection of the wealth derived from it. However, the illustrations of occupation and exercise of jurisdiction on the seabed beyond territorial waters offered by Hurst were few: either situated in bays or gulfs that were claimed as national territory or not very far from shore on shallow banks, such as the oyster beds off Ireland and the sponge beds off Tunis. Moreover, the potential interference with the right to navigation of the high seas by any national claims to extensive surface areas of the seabed cast grave doubt on the existence of such a rule in international law, except as it might be applied to certain historical fisheries and submarine communication cables. In 1932 the distinguished international legal scholar Gilbert Gidel maintained that the surface of the seabed had the same legal position as the waters above it, and that only prescriptive use over a long period or the acquiescence of other states could give rise to any national claim of jurisdiction over it.[13]

As indicated in the previous section, by the 1940s the United States had improved its technological ability to exploit petroleum resources in water depths greater than fifteen feet beyond three miles from its shores. At the same time World War II was draining American oil reserves at an alarming rate, which led the Department of Interior to suggest to the President on 3 July 1943 the start of an interagency study through which the United States might obtain for itself the reservoirs known or suspected to be found in its continental shelf. The State Department was also interested in the conservation of marine fisheries in the contiguous seas of the United States and it readily agreed to an interagency study of both problems. This study led to two proclamations by President Harry S. Truman on 28 September 1945, one on fisheries and one on the continental shelf, which have already been described in Chapter One.[14]

It should be remembered that the continental shelf proclamation opened an entirely new chapter in the history of international law with respect to the bed of the sea by declaring that "the Government of the United States regards the natural resources of the subsoil and the sea-bed of the continental shelf beneath the high seas but contiguous to the coasts of the United States as appertaining to the United States, subject to its jurisdiction and control." Where the continental shelf was shared by another state, the boundary would be determined by equitable principles, and, according to the proclamation, the character of the waters above the continental shelf as high seas and the right to their free and unimpeded navigation were in no way affected. Nothing was said about the limit seaward of the continental shelf over whose resources the United States had assumed jurisdiction, but it was suggested that submerged land contiguous to the continent and covered by no more than 100 fathoms (600 feet) of water could be considered as the continental shelf.[15]

The Truman Proclamation, of course, did not settle international law with respect to the seabed. But the unilateral United States action precipitated a resolution of the uncertain legal status of the continental shelf resources adjacent to coastal states around the world. Quickly following the United States,

Mexico declared its jurisdiction over continental shelf resources lying under water less than 200 meters in depth. Both the American and Mexican declaration had made it clear that they sought to conserve and utilize the resources of the continental shelf only and that the right to clear and unimpeded navigation on the high seas over the continental shelf were not affected. On 11 October 1946, however, Argentina declared that its "epicontinental sea and continental shelf" were subject to the sovereign power of the nations, although for purposes of free navigation the character of the waters would be unaffected. On 23 June 1947 Chile went even further, proclaiming its national sovereignty over all the continental shelf, whatever the depth, and over all the waters adjacent to its coasts to the full extent necessary to reserve, protect, conserve, and make use of their natural resources. Zones of protection would extend 200 miles from the coast out to sea, but Chile stated that it would not disregard the rights of free navigation on the high seas. On 1 August 1947 a Peruvian presidential decree followed approximately the Chilean doctrine. On 27 July 1948 Costa Rica also issued a decree-law somewhat similar to Chile's proclamation. Panama in 1946 claimed national jurisdiction over all the fisheries above the continental shelf, and somewhat similar declarations were made by Guatemala (1947), El Salvador (1950), Nicaragua (1950), and Honduras (1950). Thus while the United States had only claimed that the natural resources of the continental shelf were under its jurisdiction and control, several Latin American states had asserted jurisdiction over both the continental shelf and the resources of the seas either above the shelves or to an extent of 200 miles seaward from their coasts.

The rush of coastal states to claim the resources of the continental shelf and the water column above it beyond their territorial limits was not limited to Latin America. In 1948 Iceland unilaterally established conservation zones within the continental shelf subject to its rule and control, while Gresat Britain asserted that the boundaries of Jamaica and the Bahamas included the areas of the continental shelf. In 1949 Saudi Arabia, Kuwait, Qatar, and several Arab sheikdoms claimed control over their continental shelves. In 1950 the parade of declarations, decrees, and laws continued as Pakistan and other states brought the continental shelf, with different definitions of its extent, under their jurisdiction. Korea in 1952 proclaimed sovereignty over the superjacent waters of the continental shelf with an exclusive fisheries zone from 20 to 200 miles from its shores.

Confusion about the legal defintion of the continental shelf, as well as the rights and duties of states with respect to territorial waters, high seas, their resources, and the bed of the sea was mounting when the UN International Law Commission began to address the issues. Created by the UN General Assembly to encourage the progressive development of international law and its codification under Article 13, Paragraph 1(a) of the Charter, the International Law Commission had decided at its first session in 1949 to undertake the codification of the Regime of the High Seas, Arbitral Procedure, and the Law of Treaties.

On 12 July 1950 the Commission started its consideration of the continental shelf doctrine. The next day Manley O. Hudson suggested that the Commission follow the text of a committee of the private International Law Association, which had stated that control and jurisdiction over the seabed and subsoil of submarine areas might be exercised by a littoral state "for the exploration and exploitation of the natural resources therein contained, to the extent to which such exploitation is feasible." By 1951, after considerable discussion, the first draft article by the Commission defining the Continental Shelf read:

the seabed and subsoil of the submarine areas contiguous to the coast, but outside the area of territorial waters, where the depth of the superjacent waters admits of the exploitation of the natural resources of the seabed and subsoil.

But two years later, after comments by governments and extensive discussion, the Commission had altered its draft definition to read: ". . . the seabed and the subsoil of the submarine areas contiguous to the coast, but outside an area of the territorial sea to a depth of 200 meters."

The General Assembly of the United Nations in 1953, however, decided not to deal with any aspect of the regime of the high seas or territorial waters until all aspects of the problem had been studied. In 1954 the General Assembly again decided not to deal with the question of draft articles on the continental shelf while resolving that in the future the item should be joined to draft proposals on the high seas, territorial waters, and the contiguous zone. As a result the International Law Commission combined its draft articles under a *Regime of the High Seas* and a *Regime of the Territorial Sea* into one draft of articles subsumed under *Law of the Sea.*[16]

Another twist was given to the evolution of continental shelf doctrine when the Inter-American Specialized Conference on the Conservation of Natural Resources, the Continental Shelf, and Marine Resources met in March 1956 at Ciudad Trujillo in the Dominican Republic. The Conference found neither the exploitability limit of the continental shelf, advanced by the International Law Commission in 1951, nor the 200 meter isobath limit, proposed by the Commission in 1953, a satisfactory criterion for the jurisdiction of coastal states over the seabed. Some states wanted the right to exploit the continental shelf beyond 200 meters in water depth, if and when the technology should make such exploitation possible; others wanted to retain the 200-meter figure to emphasize the limits of the continental shelf and that the right to exploit resources of the bed of the sea did not relate to jurisdiction over the water and air column above. In the end a majority of the assembled states agreed that

the sea-bed and subsoil of the continental shelf, continental and insular terrace, or other submarine areas, adjacent to the coastal State, outside the area of the territorial sea, and to a depth of 200 meters or, beyond that limit, to where the depth of the superjacent waters admits of the exploitation of the natural resources of the sea-bed and subsoil, appertain exclusively to that State and are subject to its jurisdiction and control."

There was no agreement, however, on the juridical regime of the waters covering the continental shelf beyond national jurisdiction nor whether certain living resources (e.g. crustacea) belonged to the seabed or to the superjacent waters.[17]

Only a month after the Ciudad Trujillo Conference the UN International Law Commission met for its eighth session. During its work the Commission drafted an article that closely followed the Ciudad Trujillo formula in defining the continental shelf for the purpose of exploration and exploitation for its natural resources by the adjacent coastal state: namely, "adjacent to the coast, but outside the area of the territorial sea to a depth of 200 meters (approximately 100 fathoms) or, beyond that limit, to where the depth of the superjacent waters admits of the exploitation of the natural resources of the said areas." The Commission went on to draft articles that clearly stated (1) sovereign rights over the continental shelf should be exercised for the purpose of exploring and exploiting its natural resources, and (2) such rights do not affect the legal status of the superjacent waters as high seas or the airspace above.

Even after six years of study some members of the Commission still doubted that the General Assembly would ever adopt or endorse its project on the law of the sea. But a majority prevailed in recommending that the General Assembly summon an international conference of plenipotentiaries to examine the draft articles with a view of achieving positive international agreements on the oceans and seabed. As indicated in earlier sections, between 24 February and 27 April 1958, the representatives of eighty-six nations met in Geneva at the UN Conference on the Law of the Sea. Using drafts of the International Law Commission, the assembled nations finally approved four conventions—on the Territorial Sea and the Contiguous Zone, on the Continental Shelf, on the High Seas, and on the Fishing and Conservation of the Living Resources of the High Seas.[18]

At the opening of the Conference the fourth substantive committee had taken responsibility for the articles on the continental shelf. This committee gave ten of its meetings to general debate and thirty to reviewing and approving article by article the convention that was ultimately proposed to the plenary session. Several major amendments to the draft articles of the International Law Commission that would have either extended or limited the definition of the continental shelf over which a coastal state might exercise its sovereign rights for the exploration and exploitation of the natural resources were proposed. However, none received a majority vote, except for an agreement that all references to the continental shelf should also be understood to apply to the seabed and submarine areas adjacent to and surrounding islands.

Thus, with a few drafting changes and the minor amendment on islands, the article drafted by the International Law Commission on the definition of the continental shelf passed intact into the Convention on the Continental Shelf and was adopted in the final vote on the Convention by fifty-seven in favor, three opposed, and eight abstentions. Article 1 of the Convention reads:

For the purpose of these articles the term "continental shelf" is used as referring (a) to the seabed and subsoil of the submarine areas adjacent to the coast but outside the area of the territorial sea, to a depth of 200 meters or, beyond that limit, to where the depth of the superjacent waters admits of the exploitation of the natural resources of the said areas; (b) to the seabed and subsoil of similar submarine areas adjacent to the coasts of islands.[19]

It was further agreed (1) that sovereign rights over the continental shelf were for the exploration and exploitation of resources, and (2) that the legal status of the superjacent waters as high seas and the airspace above those waters were unaffected by sovereign rights over the continental shelf.

For the first time in history an international agreement had been endorsed by many states in the world on definitions to govern the orderly exploration and exploitation of a vast submarine area of unknown wealth. But the legal limits of the territorial sea of states and the extent of the contiguous zone for the conservation of fish by coastal states were not defined, either in 1958 or at the subsequent 1960 Geneva conference. Moreover, the Convention on the Continental Shelf had left an indeterminate jurisdiction for the coastal state over the shelf, allowing such jurisdiction to creep seaward further and further as the technology to recover resources improved. Thus, the boundary could move from 200 meters of water to wherever "the depth of the superjacent waters admits of the exploitation of the resources of the said area."

Meanwhile, in the United States a legal battle had been raging between the states and federal government over the revenues from the exploitation of offshore petroleum. When petroleum drilling began from the piers on the Summerland beach in California in 1897, the coastal landowners had granted mineral leases themselves. By 1906 there were 189 producing wells in the field. Their operations, with all their legal and economic implications, were well known to the federal government of the United States. Until 1921, when the California legislature adopted an exploration and leasing act for mineral deposits in land belonging to the state, the Summerland Oil leases owed their legal authority to common law. From 1921 to 1940 the state of California acted as if it owned the submerged lands and could control the exploitation of petroleum therein through permits and leases. Indeed, the U.S. Department of Interior during this period had refused to issue mineral prospecting permits under the Federal Mineral Leasing Act of 1920 for California offshore operations.

California and other states had long assumed that the judgment of the Supreme Court in 1845 in *Pollard* v. *Hagan*—that the original states and admitted states of the Federal Union (in this case, Alabama) had sovereign title to the shores and soils under navigable waters up to the high tide mark (in this case, the Mobile river)—would also apply to coastal areas of the sea.[20] But in the late 1930s the federal government began to question state ownership of submerged lands beyond inland waters and started to claim title for the United States itself. As the riches of petroleum reservoirs in the continental shelf became apparent just before World War II, controversy between the coastal states and the federal government over title to these resources sharpened.

On 29 May 1945 the United States started a suit agains the Pacific Western Oil Company, asking the federal district court to enjoin the extraction of petroleum in offshore leases near Santa Barbara that had been granted by California. When the U.S. House of Representatives passed a joint resolution on 20 September 1945 to have the United States quitclaim any property rights to the submerged lands lying offshore the coastal states, the United States dropped its suit against Pacific Western. The federal government then went to the Supreme Court for a declaration that the United States rather than California had dominion over the submerged lands and asked for an injunction against California and all other persons from continuing to trespass in violation of the rights of the United States. On 27 July 1946 both the House and the Senate approved the quitclaim joint resolution, but President Truman vetoed it on 1 August 1946. Finally, the Supreme Court on 23 June 1947 upheld the rights of the United States in the submerged coastal lands, reasoning that "we cannot say that the thirteen original colonies separately acquired ownership to the three-mile belt or the soil under it," and the Court refused to extend the internal water rule of *Pollard* v. *Hagan* to the bed of the sea.[21]

Nevertheless, the legal battle between the states and the federal government over property rights (and huge revenues from oil and gas exploitation) had hardly begun. Clamor and litigation by the coastal states of Louisiana and Texas again led to Supreme Court decisions in 1950 that favored the claims of the federal government. The 82d Congress once more took up the cause of the states and approved another joint resolution to yield federal offshore property rights to the states, but again President Truman vetoed it on 29 May 1951. After the election of Dwight D. Eisenhower to the White House in 1952, however, the Congress passed the Submerged Lands Act on 22 May 1953, which the President signed as Public Law 83-31. The Act recognized the property rights of the coastal states to the natural resources within the waters and submerged lands to a distance of three geographic miles from their coastlines in the Atlantic and Pacific oceans. Such rights were subject to the constitutional responsibility of the federal government for defense, navigation, commerce, and foreign affairs. The Act also provided that the boundary of the state's jurisdiction over such resources might be extended up to three marine leagues into the Gulf of Mexico or the Great Lakes if the state's historic boundary prior to joining the Union had been more than three miles from shore (Texas) or if Congress had previously approved a wider boundary when the state was admitted to the Union (Florida, readmitted in 1868). Thus Florida and Texas obtained legal possession over the resources of the waters and the bed of the sea out to three marine leagues from their shores in the Gulf of Mexico.

In order to clarify the policy of the United States with respect to the waters and the bed of the sea beyond the boundaries of the coastal states established by the Submerged Lands Act, a second statute, the Outer Continental Shelf Lands Act was approved on 7 August 1953. It closely followed the Truman proclamation of 1945 in affirming the rights of the United States to the natural resources of the continental shelf, while stating that the character of the super-jacent waters with regard to navigation and fishing remained unchanged. All property rights in the resources of the continental shelf were vested in the federal government, with power to make the necessary laws for the outer continental shelf and specification of the procedures for granting leases. Otherwise appropriate civil and criminal laws of the adjacent coastal states applied to the area.

With the major legal controversy between the coastal states and the federal government settled, offshore oil and gas production boomed. Between 1948 and 1958 some 2400 wells were drilled off the shores of Louisiana and Texas, of which 1800 yielded petroleum and natural gas. Nearly all the wells were in rather shallow waters—under a hundred feet during these years. But the constantly improving technology for drilling rigs and the pipe transmission of petroleum products from submerged lands pushed exploration and exploitation further and further out to sea. The 1953 Outer Continental Shelf Lands Act had authorized the Secretary of the Interior to grant oil, gas, and sulfur leases, in blocks not exceeding 5760 acres, to the highest, responsible bidder for a term of five years and as long thereafter as oil or gas would be produced in paying quantities. In 1954 there were 130 completed wells on the outer continental shelf under federal jurisdiction, of which 50 were actively producing oil and 20 gas; by 1960 there were 1138 wells producing oil and 210 producing gas; and by 1970 the outer continental shelf exploitation of petroleum products had dramatically increased again, with 5563 wells producing oil and 1574 producing gas.

Within barely twenty years income from the submerged resources of the U.S. continental shelf soared from virtually zero to billions of dollars, profiting both petroleum producers and the American people. From 1954 through 1970 the federal government alone received $4,375,000 in bonuses for leases, $13.1 million for minimum royalties, $100.9 million for rentals of leases, $1 million for shut-in gas payments, and $1,510,000 in royalties—or a grand total of $6 billion. About two-thirds of the sum came from wells off the Louisiana shore, about one-sixth from wells off the shores of Texas and California, and the balance from Florida, Oregon, and Washington areas. At the end of 1970 about 4.3 million acres of the 186 million acres off the mainland of the United States were under federal leases on the outer continental shelf. With 1800 fixed platforms on the outer continental shelf, more than 4000 miles of pipelines in operation, and one well in the Gulf of Mexico producing oil from under 340 feet of water some 70 miles distant from the shore, the United States was deeply involved in international policy issues as nations advanced further and further seaward on the continental shelf.[22]

Other states of the world had also entered large-scale offshore production of oil and gas. Venezuela, of course, had a long history in the development of

Lake Maracaibo's underwater resources, but by 1970 some twenty-two countries were obtaining gas or oil from their submerged lands. The total value of world offshore production then was approaching four billion dollars a year. In addition, the exploration of shelf areas for petroleum products was underway in more than seventy-five countries.

Demand for oil and gas was increasing everywhere under both the urgency of economic development in poor countries and the spread of affluence to all groups in rich countries. As nations moved inexorably seaward to tap the continental shelf for its petroleum resources, they had no international legal guidance except murky custom and the 1958 Geneva Conventions, which had been drafted under much earlier technological guidelines. Hard political questions started to be raised about the limit of national claims to the resources of the seabed. Some scholars and public interest groups began to argue that the world community had more right to the resources of the ocean floor than the economic appetite and industrial competence of any single state.

The Exploitation of Ferromanganese Nodules

Until the middle of the nineteenth century men knew almost nothing about the floor of the ocean. The depth of the seabed, its contours, and composition, were subjects of philosophical speculation rather than scientific fact. It was widely supposed that under the deep oceans without air or light, in frigid temperatures and under great pressures, organic life could not possibly exist. The first dredge to obtain scientific specimens even in shallow water had been lowered early in 1750 and as late as 1817 scholars still debated whether the bed of the sea was covered with eternal ice. Sir John Ross's expedition to the Arctic a year later, the first expedition in history to make satisfactory deep soundings and take a few samples of the ocean bottom, finally disproved the "eternal ice" theory, for Ross had succeeded in obtaining as much as six pounds of mud buried under 1050 fathoms of water in Baffin Bay, Canada.

Thus the organic and mineral components of the ocean floor were virtually unknown to man before the scientific expeditions of the last quarter of the nineteenth century. Two major types of marine deposits were then traced: *terrigenous,* generally formed from the materials washed down from the dry lands; and *pelagic,* generally consisting of organic oozes, siliceous oozes, and reddish clays. Pelagic deposits are largely made up of the remains of calcareous (mostly protozoa) and siliceous (mostly planktonic plant and animal life) organisms that have fallen to the bottom of the ocean as well as decomposed volcanic debris and reddish clays.

The first purely marine science expedition of the United States, led by Captain Wilkes in 1838, had made several deep soundings of the seas by the aid of copper wire during its four-year voyage. Then, in 1839 the British sent out an Antarctic expedition under Sir James Clark Ross. Like his uncle, Ross took soundings and bottom samples from the ocean floor during the course of his exploration of the southern polar regions. In January 1840 Ross made the first sounding of the ocean's abyss at latitude 27°26′S. longitude 17°29′W. in 2425 fathoms of water. In August 1841, moreover, at latitude 23°32′S. and longitude 167°40′E., Ross dredged at 400 fathoms and brought forth beautiful specimens of coral, coralines, flustrae, and a few crustaceous animals. He was convinced that life existed at all depths of the seabed.

An enormous impetus was given to deep-sea soundings when John Mercer Brooke, working from a principle more than 200 years old, invented a sounding apparatus in 1854. It not only detached a sinker when the weight struck the sea-bottom, but it also permitted a small deposit to be drawn up by the line. In 1851 a submarine telegraphic cable had been laid under the English Channel, and in 1856 Cyrus W. Field succeeded in connecting Newfoundland to Nova Scotia by underwater cable. To prepare the route for a transatlantic cable from America to Europe extensive surveys of the ocean floor were required, and the exploratory ships provided many samples of ooze that greatly added to scientific information about the composition of the seabed and organic life at the bottom. In 1868 the U.S. Coast Survey began a series of deep dredgings under the direction of Count L. F. de Pourtalès on the margin of the Gulf Stream that went down to depths of 510 fathoms, defining the two well-marked calcareous and siliceous deposits on the seabed from Cape Cod to Florida, with their limits marked by the course of the cold and warm currents. British deep-sea dredging from the *Lightning,* the *Porcupine,* and the *Shearwater* also took place between 1868 and 1871, while early in 1872 Louis Agassiz collected bottom samples in considerable depths off the coast of South America.

All these early sounding efforts, however, as part of Polar expeditions, the laying of submarine telegraphs, or as special task forces along coastal margins and within enclosed seas, scarcely approached the idea of a great marine science expedition to circumnavigate the globe, to probe systematically the greatest depths of the ocean, and to bring forth, for the first time in human history, a comprehensive knowledge of the oceans and the bed of the sea. It was this idea that led to the *H.M.S. Challenger* Expedition.

On 15 June 1871 Professor William B. Carpenter of the University of London wrote a letter, which was read into the minutes of the Royal Society on 29 June. He noted that other nations were entering the physical and biological exploration of the deep sea and that the British government ought to be appraised of the urgency for complete and systematic research of the oceans. On 26 October 1871 the Royal Society appointed a committee to study the matter, which included its president and officers, Dr. Carpenter and Dr. Wyville Thompson, as well as the Hydrographer of the Admiralty and others. A month later the committee proposed a voyage of circumnavigation that would (1) determine the chemical composition of sea water, (2) ascertain the physical and chemical deposits on the sea bottom, and (3) examine the distribution of organic life. On 8 December 1871 the Royal Society addressed a request for support of the expedition to the Admiralty to cover the provision of the ship, its stores, and the necessary scientific equipment and supplies. Funds were approved by the House of Commons in April 1872. Immediately thereafter the Admiralty and the Hydrographer selected a steam corvette, the *H.M.S. Challenger,* a 2306 ton vessel with approximately 1234 horsepower, in addition to its sails, for the expedition.

At 11:30 A.M. on Saturday, 21 December 1872, the *H.M.S. Challenger,* with five civilian scientists, one civilian secretary-artist, and a crew of twenty-two, from captain to carpenter, sailed out from Portsmouth, England, for a 3.5-year oceanographic cruise. The fabulous scientific work of this expedition was eventually collected in fifty volumes and reported in countless other papers, memoirs, and books, all contributing enormously to knowledge of the physical and chemical composition of the sea as well as providing extraordinary information about the ocean floor. One of the many scientific achievements of the *Challenger* expedition was the first identification and analysis of manganese nodules that lay on the red clay of the deep bed of the sea.

On 18 February 1873, proceeding from the Canary Islands westward to the Virgin Islands, at 25°45′N., 20°14′W. the dredge of the *Challenger* had gone down to 1525 fathoms, returning nothing in two soundings, for it seemed to have landed on hard ground. Another grab brought out a few small pumice stones as well as sponges and corals. The leader of the expedition, Prof. C. Wyville Thompson, noted that around the base of the corals, which had been torn off by the dredge, there were thick crusts, black on the surface, showing a fine, regular granulation. A fracture through the crusts revealed uniform dark brown color and a semicrystalline appearance. On further examination by the chemist of the expedition, "this black or brown substance which encrusted the coral and appeared to pass into and to form its bases of attachment, consisted of almost pure black oxide of manganese."

As the *Challenger* moved westward on 26 February it lowered its dredge on 3600 fathoms of rope, the deepest grab by far up to this point in the expedition, and it came up with something totally different from previous samples of the Atlantic bottom, namely, about a hundred pounds of red clay. The calcareous elements of the earlier bottom samples had greatly diminished, and this sample was almost pure clay, the silicate of alumina and the sesqui-oxide of iron with a small quantity of manganese. Finally, on 6 March 1873, about 970 miles east of Sombrero Island in the Virgin group, the dredge came up at 4:15 P.M. with a number of "very peculiar black oval bodies about an inch long with the surface irregularly reticulated . . . the whole appearance singularly like that cf the phosphatic concretions which are so abundant in the greensand and trias." On analysis "the black oval bodies" were found to consist of almost pure peroxide of maganese.

This historical event in the *Challenger* expedition heralded the discovery and recovery of many dozens of bushels of manganese nodules from the Atlantic and then the Pacific ocean, where the hauls were even greater. On 6 October 1875, for example, as the ship proceeded from Tahiti eastward, two bushels of both round types, with a concentric arrangement of layers, and large slab types, which contained volcanic tufa in their centers, came up on deck from a depth of 2385 fathoms of water. Other grabs in the eastern Pacific ocean confirmed the dispersion and abundance of the nodules.[23]

Despite the identification of manganese nodules on the ocean floor by the *Challenger* and subsequent data that were obtained on their location, formation, and composition in 1901, 1906, and 1919, further surveys and analyses of the deposits virtually stopped until the 1950s.[24] Scientific investigations had shown that the ocean floor, especially those parts covered with red clay, were strewn with grains or nodules or slabs of manganese and iron peroxides and with rocks, porous materials, and various organic debris on the ocean floor to which coatings or filings of manganese oxides were attached. Ranging from black to tan in colors, largely depending on the proportions of iron and manganese within the specimens, the potato-shaped nodules averaged about three centimeters in size, although a few very large nodules have been dredged up to deck, such as one the *Aluminaut* hoisted from the Blake Plateau in 1966, which weighed 198 pounds and in cross-section consisted of solid manganite. It was generally agreed by scientists that manganese was added to the ocean by the runoff of water over rocks into streams, submarine volcanic eruptions, submarine springs, and the decomposition of igneous rocks on the sea floor. But there have been differences of opinion on the dynamics from the time manganese and iron entered into solution to the time the elements became fixed as manganese nodules. Scientific studies in 1945 and in the 1950s addressed these problems, but until then no one had studied the practical question of the commercial value of the minerals in the nodules.[25]

Very little deep-sea dredging by either the United States or Great Britain took place during the first half of the twentieth century. Knowledge about the potential wealth of the ocean floor had been limited. Indeed, no political or economic need for the hard mineral desposits lying upon or within the bed of the sea had been demonstrated and, therefore, incentives for the improvement of ocean-mining technology to recover such deposits lagged. The International Geophysical Year 1957–1958, however, precipitated a new interest in the ocean floor. Among other events, the Scripps Institution of Oceanography at San Diego dredged and photographed the eastern Pacific basin, finding nodules almost everywhere, with one sample of 500 assayed at 30 percent manganese. In the fall of 1957 the Department of Mineral Technology of the University of California at Berkeley and the Institute of Marine Resources at Scripps, led by Henry W. Menard and Charles D. Wheelock, began to plan a cooperative ocean studies program. As their first research project the economic analysis of mining ocean floor manganese nodules was selected. Under the guidance of Professor H. E. Hawkes, John Mero of the Department of Mineral Technology was appointed Chief Investigator. Mero's original and brilliant study concluded that the mining of manganese nodules was both technologically and economically feasible.

Mero had suggested as early as 1952 that the mining of manganese nodules from the seabed might be feasible. But it was his ninety-six-page study in 1959 for the Institute of Marine Resources, expanded into *The Mineral Resources of the Sea*, in 1965 that brought manganese nodules to the attention of the mining industry, legal advisers, and the United Nations. Mero systematically brought together all that was known about manganese nodules from previous scientific expeditions and averaged out their mineral content, particularly manganese, cobalt, nickel, and copper. He speculated on the concretion process by which manganese nodules were formed and the rate of growth of these mineral resources on the floor of the sea. He described different methods of dredging nodules from the ocean floor and computed the costs of recovery. Although he recognized the difference between transforming a resource into a saleable form and the real costs of the resource imposed by transportation, technical limitations, and other economic and political constraints, Mero flatly stated that it would be "economic to mine an area bearing 1 lb. of nodules per square foot" and that sea floor nodules would "be a cheaper source of manganese, nickel, cobalt, and even copper than present land sources." Even more mind-boggling was his assertion that the mineral resources in manganese nodules, taken as a whole throughout the bed of the sea, were forming at a faster rate than the consumption of such resources in the foreseeable future. Finally, Mero perceived that title to these vast mineral resources lying on the seabed beyond the jurisdiction of any nation had to be settled in an orderly and peaceful way and suggested that the offshore boundaries for control of mineral recovery might be set at 10 miles from the coast or at a depth greater than one hundred fathoms (600 feet), whichever would be farthest from shore. "The rest of the ocean floor would be part of the general domain of the world." He then added, "An international ocean mining law could then be formulated, perhaps through the United Nations, which would spell out the exclusive rights of the discoverer . . . or grant him a franchise . . ."[26]

During the months and years that followed Mero's study of manganese nodules, some doubt was cast on his optimisitc predictions by more critical evaluations of the economic difficulties. Claims of the extremely large reserves of the minerals found in manganese nodules, for example, had been based on calculations on the total tonnage of nodules on the deep sea floor. This figure was often compared to proven *commercial* land reserves, that is, quantities of mineral both available and able to be produced at the current market price. Moreover, analysts noted that the flow of such minerals as manganese, nickel, and copper into industrial use had not been slowed by the lack of reserves, but rather by the fluctuations of worldwide demand. Price, dependent on such factors as market demand, transport costs, and government controls, often more political rather than economic, determined the operations of the mining industries to a greater extent than the quantity of metal reserves. Nevertheless, there was general agreement among the experts that at some time in the future the production of some minerals from the deep seabed would become commercially feasible.

From 1962 onward many preliminary investigations, both in the United States and other countries, examined the possibilities of mining deep-sea manganese nodules in at least four ways: by means of an air-lift or suction dredge, with its head mounted on a vehicle towed along the ocean floor by a surface vessel; by means of a self-supported flexible pipeline attached to a submerged pump and motor; by means of a self-propelled bottom mobile crawler or wheeled vehicle, which could be navigated by remote control from the surface; or, finally, by means of an entire submersible mobile mining system, that would recover ore by hydraulic dredge and load the ore into hoppers, which would then be floated to the surface. Despite these expensive research and development efforts, until the summer of 1970 not one pilot-scale deep-ocean mining project, including quantity separation of the metals in the nodules, had actually been undertaken.

In October 1968 Tenneco Inc., a diversified industrial complex with interests in manufacturing, natural gas pipelines, oil chemical packaging, and land use, founded Deepsea Ventures, Inc. The firm composed mainly of scientists and engineers, led by John E. Flipse, started to develop the technology necessary to mine, process, and market metals found in the seabed manganese nodules. By mid-January 1970, a 300-ton cargo ship had been converted to a prototype ocean mining vessel, *R. V. Prospector,* outfilled with winches, wires, dredge components, a battery of underwater cameras with videotape, a chemical laboratory, etc. The ship was prepared to view, sample, and determine the characteristics of the sea floor deposits and the ocean environment up to depths of 18,000 feet. After an exploratory cruise from January to March 1970, the *Prospector* left Charleston, South Carolina on Wednesday, 15 July 1970 and arrived fifteen hours later at a test site on the Blake Plateau, approximately 170 miles off the coast of Georgia-Florida. Several tests of the dredging system were conducted and on 30 July at 2:00 A.M. the very first piece of nodular material ever pumped from the seabed to the ocean's surface came up more than 2000 feet through the pipe to the vessel.[27]

Tenneco was not the only firm interested in seabed mining operations. The Kennecott Copper Corporation of the United States and the International Nickel Corporation of Canada also turned their attention to manganese nodules from 1962 onward. Several nodule survey cruises were completed by these firms with economic feasibility studies and some pilot plant operations. By 1972 company publicists were predicting that the commercial mining of manganese nodules from the ocean floor was only a few years away. Japanese and French groups, moreover, also started to explore the commercial recovery of manganese nodules after 1967, making extensive investigations of ocean mining sites as well as the mineral recovery and processing problems. At the same time the Soviet Union conducted several surveys of the seabed with the plain intent of eventually recovering the deepsea minerals, although information about the progress of the Russian development of that industry was scant.

In November 1972, the Ocean Mining Division of the Summa Corporation, controlled by Howard Hughes, launched the *Glomar Explorer,* with indications that it was the most efficient vessel for mining manganese nodules from the deep seabed that had ever been built. The ship was 618 feet long and 15,000 dead-weight tons, with a 46-foot draft and speed of 12 knots, with highly sophisticated electronic and mechanical equipment, including a 10,000- to 15,000-foot pipe string. Reports implied that the vessel planned to use a submersible barge, about the length of a football field and the height of an eight-story building, to collect the nodules from the sea floor through one or more dredge heads. Sailing to the eastern Pacific ocean, during the summer of 1973, the operations of the *Glomar Explorer* were shrouded in secrecy. As it turned out, the vessel, working in co-operation with the U.S. Central Intelligence Agency, attempted to raise a sunken Soviet submarine. Nevertheless, from 1973 to 1977 a number of other potential domestic and foreign mining competitors, continued to be active in planning for the exploitation of manganese nodules, possibly using continuous line bucket dredges or some hydraulic lift technique to recover the nodules, then transport them to shore, and process their mineral contents.

Riches from the sea and the expectations of ocean mining, not including gas and oil, have often been exaggerated by publicists. For example, it had been confidently expected for more than a decade that phosphorite would be commercially mined from the continental shelf and outer slopes of the seabed. The *Challenger* expedition, in addition to its dredging of manganese nodules from the deep ocean floor, had identified for the first time submarine phosphorite which it hauled aboard ship off the coast of South Africa in 1873. Phosphorite, rocks that contain calcium phosphate, has long been important to the chemical and fertilizer industries. On the ocean floor phosphorite has been found in many areas of the world and may take the form of nodules, sands, muds, and bed-rock. Phosphorite nodules, either rounded, in slabs, in irregular masses, or in coatings are the most common form of phosphorites on the seabed. They are created by the rapid precipitation of phosphate from sea water. Most nodules have been found in waters between 100 and 1300 feet deep, although some were located in depths up to 10,000 feet. A strong upwelling of nutrient-rich ocean waters, such as off the coasts of upper and lower California, where nodules were first found in 1937, and the coasts of South America, Africa, and Australia, seems to provide an ideal environment for the growth of phosphorite nodules.

Except for a brief period off the shores of California, phosphorite has not been mined from the seabed, largely because the land-minded phosphates have been purer and cheaper to market than any taken from the seabed. Some coastal states without adequate land sources of phosphorite may in the future gain from a harvest of these nodules from the seabed, but the economic limitations to many bold claims about the wealth of the oceans should be noted. Silica stone, diamonds, and amber have at one time or another been recovered from the seabed on a commercial scale. But in the mid-1970s only sand, gravel, calcium carbonate in various forms, and tin and iron sands were actually mined, with sand and gravel by far the most important in value.

By making a number of reasonable assumptions, however, the commercial mining of manganese nodules seemed imminent. Some early estimates had focused on cobalt or copper as the controlling mineral in determining the worth of exploiting the nodule for all its major minerals.[28] By 1973, however, the nickel in the nodule (with cobalt as a coproduct and copper and manganese as by-products) was touted as the key to price and profit. The demand for nickel had grown on the average of 6.3 percent per year since 1890. Such a demand rate, if continued, would require some three million more tons of the metal per year by the year 2000 than produced in the mid-1970s. Mining analysts also assumed that at least 1 percent of the deep-ocean floor held nodules with concentrations of the desired minerals great enough to warrant the costs of production within tracts of some 10,000 square kilometers.[29]

In any case, by 1977 there had been no commercial mining of deep seabed manganese nodules anywhere in the world despite the euphoric statements of the 1960s. The mineral industry was notoriously unstable, with inelastic products subject to severe price fluctuations. Speculation on the acquisition and economic worth of the concentrations of nickel, cobalt, copper, and manganese in the nodules lying on the seabed continued with vigor in the mid-1970s. At the same time considerable concern was expressed by the developing countries of the world over the effect of thrusting new quantities of these minerals on the international market and the economic hurt that might be inflicted upon the existing producers of such land-based minerals. All the assumptions about the mining of manganese nodules, however, ultimately depended on the complex political negotiations of the states of the world that had begun during the late 1960s to establish an international legal regime for the seabed. Entrepreneurial efforts to mine nickel, copper, cobalt, manganese, and other minerals were certain to be either facilitated or crimped by the legal determination of title, jurisdiction, mining rights, revenues, taxation, and environmental standards to be applied in the vast areas of the seabed that lay beyond the jurisdiction of any state.[30]

The United Nations, International Law, and the Bed of the Sea

The Geneva Convention of the Continental Shelf in 1958 had left the legal status on the bed of the sea ambiguous. On the one hand states could exercise sovereign rights over the natural resources of the continental shelf adjacent to their shores out to waters 200 meters in depth; on the other hand, they might exercise such rights over the adjacent continental shelf even further out to sea if technology permitted the exploitation of resources in deeper waters.

In 1950 the International Law Commission had not wished to encumber the exploitation of marine resources by such states as those bordering the shallow Persian Gulf by a geological definition of a "continental shelf"; furthermore, the Commission did not want to limit petroleum exploitation to a depth of 200 meters if advancing technology should make deeper-water recovery possible. But the reaction to a flexible boundary by some states and many commentators caused the Commission in 1953 to alter its text and limit the exercise of coastal jurisdiction to an absolute 200-meter water depth. Several Latin American states, however, claimed an injustice in any formulation of coastal jurisdiction based on a "continental shelf," since nature had not favored countries like Peru and Chile with wide shelves. At the same time they vigorously sought to lay claims for wider jurisdiction over their coastal fisheries. Thus, the Latin American bloc supported the proposition that coastal states should control "the seabed and subsoil of the continental shelf, continental and insular terraces, or other submarine areas" adjacent to the coast to a depth of 200 meters or beyond, where the superjacent waters admitted the exploitation of the marine resources. That was essentially the language of the 1956 Ciudad Trujillo conference, referred to earlier, which was incorporated into the final articles of the 1958 Geneva Convention.

Continental shelf, therefore, meant the seabed and subsoil of the submarine areas, regardless of geologic definition. Only two limitations were imposed on the further extension of jurisdiction by a coastal state over the resources on the ocean floor: namely, that the area be "adjacent" and that the natural resources located there be exploitable. Up to 1958, of course, public attention had been riveted on the recovery of offshore petroleum, which was still produced almost entirely from relatively shallow waters, but the study of the economic possibility of mining deep-sea manganese nodules by John Mero in 1959, which had been widely read or heard about by 1965, began to generate a clamor of concern about a comprehensive international regime for the seabed "beyond national jurisdiction"—wherever that was.[31]

Many minds turned to the tremendous challenge offered to international cooperation by the peaceful uses of the ocean and the exploitation of the resources of the seabed. In October 1965 James Roosevelt, a member of the U.S. delegation to the United Nations Twentieth General Assembly, urged the (Second) Financial and Economic Committee to start "dreaming and thinking exciting thoughts" about the role the UN could play with regard to underseas exploration. On 7 March 1966 the UN Economic and Social Council approved Resolution 1112(XL), calling for a survey on 6 December 1966 the General Assembly not only endorsed the Economic and Social Council resolution, but also called for a survey of marine science and technology as well as proposals for furthering international cooperation.

Private individuals and groups started to speak, write, and appeal for international action to regulate the seabed many months before the governments of the world were seized with the issues. In the United States in 1966 the

Commission to Study the Organization of Peace, the Marine Technology Society, the American Bar Association, the Mershon Social Science Program at Ohio State University, and the Law of the Sea Institute at the University of Rhode Island, among others, discussed or recommended public action for a new interntional regime for the seabed in the light of the potential wealth of submerged mineral resources. Statements and draft treaty articles limiting national jurisdiction over the ocean floor and conferring various powers upon the United Nations or on some international authority associated with the United Nations to regulate and manage the resources of the seabed began to circulate with increasing rapidity.[32]

Among those who were impressed by the new challenges offered to the progress of man through peaceful and orderly exploitation of the resources of the oceans and the seabed was Arvid Pardo. A member of the UN secretariat since 1945 in documents and social affairs, Pardo had served as deputy Resident Representative for the UN Development Program from 1960 to 1964 in Nigeria and in Ecuador. In 1964 he was appointed Permanent Representative of the new state of Malta to the United Nations. On 17 August 1967, Ambassador Pardo requested the Secretary General to add an item to the agenda, "Declaration and Treaty Concerning the Reservation Exclusively for Peaceful Purposes of the Seabed and of the Ocean Floor, and the Subsoil Thereof, Underlying the High Seas Beyond the Limits of Present National Jurisdiction and the Use of Their Resources in the Interests of Mankind."

Pardo pointed out that in view of the rapid progress of technology, there was fear that the seabed and ocean floor beyond national jurisdiction would become progressively and competitively subject to national appropriation and use. He urged a declaration that the seabed and ocean floor were "a common heritage of mankind" and that a treaty should embody the following principles: (1) the seabed and ocean floor beyond present national jurisdiction should not be subject to national appropriation in any manner whatsoever; (2) their exploration should be undertaken in a way consistent with the principles and purposes of the UN Charter; (3) the exploitation of the area should safeguard the interests of mankind, and financial benefits derived from exploitation should be used primarily for developing poor countries; and (4) the area should forever be reserved exclusively for peaceful purposes. Pardo believed such a treaty embodying such principles should also provide for the creation of an international agency, which would assume jurisdiction, as a trustee for all countries, over the area and which would regulate, supervise, and control all activities there in conformity with the principles of the treaty.[33]

The General Assembly requested the *Ad Hoc* UN Seabed Committee to study the scope and various aspects of the reservation exclusively for peaceful purposes of the seabed and the ocean floor, and the subsoil thereof, underlying the high seas beyond the limits of present national jurisdiction, and the uses of these resources in the interests of mankind. The Committee surveyed the past and present UN and specialized agency activities in this area and examined measures to promote international cooperation in the exploration, conservation, and use of the seabed and the ocean floor and the subsoil thereof. The Committee also considered the report that had been prepared by the Secretary-General pursuant to the resolution of the General Assembly on 6 December 1966 regarding mineral resources of the sea beyond national jurisdiction and regarding marine science and technology, as well as information notes on the economic implications of the exploitation of mineral resources on world prices, and the effect of exploitation on other uses of the marine environment.

A number of nations, including the United States, submitted various draft declarations to the *Ad Hoc* Committee, but of special significance was a proposal by fourteen developing countries from Asia, Africa, and Latin America to create "suitable international machinery" that would ensure the most appropriate and equitable benefits that might be obtained from the exploitation of the bed of the sea. No agreement was reached in the *Ad Hoc* Committee on any formulation for a legal regime to govern the seabed, but the Committee's recommendations (1) to create a permanent 42-member Committee on the Peaceful Uses of the Sea-Bed and the Ocean Floor beyond the Limits of National Jurisdiction; (2) to call for studies by the Secretary General on (a) the dangers of marine pollution and (b) the establishment of international machinery to exploit the resources of the seabed were approved by the UN General Assembly on 21 December 1968.[34]

No state in the General Assembly voted against the establishment of a permanent UN Seabed Committee; no state voted against the request for a report on marine pollution; and a resolution welcoming the International Decade of Ocean Exploration resolution had also been approved by all states without objection. But the call for a study of international machinery to exploit the resources of the seabed beyond national jurisdiction found nine states of the Soviet East European bloc solidly opposed, while twenty-five states, including the United States, Australia, Canada, New Zealand, and the major western European powers, abstained. Many states were not willing to pin down the limits of national jurisdiction over the ocean floor in 1968 in view of the rapidly changing technology for the exploitation of petroleum and other submarine mineral resources; some states felt that the fixing of marine boundaries was too soon, too complex, and too fraught with other legal consequences that required further study. Nevertheless, no one could deny the emerging international consensus that *some* area of the seabed lay beyond national jurisdiction.

During 1969 the UN Sea-Bed Committee, working through a Legal and an Economic-Technical subcommittee, considered the reservation of the seabed beyond national jurisdiction exclusively for peaceful purposes and the freedom of scientific research there, while it studied possible regimes for the exploitation of the resources of the seabed for the benefit of mankind. The Committee's work was greatly abetted by two reports of the Secretary General on pollution and on international machinery. Many states, especially the developing countries, moreover, began to point out that a legal regime for the seabed had many implications for marine boundaries, for navigation, and for resource exploitation other than minerals; many felt that the Geneva Conventions of 1958 no longer answered the need of international law for the sea and that, in any case, a number of developing countries that had since achieved independence had not participated in the formulation of those conventions. Above all, there was a strong sense among those states not engaged in ocean mineral resource exploitation or unlikely to profit from such exploitation as it extended seaward from the coasts that a halt should be called to all drilling, dredging, and digging further out to sea until an international seabed regime was established.[35]

Discussion of the UN Sea-Bed Committee Report in the First Committee (Political and Security) at the twenty-fourth session of the General Assembly led to four resolutions that were adopted by the General Assembly on 15 December 1969. Resolution 2574A (XXIV) requested the Secretary General to ascertain the views of the member states on the desirability of convening a conference on the law of the sea to review the regimes of the high seas, the continental shelf, the territorial sea and the contiguous zone, fishing, and the conservation of the living resources of the high seas, and "in order to arrive at a clear, precise and internationally accepted definition of the area of the sea bed and ocean floor which lies beyond national jurisdiction." In the General Assembly that resolution was adopted by 65-12-30, with opposition to an abstention from the resolution stemming from objection to the all-embracing purposes of such a conference.

No state in the General Assembly opposed resolutions 2574B and 2574C (XXIV) that had called on the Sea-Bed Committee to expedite the work of preparing a comprehensive set of principles based on the synthesis provided by the Legal Subcommittee and requesting the Secretary General to prepare a further study of various types of international machinery. But Resolution 2574D, which stated that all states and persons were bound to refrain from all activities of exploitation of the resources of the seabed area pending the establishment of an international regime, was opposed by twenty-eight states, including the United States, the Soviet Union, the United Kingdom, Japan, France, Italy, Norway, and Denmark, while twenty-eight other states abstained. Many of these states believed that such a resolution would retard the development of their technological capacity to exploit the seabed, create needless uncertainty about claims, and also make future international agreement on a regime for the bed of the sea more difficult, perhaps delaying or denying the share of revenues that might be available to the developing nations.

In the history of the development of an international regime for the oceans and the seabed, 1970 was a momentous year. As the United Nations began to address the complex issues of an international regime from the fall of 1967 onward, the interest of the United States in the oceans rapidly increased.[36]

In several ways the U.S. Congress had shown more initiative than the Executive Branch in the development of American policy for the oceans, notably in the creation of the National Council on Marine Resources and Engineering Development by Public Law 89-454 in 1966. Subsequent hearings before various congressional committees had brought forth extensive discussions on the issues relating to the establishment of seaward boundaries and collateral matters under study in the UN Seabed Committee. The U.S. Senate Foreign Relations Committee's Subcommittee on Ocean Space, chaired by Senator Claiborne Pell of Rhode Island, made some very special contributions to debate on the law of the sea.

On 29 September 1967 and on 17 November 1967, even before the General Assembly of the UN had decided to establish its *Ad Hoc* Committee, Pell had introduced Senate resolutions. The first stressed the need to establish reasonable rules of conduct to govern the activities of each nation "under the extraterritorial waters," and the second called on the U.S. Representative to the United Nations to take leadership by introducing to the organization an American resolution to govern the activities of nations in "ocean space." He urged a UN resolution that would declare (1) the freedom of all states to explore and exploit ocean space, (2) the freedom of all states to use the high seas, beyond a twelve-mile territorial sea, but in accordance with the 1958 Geneva Convention on Fishing and Conservation of the Living Resources of the Sea; (3) the need for a licensing authority designated by the United Nations, with the approval of the Security Council, which could grant licenses to states or international organizations for the mining of the seabed, set royalty payments, provide for safety zones of installations, and take other measures to protect the marine environment; (4) the use of the seabed for peaceful purposes only; (5) a redefinition of the limits of the continental shelf to extend seaward to the 600-meter isobath, and the provision of a Sea Guard, under the United Nations, to enforce the rules for ocean space. On 5 March 1968 Pell placed before the Senate (Resolution 263) a draft treaty of thirty-eight articles largely incorporating the principles he had enunciated on 17 November 1967.

Others in Congress, in private enterprise, and particularly in the departments of the Executive Branch were wary about a definitive treaty on the oceans and seabed in 1968. Pell responded to their doubts: "I disagree strongly with those who state that to consider an Ocean Space Treaty at this time is unnecessary or premature." In any case, the President had a comprehensive study of ocean problems under way by the Commission on Marine Science, Engineering and Resources, which was advising the National Council on Marine Resources and Engineering Development. The members of the Commission, after two years of research and reflection, recommended in January 1969 that (1) the continental shelf, be redefined under international law to extend to a depth of 200 meters seaward or 50 nautical miles, whichever was further from the shore;

(2) the United States propose a new international legal framework to govern the exploration and exploitation of the marine resources underlying the deep seas, rejecting both the doctrine of "res nullius" in which a first claim by a state might obtain legal possession and the plea that states should confer title to the entire deep-seabed on the United Nations; (3) an intermediate international zone be created, beyond the continental shelf up to the 2500 meter isobath or 100 miles from the coastal baselines, in which only the mining claims of the coastal state would be registered; (4) an International Registry Authority be created to admit claims for mining the seabed both in the intermediate zone and beyond the intermediate zone; (5) a portion of the revenues from the production in both these areas be placed in an International Fund to aid marine sciences, maricul-ture, and the developing countries.[37]

In 1969 an intergovernmental agency group, including the Departments of State, Defense, and Interior, drew on the Pell resolutions, the recommendations of the Commission on Marine Science, Engineering and Resources, and many other public and private papers that had addressed U.S. policy for the oceans and seabed to formulate an official American position paper. Its work was approved by Under-Secretary of State Elliott Richardson that winter and sent on to the White House. On 23 May 1970 President Richard M. Nixon proposed (1) that all nations renounce all national claims over the natural resources of the seabed beyond the point where the high seas reach a depth of 200 meters; (2) that they agree to regard those resources as the common heritage of human-kind; (3) that an international regime be established for the exploitation of the resources beyond this 200-meter-depth area and for the collection of mineral royalties to be used for economic assistance to the developing countries; (4) that the coastal nations act as trustees for the international community in a zone comprised of the continental margins beyond the 200-meter depths, sharing revenues in that area with the world community; and (5) that international machinery be authorized to regulate exploration and the use of seabed resources beyond the continental margins. Based on these major policy concepts the United States introduced a highly detailed draft Convention in the UN Sea-Bed Committee on 3 August 1970.[38]

The most remarkable part of the U.S. draft convention was the provision for an International Seabed Area, comprising all areas of the seabed and subsoil of the high seas seaward of the 200-meter isobath adjacent to the coasts of continents and islands; no state would have or could acquire any right, title, or interest in this area except as provided in the Convention. Moreover, part of the International Seabed Area, from the 200-meter isobath to the base of the continental slope, would be an International Trusteeship Area in which the coastal state would issue, revoke, or suspend mineral exploitation licenses, establish work conditions and would retain only between a third and a half of revenues from fees and licenses in that area. The International Seabed Resources Authority would receive the balance of the revenues.

Basically the United States sought to forestall any claims to sovereignty by coastal states to the seabed beyond the 200-meter isobath, although allowing the coastal state to control, under international standards, the exploitation of the resources from the 200-meter isobath to the edge of the abyssal ocean floor. In exchange the coastal state would deliver something between a half and two thirds of all net income from licenses and production in this "trusteeship" area to the International Seabed Resources Authority. This extraordinary scheme opened the possibility of very substantial new and independent sources of revenue for an international organization, which, if realized, would have been a totally unprecedented and a spectacular giant step forward in the development of international institutions.

The detailed U.S. draft convention described the main organ of the International Seabed Resources Authority, including a Council in which a majority vote of the six most industrially advanced nations would be essential for important decisions, an Assembly, and a Tribunal. In 1970 the United Kingdom and France also submitted working papers on the international regime for the exploration and exploitation of the seabed. Despite the increasing number of studies and the availability of draft proposals, the UN Seabed Committee, in its report to the General Assembly, felt obliged to state that "many differences remain on issues and problems which are of great importance." The chief dilemma lay in the impossibility of fixing a regime for the seabed without opening questions about the width of territorial waters, passage through international straits, new protective zones of maritime jurisdiction for the conservation of living resources, and the hazards of marine pollution. Without a conference to consider *all* these issues in their reciprocal effects most nations felt an international regime for the seabed could not be achieved. Nevertheless, the time was ripe for a declaration of principles that could guide the world community in reaching treaty agreements about the seabed.

On 17 December 1970 the General Assembly, therefore, adopted the Declaration of Principles Governing the Sea-Bed and the Ocean Floor, and the Sub-Soil thereof, beyond the Limits of National Jurisdiction by a vote of 108 in favor, none against, and 14 abstentions. The draft had been recommended by the First Committee where patient negotiation crystallized all the efforts and compromises of the UN Sea-Bed Committee into an agreeable text. The General Assembly solemnly declared that

1. The sea-bed and ocean floor, and the subsoil thereof, beyond the limits of national jurisdiction (hereinafter referred to as the area), as well as the resources of the area, are the common heritage of mankind.

2. The area shall not be subject to appropriation by any means by States or persons, natural or juridical, and no State shall claim or exercise sovereignty or sovereign rights over any part thereof.

3. No State or person, natural or juridical, shall claim, exercise or acquire rights with respect to the area of its resources incompatible with the internal regime to be established and the principles of this Declaration.[39]

There were other parts to the declaration, but most significantly the General Assembly called for the establishment of "appropriate international machinery" by an international treaty "of universal character generally agreed upon," which would provide for the character generally agreed upon," which would provide for the safe and orderly development of the seabed area and its management, both to expand opportunities for its use and to insure the equitable sharing by states, particularly the developing states, in the benefits to be derived from the exploitation of the resources. Finally, the declaration made it clear that nothing within it affected the legal status of the waters superjacent to the seabed area, or the airspace above those waters. It also maintained that, subject to the international regime to be established, states retained their rights to take measures to prevent, mitigate, or eliminate grave and imminent danger to their coastlines.

As indicated in previous chapters, when the Third UN Law of the Sea Conference met in its first substantive session in Caracas in the summer of 1974, it was organized into three main committees, the first of which dealt with the international regime for seabed beyond national jurisdiction. Fundamental to the work of the first committee, of course, was the 1970 UN declaration on legal principles for the seabed beyond national jurisdiction and the call for "appropriate international machinery." In general, developed countries at first perceived this "machinery" as primarily a licensing authority to ensure orderly claims for mining the seabed under general international standards with some formula for a royalty from the successful recovery of seabed resources to be paid into an international development fund. But many developing countries, proceeding from the idealistic dictum that the resources of the seabed beyond national jurisdiction were the common heritage of mankind decried the probability that the technologically advanced countries would quickly exploit the manganese nodules and leave little for the other nations of the world. Led by Latin American, African, and South Asian states, the "Group of 77" called for the direct exploitation of the seabed beyond national jurisdiction by the International Seabed Authority itself. It should be remembered that the dense and voluble Caracas session of the Law of the Sea conference yielded hundreds of documents, some main trends, but hardly a text of articles to which any state agreed either in part or whole.

The Geneva session of the Law of the Sea Conference from 17 March to 9 May 1975 produced a single negotiating text, but so far as the international regime for the seabed beyond national jurisdiction was concerned the gap between the developed and developing states barely narrowed. As stated by John R. Stevenson, the head of the American delegation, some nations were not prepared to subject their access to the seabed to a system in which they might not have reasonable assurances of security and in which their views would be inadequately represented in the decisionmaking process. In his judgment it did not seem possible "to agree to give ultimate powers of exclusive exploitation to a single new international entity."[40]

Yet further informal negotiations and a reevaluation of the situation led the United States to concede by the summer of 1975 that if the international organization which set the rules for deep seabed mining would (1) preserve the rights of all states and their nationals to exploit seabed resources directly, (2) ensure adjudication of conflicting interests, (3) guarantee the security of investment, and, in its management, (4) reflect the balance of interests of the participating states, then the United States would agree that the international organization itself could also conduct mining operations on behalf of the world community. In fact, the United States suggested that a state or person applying to mine a tract should permit the International Seabed Authority to choose one-half that tract for itself to mine or hold in reserve for mining while allowing the other half to be mined by the applicant. "The organization should not have power to control prices or production rates."

That last sentence irritated several developing countries, whose economies were severely dependent on the export of manganese, copper, nickel, and cobalt, and it also bothered a few developed countries, like Canada, with land-based production of such commodities. In the mid-1970s among the developing countries exporting substantial quantities of manganese were Gabon, Brazil, and Ghana; exporting-copper countries were Zambia, Chile, Zaire, Peru, and the Philippines; exporting-nickel countries were Cuba and Indonesia; and exporting-cobalt countries were Zaire, Zambia, and Greece. Supported by other states that viewed the mining of the manganese nodules as an attempt of the industrialized states to capture the wealth of the seabed for themselves, the "Group of 77" (really a larger bloc of developing countries) obtained a provision in the Revised Single Negotiating Text at the 15 March–7 May 1976 session in New York that limited mineral production. In an interim period of twenty years, which might be extended to twenty-five, total production in the international seabed area would not exceed a projected cumulative growth segment of the nickel market, provided that the computed rate of increase was at least 6 percent per year. It was hoped that the rates of seabed production would not unbalance the existing worldwide demand for nickel from land-based producers, but there was some dissatisfaction on the formula, such as the view of Canada, a large nickel-producing country, which wanted the Authority to be able to exercise a production control at a lower limit.[41]

A whole statute for the Enterprise, which would mine seabed minerals directly for the International Seabed Authority, and procedures for dispute settlement in the area beyond national jurisdiction had also been included in the Revised Single Negotiating Text. But progress in reconciling strong national views on access, security, rents, production, and decisionmaking power in the international seabed area went slowly. With none of the fanfare that had marked the first substantive session at Caracas in 1974, the delegates to the Law of the Sea conference plodded through the negotiating text again from 2 August to 17 September 1976, arguing whether the International Seabed Authority and Enterprise, even if legally capable of exploiting the area, would have the capital and skill to do so, and gaining a promise from Secretary of State Kissinger of some American endeavor to gain financial assistance for the Enterprise.[42]

Following a two-week informal meeting at the end of March 1977, specifically on the issues of the international seabed area, the delegates to the Third UN Law of the Sea Conference resumed their work on 23 May 1977 in New York. They looked forward with hope to the prospect of bringing the mineral wealth of the seabed under the titular control of an international organization, yet they were fearful that disagreement and discord might unravel the intricate web of articles and expose the area to the prompt claims of competent national entrepreneurs.

Problems and Issues

Meanwhile in the mid-1970s, U.S. policy for the mineral resources in the continental shelf and on the deep seabed underwent some fundamental changes. The revision of policy was induced, in part, by the developing energy shortages that occurred in the United States during these years; in part, by officials, businesspersons, and marine experts who were skeptical of the efficacy of the 1970 detailed American draft convention on the seabed; and in part, finally, by the lack of support of that draft convention by other nations of the world.

On the verge of the Third UN Law of the Sea Conference in the fall of 1973, the American public suddenly faced an energy crisis that had been engendered by an extravagant use of oil and gas. Anxiety about heating and automobile fuel shortages quickly spread through the nation, leading to new energy policies that sharply affected the future use of the oceans and the seabed.

Although a few energy shortages had appeared in the United States in the winter of 1962–1963 the American public was first aroused to the long-pending eclipse of supply by demand in the fall in 1973. The Arab governments, protesting the partiality of the American government for Israel during the Egyptian-Syrian-Israeli war, stopped their oil shipments to the United States and thereby triggered long lines of motorists waiting for rationed gasoline. Suddenly public attention focused on petroleum and gas shortages, while several Congressional investigations were started amid a spate of new policy proposals. But the U.S. energy crisis had long been brewing. Between 1947 and 1970 Americans had tripled their demand for products refined or processed from crude oil for use in the household and business; they had doubled their demand for such products for industry, tripled it for transportation, and almost quadrupled their demand for petroleum to generate electricity. Expressed simply, the U.S. demand for petroleum had grown from 1,959 million barrels in 1947 to 5,364 million barrels in 1970.

From 1968 through 1971, moreover, the production of natural gas had only increased slightly while the amount of proved natural gas reserves had been declining. As indicated earlier in this chapter, although the United States had been an exporter of crude oil right up to World War II, the depletion of domestic stocks, increasing domestic costs, national security consideration, and other complex factors led to the importation of oil by America. Imports rose slowly in the post-World War II period to reach about 500 million barrels in 1970, 600 million barrels in 1971, and then about 800 million barrels in 1972. Imports from Mexico, Chile, Colombia, and Venezuela tended to decline or cease while imports from Iran, Indonesia, Algeria, Libya, and Saudi Arabia, as well as Canada, tended to rise. Although Arab oil was not a large part of total U.S. production and refining, the imports aggravated U.S. dependence on the volatile Middle East countries.

In any case, Americans had been consuming energy at unprecedented historical growth rates. The insatiable appetite of the United States can be seen in a calculation of total demand for energy units. From 1947 to 1960, the net energy input to the American economy, expressed in British Thermal Units (BTUs), remained more or less constant at 200 million BTUs *per capita.* From 1960 to 1970, however, the net energy input soared to about 275 million BTUs per capita. On a gross basis, including conversion losses, U.S. energy consumption rose from 30 quadrillion BTUs in 1947 to almost 70 quadrillion BTUs in 1970.[43]

Moreover, the utilization of the major energy sources in the United States had changed radically in the twenty-five years following World War II. Coal, which had accounted for 15,824 trillion BTUs in 1947, accounted for only 12,922 trillion BTUs in 1970. Petroleum and natural gas, on the other hand, which had provided only 15,885 trillion BTUs to the American economy in 1947, contributed 51,633 trillion BTUs in 1970. Petroleum alone accounted for about 29,000 trillion BTUs, of which more than half went into transportation, notably the internal combustion engine of the automobile.

Another way of looking at the global shift of energy resources and the American share of the world oil and gas is through figures on production and "proved" reserves, that is, reserves that are both known to be in place and commercially recoverable. Through 1971 the cumulative world *production* of oil had been 264 billion barrels with the United States accounting for 97 billion barrels; through 1971 the *proved reserves* of world oil had been 632 billion barrels with United States accounting for only 38–45 billion barrels. Through 1971 the cumulative world *production* of gas had been 620 trillion cubic feet, with the United States accounting for 415 trillion cubic feet; the *proved reserves* of natural gas worldwide were 1,725 trillion cubic feet with the United States accounting for only 279 trillion cubic feet.

In 1971 President Richard Nixon had sent to the Congress the first presidential message ever devoted to the energy question. Then, on 15 February 1973, he indicated to Congress that one of the highest priorities of his Administration would be a concern for energy supplies during the coming year and said, "We must face-up to the stark fact in America: we are now consuming more energy than we produce." On 11 October 1973 the President sent a further message to Congress in which he proposed legislation to create a Department of Energy and Natural Resources as well as an independent Energy Research and Development Administration.

These events inevitably swayed the oceans policy of the United States. Until 1973, although there had been an interagency task force on the Law of the Sea, the underlying philosophy of the American approach to the future regime for the seas had been guided by the Department of State, particularly the Office of the Legal Adviser and its consultants. In the spring of 1973, however, the emerging energy crisis, with its prospects of higher costs for imported fuel and unfavorable impact on the U.S. balance of payments, prompted the Treasury Department to call for a reassessment of U.S. policy on issues before the Law of the Sea Conference. In particular, the Treasury Department wanted further study of such issues as offshore oil and gas development, the feasibility of international revenue sharing in the coastal economic seabed area, and the functions of an international organization with authority over seabed minerals. By 1974, therefore, the U.S. delegation, guided by the 100-member interagency task force on the Law of the Sea, but especially the executive committee of that task force, was receiving a substantial input from the Treasury Department.

A number of studies by the task force itself were also initiated to examine new initiatives and alternatives to policies that might be taken by the United States. Clearly both the deep seabed, with its manganese nodules, and the continental shelf, with its oil and gas reserves, had assumed a greater importance in the American economy. In 1972 the total production of crude oil in the United States had amounted to 3,455 million barrels, of which 608 million barrels had come from offshore wells. In the same year 22,533 billions of cubic feet of natural gas had been produced in the United States, of which 3,353 billions of cubic feet had come from offshore reservoirs. Estimates of the amount of gas and oil lodged in the continental shelf of the United States were bound to be uncertain. But potentially recoverable oil in the shelf was calculated at 400 billion barrels and natural gas in place estimated at 300 trillion cubic feet. Making many assumptions about prices, leasing policies, and technological improvements, it seemed possible to obtain as much as 1.5 billion barrels a year from offshore wells by 1990.

Everywhere technological developments, spurred by the worldwide demand for oil and gas, had outstripped the early international hopes for limited national jurisdiction over the seabed by coastal states. By the early 1970s leases had been granted by more than 50 countries, including the United States, to tracts beyond the 200-meter isobath noted in the 1958 Geneva Convention on the continental shelf and the United States already was producing oil in water depths up to 400 feet. Indeed, it was technologically feasible to pump oil up from wells in far deeper waters.[44]

The awareness of the energy shortages looming for the United States in the future provoked debate on whether the United States should begin to favor a 200-mile limit to the coastal economic seabed zone or even a broader zone that included the entire continental shelf. Doubts were raised about the advisability of sharing revenues from this area with some UN authority, agency, or development fund. On 16 July 1973 the United States introduced to Subcommittee II of the UN Seabed Committee meeting in Geneva draft articles for a chapter on the rights and duties of states in the "coastal seabed economic area." In this draft the American delegation left blank the limits of the coastal seabed economic area. The United States proposed, however, that the coastal state should have the exclusive right to explore and exploit—and to authorize the exploration and exploitation of—the natural resources of the seabed and the subsoil in this area under the laws and regulations of the coastal state. The draft articles also gave to the coastal state the exclusive right to authorize and to regulate, both on the seabed and in the superjacent waters, the construction, operation, and use of offshore installations affecting its economic interests as well as any drilling for purposes other than the exploration and exploitation of resources.

U.S. seabed policy had clearly shifted. Far greater authority for the coastal state over the seabed was suggested in the 16 July 1973 draft articles than ever envisaged in the 1970 American draft articles. The new proposal embraced not only the exploitation of the resources on the seabed, but all construction, structures, and installations to be located in the coastal seabed economic area. The United States acknowledged a prescriptive role for the future international Seabed Authority and the International Maritime Consultative Organization in setting minimum standards for navigational safety and for protection of the marine environment to be observed by the coastal state in the area. But essentially the idea of a "trusteeship zone" between the end of national jurisdiction over the seabed at the 200-meter isobath and the beginning of the deep seabed under international authority was abandoned.

The U.S. draft proposal also included a paragraph that pledged coastal states to guarantee that the terms of licenses, leases, and other contractural arrangements for the purpose of exploring or exploiting seabed resources would be strictly observed, and to provide for prompt, adequate, and effective compensation for any expropriations. With regard to a share of revenues from the "coastal seabed economic area" for the international community, the United States merely indicated that the coastal states ought to make available some share of revenues in accordance with the provisions of an article yet to be written. Disputes with respect to the interpretation or the application of the provisions for the "coastal seabed economic area," moreover, were to be resolved by a compulsory dispute settlement procedure. But the U.S. draft left the details of that procedure to be written in another article in another chapter. Finally, the United States made it clear that none of its provisions for the area would affect the rights of freedom of navigation and overflight as well as other rights unrelated to seabed resources exploration and exploitation under general principles of international law or as might be otherwise provided in the Law of the Sea conventions.[45]

Thus, as with fisheries, the U.S. delegation had yielded to both internal American political pressures and the concerted efforts of many states in the UN Seabed Committee to give greater control to the coastal state over a wider seabed area for the exploration and exploitation of resources.

In 1975 the pressure both domestically and internationally to give the coastal state virtually complete control over the resources of the ocean and the seabed within a 200-mile "exclusive economic zone" became inexorable, and the United States continued to yield to this movement, while stoutly upholding the right of free navigation on the high seas and transit through international straits. At the Geneva session of the Law of the Sea conference, an informal group, led by Jens Evensen of Norway, had completed a text on the zone, which was largely acceptable to the United States. Only a trace of revenue sharing with the international community remained, and that would be in the area of the continental margin. Only in the area beyond the 200-mile zone and down to the ocean floor, which a state might claim as part of its continental shelf, the United States proposed that a share of the well-head value of petroleum production from 1 percent up to a maximum of 5 percent be given to an international development fund. And by 1977 there was scarcely any debate over the Revised Single Negotiating Text of the Third UN Law of the Sea conference, in which the coastal state was given sovereign rights for exploring, exploiting, conserving, and managing all living and nonliving resources in the exclusive economic zone; exclusive rights and jurisdiction over artificial islands, installation, and structures; and exclusive jurisdiction over other activities such as energy production from the water and winds. A number of questions arose, however, about the delimitation of these exclusive economic zones; their legal status as high seas or some other juridical norm to provide for the passage of vessels and the overflight of planes in the zone; and the extent to which jurisdiction over scientific research in the zone might be exercised; whereas the status of the continental shelf beyond the 200-mile zone and sharing its resources with the international community remained debatable.[46]

From the point of view of the United States, with the fourth-largest coastline in the world, the problem of the exploitation of offshore oil and gas in the mid-1970s largely fell into the domestic political arena. The urgency of action to meet the national energy crisis met complaints from various seaside towns and environmental groups that drilling, pipelines, and tankers on the continental shelf would seriously harm nature and community life in the coastal zone.

Although President Nixon had directed the Secretary of Interior to increase the acreage leased on the outer continental shelf to ten million acres, beginning in 1975 (which would have been equal to all the lease sales between 1954 and 1974), the oil companies were hardly prepared to handle (and bid enough) for such a huge acreage. And opposition from state and local leaders, fearful of both exploitative profits by the companies and the environmental effects, deterred rapid leasing. In fact, in 1975 only a little more than 1.5 million acres were leased off California and in the Gulf of Mexico, less acreage than in 1974. It was not until 17 August 1976 that the first lease was granted on the outer continental shelf under the Atlantic ocean. Forty tracts from 47 to 92 miles off the coasts of New Jersey and Delaware, comprising some 800,000 acres under water from about 115 to 570 feet deep were auctioned by the Department of Interior for more than a billion dollars. But the leases were immediately challenged by environmental groups, who sought early in 1977 a permanent injunction to prevent the exploration of oil and gas as well as the rescinding of the leases themselves.[47]

Beginning in 1970 the American Mining Congress had expressed concern about U.S. policy for the seabed beyond national jurisdiction, suggesting that it might not be in the best interest of the United States for a UN Law of the Sea conference to fix the limits of jurisdiction and that in any case interim arrangements for mining should be based upon the 1958 Geneva Convention. Further lobbying action by the American Mining Congress led to the introduction of bills in 1972 (S.2801) and in 1973 (S.1134) "to promote the conservation and orderly development of hard mineral resources of the deep seabed." Although several Congressional committees held hearings on U.S. oceanography and international issues in the early and mid-1970s, the most receptive to the views of the hard minerals industry was the Subcommittee on Mines, Minerals, and Fuels, chaired by Lee Metcalf of Montana, under the Senate Interior and Insular Affairs Committee.

The spokesman for the American Mining Congress declared that industry needed security of investment, security of tenure, financial protection against interference from others, and the control of ocean mining activities of persons subject to U.S. jurisdiction. He added that it might also establish a customary pattern or rules and regulations that could be the basis for an agreement with like-minded nations.

Essentially the hard minerals industry wanted Congress to authorize the Secretary of Interior to grant immediate 15-year mineral exploration licenses in blocks up to 40,000 square kilometers to American entrepreneurs on the ocean floor beyond national jurisdiction. Such licenses would be exclusive for all persons subject to U.S. jurisdiction, and the bill provided that they might be exclusive with respect to other states that entered into reciprocal agreements with the United States during this interim period. If commercial recovery were achieved, the license would remain in effect as long as commercial recovery continued, although the licensee would relinquish 75 percent of the tract. Most importantly, although these American licenses would be subject to any international regime to be established for the seabed beyond national jurisdiction, the United States would not agree to such an international regime unless the right of the prior licensees to develop their tracts under the terms and conditions originally set by the Secretary of Interior were recognized.[48]

The State Department did not object to S.1134 on the grounds that it violated international law, since neither treaties nor universal custom prohibited the mining of the seabed beyond national jurisdiction, but because the bill would prejudice the negotiation in the Third UN Law of the Sea conference in 1974 of a comprehensive law of the sea treaty that would, inter alia, provide for the orderly conservation and development of the resources of the seabed. Enactment of S.1134 by Congress, it was argued, might lead to a "free-for-all" that would be harmful to American industry insofar as unregulated mining of the seabed would lead to conflicting claims by different states and their nationals.

Private environmental protection groups and world order associations that testified before Congress on seabed mining legislation tended to share the views of the Department of State. But neither the mining industry nor a large number of congressional members were convinced that the UN Law of the Sea conference would, in fact, arrive at a timely international agreement on the seabed regime beyond national jurisdiction. The pessimism of the minerals industry was exacerbated by the failure of the Caracas session to produce a text and the blatant biases of both the Single Negotiating Text in 1975 and the Revised Text in 1976 against early exploitation of the manganese nodules by the nationals or agencies of the developed countries.

Neither S.1134 nor H.R. 9, its counterpart, had emerged from Committee in 1973. In 1974 new bills, H.R.1223 and S.2878, as well as Amendment 946 to S.1134, were presented. The license fees for the lease of blocks was rasied, and all commercial recovery from such blocks was forbidden until 1 January 1976, when it was felt the Third UN Law of the Sea Conference would have concluded its work. Some of the objections to the earlier bills on mining hard minerals from the deep seabed were met. But critics pointed out that the self-denial of commercial mining before 1976, tied to a clause that the United States would guarantee such rights under any future regime, essentially thwarted the idea of international control.

In 1973, however, the Arab embargo on oil exports emphasized the dependence of the United States on foreign commodities and the dangers of both price escalation and political reprisals. With prompting from the mining industry and others interested in seabed exploitation, the attention of the Congress and the public focused on the fact that virtually all manganese and cobalt used in the United States in the mid-1970s was being imported; that about 70 percent of the nickel used came from foreign sources; and that the imports of copper, although the United States had the largest known reserve of the ore, amounted to about 15 percent of American use. By mining manganese nodules from the seabed, it was said, the United States could not only free itself from politically volatile sources of supply, but also greatly improve its international balance of payments, a persuasive argument in years when American energy imports and prices were skyrocketing.

On 14 November 1974 Deepsea Ventures actually filed a "Notice of Discovery and Claim of Exclusive Mining Rights" with the Secretary of State and requested diplomatic protection for the claim and investments in a tract of seabed in the East Central Pacific ocean. A year later testimony before the Subcommittee on Minerals, Materials, and Fuels of the Senate Interior and Insular Affairs Committee, indicated that at least three major groups (led by Tenneco, International Nickel, and Kennecott, with participation by British, Belgian, Japanese, and West German companies) might be ready to proceed to seabed mining if their legal rights were assured and their investments were protected against expropriation. Mining equipment had been tested in depths of 15,000 feet of water, and hydrometallurgical processes for obtaining metal from the nodules were available. To build prototype equipment for actual mining required a minimum capital of $300 million, a sum banks or investors were not likely to advance without greater assurances about the security of the property itself.

Again in April 1976 the Interior and Insular Affairs Committee looked favorably on a bill, S.713, that would have started seabed mining by American entrepreneurs. However, when the bill was referred to the Armed Services Committee, the Commerce Committee, and the Foreign Relations Committee of the Senate, none recommended it favorably, so that on 15 September 1976 the bill was removed from the Senate schedule.

The issue was hardly dead. Early in 1977 both the House Merchant Marine and Fisheries Committee and the International Relations Committee had bills before them on deep seabed mining. One emphasized the right of the United States to mine the seabed, with a system of mutual recognition of claims by other states; the other maintained that if no treaty on the international seabed area had been reached by 1980, the United States could proceed unilaterally to mining it.

What was at stake? Title to all the seabed of the world under all the oceans of the world beyond the rim of the national jurisdiction of states, an immense deep and dark area of unknown wealth. Would it be possible to place that potentially enormous asset, with uncertain consequences for control of the superjacent waters, under the jurisdiction of an international organization, whose composition and authority had to be determined? Would states submit to an arbitral or judicial settlement of disputes arising from the allocation of rights, the management of operations, or the distribution of rewards for all the seabed? Certainly the United States had to proceed with caution, recognizing that the appropriation of any part of the seabed beyond present national jurisdiction by a single state would challenge all the presumptions about the common heritage of mankind that had echoed through the chambers of the

United Nations and captured the imagination of millions of its own citizens. Yet realistically Washington had to acknowledge that delay and limitations of its own interests were being imposed by endless international negotiations and that an international management scheme might utterly fail to provide incentives for American industry to benefit American consumers.

6   Marine Pollution

Man and Nature

For the last quarter of a century the United States has confronted a fundamental value choice beset by ignorance, doubt, and fear: essentially, in what way and at what rate should the American economy be developed with what effect upon or at what cost to the balance of nature? Put another way, how can the maker of policy encourage a productive and prosperous life for the public while protecting the chemical and biological system of the earth that sustains plant and animal life, including *homo sapiens?*

Such questions are hardly so novel as they appear to a callow student fuming over dirty rivers and blighted cities. Yet because the magnitude of the issue has grown to national and international proportions, because the complexity of environmental degradation has increased with industrialization and advancing scientific knowledge, it is important to search back for the philosophical underpinnings that have determined the policymakers' choice. And it is equally important to examine the genesis of the American movement to curb abuses of the environment with their present effect on legislation, which is reordering the priorities of American society.

The giants of classical wisdom, Plato, Aristotle, and their disciples, had developed theories about the order and purpose of the universe many centuries before the modern controversy over the right relationship of man to his environment. Aristotle, for example, saw a clear purpose in nature, which strove to realize the end, the future, and the form for which all creatures had been designed. Thus, nothing in nature was incomplete or in vain. The Aristotelian conception of harmony in the universe, whether due to an omniscient creative God or some in-dwelling force of nature that was bent on teleological design, has persisted throughout human history. In the world of the twentieth century, ecologists, publicists, and politicians have alleged that man's insults to the biosphere and his disturbances of the balance of nature will have dire consequences. Although the language and the observations have been cast in "scientific" terms, the philosophical undertone on the essential harmony of nature still rings sweetly to the ear.

Not all the philosophers of antiquity, however, accepted the idea of the earth as a designed and appropriate environment for life. For Lucretius, with his Epicurean bias, the very imperfections of nature, which could be seen in the wasted deserts, the barren rocky crags, the superfluous oceans, and in the

211

characteristics of man himself, cast doubt on the portrayal of God as a beneficent harmonizer. Nothing, indeed, seemed to have been born for its own use or end, but rather whatever had been born seemed to have created the required skills, habits, or artifacts for its own survival. In the twentieth century, it is a matter of debate as to whether those profound adaptations of humans to the physical universe, as suggested by Lucretius, to maintain and develop society, have in fact endangered the life support of the species itself.

For centuries thoughtful men had been aware of the ways in which the forests, the plains, the shores, and the streams were altered by human cultivation and industry. In the earliest histories, for example, Herodotus and Strabo, writing about the Egyptians, had noted the way in which they had mastered the Nile with canals and embankments for the annual cultivation of the shores and for transportation on the river; Theophrastus had observed that changes of climate had occurred in Thessaly as a result of human intervention by the cutting of trees and the draining of marshes. Thus, even in ancient times geographers had commented on the ways by which agricultural and industrial man had reshaped nature to his purposes. But with small populations, limited sources of energy, and modest tools to scratch the surface of the earth, reshape rivers, or change the atmosphere the effects of human society upon nature seemed small and local.

Beginning with *Air, Waters, Places,* attributed to the physician Hippocrates, a long line of classical scholars had also commented on the effects of the environment on human health, as well as temperament, culture, and social organization. To climate, in particular, the characteristics of individual and national indolence or activity had been attributed. The passivity or inventiveness, the ferocity or gentleness, the freedom or slavery of different peoples in different locations were examined in the light of different climates and terrains. Aristotle wrote extensively on the influence of climate. Plato, Aquinas, and Bodin all dealt with the necessity of having law-givers who appreciated the nature of their people and the physical conditions that shaped their environment. Again these commentaries were analytical of the effects of environment on men and society, but they could hardly deal with man's deliberate alteration of nature on a large scale.

From the fifteenth to the eighteenth centuries such European discoveries as the motions of the planets, the new continents on the earth with strange peoples, the reproductive and circulatory systems of animals, and hundreds of other "natural" phenomena gradually deflated the physico-theological concept of God the Designer or Nature the Harmonizer. More and more, man himself was thrust forward by philosophers as the rectifier and arbiter of nature. Man was seen as the creature best suited to comprehend and tame a savage world and to unlock the resources of the planet's wealth by modifying its physical environment. Thus, the clearing of forests, the damming of floods, the draining of swamps, the burrowing of the earth, and the building of canals all attested to human ingenuity, industry, and power to shape the environment. In particular, Montesquieu, whose works emphasized the effect of climate and other geographical factors upon man and his society wrote in *De l'Ėspirit des Lois,* "Mankind by their industry and by the influence of good laws, have rendered the earth more proper for their abode."

Epitomized by Montesquieu, theories of the effect of climate or environment on religion, customs, habits, and character were remarkably revived in the eighteenth century. An English physician, John Arbuthnot, reaching back to Hippocrates, wrote an essay in 1731, *Effects of Air on Human Bodies,* analyzing the influence of heat, cold, humidity, and blood circulation on the human body, which led to generalizations about national characteristics. Others like Hume and Kant, dealt with the influence of climate as well as human activities on physical changes of the earth. As early as 1760 Hugh Williamson read a paper before the American Philosophical Society alleging that the climate of Pennsylvania and the neighboring coastal colonies had changed over forty years due to the clearing of land and suggesting ways in which the climate might be altered to gain more moderate temperatures and salubrious airs.

The most pervasive analysis of the ways in which men had modified their environment up to the nineteenth century, however, was the work of Comte de (Georges-Louis de Clerc) Buffon in 40 volumes *Histoire Naturelle, Générale et Particulière,* published in Paris between 1749 and 1804. Buffon's enormous curiosity and diligence led to infinite observations of the entwinement of nature and man, whether it involved the clearing of forests, the cultivation of plants, the domestication of animals, the channelling of rivers, or the mining of minerals. Central to his thought was the improvement of man as he mastered the wildness of nature, domesticated the savage environment, and bent the earth and its creatures to the betterment of civilization. Buffon recognized the need to conserve resources, like forests, after the necessary clearance for agriculture and climatic improvement, and he also wistfully admitted that men had depleted wild animal life, including marine species, such as the seals and the walruses, which had apparently been driven to deserted coasts and the extremities of the continents. Nevertheless, in that age of enlightenment, with its sublime faith in human progress, preached by contemporaries like Rousseau, Condorcet, and Goodwin, the Comte de Buffon perceived nature as malleable to human use, to be improved by human intelligence, tools, and industry. For Buffon the history of man was the productive domination of the earth's environment.[1]

Nevertheless, at the very moment when western European society seemed to be taking its greatest leap forward in a rise of material living standards by the application of human intelligence to the exploitation of natural resources, doubts about such progress started. The first dramatic caution on a large and theoretical scale came in 1798, when the thirty-two-year-old Thomas Malthus argued that men too were limited by the forces of nature and that "progress" depended on finite resources of the earth. Basically Malthus saw the reproductive drive of all living things tending to outrun their food supply and therefore level down their economic gains. This phenomenon would either limit or deny progress. Other scholars had also analyzed population growth. The law of diminishing returns was not a new principle for economists. But Malthus dramatically brought the relationship of resources, population growth, and the advance of human society into public discussion, with some of the same strengths and weaknesses of argument that was to characterize all future debate on the subject.

Malthus had focused on population and food supply. Others had generally noted the depletion of natural resources. Throughout the Middle Ages and early modern times many keen farmers, gamekeepers, hunters, herdsmen, and administrators of feudal or royal estates, for example, had observed the use and abuse of forests as they had been cut and cleared for fuel, construction, and agricultural fields. Climatic and erosion effects on the environment did not go unnoticed. Moreover, individual commentaries on soil exhaustion and on some of the side effects of artificial dams or drainage projects appeared from time to time. From the Middle Ages onward forest preserve laws had been enacted, mostly to maintain the game and other forest goods of the privileged nobility and the prelates of the Church, although in the seventeenth century the King of France himself decreed the preservention of forests to conserve the wood so badly needed for fuel and ship's timber.

Until 1864, however, no one had comprehensively examined woods, waters, and sands as modified by human action. Then George Perkins Marsh sounded an alarm: although man must dominate nature, he had "too long forgotten that the earth was given to him for usufruct, not for consumption, still less for profligate waste." Marsh was an extraordinary man who wrote an extraordinary book, *Man and Nature.* He influenced generations of conservationists, and he must surely be regarded as the American pioneer of the twentieth-century movement to protect the human environment. Professor, lawyer, U.S. Congressman, print collector, architectural authority, master linguist, philologist, ambassador to Italy for twenty-one years, Marsh was a person of prodigious talents and great intellectual curiosity. He made it clear to every reader that man, by his actions in reshaping nature to his own uses, could destroy nature. Man could leave barren hills never to be forested again, vast deserts never to flower again. Following the intellectual tradition from Aristotle to Buffon, Marsh had originally entitled his work, "Man the Disturber of Nature's Harmonies." He too believed that there was a balance in the earth's natural environment. As an American of the nineteenth century, however, he felt neither repugnance nor despair about the economic activities of people in their search for progress. But Marsh wanted to illuminate the notion that consciously or unconsciously men were destroying their patrimony, that the great power of man to alter his environment could throw nature into disequilibrium and thus destroy the heritage of a bountiful earth for the coming generations.

Marsh had faith in the power of science and agricultural technology to increase the food supply to meet population growth, and he exonerated a certain measure of transformation of the terrestrial surface by man as necessary for subsistence and a rise to higher potentials of life. But he argued that man was going too far: he noted the wanton felling of forests without leaving belts of woodland for spontaneous propagation; the destruction of mountain reservoirs that fed streams and the failure to maintain cisterns and canals; the loss of the thin top soil by poor cultivation and erosion; the killing of semiaquatic plants that skirted the coasts and checked the spreading of dunes; and the dispersion or death of birds that preyed upon the insects most harmful to harvests.[2]

Deforestation and overgrazing received most of Marsh's attention, soil exhaustion rather little, and the problem of nonrenewable resources, such as minerals and fuels, none at all. Yet he laid the foundation for the conservation movement in America—and from that concern with the balance of nature on land it was a short step to discover the effect of human activities on rivers, estuaries, and the great oceans themselves.

In 1873 the American Association for the Advancement of Science first petitioned Congress to conserve the natural resources of the United States. Not until the last quarter of the nineteenth century, however, did the public begin to recognize the importance of trees and forests to human ecology. In fact, as late as 1885 there had been practically no forestry management in the United States. But thanks to the work of Gifford Pinchot and others, by 1897 a legal base for the U.S. national forest system had been laid, allowing the President to set aside reserves and to license prudently their productive use. Under President Theodore Roosevelt, moreover, the conservation of natural resources became a watchword. The U.S. Forest Service was established in 1905, and all forest reserves were transferred from the Interior Department to the Department of Agriculture. The national forest reserve increased from 43 million acres in 1901 to 194 million acres in 1910, while another 85 million acres in mineral lands in Alaska were set aside for conservation. The Reclamation Act of 1902 brought millions of acres of flooded land under the protection of dams and provided irrigation for arid fields with funds derived from the sale of public lands. Finally, the Antiquities Act of 1906 empowered the President to reserve areas that contained scientific and historic features of national importance.

In his Conservation Message of 1907 President Rossevelt said, "The conservation of our natural resources and their proper use constitute the fundamental problem which underlies almost every other problem of our national life" and "we must substitute a planned and orderly development of our resources in place of a haphazard striving for profits." In addition to forest preservation, flood control, and irrigation laws, Roosevelt established fifty-one national bird sanctuaries and transferred the disappearing American buffalo stocks to both Yellowstone Park and the National Bison Range in Montana.

President William Howard Taft, buffeted by the complaints of timber and mineral interests in the West, which were reflected in Congressional pressures, did not bring Roosevelt's dramatic leadership to the progressive movement and yielded more easily to the doctrine of "states rights" against federal intervention. Conservation was not abandoned by Taft, but it was tempered. Although conservationists fumed against some Taft appointments and several scandals erupted over the spoliation of natural resources by big business expansion, trusts, and monopolies, the Weeks Act of 1911 enabled the federal government to cooperate with states in preventing floods and soil erosion. Moreover, Taft set aside in 1912 the Naval Oil Reserves, as America sped into a new age of energy with petroleum as a major source of power—and pollution.

The political support for the early twentieth-century conservation movement in America, however, came paradoxically from two camps: the followers of the gospel of efficiency who saw great material benefits for society in the wise planning, utilization, and thorough exploitation of resources; and the followers of the gospel of esthetics, who perceived beauty, harmony, and tranquility in nature as necessary to spiritual well-being. On the one hand, engineers saw in conservation better ways to control floods, irrigate farms, increase agriculture, expand industrial production, facilitate transportation, and raise the power of machines to do labor; on the other hand, many upper- and middle-class citizens viewed conservation as the way of restoring nature's beauties maintaining a cultural heritage, providing parks for repose and recreation, reducing industrial blights, urban congestions, and limiting the mad drive for economic development through resource exploitation.

Men like Pinchot were not unconscious about the preservation of natural scenery and historic sites, but such a goal in their view was definitely subordinate to the scientific management of timber to sustain an optimum yield. Members of the General Federation of Women's Clubs and the Daughters of the American Revolution, among others at this time, were not unaware of the economic facts of life, but they deplored commercial development as an exaggeration of materialism in American life. They sought to save resources from use rather than to exploit them further—even if more rationally. Like other pieces of legislation under representative government, the early twentieth-century conservation measures were passed by combinations of constituencies with rather different objectives in mind.[3]

World War I and World War II were ten years of monstrous waste of resources—both human and material. During the twenty-one years intervening between these calamities, the leading nations of the world were frantic to rebuild and develop their economies. Especially during the Great Depression governments were desperate to increase the demand for goods and services and to raise living standards at almost any price.

President Franklin D. Roosevelt's philosophy on the conservation of resources paralleled that of his distant cousin Theodore Roosevelt. But the time and reasons for conservation in the 1930s were different. The purchasing power of American farmers had declined some 50 percent between 1929 and July 1932; industry was operating at only one-half the volume of 1929; and monthly wages had dropped 40 percent as the average number of unemployed workers in 1932 hovered about twelve million. In 1933 the Civilian Conservation Corps was established to put young men to work on reforestation, soil erosion, flood control, and other public works projects. When the most devastating drought of American history in the Midwest further dramatized the effects of soil erosion by turning farms into dustbowls in 1935, Stuart Chase wrote that the continental soil was widely and rapidly declining and that the skin of America had been laid open. He warned that the forest cover had been stripped away and the natural grass cover had been torn to ribbons by the steel plow and the hooves of cattle. "Streams have lost their measured balance, and, heavy with silt, run wild in flood to the sea at certain seasons, to fall to miserable trickles in drier months." In the same year Paul B. Sears wrote that man was attempting to rule the earth as a god might do, not only seeking what he needs, but manipulating everything about him. "He no longer accepts, as living creatures before him have done, the pattern in which he finds himself, but has destroyed that pattern and from the wreck is attempting to create a new one. That, of course, is cataclysmic revolution." Sears foresaw the need for taxation by the government to encourage the good management of soil. The conserver of resources would be "a trustee for the future" and assisted by subsidies while the despoiler of nature's heritage would be penalized.

The Roosevelt Administration had created a U.S. National Resources Commission to collect data and plan the use of natural and human resources. Legislation for flood control through dams, financed by federal monies under the authority of regional river basin commissions, had also provided cheap hydroelectric power to impoverished rural communities. Furthermore, the Soil Conservation and Domestic Allowance Act of 1936 sought the restriction of agricultural production and a renewed fertility of the farmlands. But valuable as all these actions were to the environment, their main object was to increase employment and revive the economy. Water pollution due to poor sewerage also became a political issue in the 1930s yet hardly aroused a nation in economic distress. The administration's policy was to advocate grants-in-aid to local communities and loans to industries to help them control their wastes, but Roosevelt rejected federal water quality standards and felt that regulation should be left to the states or interstate compacts, particularly under regional water authorities.

By 1939, however, the country was forced to concentrate on the threat of worldwide conflict and the need to mobilize resources, increase production, and manufacture arms with scant attention to environmental consequences. On 5 January President Roosevelt presented a budget for Fiscal Year 1940 to Congress that called for $1.32 billion for defense, and only seven days later he asked for an additional $500 million for national security. Thereafter, the output of American coal, oil, timber, food, and minerals for the Allies and the U.S. war effort was prodigious, only measurable in terms of sacrifice and victory, not environmental costs.

No sooner had the din of battle died down, however, than new prophets warning of the damage to nature by man's activity appeared on the American scene. The arguments, however, had now acquired a far more philosophical dimension due to the speculations of a number of scientists. In truth, the political battles over the conservation of resources in the early twentieth century had stemmed from the plain historical observations of Marsh and his successors over the ruin of forests, farms, beaches, streams, and wildlife, which had been visible to everyone. But science began to pose far more profound questions about the nature of the universe and the relation of organic life to it.

The end of the nineteenth century had witnessed the general acceptance of Darwin's natural selection principle, with its brilliant explanation of the way in which organisms throughout history had adapted to their environment. Then, in 1915, Lawrence J. Henderson wrote a remarkably seminal work, *The Fitness of the Environment,* which was subtitled "an inquiry into the biological significance of the properties of matter." Henderson suggested that no one had yet speculated "if by chance the material universe also may be subject to laws which are in the largest sense important in organic evolution." After examining the unique characteristics of water and carbon dioxide, as well as the elements of carbon, hydrogen, and oxygen, Henderson concluded, "The properties of matter and the course of cosmic evolution are now seen to be intimately related to the structure of the living being and to its activities . . . the biologist may now rightly regard the universe in its very essence as biocentric."

In the spring of 1933 Harold F. Blum discussed Henderson's book with his class in General Physiology at the University of California. Thereafter Blum began to concentrate on the relationship between the second law of thermodynamics and organic evolution. In August 1950 he finished *Time's Arrow and Evolution,* which contained a chapter entitled, "The Fitness of the Environment." Blum pictured evolution as a great tapestry that had a strong unyielding warp formed by the essential nature of elementary nonliving matter, including the way in which it had been brought together on this planet and wherein the second law of thermodynamics played a predominant role. The tapestry of evolution also had a woof, which had been formed by mutation and natural selection and which showed the beauty and the variety of ways in which organisms fit their environments. Following Darwin, scientific inquiry had been directed toward the woof, but the warp actually established the dimensions and supported the whole process. Blum wrote, ". . . this life-stuff is something to be cherished as our proper heritage. . . . It should be guarded from destruction by the activity of man who, as a species of the living system, has risen to power and dominance through his intelligence." Blum concluded that the very development of man had apparently given this particular system of evolution the ability to determine its own destiny to a certain extent, although he glumly noted that there were all too many signs that man at the moment lacked the ability to exercise the self-control that might be necessary for survival.

The term "biosphere," meanwhile, had been popularized in international circles by V. I. Vernadsky in 1926 through his book *Biosfera*. He too followed the notion that man was inseparably connected to the material and energetic structure of the atmosphere, waters, and earth of the planet. Vernadsky posed an important policy question: how should man, with all his molding and manipulating activities, reconstruct the biosphere "in the interest of freely-thinking humanity as a totality." Such ideas were further stitched together in the 1950s by the Catholic paleontologist-philosopher Pierre Teilhard de Chardin in a metaphysical system that was based on the preeminent significance of man in nature and the organic nature of mankind. Recognizing the deep disturbance that human society had inflicted on the biosphere through the economic domination of nature, Teilhard saw hope by pooling and unifying the knowledge of mankind as the species sought, in an evolutionary way, to reach its full potential. Thus, he concluded, "it is not so much on the quantity of our economic resources, but rather on the increased intensity of our reflective and affective powers that the ultimate success or failure of humanity depends."[4]

For most Americans, however, the dramatic prose of people like William Voigt on similar themes received greater attention. In 1948 Voigt argued that the United States was face to face with a serious depletion of resource capital. Noting that 286 million acres of land had been destroyed for crops and ranges, he deplored the wastes of gas, water, and metals. In a preface to Voigt's book, *The Road to Survival*, Bernard Baruch wrote, "mankind must reach a sound, healthy relationship with its total environment." Voigt then urged that men find a "favorite biophysical relationship to the earth." Neither the word "ocean" or "sea" appeared in the index of the book.

In 1952 Fairfield Osborn, primarily worried about soil erosion, repeated the idea that "man is part of one great biological scheme," and that he must recognize the sovereignty of nature, or destroy his own life source. Osborn said that "the tide of the earth's population is rising, the reservoir of the earth's living resources is failing." A year later Samuel H. Ordway, Jr. took issue with the prevailing dogma that growth was the bulwark of American strength, that expansion was the very essence of the development of the United States, and that any other policy opposed to growth would mean stagnation and decay. These views had been vigorously espoused by such leaders as the President of the U.S. Steel Company and the Secretary of the Department of Interior, as well as in the Report of the Paley Commission at that time. Ordway's book, *Resources and the American Dream*, included a chapter entitled "The Limits of Growth," and he wrote that growth must give way to a "truer, less aggressive faith that to prosper we do not need more than the earth produces," and concluded that consumption must be limited to a continuing supply.[5]

The beginnings of the post–World War II environmental protection movement, however, may be traced to those nuclear physicists who were deeply concerned that the very weapons that had so remarkably changed the dimensions of international power might also alter or destroy the human race. Their anxieties, at first stemming from the grim prospect of the permanent maiming of populations by an atomic bomb dropped in battle, were increased by evidence that radioactive particles, as a result of testing in the atmosphere in the 1950s, might be accumulating in the food chain. Example of radiostrontium found in the bones of young chilren tended to support this fear.

The U.S. Congress had decisively placed responsibility for the further development of atomic weapons into the civilian hands of the Atomic Energy Commission in 1946. But the atmospheric testing of weapons continued. Between 1946 and 1963 the United States conducted 256 tests; the Soviet Union 145; Great Britain 23; and France 5. Moreover, the intention of industry to build nuclear-fueled electric power stations aroused further alarm about radioactive fallouts, runoffs, and accidental explosions. While the Bulletin of the Atomic Scientists continued to draw attention to the consequences of nuclear explosions and nuclear energy uses, other groups, such as the St. Louis Committee for Atomic Information formed by the biologist Barry Commoner,[6] and other scientists, such as the microbiologist Rene' Dubos, took an increasing interest in the environment and the means of educating the public to dangers of abusing man's habitat.[7]

On 10 October 1963 a treaty banning nuclear weapon tests in the atmosphere, in outer space, and under water (but not underground), including the high seas, entered into force between the United States and the Soviet Union. The treaty ended for the moment the extraordinary danger of radioactive fallout from experimental explosions, although France was not a party and continued its atmospheric testing over the high seas. Some of the groups that had originally started to alert the public to radioactive contamination widened their interests to other insults to the environment: for example, the St. Louis Committee for Atomic Information became the St. Louis Committee for Environmental Information in 1964.

Meanwhile, the United States continued to grow: from 150 million people in 1950 to 180 million people in 1960; in one decade the output of refined petroleum products rose from 2,190 to 3,119 billion barrels per year and the net generation of electricity by fuels soared from 232,813 to 640,178 million kilowatt hours. A striking change also occurred in American agriculture as a consequence of better technology and management, involving genetics, irrigation, fertilizers, and pest controls. From 1946 to 1950 it had taken an average of more than 70 million acres of farms to produce a little more than one million bushels of wheat annually. But from 1956 to 1960 only 50 million farmed acres produced about the same amount of wheat. Productivity per acre also increased in several other crops. The total acreage planted with cotton, for example, was reduced by one-third between the late 1940s and the late 1950s, yet more than 12 billion bales continued to be harvested each year. Part of this increased agricultural output was due to the phenomenal increase in the use of synthetic pesticides. The production of pesticides in the United States rose from 124,259,000 pounds in 1947 to 637,666,000 pounds in 1960. Moreover, from 1950 to 1960 the number of acres sprayed by chemicals from the air increased almost 56 percent to cover some 50 million acres. In liquid form alone the amount of pesticides sprayed increased from 49 million gallons to 113 million gallons.[8]

This extravagant application of pesticides to the soil, with its consequential fallout or transfer to streams and rivers as well as to human settlements opened a new and dramatic chapter in the historical dialogue between the exponents of economic progress and the exponents of balance between man and the physical environment.[9] A series of three articles by Rachel Carson in the *New Yorker* magazine beginning in June 1962 gave a dramatic impetus to the environmental protection movement of the 1960s and 1970s.

Carson, a marine biologist and science writer and editor-in-chief of the United States Fish and Wildlife Service, had first achieved a national reputation in 1951 with her book, *The Sea around Us.* Although three pages were devoted to the latent petroleum resources in the seabed, the index of the book did not contain any words like "contamination," "pollution," "chlorinated hydro-carbons," "environment," and so forth. The subject was simply not considered by Carson in her poetic-scientific descriptions of the marine ecosystem. Ten years later, however, with exquisite literary skill, she took up the theme of man's modification of the environment in the twentieth century. Focusing on the item of "some six hundred basic chemicals . . . created for the purpose of killing insects, weeds, rodents" and other pests between 1945 and 1960, Carson dramatically invented a future time when, due to insecticides and pesticides, the cattle would die, the flowers would not bloom to nourish fruit, fish would perish in streams, vegetation would wither, people would be sick, and no birds would sing. It would be a "silent spring."[10]

Carson had gathered many disturbing reports on the effects of dichloro-diphenyl-trichloro-ethane (DDT), chlordane, dieldrin, aldrin, endrin, parathion, malathion, arsenic, phenols, and other chemicals on the basic food chains of nature and the health of domesticated animals, wild life, and human beings. Her message came through with a shock to the sophisticated readers of the *New Yorker,* "The most alarming of all man's assaults upon the environment is the contamination of the air, earth, rivers, and seas with dangerous, and even lethal, materials."

Carson did not contend that moderate chemical controls should never be used in any circumstances, but rather that their use ought to be reduced to a minimum and that biological controls should be developed. Her final words were a ringing challenge that public officials "in an era dominated by industry" should declare public welfare to be more important than dollars. Only then would there be relief "from this poisoning of the environment."

Thus, following the path of Marsh, Chase, Sears, Voigt, Osborn, and others, who had warned of the consequences of man's insult to natural resources, Carson had raised a bold, bright banner against pollution of the environment. Many American public interest groups quickly joined the call for the reform of industrial and agricultural technologies, and the "environmentalists" soon made a remarkable impact on public policy, both nationally and internationally.

In 1954 only one lobbyist in Washington was registered specifically to influence environmental legislation. By 1969 some thirty organizations interested in conserving nature or protecting the environment in one way or another had registered as lobbyists. True, a number of state laws had been enacted in the late 1960s which were aimed at abuses of land, water, and air. But national attention focused on the environment only a few days after the inauguration of Richard M. Nixon as President in 1969 when a disastrous oil well blowout off the coast of Santa Barbara caused an 800 square-mile ocean slick. In May the President created a Cabinet-level interagency Environmental Quality Council. Moreover, the Senate, on 10 July, and the House of Representatives on 23 September, approved far-reaching bills that were finally adjusted and passed on 20–22 December (P.L.91-190) as the National Environmental Policy Act (NEPA).

NEPA, which the President signed on 1 January 1970, declared that it was the national policy of the United States to protect the environment. It required every federal agency henceforth to take environmental impacts into account in any of its programs and to provide statements of such impacts to a new three-member Council on Environmental Quality in the Office of the President. The Council had general oversight of environmental policies and might recommend legislation to the Congress. The President was also required to make an annual report on the environmental quality of the nation. About his first report on the environment, as transmitted to Congress in August 1970, the President said, "It represents the first time in the history of nations that a people had paused, consciously and systematically, to take comprehensive stock of the quality of its surroundings." The President then went on to crystallize all the previous warnings of naturalists, scientists, and philosophers in the past by stating that man had been too cavalier in relations with nature and that unless he arrested the depredations that had been made upon the systems of nature, the United States would face an ecological disaster.

President Nixon had also said that historians might one day regard 1970 as the "year of the environment." The administration proposed on 10 February 1970 a thirty-seven-point program for environmental improvement and twenty-nine specific proposals for legislation. A remarkable number of environmental laws and agency reorganizations were approved during the next month. One of the most notable was Reorganization Plan 3, which the President submitted to Congress in July 1970, which created the Environmental Protection Agency

(EPA). Among other things EPA was given responsibility for setting standards for and monitoring air and water pollution, pesticides, certain radiation emissions, and solid waste management that had been under the Department of the Interior, the Department of Health, Education, and Welfare, and the Department of Agriculture, the Atomic Energy Commission, and the Federal Radiation Council. Responsibility for general oversight and coordination of environmental policies of the federal government was left to the Council on Environmental Quality.

In 1972 six major bills on the environment cleared the 92d Congress, a truly historical record, reflecting both the national will and the exuberant international mood that led to the UN Conference on the Human Environment in Stockholm in June of the same year. The Federal Water Pollution Control Act Amendments (P.L.92-500), the Marine Protection, Research, and Sanctuaries (Ocean Dumping) Act (P.L.92-532), the Coastal Zone Management Act (P.L.92-583), the Noise Control Act (P.L.92-574) the Pesticides Regulation Act (P.L.92-516), and the Sea Mammals Protection Act (P.L.92-522) were remarkable that year. And there were other acts, such as the Port and Waterways Safety Act (P.L.92-340), which set standards for vessels carrying hazardous cargo, and P.L.92-421 which authorized $65 million a year over fifteen years for reforestation, that affected the environment in the United States.

Not everyone had been enamoured of conferring broad regulatory powers over industry, commerce, construction, and other private or local public activities on a federal agency in the name of the environment. Some had held that the proofs of environmental degradation by scientific method were inconclusive or contradictory; others measured the need for economic development, as a part of human progress, against the obvious changes in the environment and found the costs to be reasonable. In testifying against the Reorganization Plan 3 that created the Environmental Protection Agency in 1970, a sanitary engineering consultant of long experience, John E. Kinney, said, ". . . I think with the emotional and political climate, undoubtedly the reorganization will go through as something which is a step in the right direction. I am reminded of the old remark that if you do not know where you are going, it does not make any difference which road you take."

In fact, a sharp change in attitudes did take place in 1973 for at the beginning of that year there seemed to be ample energy for all Americans to prosper with strict environmental controls. However, at the end of the year gasoline and fuel oil prices had skyrocketed, affecting every facet of American life that enjoyed cheap lighting, heating, factory power, and transportation. Not only had the rate of the demand for energy, particularly natural gas, fuel oil and gasoline been increasing in the United States beyond the rate of growth of national reserves, but the petroleum exporting countries in the Middle East, Southeast Asia, and Latin America had united in the Organization of Petroleum Exporting Countries (OPEC) to demand substantially higher prices for their resources. The administration responded by seeking to decontrol the price of natural gas, increase the exploitation of offshore petroleum resources, consider the construction of deepwater terminals off the coast of the United States in order to accommodate very large oil tankers, and expand appropriations for research and development of other forms of energy. Significantly the only bill on the environment to clear Congress in 1973 was an act to protect certain endangered species of wildlife.

In the past decades shrill alarms have been raised about radioactive elements, chlorinated hydrocarbons, oil, heavy metals, and other potentially noxious materials that have fallen or been washed or deposited into the environment through man's activities. Clearly some of the evidence has been poetically exaggerated rather than scientifically linked to objective conclusions. Moreover, the economic costs have been far more burdensome than propagandists would admit or the public would bear if given a simple choice. Nevertheless, the history of the past decades seem to indicate a slow reordering of the value system of American activities with respect to choices between economic productivity and the preservation of a healthy and agreeable environment.

The consequences of this shift of attitude in the United States—whether wrongly foisted upon the government or rightly recognized to be in the interest of a greater public good—could be extravagant. Although Americans may be willing to pay the economic costs for an improved quality of life in their own land, sea, and air, other countries with other value systems could make comparative economic and military gains, not only detrimental, but even destructive to the American way of life. Only international cooperation ending in international agreements to fix minimum standards for all states of the world could provide a way out of that dilemma.

Sewage and Oil in the Rivers

From the most ancient times people have been plainly aware of the need to dispose of their wastes and to provide in closely settled communities some means for burying or transporting urine and fecal matter out of sight, touch, and smell. Babylon, Ninevah, and Jerusalem, as well as the later Greek and Roman cities, had sewers, which were often great underground drains. But such sewers were not connected to private buildings, which had their own cesspools, and the bulk of the poor population used public latrines or gutters that were washed, more or less, sooner or later, into the sewers. From the beginning of the Christian era to the middle of the nineteenth century there was practically no progress in sewerage.

With their primitive knowledge of medicine the public authorities of the Middle Ages in Europe never properly connected disease with water pollution. Yet any sensitive person could observe the noisesome effects of human waste, garbage, and other dumpings of spoils on neighboring properties, streets, and highways. Streams running into rivers and out to the sea were the natural sewers of civilization. For the drainage of those ditches and sewers that ran into the streams and rivers, however, landowners and townships were held responsible. For example, many appeals against negligence of such public works in England went to the King in medieval times. However, once waste or refuse had reached the Ouse, the Humber, the Lea, or the Thames, there was, considering the small population and little industry, no public interest in the condition of the river water, let alone the apparently bottomless, heaving ocean. Several statutes on local drainage were approved under the Tudor dynasty, and, in fact, the legal basis for all sanitary works of sewage in England up to the middle of the nineteenth century depended on a statute passed in 1531, amended during the reign of William and Mary.[11]

In 1832, however, cholera invaded England, claiming 6729 lives in London alone. Fifteen years later, alarmed by word of a new outbreak of cholera in India, a Royal Commission was appointed to inquire into the sanitation of London. In 1847 John Phillips made the first comprehensive engineering study of the sewerage needs of the city of London and observed that thousands of houses emptied into stinking, overflowing cesspools with no drainage whatsoever. "I have visited very many places where filth was lying scattered about the rooms, vaults, cellars, areas, and yards, so deep that it was hardly possible to move for it," and ". . . human beings living and sleeping in sunk rooms with filth from overflowing cesspools exuding through and running down the walls and over the floors . . ." According to Phillips, hundreds of streets, courts, and alleys lacked any drains or sewers, and "how the miserable inhabitants live in such places it is hard to tell."

The stench of the Thames in the seventeenth century had been so foul that King James threatened to move the court to Windsor while Queen Anne, in the next century, found the river so rancid that she considered transferring Parliament from London to Oxford. And in the nineteenth century, during the reign of Queen Victoria, sheets dipped in chlorine were hung from the windows of Parliament to mask the smell rising from the putrid Thames.

During the cholera epidemic in London in 1848–1849, all the water companies delivered their water to the city without filtration. They took tide-water from the Thames, which, at that time, was subject not only to all the sewage impurities of London, but also the discharges into the river from the banks about the city. During the cholera epidemic of 1853–1854 it was finally demonstrated that in those parts of London that had used water taken from river areas not subject to the direct influence of sewage, the inhabitants had suffered far less than in other parts of the city to which less pure river water had been delivered.

In Paris until the middle of the eighteenth century all the drains were uncovered, generally carrying off the contents of the streets through a conduit in the middle of the road into a great drain and thence into the Seine. The first comprehensive effort to study the needs of the city for sewerage seem to have been made about 1808, but the ravages of cholera in 1832, as in London, finally awakened the authorities to the need for a more sanitary system. From 1833 onwards new, six-foot high sewers, of legendary fame in Parisian crime stories, were built underground.

Early sewers, whether at public expense or private responsibility, were not designed for the removal of excreta, but solely for the rain waters washing down from roofs and collecting in the streets. London sewers did not collect human wastes until 1815, nor in Boston until 1833; and Paris sewers were filled only by rainwater and street washings until 1880. In Baltimore in 1922 there were still some 20,000 houses that had no connection to the public sewers. Linked to the discussion over the merits and problems of separate sewerage for rain-water-washed wastes and human excretions by the engineering experts were a number of experiments that used sewage to obtain nutrients beneficial to agriculture through its irrigation on farm lands. This method could also provide useful disposal sites that put fewer pollutants directly into the streams. But the rapid growth of towns and cities in the nineteenth century, with rising land values close to population centers, not to mention some noisesome effects, tended to discourage this trend.

In the United States, endowed with ample land in its early history, with many streams discharging into rivers that moved briskly into the oceans, and with inexpensive building materials to construct simple channels, the disposal of sewage gained no widespread public attention until almost the end of the nineteenth century. Indeed, the first systematic and large-scale inquiry on American sewerage took place in 1875. The Massachusetts State Board of Health, which had discussed the sewerage of towns and the pollution of rivers generally in previous annual meetings, was empowered by the General Court (legislature) of Massachusetts to investigate the correct method of drainage and sewerage of the cities and towns of the Commonwealth. The Board was also charged to examine the pollution of rivers, estuaries, and ponds. Thereafter, James P. Kirkwood, a civil engineer of Brooklyn, New York, made a special report to the Board in which the results of replies to a circular sent to all the cities and to 169 towns were analyzed.

Forty streams and eleven ponds in Massachusetts were receiving sewage. Although forty-eight cities and towns, embracing about one million people, had provided partial or complete water supplies, only half of them had provided even partially for the removal of such water by sewers. Forty-six cities and towns reported that their present methods of dealing with sewage were objectionable and nineteen reported that their sewage "seriously pollutes the atmosphere." One hundred and twenty reported wet or damp cellars from inadequate drainage. In Salem, Lynn, Haverhill, Worcester, and Boston, with its adjacent cities, the nuisance from putrefying sewage incompletely removed had become a serious evil.

"In all these cases," said the report, "the law fails to provide a prompt and efficient remedy." The report also recognized the problem of industrial pollution of streams, such as the runoffs from the tanneries of Worcester, and commented that certain small streams in New England had already become unfit for any domestic (household) purpose.[12]

Some of the recommendations to the Massachusetts General Court finally adopted by the Board of Health were that no city or town should be allowed to discharge sewage into any water course or pond without first purifying it "according to the best process at present known;" that no sewage, processed or not, be allowed to enter any pond or stream used for domestic purposes; that the irrigation of sewage upon the land be undertaken experimentally; and that laws should be provided for cases of serious annoyance arising from the proved defective disposal of sewage. However, the experts and the Board also recommended that no sweeping laws for the general and immediate purification of all the streams were warranted or justifiable.

The State Board of Health of Massachusetts, in retrospect, need not have feared any overzealous legislation: good sewerage was costly, and representative governments moved slowly, if at all, on public expenditures that could not be connected to an absolute immediate danger or a proved commercial-industrial gain. The first extensive sewage treatment plant in the United States, using chemical precipitation, was not completed in Worcester, Massachusetts until fourteen years after the 1875 report of the Board of Health. And in other less developed states of the Union, lacking the industry and population density of Massachusetts, progress toward a safe, healthy, efficient disposal of sewage was even slower.

Resort to the common law, whether by individuals or communities, for relief against water pollution proved ponderous and offered little help. At the beginning of the twentieth century, for example, the State of Missouri tried for several years to prevent the Sanitary District of Chicago and the State of Illinois from draining Chicago's sewage into the Des Plaines River (previously carried into Lake Michigan) thence to the Illinois into the Mississippi. Carrying its plea for an injunction to the Supreme Court of the United States, Illinois failed to receive any satisfaction. The Court studiously examined the conflicting opinion of experts, but found them to "differ as to the time and distance within which a stream would purify itself." While the Court accepted the prevailing scientific explanation of the cause of typhoid fever, the statistics on the incidence of death along the Mississippi river from the disease were strongly contested. River pollution of this kind, of course, had never been recognized by the old common law, since there was "no visible increase in filth, no new smell." Indeed, the defendants alleged that the Mississippi river water had been improved by the mixture of large volumes of Lake Michigan water into the discharge of the Sanitary District canal. In sum, the Court said, "What the future may develop of course we cannot tell. But our conclusion upon the evidence is that the case proved falls so far below the allegations of the bill that it is not brought within the principles heretofore established in the cause."[13]

Similarly, in 1921, when the State of New York sought to enjoin the State of New Jersey and the Passaic Valley Sewerage Commissioners from discharging sewage into the Upper Bay, the Supreme Court commented that regrettably "any forecast as to what the effect would be of the treatment . . . for this large volume of sewage must depend almost entirely upon the conflicting evidence of expert witnesses," who only agreed upon one point: namely, that the best index of pollution by organic substances was the amount of dissolved oxygen in the water. The Court, therefore, found that the complainant had failed to prove that the discharge of the sewage would create a public nuisance by causing offensive odors or unsightly deposits on the surface or that it would seriously add to the pollution of it.

Apart from sewage, the discharge of refuse from ships and shore into the streams of the United States was a long-standing problem. The Army Corps of Engineers had been asked by Congress as early as 1824 to improve the navigation of American waters and thereafter the Corps had conducted a number of hydrographic studies towards that end. In 1877 the Chief of Engineers and the Secretary of the War Department called to the attention of Congress some of the instances of serious injury to navigable waters that were due to the discharge of sawmill wastes into streams and the harm to harbors and channels caused by deposits of ballast, steamboat ashes, oysters, and rubbish from passing vessels. The first national regulation of discharges into American rivers stemming from the federal power over interstate commerce and navigable waters resulted from an Act of Congress in 1886 to make appropriations "for the construction, repair and preservation of certain public works on rivers and harbors." The Act specified that "it shall not be lawful to cast, throw, empty, or unlade" from or out of any ship or from the shore, pier, or wharf "any ballast, stone, slab, gravel, earth, slack, rubbish, wreck, filth, slate, edgings, sawdust, slag, or cinders, or other refuse or mill waste of any kind, into New York harbor."

In 1888 a somewhat similar bill that would have applied to all navigable rivers passed the Senate, but the House of Representatives sent it to its Committee on Commerce, from which it never returned. In both 1890 and 1894, however, restrictions upon the discharge into navigable streams of certain enumerated wastes that might impede or obstruct navigation were passed by Congress as part of the public works appropriations for rivers and harbors. Finally, in 1899 Congress approved the appropriations act for rivers and harbors, sometimes called the National Refuse Act, that comprehensively prohibited for the first time the discharge of wastes of any kind into American waters, whether navigable or tributaries to navigable waters and whether shown to obstruct navigation or not. Borrowing from previous acts, the Congress also made in unlawful to place upon the banks of any navigable river or tributary any material that might be washed into such rivers or their tributaries. The only exception to the law was matter that flowed "from streets and sewers and passed therefrom into a liquid state into navigable waters of the United States." And that was a large exception, for it permitted almost any matter in "a liquid state," such as raw sewage or chemical-industrial wastes to pass into streams or rivers, absent local ordinance or prohibition.[14]

The National Refuse Act, therefore, did not attack the problem of water quality itself. It was not addressed to any liquid wastes running through some system of sewerage and for a long time it was not used to control bilge water, oil, grease, human excretions, and other filth that passed from vessels into the rivers.

In 1901, meanwhile, a Hygienic Laboratory had been established under the U.S. Public Health and Marine Hospital Service. When in 1912 Congress acted to change the name of the Public Health and Marine Hospital Service to the Public Health Service, to increase the pay of its officers, and "for other purposes," it also provided that

The Public Health Service may study and investigate the diseases of man and conditions influencing the propagation and spread thereof, including sanitation and sewage and the pollution, either directly or indirectly, of the navigable streams and lakes of the United States—and it may issue information of the use of the public.

In conjunction with the Act the Hygienic Laboratory, located in Cincinnati, began research on water pollution. This led in 1914 to the promulgation of the first safe drinking water standards in the United States. In fact, only between 1912 and 1920 did the American people begin to obtain the scientific information on the degradation of streams by refuse and liquid wastes; however, no federal law for the enforcement of water pollution controls was enacted. Congress did consider providing such authority as early as 1912 but rejected the proposal and laid aside the idea for 36 years.

As indicated in Chapter 5, the introduction of petroleum as a fuel for engines in the last quarter of the nineteenth century and especially the rapid development of the automobile in the early twentieth century had revolutionized western industry and society. Shipping was equally affected. Diesel-fueled engines were introduced for the propulsion of both naval and merchant ships, and tankers were built to carry petroleum across waters from areas of supply to areas of demand. The beneficial consequences of petroleum fuel for western Europe and the United States were obvious, but the attendant evils of marine pollution from ships that burned or transported oil soon became evident in the harbors of England, France, Germany, Italy, Denmark, Holland, and the United States.

Complaints against such pollution prior to World War I had been few, but the rapid increase in numbers of oil-burning ships during the war greatly aggravated the conditions of the harbor waters, especially around New York. By

1920 there were 1731 vessels of 500 gross tons or more that were moved directly by oil-fueled engines. Working from the 1888 law that prohibited obstructive
and injurious deposits within the harbor of New York and its adjacent waters,
the supervisor of that harbor found 125 cases of oil pollution between 22 May
1919 and 16 December 1922, of which 88 were ascribed to ships, 6 of them
tankers. Needless to add there were other contaminations by oil that were not
discovered or reported.

Until 7 June 1924 there was no federal law that specifically prohibited the
discharge of oil into the navigable waters of the United States. Although the War
Department had maintained that the 1888 Act applied to the discharges of oil
into the harbor of New York, legal opinion of the time held that the 1899
National Refuse Act did not apply to oil released into the navigable waters and
their tributary streams throughout the United States. New legislation was required. The Oil Pollution Act of 1924, made it unlawful to discharge oil into
the coastal navigable waters of the United States from any vessel that either
used oil as fuel for the generation of its propulsion or that carried oil in excess
of that necessary for its lubricating requirements, such as tankers. The only
exceptions were cases of emergency imperiling life or property, or unavoidable
accidents like collision and stranding. Authority for the supervision and enforcement of the Act was given to the Secretary of War and his assistants for rivers
and harbors improvement, assistant engineers, and inspectors, while the Customs and Coast Guard service was also provided with powers of arrest.

All accounts indicated a noticeable improvement in U.S. harbor waters
immediately after the enactment of the 1924 Oil Pollution Act. But whatever
the Act's success in the navigable waters of the United States, it had no effect
beyond the three-mile territorial sea. The pumping out of ballast and bilge
waters contaminated by oil from oil-burning and oil cargo ships; the cleaning
and flushing of their oily tanks with sea water; and the accidents of collision,
stranding, or sinking that could release oil into the ocean were under no regulation in the contiguous zone or high seas adjacent to the United States. As the
U.S. Bureau of Mines reported in October 1925, many of the maritime nations
had taken action to prevent or reduce to a minimum the pollution by oil of their
territorial waters, but there was nothing to prevent the discharge of waste oil
on the open sea, with the likelihood that winds and waves would carry it into
territorial waters only to become a source of damage and possible danger. Thus,
"the problem of oil pollution of navigable waters is one which must be solved
internationally."

On 1 July 1922 President Warren G. Harding had signed a joint resolution
of Congress that requested him to call a conference of maritime nations to seek
the adoption of effective means for the prevention of pollution of navigable
waters. The Congress noted the fire hazards due to floating oil at the piers; the
destruction of ocean fisheries from the discharge of oil wastes and particularly
the harm to oysters, clams, crabs, and lobsters; and the ruination of valuable

bathing beaches and seaside properties. The resolution emphasized that "pollution takes place on the high seas as well as within territorial waters." In response the Secretary of State requested the departments of Treasury, War, Navy, Interior, Agriculture, and Commerce, and the U.S. Shipping Board to join with the State Department in an interdepartmental committee to study the problem. Almost three years later on 13 March 1926 the committee concluded that in the light of its several studies and investigations the government of the United States was warranted in convening a preliminary conference of experts from the several maritime countries concerned to exchange technical views and "to consider the formulation of proposals for dealing with the problem of oil pollution of navigable waters through international agreement."[15]

From 8 to 16 June 1926 the representatives of nine European countries, the British Empire, Canada, Japan, and the United States met in Washington to consider proposals for dealing with the discharge of oil on the high seas contiguous to coastal states. The conference had before it the report of the U.S. interdepartmental committee. But the Netherlands felt that oil pollution off its coast had been reduced to "negligible proportions" and was "no longer troublesome." Canada believed that bilge water was the most important factor in pollution. And all remarked that there had been a noticeable decline in the pollution of their navigable waters ever since public attention had been called to the problem and national legislation had curbed oil discharges in navigable waters. There was general agreement, however, that maritime states might wish to declare certain areas up to fifty miles from their coasts and on recognized fishing grounds as places where no discharge containing more than 0.05 of 1 percent of oil would be permitted. Other states, of course, would be notified of such areas. Alleged violations of the prohibition by a ship on the high seas would be reported to its flag state for action. All war vessels, however, would be exempt from any regulations save those of the flag state, and it was further advocated that no ship would be penalized on tonnage measurements because it had installed equipment to separate and store oil wastes. Finally, it was urged that some central international agency should be established to collect data, coordinate information, and circulate information about the restricted areas and pollution of the seas by oil. But when all was said and done in 1926, the majority of the states did not support the draft international convention. None of the states adopted it during the following years and thereafter they relied solely on an educational campaign to prevent pollution of the high seas by oil discharges.[16]

During the 1920s the 1930s, moreover, very slow progress had been made toward any abatement of the pollution of American rivers by human, agricultural, or industrial wastes. Generally these wastes poured through pipes or drains or simply were washed off with the rain into nearby lakes, streams, and rivers. About 26 million inhabitants of the United States had been served by sewers at the turn of the twentieth century, but only 1 million of them had been served by a system in which some treatment of wastes took place; by 1920 somewhat over 47 million inhabitants were served by sewers, but only 9 or 10 million used systems that treated wastes; by 1935 more than 60 million inhabitants were served by sewers, yet only 28 million had systems that treated wastes. In fact, as late as 1950 about 26 million people in America were still discharging raw wastes into the lakes, streams, and rivers of the United States, not only from their bodies, but also from their manufacturing, transportation, commerce, communications, farming, and leisure activities.[17]

Congress was not unaware of the need for federal water pollution control legislation, and from the late 1930s onward water pollution control bills were introduced, even passed, by the House and the Senate. Because of technicalities, however, one Act was vetoed by the President, and another bill failed to get agreement in a conference committee of the House and Senate. World War II interrupted the thrust of several groups seeking such legislation, but finally on 30 June 1948 Public Law 85 was enacted to "provide for water pollution control activities in the Public Health Service of the Federal Security Agency and in the Federal Works Agency." This was the first federal water pollution control legislation in the history of the United States—and it was modest.

During the hearings on the bill the case was strongly made that water pollution endangered the health of Americans, damaged the shellfish industry, and contaminated beaches. The Surgeon General of the United States introduced evidence showing that although typhoid fever incidence had been reduced dramatically since 1900 many outbreaks of water-borne typhoid had occurred in the last decade along with thousands of cases of diarrhea and amoebic dysentery. The chief causes of the polluted waters were defects in the collection, treatment, storage, and distribution of water for public consumption, particularly in town and city populations. Senator Thomas Green of Rhode Island, moreover, pointed out the damage of pollution to the oyster industry in his state. The harvest had been reduced from 8.5 million pounds in 1908 to 1.5 million in 1943, representing at then current prices a loss of almost 3 million dollars a year to the industry. The Commissioner of Public Affairs of Camden, N.J. was more blunt: "As it is right now, the (Delaware) river stinks to high heaven. I mean you can actually go on that river and take your hand, there in the summertime, and pick up the foul debris . . . you could just see the fumes coming up from the river . . . there have been occasions when it smells as if someone had exploded a bomb, a stink bomb . . ."[18]

The original bill had given great power to the Surgeon General in a program to control water pollution and had provided swift legal remedies for ensuring abatement. But several witnesses before Congress, not only from industrial interests, but also from municipalities, strongly objected to the entire bill. For example, the Passaic Valley Sewerage Commissioners, representing twenty-seven municipalities, argued that "there are adequate local laws and agencies now in practically all the states to prevent stream pollution . . . very great progress has been made in recent years by local agencies in the elimination of pollution . . .

there is actually no necessity for Federal legislation," which would place the municipalities and their taxpayers "at the mercy of the Surgeon General." The Surgeon General might determine that the combined sewerage through which storm water and sanitary sewage flows should be replaced by separate systems at a "staggering" cost. And why should the taxpayers of one district who had attended to their sewage needs be forced to pay through federal taxes for grants and loans to far-distant municipalities, which had shirked their responsibilities? To the question of legal remedies against one state polluting an interstate stream to the detriment of another state, the Commissioners—and others—replied that the Supreme Court provided an adequate and effective avenue for redress. "No new legislation is needed to give such right or remedy." In the end Congress compromised, amending the bill to restrict the powers of the Surgeon General and virtually frustrate federal suit against alleged polluters of interstate streams.

The Water Pollution Control Act of 1948 sought, among its purposes, "to recognize, preserve, and protect the primary responsibilities and rights of states in controlling water pollution." It enabled the Surgeon General to prepare and adopt comprehensive programs to eliminate or reduce the pollution of interstate waters and their tributaries. It created federal grants to states for water pollution studies and it established a Federal Water Pollution Control Advisory Board. It encouraged interstate compacts. It allowed the Federal Works administration to make loans (up to $250,000 each) to provide for no more than 30 percent of costs to states, municipalities, or interstate agencies for the improvement of their sewage treatment facilities under programs that were approved by the Surgeon General. But it emasculated any enforcement of water pollution standards within the states. While the pollution of interstate waters that endangered the health or welfare of a person in a state other than that from which the discharge stemmed was declared "a public nuisance" and subject to abatement, two separate notices had to be given by the Surgeon General to the alleged polluter, followed by a public hearing. Then, if no action had been taken, and only "with the consent of the water pollution agency . . . of the State" could the Federal Security Administrator request the Attorney General to bring a suit on behalf of the United States to secure abatement.

Under the 1948 Act the Congress had authorized $22.5 million a year for fiscal years 1949–1953 for construction loans; $1 million a year for pollution studies; and $800,000 a year for grants to aid the drafting of construction plans for water pollution control projects. The provisions of the 1948 Act were extended for an additional three years in 1952 by the enactment of Public Law 82-579. Finally, in 1956 a national water pollution control program on a permanent basis took shape through the enactment of P.L. 84-660, the Federal Water Pollution Act.

The Act was designed to strengthen and expand the Water Pollution Control Act by continuing in form and language many of its provisions and by also increasing the annual authorizations ($3 million) of grants to states for establishing and maintaining adequate measures for the prevention and control of water pollution. It also increased the annual authorizations ($50 million) for construction loans to states. Additionally the new act modified the procedure for securing the abatement of pollution in interstate waters. It was categorical in declaring that the "pollution of interstate waters in or adjacent to any State or States . . . shall be subject to abatement." But it still emphasized the priority and primary responsibility of the states to control water pollution. Once more the Surgeon General was entitled to give notice to a state water pollution agency of a discharge under its jurisdiction that endangered the life or welfare of inhabitants in another state. But he was further empowered to call a conference of the involved state water pollution agencies and to provide a summary of the occurence of water pollution, the measures taken, and the nature of the delays in controlling it, with his recommendations. If no remedial action had been taken within six months, the Secretary of Health, Education, and Welfare could appoint five persons to hold a public hearing and make findings to be followed by a notice from the Secretary to the state water pollution control agency. If, again after six months, no action had been taken, the Secretary, with the written consent of the state water pollution control agency, could request the Attorney General of the United States to institute suit.

Criticisms of the gradual entry of federal controls, federal bureaucracy, and federal taxation into the rights of the states and municipalities to manage water pollution continued. But by 1961, with the environmental movement gaining national attention, pressure for a strong water pollution control program increased. After extensive public hearings, the Public Works Committee of the House of Representatives recommended to Congress a bill that was enacted as an amendment to the Federal Water Pollution Control Act, Public Law 87-88. Among other things the amendment altered the balance between states rights and federal prerogatives. First, the Secretary of Health, Education, and Welfare (rather than the Surgeon General) was invested with the substantive power of appointments and reviews under the program; second, it required the Corps of Engineers, the Bureau of Reclamation, and other Federal agencies to take water pollution control into account in their reservoir programs; third, it authorized grants to local communities for sewage treatment in amounts of $80 million, $90 million, and $100 million for fiscal years 1962, 1963, and 1964–67 respectively, raised the total cost allowable to a single project from $250,000 to $600,000, with the federal share up to 30 percent, and, fourth, extended pollution abatement procedures to "navigable" waters, whether intrastate or interstate. Virtually all the procedures to bring about abatement that had previously been enacted were retained, except that after the public hearing and the Secretary's final notice to bring about abatement, he could, if no action had been taken, request the Attorney General to bring suit on behalf of the United States *without* the permission of the state from which the pollution originated *if* such pollution were endangering the safety or welfare of persons in another state.

Congress, therefore, was well on the way to new and bold federal measures for water pollution control in the streams and rivers of the United States by the early 1960s. Yet it seemed that the more that was done for research, for grants in aid of construction, and for enforcement actions against water pollution, the more that was needed. Beginning on 21 May 1963 a subcommittee of the House Committee on Government Operations held an extensive inquiry into water pollution control and abatement with hearings both in Washington and in various regions throughout the country. In its final report, completed some two years later, the Committee said, "By 1960, the municipal sewage discharged into our streams, treated and untreated, was almost 5 times the amount discharged in 1900, and its pollutional effect was equal to the untreated sewage from more than 75 million people, or triple the amount in 1900."

Substantial progress, of course, had been made over a seventeen-year period from 1945 to 1962 during which time the number of American sewered communities had increased from 8,917 to 11,420 and the U.S. population served by sewers had increased from 74,740,887 to 118,371,919. Moreover, the population discharging raw sewage into streams and rivers had declined from 27,867,783 to 14,686,941. Nevertheless, more than 14 million people in more than 2000 sewered communities still poured their untreated wastes into nearby waters. And another 2704 plants, serving more than 40 million people, provided less than a secondary treatment of its sewage.[19]

The report of the House Committee on Government Operations concluded that better sewage treatment methods for municipal wastes had to be developed, and that although the construction grant program had substantially increased the number and quality of facilities, it had hardly ended the problem of water pollution. Sewerage required more systematic sewage planning and more efficient operations and the report added that more research was required. The report also concluded that the federal construction grants program had been endorsed by state and local authorities.

But not every member of the Committee on Government Operations agreed with these findings. Congressman Robert McClory, who had been a member of the Natural Resources and Power subcommittee that had studied the subject for the full Committee, stated, "The report reflects only the view held by the Public Health Service that there is little or no progress in controlling municipal sewage and that increased Federal funds—and increased Federal authority—provide the sole answer to the problem." He further pointed out that the report relied upon an inventory of municipal waste discharges and theoretical degrees of treatment rather than upon measuring water quality itself—and that there was duplication by several federal agencies in monitoring streams. In his view one agency, logically the U.S. Geological Survey, should have primary responsibility for this function. Finally, he questioned the entire premise that federal construction grants to the states had helped obtain efficient facilities more quickly, saying, ". . . at least 75% and possibly more would have been built without Federal aid." He further argued that the lure of a 30 percent federal grant toward costs, even a 75 percent grant under the accelerated works program, had dampened local initiative and the willingness of local authorities to tax their constituencies to control local water.

In his State of the Union message to Congress in 1964, President Lyndon B. Johnson said not a single word about environmental pollution. But in January 1965 his message boldly called the nation to "end the poisoning of our rivers and the air we breathe," to "provide legal power to prevent pollution . . . before it happens," and to "give first priority to the cleanup of our contaminated rivers." Shortly thereafter the President delivered a special message to Congress on conservation and the restoration of natural beauty in which he suggested a "Natural Wild Rivers System" with large free-flowing stretches of unspoiled waters.

Indeed, 1965 was a banner year for water resources with five pieces of legislation on that subject, the most important of which was the Water Quality Act, P. L. 89-234, which had the endorsement of the administration. As in other areas of federal-state relations under the peculiar system of American government formulated by the 1789 Constitution of the United States, the debate between federal control and state independence continued. However, the complaint of Congressman McClory that the abatement of pollution could only be measured against some standard of water quality was compelling and was incorporated in the Water Quality Act.

Under the previous laws there had been no "purity" standard against which pollution could be measured so that abatement measures could only be started after *prima facie* evidence, and then on a case by case basis. Under the Water Quality Act, which again amended the Federal Water Pollution Control Act, states were required to establish water quality standards for interstate waters or portions thereof within their boundaries and adopt a plan for the implementation and enforcement of such standards by 30 June 1967. If the state failed to do so or provided standards that were unsatisfactory to the Secretary of Health, Education, and Welfare, he could, following informal conferences, propose water quality standards. If a state objected further, there would be a public hearing before a board of five persons, appointed by the Secretary, but representing both the federal and the state governments which would approve or modify the standards. If discharges into streams reduced the water quality below the standards that had been set, then abatement measures could be taken as previously described under the Water Pollution Control Act. Appropriations of $20 million a year for fiscal years 1966–1969 were authorized for federal matching grants to states, municipalities, and interstate or intermunicipal agencies for projects to help develop improved methods for treating sewage, and $150 million a year was authorized for federal grants toward construction of community sewage treatment plants. Finally, a new Federal Water Pollution Control Administration was established in the Department of Health, Education, and Welfare.

Nevertheless, the 89th Congress in 1966 still had before its Senate and House committees a score of bills to amend the federal Water Pollution Control Act once again. Senate Bill 2947, sponsored by Edmund S. Muskie of Maine and forty-seven other senators, became the nucleus of Public Law 89-753, which was enacted on 3 November 1966 as the Clean Water Restoration Act. In a prelude to the hearings of Subcommittee on Air and Water Pollution on that bill and others, Muskie said that the committee had found that the dollar limitation on federal grants for sewerage improvements had discriminated against the large cities; that the states were not moving rapidly enough under the matching funds program to upgrade their sewage disposal facilities; that the costs were greater than expected; and that 20 billion dollars would be required just to bring municipal sewage discharges to acceptable levels. While acknowledging that the Water Pollution Control Act had been a major achievement, he concluded, "our task is to provide the necessary funds—and it is a money problem . . ."

With flourishes of political rhetoric for the popular theme of "cleaning up our rivers" and with the backing of interested local agencies in quest of federal funds as well as the mounting support of the environmental groups, Congress authorized a magnificent total expenditure of 3,550 million dollars for fiscal years 1967–1971 under the Clean Water Restoration Act. As it turned out, Congress appropriated only a little more than half that amount in that period, which was still substantial. Indeed, criticism of the Clean Water Restoration Act was not lacking, although muted under the wave of enthusiasm for reducing water pollution. Again experts in sanitary engineering, business and agricultural interests, and some local agencies protested that water quality conditions and waste absorption were often misinterpreted; that more federal money for sewerage systems meant more federal control and less local initiative; and that delays in improvements were often due to the clumsiness, uncertainty, and sluggishness in the federal bureaucracy itself. Under the Act a majority of the conference called by the Secretary to consider allegations of pollution in which no abatement or insufficient action seemed to have been taken could request the alleged polluter to furnish materials on the character, kind, and quantity of discharge from the source—and a refusal to file a report could be subject to a fine of $100 a day.

In the midst of these rapid developments to reduce water pollution, in fact, just after the Water Quality Act had been enacted in 1965 and just before the enactment of the Clean Water Restoration Act in 1966, Reorganization Plan No. 2, effective 10 May 1966, transferred the Federal Water Pollution Control Administration as well as most of the functions of the Secretary of Health, Education, and Welfare under that Act to the Secretary of Interior.

The Clean Water Restoration Act dwelt for the first time on the importance of the estuaries of the nation to the economic and social well-being of the people of the United States. It called for a three-year study by the Secretary of the "major economic, social, and ecological trends in estuarine zones" as well as recommendations for a "comprehensive program for the preservation, study, use, and development" of the estuaries of the nation. For the first time the importance of stream and river pollution upon the wetlands, bays, inlets, and other territorial waters affected by the interface of ocean tides and outpouring rivers was recognized in legislation. Finally, the Act amended the Oil Pollution Act of 1924, not only making it unlawful to discharge or permit discharges of oil by any means into or upon navigable waters of the adjoining shoreline, but also requiring the removal of all such pollution by an offender. The failure to remove the pollutants made the offender liable for all the costs of removal and allowed liens upon vessels for payment, while failure to comply with the Act made an offender subject to fines and imprisonment. Just beyond the estuaries and the territorial waters of the United States lay the oceans themselves, once regarded as the ultimate, bottomless drain for the wastes of all the earth, slowly being recognized as a part of a fragile ecosystem that could be permanently damaged.

Pollutants in the Estuaries and Oceans

"It is the last pollution. Last to seep into public consciousness; last to be treated by the rule of law; last to be analyzed by science." Thus began an article in the New York *Wall Street Journal* on 2 October 1973 that was headlined: "Pollution of Oceans is Enormous Threat, but Few People Care."

Plainly the problem of stream and river pollution had not captured public attention until the latter part of the nineteenth century and few regulations were imposed on the filth delivered to inland or coastal waters until well into the twentieth century. But the oceans? Enormously wide and deep, tossed and aired by the endless wind, with great waves and sweeping currents, so desolate of visible creatures over most of its expanse and, above all, not the possession of any state of the world, how could the oceans become polluted and harmful to man?

For millenia the oceans had received the silts of the dry earth of the planet either washed down through crevices, gullies, and river valleys, or pouring over the banks of the continents. And for millenia the crust of the earth, submerged below the seas, had either cracked and crumbled, causing mountainous upwellings of turbidity or it had let seep up through its pores into the ocean the deeper sediments of liquids and gases under pressure. Changes in the temperature, currents, opacity, and chemical composition of the seas took place over geological time with marked effects upon the biota, unquestionably altering the appearance of marine plant and animal life. Some growths were encouraged, others were destroyed, while nature created abysses and shallows, wearing away one shoreline and extending another with accretions of mud, sands, soil, grass, and vegetation. The sparse settlements of mankind had but little effect upon these titanic workings of the earth, the skies, and the seas. The puny ports for marine commerce, the small clearings of brush and forest for agriculture, and the minor wastes from industry and human bodily functions only moderately affected the coastal waters until very recent times and scarcely ruffled the oceans.

The agricultural and industrial revolutions of the past two centuries, however, produced a dramatic increase in the human population of the earth. Starting from both philosophical and economic motives, particularly in Europe, science and technical innovation radically changed the patterns of the production, distribution, and consumption of goods in human civilization. The effects, such as deforestation with its concomitant soil erosion and floods, were rapidly perceived on the land. But it took longer to perceive the blights that people were inflicting on the ocean, not only because the watery part of the planet was so vast and distant, but also because the pollutants to reach the seas through human activity had at first been small, hardly recognizable, and of little interest to a world society out of sight, smell, and touch with the marine environment.

It should be emphasized that knowledge—strict and demonstrable cause and effect data—about the number, kind, and effect of pollutants in the oceans is very far from being either complete or certain. One reason is the amplitude of the marine environment, requiring many difficult observations, which often lack any baseline of data to make comparisons or extrapolations. Another reason for the absence of conclusive findings about pollutants in the marine system comes from the faults or imperfections in the technology of investigation itself. For example, until 1952, when chromotography began to be widely used as a laboratory tool for analyzing organic molecules, there had been no way to detect chlorinated hydrocarbons at the minute levels of concentration found in the environment as residues from the use of pesticides. Indeed, it was the ability to determine such residues in such fractions as parts per billion or even parts per trillion that sharply focused scientific attention upon the role of pesticide contaminants. Sound physical and chemical methods of analysis are essential for a wide range of pollution research and monitoring. Only in recent years, and most often due to basic research for other purposes, have scientists had available the instrumentalities, not to mention the public interest and funds, to detect the existence, dispersions, and effects of contaminants in the marine environment.[20]

Any definition of pollution of the oceans is bound to stir controversy, first, because nature itself, long before man made his imprint upon earth, releases substances into the marine environment that can be disturbing and even lethal to life in the oceans. Rainfalls, for example, have always carried some contaminants absorbed from the dry land to the seas or washed some miniscule concentrations of chemicals into waters. Natural seeps of petroleum from the ocean shoreline or submerged lands have existed for eons, and heavings of the earth's crust in its mighty mountain building process or subsidence have caused violent water motion, turbidity, rapid thermal changes, and massive upwellings of foreign elements into the seas. The point of any definition of marine pollution, therefore, lies in the contribution that man has been making deliberately or unwittingly, to a degradation of the marine environment.

In 1969 a group of scientists concerned about oceanographic research and the resources of the sea formulated a definition of marine pollution that has since been widely accepted in the United Nations system, and, in one phrasing or another, has found its way into a number of declarations, treaties, and national laws: namely, "the introduction by man into the marine environment (including the estuaries), directly or indirectly, of substances or energy, which bring about deleterious effects, such as damage to the biological resources, hazards to human health, a lessening of the quality of the sea water for use, and a reduction of the possibilities offered for its enjoyment."[21] Such a sweeping definition of marine pollution, of course, is open to many objections, from the point of view of both science and law. Nevertheless, it provides a concept that both illuminates the problem and suggests the need for controls.

Pollutants from the activities of man enter the marine environment in a variety of ways. As already indicated vast quantities of human sewage and agricultural-industrial wastes have either passed through pipes or simply run off the land into streams and rivers into the estuaries of the oceans. Heavy and lacking inertia, however, these wastes generally sink into nearshore sediments, combining with natural silt, which must be dredged to maintain the navigation channels of rivers and ports.

Such wastes, of course, have always been deposited in streams, lakes, and bays by human communities, but the magnitude of the materials has enormously increased in the last two or three decades. For example, it was estimated in 1970 that the transport of iron due to natural erosion and washings from rivers to the ocean was about 25,000 metric tons a year. Due to the activities of man, however, another 319,000 tons of iron was reaching the seas. The transport of lead to the oceans under natural conditions may have amounted to 300 metric tons, but the activities of man were probably adding another 2330 metric tons of lead to the seas. Similar comparisons were made for copper, zinc, phosphorous, mercury, and other minerals.[22]

The variety of substances reaching the oceans recently has also multiplied. Oil pollution is a twentieth-century phenomenon. The contamination of the rivers and atmosphere with transuranic elements that pour into or fall upon the oceans only began after World War II with atomic bomb tests and nuclear reactors for generating power. Only in the last few decades has the petrochemical industry flourished with plastics, synthetic fibers, and artificial rubbers, while halogenated forms of hydrocarbons began to be used for pesticides, solvents, or heat exchangers. Chlorinated hydrocarbons started their big commercial growth in the 1920s with the growing use of liquid chlorine and only obtained a dominant position in the chemical industry after World War II. About 70,000 tons of chlorinated hydrocarbons were produced in 1948; about 8,200,000 tons were produced in 1970.

The effects of such wastes have been dramatized a thousand times in popular literatures, sometimes with fact and often with fancy based on probabilities that take little account of the celerity of human intervention to modify, reshape, or terminate harmful activities once the evidence of their danger is reasonably apparent. In any event it is mandatory that policymakers be alert to the possibility that some of the great mass of materials reaching the marine environment, whether by design, inadvertence, or ignorance, may be toxic to marine biota. Moreover, little argument should be needed to convince public leaders that the pollution of ocean waters can be a nuisance to fishing, boating, swimming, and shoreline properties. Far more troublesome—and far more difficult to demonstrate—is the notion that such gross changes in the chemical composition of waters of the world through pollutants are taking place that they could have enduring effects upon the envelope of the earth's physical system by interrupting photosynthesis on the ocean's surface, thereby increasing the carbon dioxide and reducing the oxygen in the atmosphere.

One way in which pollutants have entered the oceans as a result of human activity is the runoff of human and industrial wastes into streams and rivers and thence into the oceans. This includes millions of gallons a day of dissolved organic and inorganic materials that either become part of the sedimentary deposits of a river bed or flow directly into the nearby seas. In 1975 Americans used an estimated 384 billion gallons of water *per day,* of which about 127 billion went for irrigation, 30 for public systems, 5 for rural-domestic household use, 65 for industrial-commercial uses, and 157 for electric utilities. These enormous torrents of water wash down from the land or pour through pipes all the powders, clippings, shavings, grimes, greases, oils, urine, slime, scum, filth, fragments, feces, spoils, acids, dregs, and countless other dirty residues of human civilization. For example, of the four million metric tons of oil estimated to have been placed into the oceans of the world as a result of man's activities in the early 1970s, about half probably came from refinery and petrochemical plant wastes, industrial machinery waste oil, and automobile crankcase oil, all running or seeping off the land, both inside and outside piping systems. Many seaside communities pour their wastes directly into the oceans: In the early 1970s, New York City was discharging about four million tons of waste water a year into the ocean, and California was discharging more than one billion gallons of effluent a day or about thirty percent of the total discharge of the United States into the oceans. In 1975 the island of Oahu in Hawaii was discharging sixty million gallons of raw sewage a day into forty feet of water only 3600 feet from the shore.

Much of the vast volume of water consumed in the production of foods and fibres, in commerce, and in individual human use returns to the rivers and seas with only slight adulteration. Moreover, some of the water consumed, such as that used by electric utilities, is drawn from saline river or ocean waters. Nevertheless, the outpouring of wastes from land into the seas has steadily mounted in the twentieth century and has brought with it a load of pollutants that can manifestly harm the marine environment if not monitored and, where appropriate, regulated.

A second way in which pollutants have entered the ocean is through the atmosphere. The fallout of transuranic elements into the seas was first dramatized by the testing of atomic weapons in the atmosphere, but other chemicals and metals may be blown off the earth into the oceans or drawn into vapors and rained upon the seas, sometimes many hundreds of miles from their point of origin. Among the synthetic organic chemicals, DDT, used as a pesticide, and PCBs, used in heat transfer systems and electrical devices, both chlorinated hydrocarbons, tend to be transported by the atmosphere into the oceans. The same is true of volatile organic liquids and gases, such as Freon and dry cleaning solvent.

A third way in which pollutants enter the ocean is the deliberate discharge or dumping of materials, either collected from the land or dredged from inland waters, into offshores areas.

For more than a century the U.S. Corps of Engineers has been responsible for preventing or removing obstructions to the navigation of rivers of the United States. As sediments collect on the beds of a watercourse from the land erosions or the dissolved solids discharged from pipes, channels become more narrow and shallow. A constant program of dredging has been required to meet the needs of navigation. By far the largest amount of dumping into the ocean has been the spoils dredged from navigation channels by the Corps or by private companies under contract to the Corps. In 1968 it was estimated that 80 percent of all ocean dumping—believed to aggregate 48 million tons of waste a year—consisted of dredge spoils. These spoils were generally deposited in coastal waters under 100 feet in depth and, according to the Corps of Engineers, about a third of the material was polluted.

Another deposit dumped directly into the ocean has been sewage sludge. At wastewater treatment plants that receive the millions of gallons of sewage from communities in the United States the amount of suspended solids load can vary from one-quarter to one-half a pound per capita. Heavy industrial wastes, a widespread use of garbage grinders, or the deliberate addition of chemicals to wastewater in order to improve in some way the quality of the effluent can add to the weight of the suspended solids and increase the problem of handling the residual sludge. About 60 percent of the suspended solids load may be removed in the primary treatment of the effluent when it is mixed with aerobic microorganisms and large volumes of air; and it is possible, always at more cost, for a third treatment by heated amerobic digestion, to complete the capture of up to 95-98 percent of all the suspended solids load reaching wastewater treatment plants.

The very large amounts of sewage sludge whether in primary (raw) or secondary (waste activated) or tertiary (digested) form must be removed from the waste treatment plant and deposited somewhere. In the United States most of the sewage sludge has been either incinerated or put into land fills, but on the Atlantic coast cities have dumped their sewage sludge into the seas. In the early 1970s New York was dumping almost four million wet tons a year off its harbor, and Philadelphia was dumping about 500,000 wet tons a year outside the Delaware Bay. Such wastes not only have a high oxygen demand, but they also concentrate significant quantities of heavy metals found in the effluent of industrial and commercial wastes.

Industrial chemical wastes, which include acids, sludges, cleaners, spent caustics, waste liquors, and plating solutions, have also been dumped at sea. Such industrial wastes amounted to 2.2 million tons in 1959, but by 1968 they had increased to 4.7 million tons—with New York City alone accounting for the disposal of 2.7 million tons at sea. Chemical industries, paper mills, pesticide manufactures, refineries, pharmaceutical plants, and others all contributed to such residues. Highly toxic wastes have generally been packed into drums and dumped in deep water some miles offshore. Until 1962 radioactive wastes were handled this way by the Atomic Energy Commission, and until 1964 the primary method for disposing of unserviceable or obsolete military ammunition, shells, mines, solid rocket fuels, propellants, and other chemical agents was by dumping at sea. From 1964 to 1970 Liberty ships were loaded with such military material and scuttled in more than 4000 feet of ocean water.

Garbage, trash, commercial cannery wastes, and construction-demolition debris have also been barged and dumped into ocean waters, largely due to the lack of availability of suitable land-fill areas, but these materials form a rather small part of the refuse placed into the seas and, with some exceptions, pose the least threat to marine life.

In proportion to the total amount of contaminants that run or blow off the land, dumping probably has not been a major source of ocean pollution. However, the concentration of dumping into a few localities combined with the toxic character of some wastes have seriously menaced the marine environment. For example, the constant deposition of huge quantities of sewage sludge in the New York bight grossly degraded the quality of the seabed and superjacent waters, causing infection and death for marine life, danger for human health, and ruin for public amenities.[23]

A fourth way in which pollutants enter the oceans is the discharge of vessels. Ships at sea and in coastal waters either deliberately pump out their wastes or through accidents of collision, grounding, or storm unloose cargoes of contaminants, chiefly oil, into the oceans. In the early 1970s about 75–80 percent of all the oil tankers in the world were collecting their tank washings and oil-contaminated ballast into special slop tanks, waiting for the oil and water to separate in such tanks, and then pumping the water out, leaving an oil residue on top of which new oil was loaded. Even with this "load-on-top" method to reduce oil pollution of the seas, the cleaning of other tankers, the bilge-cleaning and ballasting of different types of vessels, and a variety of spills and leakages in the course of maritime operations accounted for more than one million metric tons of oil pollution of the seas in one year.[24]

More dramatic, of course, have been the great oil discharges into the seas due to maritime disaster, such as the grounding of the *Torrey Canyon* on the rocks of the English Channel on 18 March 1967. The ruptured vessel disgorged 119,193 tons of crude oil into the sea, much of which drifted to the shores of Great Britain and France, requiring millions of dollars for clean-up operations. Another major disaster was the hull failure of the tanker *Keo* on 5 November 1969 some 120 miles southeast of Nantucket Island, which unloosed about 30,000 tons of No. 4 fuel oil into the sea. On 9 August 1974 the *Metula,* a 207,000 DWT tanker under a Dutch flag, ran aground in the eastern entrance of the Strait of Magellan. Five of the vessel's forward compartments, including two cargo tanks, were ripped open, and 16 million gallons of crude oil gushed into the sea. On 6 January 1975 the *Showa Maru,* a 238,000 DWT tanker under the Japanese flag ran aground eight miles south of Singapore in Indonesian waters and released about a million gallons of crude oil in the water. In addition to these catastrophes, a large number of small accidents on vessels and from on-shore facilities caused marine pollution by oil. In the United States in 1975, for example, about 12,812,000 gallons of oil were accidentally spilled into the rivers, estuaries, and coastal waters by vessels and pipeline, dock, and port operations. Unfortunate as these major and minor accidents may be, they still represent on the average about 200,000 metric tons of oil discharged into the oceans a year, considerably less than the losses occurring through normal tanker and transfer activities at terminals and in bilging or bunkering operations.

A fifth source of marine pollution has been the production of petroleum products in offshore areas. The worldwide input of oil to the oceans from off-shore drilling has been estimated at 80,000 tons a year, of which about 20,000 tons may be lost through minor spills of 50 barrels or less and through the discharge of oil field brines during the course of drilling and recovery operations. The balance of 60,000 tons a year which has been lost to the oceans comes from major accidents, that is, spills that exceed 50 barrels from blowouts, ruptured pipelines, and other accidents. The most sensational of such calamities in the United States occurred in the Santa Barbara channel on 28 January 1969 when about 14,000 tons of crude oil started to escape into the sea from a drilling operation. Eventually a strip forty miles along the California coastline was contaminated.

As indicated in Chapter 5, exploration for and exploitation of petroleum resources in shallow basins and on the continental shelf has been rapidly increasing around the world. Rigs and drilling vessels are becoming more capable of penetrating the crust of the earth at depths under the sea. Hazards to the marine environment from such exploitation have in turn mounted, although the technology for safe recovery and shut-offs in the event of accident have also improved. In the near future, the marine environment may also be endangered by the mining of manganese nodules from the deep ocean floor, the placement of more and more nuclear powered electric generating stations at sea, the building of deepwater ports as terminals for petroleum products, and various other schemes to utilize the oceans for security, industrial, or maricultural purposes.

The commercial recovery of manganese nodules from the deep ocean floor had not started by 1977, yet many years had already been devoted by scientists and entrepreneurs to the exploitation of the seabed in quest of the most lucrative collection of copper, nickel, and cobalt-rich manganese nodules. The nodules of greatest commercial interest appeared to occur in water depths between 3000 and 6000 meters at least 1000 miles from shore in the north equatorial central Pacific ocean. Technology for their recovery had advanced to a point where profitable mining seemed possible if legal title, which involved the security of investment, could be assured. All systems of recovery require some separation of the nodules from the sediment upon which they lie whether by a rake tines, a radialtooth roller, harrow blades, water jets, or suction. Perturbation of the local sediments will almost certainly occur. Yet marine flora and fauna seem to be sparse in the great depths of water in which the nodules are located and would probably be little affected over time by sweeping or dredging. Temperature, salinity, and particle dispersion of the superjacent waters could be changed during the recovery of the nodules, but scarcely enough, on the basis of present mining plans, to harm the enormous masses of the surrounding oceans or their biota. In the mid-1970s the leading entrepreneurs were planning to utilize land-based plants for the metallurgical processing, in which case the disposal of wastes would not differ from existing activities.[25]

The siting of nuclear-powered electric generating plants on rivers, on the coasts, and, under some well-advanced plans, on the sea itself could also affect the marine environment. In the face of outcries from public interest groups, requirements for environmental impact statements, delays in construction, and so forth, the generation of electricity from nuclear power in the United States had advanced rapidly. In 1960 the demand for all energy outputs in the electrical sector that was met by nuclear power had been less than one percent; by 1975 nuclear power was accounting for more than 6 percent of that demand, with coal, oil, gas, and water power making up the rest. Put another way, in 1957 nuclear powered electrical plants supplied only 9.86 million kilowatt hours; ten years later the figure was 7,655.0; and the estimate for 1980 was 131,600.0 million kilowatt hours. This phenomenon, of course, has not been confined to the United States, and the foreseeable worldwide growth of nuclear-powered electrical energy stations must be regarded with caution by anyone concerned about marine pollution.

For public opinion and the policymaker in the 1970s it has not been easy to separate the hard fact of scientific evidence of marine pollution from the surmises, inferences, extrapolations, and allegations that stem from scanty data, limited samples, and unproven causality. There can be no doubt that certain substances like radioactive materials, synthetic organic chemicals, and heavy metals can have a deleterious effect upon the marine environment, degrading private, and public uses of the sea for recreation and commerce while endangering plant, animal, and human life. Yet estimates of the actual damage of these potentially hazardous materials, and reasonable regulations for their control in the face of their value to national security or industry depends upon a good knowledge of their rates of release to the environment, the length of time they persist in the environment, their concentration, and their levels of toxicity. None of this information has been easy to obtain. For example, practically nothing has been known of the biological or environmental significance of transuranic elements once they are incorporated into marine sediments.

One important source of radioactive pollution of the oceans was the nuclear explosion in the atmosphere initiated by the United States in 1945, followed by others set off by Washington and Moscow until stopped by treaty in 1963. France, China, and India, however, have each detonated nuclear materials since then. Hundreds of radioactive isotopes, most of which become harmless in a very short time, have fallen through the atmosphere upon land and sea, roughly 70 percent of them descending into the oceans. Some of the radioactive elements take years to decay into a stable form: Strontium-90, for example, has a half life of 28 years; Carbon-14 a half life of 5500 years; and plutonium-239 a half life of 24,400 years. These elements may have properties that tend to concentrate in marine organisms and possibly move up the food chain to damage man. But the present situation, which should encourage caution, need not inspire strident fears. It has been estimated, for example, that the total amount of radioactive pollution in the oceans due to nuclear explosion fallout amounts to 10^9 curies, yet the natural radioactivity of the oceans, principally potassium-40, is about a thousand times greater. Moreover, if nuclear testing in the atmosphere is not increased in the coming years, the 10^9 curies from this source in the oceans should not increase. It may decrease.

Other important sources of radioactive pollution in the oceans have been nuclear reactors, the reprocessing of fuel, and the management of the wastes. Reactors have been employed for vehicle propulsion and used for special research. They could have other uses where great energy is required, but electric power generation has appeared to be their most immediate and greatest application. Reactor cores require extensive cooling. River and ocean waters are drawn into and expelled from the system for that purpose. Apart from any problems arising from the differential rise in heat in the ambient waters at the outfalls, impurities in the cooling water can be activated and then enter the sea.

A greater danger, for marine pollution, however, lurks in the reprocessing of the nuclear fuel, which must be purified of the fission products in order to reuse the very expensive fuel. The fission products recovered in this process are highly radioactive and longlived. Together with some components of the spent fuel these wastes must be contained and, in the United States, they have been placed in remote cemetaries in the western states. Low level wastes associated with the reprocessing of the fuel, however, have been run off to the seas—and it has been estimated that their contribution to the radioactivity of the oceans amounts to about one million curies, a figure that will doubtlessly increase as the number of nuclear powered plants for electric generation grows through the century. The most fearful uncertainty about marine pollution from radioactive elements is an accident to a power station, particularly those located at the seashore or on an artificial island, or an accident in the course of reprocessing, transporting, or burying wastes. Yet, in sum, there is still insufficient information on chemical and biological behavior of a number of radioactive elements in the marine environment, no clear and present danger from present activities, yet an imperative need to be conservative in the discharges of wastes to the sea and vigilant against any accident.[26]

In the early 1970s the United States petrochemical industry was selling more than nineteen different halogenated forms of the basic fossil-fuel derived hydrocarbons. Among the many kinds of synthetic organic chemicals that had been developed over the past fifty years to improve agriculture, industry, and the standard of living of mankind, some chlorinated hydrocarbons and volatile organic liquids or gases seem to have presented the greatest danger to the marine environment.

Pesticides, such as DDT, chlordane, dieldrin, and endrin, have been most publicized for their persistence after they wash off the ground or are blown into the atmosphere and thereafter enter rivers, estuaries, bays, and the oceans. DDT, for example, was produced in very large quantities for insect control in the United States until it was banned in 1972. With a low solubility in water, DDT tends to be absorbed on soil and silt particles where its half life can be about ten to fifteen years. In the presence of oxygen, however, DDT rapidly degrades to DDE, its most persistent degraded form. In the early 1970s DDE was probably the most abundant of the synthetic organic pollutants in the oceans. The problem with DDE apparently is that no marine organism is able to metabolize it. Thus it may accumulate in fatty tissues and be passed on up through the food chain through ocean plankton, small fish, large fish, and sea birds.

There seems to be sufficient evidence that some fish and fisheating birds, like the brown pelican and the herring gull, have been affected by DDT. Yet different species of fish in the same waters appear to have different abilities in concentrating and tolerating chlorinated hydrocarbons, with some carrying high residues and others rather low residues. No real evidence of damage from these chlorinated hydrocarbons in their normal use has been produced, and, there is even a question about the cumulative residence of DDT in the fatty tissues of animals. For example, if DDT were no longer entering the bloodstream of a man, some of the fatty tissue concentrates might be slowly released and eventually excreted.

The polychlorinated biphenyls (PCBs), which have good resistance to heat, fire, and explosives, have found valuable uses in capacitors, transformers, and other electrical devices, and as additives to paints, plastics, and coating compounds. Perhaps 20 percent of the worldwide production of PCBs leak to the atmosphere due to their high volatibility; another 5 percent is swept into sewers and rivers. Rather little was known in the early 1970s of the effects of PCBs on marine organisms, although these chlorinated hydrocarbons also tended to accumulate in the fatty tissues of animals. Scientific certainty here has been less than in the case of the insecticides, and prior to 1968 some measurements even failed to differentiate between DDT and PCB concentrations in tissue.

Speculation about the effects of chlorinated hydrocarbons upon the marine environment has been encouraged. In 1973, for example, a group of scientists examined in detail four low molecular weight chlorinated hydrocarbons (LMCHs); tetrachloro-ethylene (Per); 1.1.1-trichloroethane (1.1.1-TCE); di-chlorethane (EDC); and 1, 2-dichloropropane (PDC) in an effort to identify compounds whose effects on the marine environment may not yet be obvious, but which could signal danger. Per and 1.1.1-TCE have been used for dry cleaning and degreasing processes while EDC and PDC have been mainly used as chemical intermediates, such as lead scavengers in tetraethyl lead mixtures or in the production of vinyl chloride, Per, or carbon tetrachloride. Smaller amounts of EDC and PDC have also been used in solvents, degreasants, films, paint removers, and fumigants against insects.

The study panel concluded that the effects of the low-molecular-weight chlorinated hydrocarbons were "poorly understood." Most of the published literature dealt with acute exposure to selected LMCHs. Generally, the LMCHs seemed to have "a low potential for accumulation in aquatic systems." The panel felt that the atmospheric release of these LMCH's would not be hazardous because photolysis is very rapid in the higher atmosphere and takes only a few days at sea level. However, the scientists noted that hydrolysis would be slower. River or ocean disposal, therefore, might be "of greater concern."

In sum, the chlorinated hydrocarbons need to be watched with care for their rate and method of release into the marine environment while research continues to examine their effects upon all parts of the marine system. But there seemed to be little cause for public alarm, let alone panic, so long as the government had a constant opportunity to regulate the production, use, and disposal of the chlorinated hydrocarbons as better evidence of their behavior in the marine environment came to light.

Heavy metals in the marine environment have been another cause of concern to the public. In 1932 the Chisso company in the small Japanese city of Minamata first began producing acetaldehyde, to be used in manufacturing plastics, drugs, photography, chemicals, and perfumes. However, the inorganic mercury used as a chemical catalyst in making acetaldehyde, was converted into methyl mercury. This poisonous substance was continually flushed into the nearby bay in ever-increasing amounts in the early 1950s. The methyl mercury entered the fish which, in turn, were eaten by cats and by people in Minamata. First, the cats staggered crazily, had convulsions, and died; then, in 1956 a five-year old child, incoherent and in delirium, was taken to the factory hospital. Before the Minamata tragedy ended more than 100 people had died and about 3000 had chronic ailments, some quite severe. Even unborn children were affected: a few began their lives as hopeless cripples. These horrifying events in Minamata attracted the attention of the world to the great peril of heavy metals in the marine environment.[27]

All the heavy metals are found naturally throughout the crust of the earth and in seawater in greatly differing concentrations. Indeed, some of them, when in the proper form and concentration, are essential to life itself. However, the problem with heavy metals, such as mercury, cadmium, selenium, nickel, lead, copper, chromium, arsenic, tin, or manganese is that they can be toxic to marine organisms. Metallic mercury and most mercury compounds may be biologically converted into the poisonous methyl mercury, and some of the food chains may concentrate methyl mercury. Even though no harmful connection between the lead presently in the oceans and marine organism damage has yet been demonstrated, lead is known to be toxic to creatures at rather low levels. Cadmium has killed the larvae of crabs and fish, and cadmium also can be concentrated in tissues.

Any of the heavy metals may be hazardous to the environment when poured, dropped, or floated in quantities exceeding the parts per million ordinarily found in nature. In recent decades the increase of agricultural, industrial, and commercial products that utilize metals has been phenomenal. Either through the disposal of these products as refuse or through the processing of the product itself, very large quantities of heavy metals have been running into the rivers or poured into the oceans. In addition, the fossil fuels contain some of these metals, which combustion liberates into the atmosphere only to fall upon oceans through wind transport. For example, of the world production of 8800 tons of mercury in 1968 it was estimated that 4000 tons went into the environment from losses in industrial and agricultural uses, and another 1,600 tons entered the atmosphere through fossil fuel combustion. The natural flows of mercury by degassing of the earth's crust or by natural oil erosion and runoff to the rivers was probably several times that amount, but the problem lies in the concentration and disposal of the metal.

Undoubtedly most of the heavy metals find their way into sediments, and, if undisturbed, seem to cause little harm to marine organisms or to man. Yet the Minamata disaster is a constant reminder of the penalty of carelessness in not attending to the recycling of heavy metals into an environment which can tolerate, in fact, utilize their presence.

In testimony before the Subcommittee on Oceans and Atmosphere of the U.S. Senate Committee on Commerce Dr. Thomas Owen of the National Science Foundation made the point that while much publicity had been given to the toxicity of heavy metals, there was no evidence that the concentration of these elements in the open ocean had been increased. He suggested that their removal had been sufficient to maintain constant concentrations in the seas. Undoubtedly the parts per million of these metals have increased in the estuaries and their sources, but Dr. Owen ascribed this phenomenon to the natural erosion of the watershed. One thing was clear. There was scarcely enough evidence from research to arrive at many, if any, conclusions about tolerable levels of heavy metal concentrations in the 1970s. Certainly the effect of each metal upon different plant and animal life had to be examined separately, and the great gaps in hard knowledge hardly provided a strong bridge to general conclusions. After Minamata no one could be indifferent to the presence of heavy metals in rivers, bays, and coastal waters, but the evidence pointed to the need for patient and cautious research without public anxiety.

The effects of petroleum upon the marine environment have been the most obvious to the public. Oil is the most prevalent, the most visible, and the most tangible of the persistent pollutants in the oceans. People who may be unaware of the toxic effect of a contaminant upon marine organism easily recognize oily waters when they see or smell them. And they are both repelled and angered by oil slicks washing up on a sandy beach. But apart from appearances and an abuse of the amenities, like bathing in the surf, how much damage has oil inflicted upon the marine environment?

Again the response, as with other pollutants, has been one of uncertainty. Much depends upon whether the oil is crude or refined. In a West Falmouth oil spill of 1969 about 110,000 gallons of #2 Fuel Oil exacted a deadly toll of many of the organisms that it touched at the time of the spill; then, as the oil spread in succeeding days, the kill was extended, although more slowly; degradation of the fuel oil by biological and physical processes followed, but the shellfish of the area were unacceptable for a long time and evidence of hydrocarbon pollutants in the sediments persisted. On the other hand, when a barge sank in the mouth of the Potomac River on 2 February 1976 and spilled 250,000 gallons of crude oil, after a six-week clean-up of the mess in the water and on shore in the Chesapeake Bay, the marsh grass grew wonderfully well and later a study showed no effect on mussels and oysters.

Oil in the marine environment could affect the metabolism, the reproductive potential, or the genetic make-up of organisms; however, little proof has been available. Laboratory experiments have demonstrated that high concentrations of refined petroleum residues can be lethal to salmon, both in egg and adult form, to striped bass, anchovy, the tanner crab, herring, and trout. Studies of mussels have indicated that even small amounts of crude oil in the habitat can decrease the amount of energy available for maintenance growth, and reproduction. Far more is known about the short-term effects of recent dramatic oil spills upon marine organisms than the long-term chronic effects which may—or may not—endanger the marine environment.

The overwhelming amounts of petroleum lost to the sea by man's activities through exploitation and transfer have been crude oils. Slicks and tar lumps on the surface of the sea may evaporate or decompose in the atmosphere, disperse into the water column, adhere to and incorporate with sediments, or be oxidized by chemical and biological action into carbon dioxide. Some microorganisms capable of oxidizing petroleum seem to be present everywhere; however, while some fractions of oil are easily degraded, others seem to be more hardy. Fish can swallow hydrocarbons or take them through their gills, metabolize the elements, and excrete them. However, invertebrates and benthic organisms seem to have much more difficulty in the metabolic process. Hydrocarbons may be stored in the fats of many organisms, but there is little evidence of the magnification of petroleum hydrocarbons through the food web chain.[28]

In the record of the effects of oil spills and other sudden discharges of petroleum into water, the greatest damage has occurred to the biota where the quantity of oil released has been great relative to the affected area. Plants and animals in enclosed or semi-enclosed areas of comparatively shallow water have suffered the most. As indicated above, different types of oil inflict different kinds of casualties; moreoever, some organisms seem to be affected by persistent hydrocarbons in the environment, but others not at all. Some birds have been killed by a single coating of crude oil; some marsh plants have sustained several coatings without much harm; and oyster shells have not been affected at all. Intertidal species seem to endure better in the presence of petroleum than subtidal species. Practically no data have been available on pelagic species.

With regard to the effects of oil on human health as a consequence of eating marine organisms, the best scientific judgment has led to a "modest concern rather than alarm" for the amount of carcinogens in petroleum that might be ingested by a meal with shell or fin fish seems to be no greater than the amount ingested in any ordinary meal.

As with radioactive elements, chlorinated hydrocarbons, and heavy metals, caution is required in assessing the pollution of the marine environment by petroleum. But dire forecasts about the death of the oceans and the destruction of life upon the planet as a result of the exploitation or transport of oil, with the present spills and wastes, seem far-fetched, sounding false alarms, diverting scare resources, and running the risk of self-defeating regulation.[29]

In all environmental matters, including marine pollution, a balance must be struck between the benefits and the costs. At one time, a society may regard its national security as so endangered that it will risk and even pay the costs of radioactive pollution. At another time, a people, scourged by malaria or weak with famine from the ravages of rodents and insects, will gladly accept the long-term risks of pesticides. Modern society would be thrown back to a far lower standard of living, completely unacceptable to the public, by the elimination of heavy metals from industry and the ban of oil as an energy source. The issue, therefore, cannot be one of elimination, but accommodation. Anything in life that is too abundant in the wrong place can be called a pollutant and a threat to the environment. Agriculture, for example, requires water—but too much brings a flood and severe damage to crops while too little brings drought and destruction. Marine organisms too have optimum environments, often disturbed by natural causes beyond the control of man, but more recently threatened by human activities that have permitted a plethora of wastes to fly, wash, drift, or be dumped into the wrong places.

The most significant element in either the adaptability of man to his environment or in his change of the environment to suit his prevailing needs lies in rationality. Properly informed by objective analysis the public can (there is no guarantee that it will) exercise control over its agricultural, industrial, or other commercial activities through law and regulations. The response of the American government has not been slow, as this chapter indicates. Whether legislation has been sufficient for the protection of a safe, healthy, and pleasant environment within the economic needs and goals of the United States is a debatable policy issue. The problem is complicated not only by the federal-state system of law and administration on the national scene, but also by the necessity of international regulations for pollutants that spread across the skies and seas, transcending all political frontiers.

U.S. Policies on Marine Pollution

In the late 1920s and 1930s the discharge of oil by ships into the high seas had been somewhat mitigated by a "gentlemen's agreement" that obtained among the private shipowners' organization. Certain ocean zones contiguous to coastal states were recognized as places where discharges were prohibited. After the failure of the 1926 international conference in Washington to reduce the pollution of the seas outside territorial waters, however, no legal constraints bound the use of the high seas for the washing, dropping, dripping, leaking, or dumping of oil. But after World War II the use of the oceans by shipping changed dramatically. Responding to the rising demand for petroleum as fuel for the reviving economies of western Europe, the importation of oil by sea-going vessels to Great Britain, Scandinavia, Western Germany, Belgium, the Netherlands, and France, as a bloc, increased about 300 percent in three years from 1950 to 1953. The rapid increase of oil pollution in the contiguous water of these countries led to a second international conference on this subject, which adopted the International Convention for the Prevention of the Pollution of the Sea by Oil in 1954 at Brussels, signed by 28 states, including the United States.

The Convention came into force in 1958, but the United States did not ratify it until 1961. In fact, between 1924 and 1960 the U.S. Congress had passed no law specifically dealing with the discharge or spillage of oil into the sea. The Oil Pollution Act of 1961 was approved by Congress to implement the provisions of the Convention.

Under the Act for the first time in American history the discharge by any person from any ship of oil or any oily mixture, in which the oil "fouls the surface of the sea," became unlawful in a number of prohibited zones around the world. These prohibited zones were all sea areas within fifty miles from land, but in some cases, like the coasts of northwest Europe and parts of the coast of Australia, the prohibited zone went as far as one hundred or one hundred and fifty miles out to sea.

Each ship was required to carry an oil record book and tankers were compelled to enter data about their tanks, the cleaning of tanks, the settling in slop tanks, and the disposal of oily residues. Ships other than tankers were required to enter information about the ballasting or cleaning of bunker fuel tanks and the disposal of oil residues. All ships had to record any accidental or exceptional discharges or escapes of oil especially in a prohibited zone, with details of the circumstances and reason for the discharge signed by the officer supervising the operation and by the master of the ship. Finally, the Coast Guard was empowered to draft regulations for ship fittings, equipment, and operating requirements to help prevent leakages.

Although the Act, belated or not, was a step forward in the reduction of the pollution of the sea by oil, it reflected the caution of the shipping industry and followed the language of the international convention which it implemented. Naval auxiliaries and ships, under 500 tons gross tonnage were not covered by the Act while ships engaged in the whaling industry or navigating the Great Lakes were exempted "for the time being." Moreover, discharges for the purpose of securing the safety of the ship, preventing damage to the ship or its cargo, or saving life at sea; or the escape of oil or an oily mixture resulting from damage to the ship or unavoidable leakage, assuming all reasonable precautions had been taken; or the discharge of sediments were not illegal provided that such discharges had been made "as far from land as is practicable." Finally, the U.S. Senate, while agreeing to the ratification of the Convention, had not accepted Article IV, which had provided that within three years of the Convention's entering into force each state would provide in each main port facilities adequate for the reception of residues from oil ballast water and tank washings.[30]

Nothing in the Oil Pollution Act of 1961 had amended or modified the Oil Pollution Act of 1924. The next important legislation in this area came five years later when the Clean Waters Restoration Act of 1966, which did amend the Oil Pollution Act of 1924, made it unlawful to discharge or permit discharges of oil *by any means* into or upon navigable waters of the United States or the adjoining shoreline. Moreover, offenders were required to remove the pollutants and if they failed to do so could be held liable for the costs of removal.

By 1969, however, experience with an increasing number of oil spills and a few tremendous accidental discharges had demonstrated the delay or the inability of the responsible parties in undertaking clean-up operations. The payment of costs was further complicated by the problem of fixing liability under the law. With this background the House and Senate examined new legislation to regulate the pollution of navigable waters by oil, but the committees of Congress found themselves deadlocked for five months on some issues, notably the fixing of liability on owners or operators. The House preferred liabilities only in cases of willful or negligent discharges. Reports of new accidents of oil spills, however, finally led the House and Senate to come to an agreement on the Water Quality Improvement Act of 1970, (P.L. 91-224).[31]

Legally, as amendments to the Federal Water Pollution Control Act as amended, the Water Quality Improvement Act provided that no oil of any kind or in any form could be discharged into the navigable waters, the territorial sea, or the contiguous zone of the United States from vessels, offshore, or onshore facilities. Failure to report a spill made an owner or operator liable to criminal penalties up to $10,000 or up to a year in imprisonment; for the "knowing discharge of oil" a civil penalty of up to $10,000 could be assessed. Most importantly, unless the responsible owner or operator immediately cleaned up the pollutant, the President was authorized to take the necessary removal action and to hold the operator or owner liable for the costs incurred by the federal government up to $100 per gross ton of the vessel or a maximum of $14 million, whichever was less. Owners of onshore or offshore facilities could be held liable for amounts up to $8 million. The Act also adopted the Senate view of "absolute" or strict liability, that is, no excuses by the owner or operator from liability, except for an act of war, an act of God, negligence of the federal government itself, or an act or omission of a third party. To make certain that owners or operators would have the financial capacity to pay for clean-up costs, every vessel transiting the navigable waters of the United States was required to show evidence in one form or another of an ability to secure payment up to $14 million. There was one other important exemption from absolute liability for owners and operators, namely, in the discharge of oil in the contiguous zone of the United States in so far as it was permitted by Article IV of the International Convention for the Prevention of Pollution of the Sea by Oil (1954). Under that Convention the jettisoning of oil to secure the safety of ship and cargo and to save life at sea was allowed as well as any escape of oil that resulted from damage to a ship or an unavoidable leakage.

Other provisions of the Water Quality Improvement Act of 1970 established a Federal revolving fund for use in clean-ups, stated that nothing in the Act prevented states from imposing any requirement or liability with respect to discharge in their waters, or prevented further suits against operators or owners for damages to private or public property. Moreover, any facility that required a federal permit or license must first have approval from a state that its discharges, if any, would meet the state's water quality standards. Marine sanitation device standards were to be established for all new vessels and demonstration-research projects were authorized for mine acid elimination, the reduction of pollution of the Great Lakes, and methods to control pesticides released into the environment, particularly the marine environment.

By 1972 the United States had reached the apogee of the arc of environmental legislation. A spate of major laws culminated the bold campaign by the outspoken environmental groups to gain public recognition of the value of clean air and water to American society. Three acts of Congress in that year particularly addressed themselves to the problems of marine pollution: namely, the Ports and Waterways Safety Act (P.L. 92-340); the Federal Water Pollution Control Act Amendments (P.L. 92-500); and the Marine Protection, Research and Sanctuaries (Ocean Dumping) Act (P.L. 92-532). Another law of long-range importance to the uses of the shoreline and near-shore waters was the Coastal Zone Management Act (P.L. 92-583).

Not the least of the problems that had plagued the marine environment in the 1960s was the increasing density of traffic of vessels entering the ports of the United States, the growth in the tonnage and draft of ships, particularly tankers, and the dangers of explosion, fire, and water-shore pollution from ruptured cargoes of oil, gas, and other hazardous cargoes. The Ports and Waterways Safety Act, which became law on 10 July 1972, was enacted to safeguard further the navigable waters and the shores of the United States against hazardous cargoes aboard vessels. Henceforth, the design, construction, alteration, repair, maintenance, and operation of any vessel carrying hazardous cargoes and using or entering the navigable waters of the United States were subject to minimum standards set by the Secretary of Transportation through the U.S. Coast Guard. Hazardous cargoes were described as inflammable or combustible liquids or gases, or such other cargoes as the Secretary of Transportation might designate as hazardous. Regulations were made applicable to foreign vessels as well as those under the U.S. flag, with discretion given to the Secretary to accept such certificates or documents from foreign vessels as might be agreed upon in a treaty. In any case the Secretary was authorized to deny the use or entry into the navigable waters of the United States to any vessel that did not meet the minimum standards.

Because the International Maritime Consultative Organization (IMCO) was holding an International Conference on Marine Pollution in London in October 1973, the Act allowed the U.S. Coast Guard until 1 January 1974 to promulgate its regulations. With regard to tankers, the obvious and ubiquitous source of marine pollution by oil, there was agreement in the U.S. Coast Guard—and at the international conference in London—that segregated ballast tanks in new ships would gradually eliminate one of the major sources of oil discharge into the seas. With segregated ballast tanks the washing out of oil storage tanks by seawater and the use of the same tanks for water ballast would be stopped. The Convention provided that all tankers larger than 70,000 DWT ordered after 31 December 1975 be equipped with segregated ballast tanks large enough to provide adequate operating draft without having to carry ballast water in the cargo oil tanks.

On another issue of construction design, however, whether all new tankers should be required to have "double bottoms" in order to protect their cargoes of oil from release upon accidental groundings, a fairly common form of marine hazard, international opinion was strongly divided. The U.S. Coast Guard had taken the position that double bottoms in tankers were desirable. It had presented a paper at the London international conference indicating that such construction would have prevented oil discharges in 90% of the cases or avoided about 11,000 of the 12,499 tons actually spilled in U.S. navigable waters between 1969 and 1975 by grounding. Nevertheless, the IMCO conference in 1973 approved the International Convention for the Prevention of Pollution from ships without any provisions for "double bottoms."[32]

By July 1974 the U.S. Coast Guard had ready its rules for segregated ballast tanks, pumping, piping, and discharge arrangements, slop tanks, and oily residue tanks for U.S. vessels—not public vessels—"engaged in the carriage of oil" to meet the Convention and its responsibilities under the Port and Waterways Safety Act of 1972. The Coast Guard proposed that segregated ballast tanks be built into vessels, 70,000 tons or more, contracted for after 31 December 1974, or which were under construction by June 1975, or delivered after 31 December 1977. Following the International Convention, nothing was said of double bottom construction.

In Congress, however, the proponents of a mandatory requirement of double bottoms for tankers were not hushed. A few of the leading American shipbuilding companies had actually built more than a score of large tankers with double bottoms and had indicated that the additional costs ran to only two or three percent of the contract price. On 23 January 1975 Senator Warren G. Magnuson of Washington, a leading advocate of double bottoms, introduced a Tanker Safety Improvement Act as an amendment to the Ports and Waterways Safety Act of 1972. His bill required that any vessel more than 20,000 deadweight tons, under the U.S. flag, engaged in the carriage of oil to U.S. ports situated in internal waters or straits, and which was contracted for or commenced construction after 30 June 1975, be fitted with a double bottom. This issue seemed likely to divide opinions, with national and international ramifications, in the immediate years ahead.

The second major Act that addressed the problem of marine pollution in 1972 was the Federal Water Pollution Control Act Amendments.

The 1899 "Refuse Act" had made the discharge or dumping of any refuse matter into the navigable waters of the United States illegal, except for discharges in liquid form through the streets or sewage systems. The Secretary of the Army had also been empowered to make other limits, conditions, or exceptions to the Act, but until 1970 no system for monitoring such discharges had been formulated. Moreover, "refuse matter" was consistently interpreted by the Army Corps of Engineers as materials that would actually impede navigation.[33]

Marching along with the fervor of the environmental movement President Nixon on 23 December 1970 issued an executive order to utilize the Refuse Act "whose potential for water pollution control has only recently been recognized," to require industry to submit both to state authorities and the federal government data concerning their effluents. Henceforth permits would be required from the Corps of Engineers for all industrial discharges and applications would be reviewed to meet both state and federal water quality standards. The Environmental Protection Agency was designated as the responsible agency for this final review on the federal side.

The permit system ran into trouble almost immediately. The Corps of Engineers itself had failed to file environmental impact statements for its actions as required by the National Environmental Policy Act of 1969, so permits were blocked by litigation. Out of 20,000 applications, only 20 permits were issued. Moreover, all enforcement actions had to be delayed pending the review of a key case by the Supreme Court in which the government alleged that a company could be held criminally liable for the discharge of certain kinds of industrial wastes into the Mononagehela river. The defendant protested that the Corps of Engineers had always led it to believe that such wastes did not interfere with navigation and, therefore, were not illegal.

Meanwhile the federal water pollution control program had technically expired on 31 October 1971. The fiscal year 1970 authorization of grants to aid local community sewage systems elapsed on 30 June 1971. Although the President, eight days later, signed a new Congressional authorization of funds until September 1971 and although there was a further extension of the authorization for one month in September, a third extension of the grants program, which the House approved on 28 October, failed passage in the Senate. In fact, the Senate had under consideration during these months far-reaching legislation on water pollution control that would become famous in the history of the environmental movement.

On 2 November 1971, after extensive hearings, the Senate voted 86-0 for S. 2770, a bill establishing as a goal the clean-up of the nation's waters to make them suitable for fish propagation and recreation by 1981 and as "federal policy" the complete elimination of the discharge of pollutants in navigable waters by 1985. The amount authorized for construction grants for water pollution treatment plants was a staggering $14 billion, more than twice the sum requested by the President for this program, while additional hundreds of millions of dollars were authorized for research, enforcement, and a new permit system for discharges under the authority of the EPA. The House of Representatives failed to act on that bill in 1971. But on 14 March 1972 the House Committee on Public Works reported favorably on a bill (HR 11896) with the same intention of cleaning up the waters of the United States over the same years. It too provided for a permit system under the EPA, ending the issuance of permits under the Refuse Act.

Still there were wide differences between the Senate and the House bills, which were not resolved until 14 October when the Congress overwhelmingly approved the Federal Water Pollution Control Act Amendments of 1972. The

Act was an entirely new and forward step in the progress of American environmental legislation, more comprehensive and by far more expensive than any previous legislation for reducing the pollution of the waters of the United States. Indeed, the Act authorized expenditures of $24 billion, three times the amount the President had requested in 1971 for similar purposes. Therefore, President Nixon vetoed it, saying that legislation to continue the nation's efforts to raise the standards of water quality "through extreme and needless over-spending, does not serve the public interest." But within a day, on 18 October 1972, both the House and the Senate overrode the President's veto by very large margins.[34]

The Federal Water Pollution Control Act Amendments of 1972 established as a "national goal" the elimination of pollutant discharges into U.S. waters by 1985. The key to the strength of the amendments, however, lay in assigning to a single federal agency the power to limit all effluents from "point sources" such as industrial plants. The law required the EPA to determine by 1 July 1977 the limits on effluents from all point sources on the basis of the "best control technology currently available." Furthermore restrictions on the discharges of publicly owned sewage plants by that date were to be based on a secondary treatment process. Moreover, the law required effluent limitations from point sources to be based upon the "best available technology economically achievable by 1 July 1983."

The administrator of EPA was also directed to list categories of industrial pollution sources and set national performance standards for each new source; to list toxic pollutants and prohibit their discharge; and to set pretreatment standards for discharges into publicly owned treatment plants. Furthermore, the administrator of EPA was given the right to enter pollution sources and to inspect and monitor equipment to control pollution. In addition, at the request of the Secretary of State, the administrator could take action necessary to stop international pollution originating in the United States. For violations of EPA standards or orders, penalties of between $2,500 per day to $25,000 per day or a year in prison or both were provided for criminal acts, with $50,000 a day or two years in prison, or both for second offenses. Civil penalties could be as high as $10,000 per day.

All discharges of radiological, chemical, or biological warfare agents, as well as high-level radioactive wastes, were prohibited, while it was declared U.S. policy that there should be no discharge of oil or hazardous substances into U.S. waters, adjoining shorelines, or contiguous zone waters. Such discharges could be penalized at $50,000 per discharge, with no limit to fines for willful discharges. Furthermore, the cleanup costs of such discharges from vessels, onshore, or offshore facilities would have to be paid by the owners or operators—unless they were caused by negligence of the federal government, an act of a third party, war, or God. The Act also provided that a citizen in a geographic area who had been adversely affected by pollution or who had been actively engaged in the administrative process about an alleged violation of the Act could bring suit against the federal government or its agencies, including the EPA administrator.

A large part of the legislation, which essentially set forth amendments to the previous Water Pollution Control Act, continued to deal with research and construction grants. But the provisions went far beyond previous enactments in directing the administrator to conduct research, such as studies of the special water pollution problems of oil spills, marine sewage equipment, pesticides, waste oil, estuary pollution, river systems, and thermal discharges, and authorizing research and development grants as high as 75 percent of total costs for problems connected with storm sewers, water recycling methods, agricultural pollution, and mine acid or mine water pollution control. For the first time, moreover, grants to state or local agencies for the construction of publicly owned treatment works could be allocated to states on the basis of need, rather than population, with the federal share reaching a maximum of 75 percent of the costs. Areawide planning processes and agencies for waste treatment management could be funded from federal grants at 100 percent of costs for a period of three years—and 75 percent thereafter.

Under the Act states were authorized to conduct their own discharge permit programs if approved by EPA. In fact, EPA encouraged the states to assume the administration of the new National Pollutant Discharge Elimination System, but states were required to adopt regulations for public notices, enforcement, and other procedures as may be specified by EPA. In April 1973 California became the first state to receive permanent approval for its permit system. However, each permit under a state program, except for some categories that may be waived by EPA, has been subject to review and possible veto by EPA on grounds of inconsistency with the statute or effluent guidelines.

Many other provisions of the Act moved vigorously—far too vigorously and expensively in the eyes of the President, some members of Congress, and industrial groups—"to restore and maintain the chemical, physical, and biological integrity of the nation's waters." Three months before the enactment of the 1972 Federal Water Pollution Control amendments, the Council on Environmental Quality had estimated that a total of $287 billion would be required to reduce pollution in the United States to tolerable standards by 1980. Of this amount $87 billion would have to be spent for water pollution control alone. In September 1973 the CEQ reported, "It is clear that our national commitment to a cleaner environment will be very costly," amounting to about $275 billion or 2.5 percent of the gross national product during the next decade. At the end of 1973 the administrator of EPA reported that industry would have to invest about $12 billion in treatment facilities "within the next few years" to meet the 1977 standards set under the Federal Water Pollution Control Act. Put another way, industry would have to increase the average annual amount invested for water pollution control per year by about three and one-half times. Finally, investments by utilities and other plants to prevent thermal pollution, depending on the number of plants exempted from thermal standards, were estimated at $2.3 to $9.5 billion.

These extraordinary costs hardly stemmed the rush of rhetoric and regulations in Washington to seek an end to the pollution of the streams, rivers, estuaries, and coastal waters of America. In a study of twenty-three industries that were discharging wastes directly into the waters of the United States, EPA gave its opinion that "in most cases" they would be able to recover the costs of "the best practical waste water treatment" by an increase in prices. However, continued EPA, some smaller and older plants might not be able to pass on the costs and might decide to close by 1977.

Everything has not gone smoothly under the Federal Water Pollution Control Act Amendments of 1972. Complaints of stringent regulations and more than usual bureaucratic red tape in the implementation of the Act were plentiful from 1973 to 1977. EPA suffered the disdain of both industry and the ardent environmental movement for its procrastination in issuing effluent limitation guidelines. And many communities, as in the past, still had difficulty in raising the local funds required for sewage treatment facilities despite the generous share of federal aid for this purpose.

Nevertheless, more than 90 percent of major dischargers and 67 percent of all industrial dischargers had received permits by the middle of 1976. Between 1957 and 1977 about $18 billion was obligated by the federal government for municipal treatment of waste water. Controversy over how to allocate these funds to states never ceased. Public Law 92-24, signed by the President on 3 January 1974, established a new formula for allotting federal funds for sewage treatment facilities with 50 percent based on the "needs" of the states and 50 percent based on the ratio of costs of three specific categories of pollution control facilities. But another formula based on population and future growth was also considered by Congress.

The Federal Water Pollution Control Act Amendments fundamentally ensured the control of point source pollution of river and coastal waters and accelerated the development of public sewage plants that would provide secondary treatment for all wastes. The amendments, moreover, did not ignore the problem of the deliberate dumping of pollutants from vessels into coastal waters or the oceans, for the Act had authorized EPA to establish procedures to grant permits for such dumping and had also authorized the Secretary of the Army to grant permits for dredged or fill material at certain sites. However, the basic law that prohibited for the first time in American history the unregulated dumping of waste materials into coastal waters and the oceans was the Marine Protection, Research, and Sanctuaries Act, PL 92-532, better known as the Ocean Dumping Act, of 1972.

President Nixon, in a special message to Congress on the environment on 8 February 1971, had urged that "national policy should be to ban unregulated ocean dumping of all wastes and to place strict limits on ocean disposal of harmful materials" and had suggested appropriate legislation. Nevertheless, for almost a year the House and the Senate could not agree on the same bill for this purpose. Among other things, the committees of the two houses had differing views about the definition of the waters to be covered, the dumping of fish wastes, the primary responsibility for the dumping of dredged materials, and the amount of funds to be authorized. Finally the Ocean Dumping Act was cleared by Congress on 13 October and became law on 23 October 1972, just five days after Congress had overridden the President's veto of the Federal Water Pollution Control Act Amendments.

The Ocean Dumping Act made it the policy of the United States to regulate the dumping of all types of materials into ocean waters and to prevent, or strictly limit, the dumping of any material that would "adversely affect human health, welfare, or amenities, or the marine environment, ecological system, or economic potentialities." The transportation out to sea and the dumping of any radiological, chemical, or biological warfare agents, or high-level radioactive wastes in the territorial waters and the contiguous zone (from three to twelve miles out to sea) was absolutely forbidden. Indeed, federal employees and agencies were forbidden to transfer such materials from *outside* the United States to the ocean for dumping. Rep. Charles A. Mosher, one of the members of the House-Senate conference committee that had finally reported favorably on the compromise bill, observed that the Ocean Dumping Act "marks a turning point in man's destructive use of the seas as a garbage dump."

In the issuance of any permit for dumping materials into ocean waters, the Act specified that criteria of the need for such dumping, its effect on human health and welfare, including esthetic and recreational values, its effect on fisheries resources, its persistence, volume, and nature, the location and other possible dump sites, and the effect of such dumping on alternate uses of the oceans must be taken into account. Except for dredge spoil, there was little debate that EPA should be the permitting agency. Congress was divided, however, over whether the Corps of Engineers, which had always been responsible for dredge spoil, should be ultimately responsible for permits to dump that material. In the end the Corps was granted authority to prepare permits for dredge spoil, but required to notify the EPA of its action before the actual issuance of the permit. If disagreement arose between the Corps and the EPA, the determination of the administrator of EPA "shall prevail."

By the spring of 1973 EPA had ready its interim regulations for the permit system and the criteria to be used in the evaluation of applications. On 15 October 1973 EPA published these in final form, which also satisfied the Federal Water Pollution Control Act Amendments of 1972 that had required EPA to promulgate guidelines for determining the degradation of the waters of the territorial sea, the contiguous zone, and the oceans. The Corps of Engineers published its revised regulations for permits for the transportation of dredge spoil to be dumped into ocean waters on 10 May 1973. By the end of that year EPA had designated 118 dumping sites, mostly for the dumping of dredge spoil as well as mud, sand, and chemical wastes. Three sites were marked for the disposal of toxic wastes: one off the Massachusetts coast, one off the Delaware Bay, and one off the coast of Los Angeles.

In addition to the materials expressly forbidden to be dumped by the Act, EPA regulations have banned the dumping of certain substances whose effect on the marine ecosystem cannot be determined, which have persistent inert materials that float or stay suspended on the surface, or which have more than trace amounts of mercury, mercury compounds, cadmium compounds, cadmium, and orthohalogens, as well as crude oil, fuel oil, heavy diesel oil, lubricating oils, and hydraulic fluids. To dump other materials such as those formed of arsenic beryllium, chromium, or lead, or low level radioactive wastes, organo-silicon compounds, organic and inorganic processing wastes, oxygen-demanding wastes, petrochemicals, and organic chemicals henceforth required a special permit. The Act also provided that no state "shall adopt or enforce any rule or regulation related to an activity regulated by this title." But states can propose and EPA can adopt special regulations for marine waters within a state's jurisdiction.

Two other federal agencies also have had responsibilities in connection with ocean dumping under the Act. Research and the monitoring of ocean dumping fell within the province of the National Oceanic and Atmospheric Administration while surveillance and enforcement functions were assigned to the Coast Guard. In April 1973 an Ocean Disposal Coordinating Committee, consisting of the four responsible agencies under the Act and chaired by EPA, was established for joint research and monitoring strategies on all aspects of ocean dumping.

On 29 December 1972 the United States had signed the Convention on the Prevention of Marine Pollution by Dumping of Wastes and Other Matter. The Senate consented to the ratification of the convention on 3 August 1973, and it then became necessary to amend the Ocean Dumping Act to conform to the treaty responsibilities of the United States. The most significant changes were the extension of U.S. law to include not only the regulation of the carriage and dumping into the ocean of waste materials from the United States, but also from any foreign territory by a U.S. vessel or aircraft, and the widening of the definition of "material" to include any oil taken aboard a vessel or an aircraft for the purpose of dumping at sea. In October 1973 EPA published its final regulations for ocean dumping, which generally provided permits for limited periods. Where the dumping of wastes exceeded the criteria set forth in the Ocean Dumping Act because alternative disposition was not available, the permit required a plan that would lead to eventual disposal within the limits set by the Act. Because of the new regulations, forty dumpers of industrial wastes in the New York area stopped their ocean disposal practices.

During 1973 almost 12 million tons of wastes were dumped into the oceans, of which over 10.5 million tons went into the Atlantic, 1.4 million tons into the Gulf of Mexico, and only 240 tons into the Pacific. Over 90 percent of the wastes were sewage sludge and industrial wastes. By 1975 ocean dumping had been completely eliminated in the Pacific and reduced in the Gulf of Mexico. But in the Atlantic, although industrial waste dumping had declined slightly, the total figure of 8.7 million tons was still higher than the 1968 figure. This was because of the increase in sewer sludge dumping.[35]

Another law reflective of the American people's concern for the marine environment was the Coastal Zone Management Act of 1972. Interest in national land use planning for the seashores of the United States dated far back into the 1950s and 1960s. By 1955 of the 127 million acres of wetlands estimated to have been part of the 48 contiguous states, only 74 million acres remained. Over a twenty-year period California alone lost 67 percent of its coastal estuarine habitats. In 1961 Congress had taken a first step in the preservation of the wetlands through the Wetlands Loan Act, which authorized funds to accelerate federal acquisition of a portion of such lands needed by migratory waterfowl. But that program ran into such strong opposition by state and local interests that it had to be amended in 1967 to permit a state veto of any federal acquisitions. In September 1966 Vice-President Hubert H. Humphrey, chairman of the Cabinet-level National Council on Marine Resources and Engineering Development (created to recommend long-range ocean policy), put forth as a major goal the reduction of the hazards of pollution of bays and seashore areas. In January 1959 the Commission on Marine Science, Engineering, and Resources recommended that a Coastal Zone Management Act be enacted to provide policy objectives for the Coastal Zone and to authorize federal grants-in-aid to facilitate the establishment of State coastal zone authorities "empowered to manage the coastal waters and adjacent land."[36]

Meanwhile the Clean Water Restoration Act of 1966 had authorized the Secretary of Interior to study and present recommendations to Congress for a comprehensive national program for preserving, studying, using, and developing the estuaries of the United States and to delineate the respective responsibilities of the federal and state governments. At the end of 1969 Secretary Walter J. Hickel reported that 70 percent of the U.S. population lived in the coastal states, including the Great Lakes. Moreover, the population of the coastal states had increased by 78 percent over the last thirty years compared to a national growth rate of 46 percent—and coastal state population was expected to be doubled by 2020. He recommended a National Estuarine and Coastal Zone Management Act.

Two problems faced any national legislation dealing with the coastal zones. First, the regulation of land use had always been a prerogative of the states. In turn, the states had delegated zoning powers to local governments or authorities. Second, the abuse of land was hardly confined to coastal areas. Indeed, the management of coastal land resources for the public good could not, in the minds of many planners, be separated from the entire economy or community of interests in a state or region. Secretary Hickel in his testimony for a National

Estuarine and Coastal Management Act had indicated that what was "really needed" was a land-use management act.[37]

On 19 September 1972 the Senate passed a bill to establish a national land-use policy. It would have provided grants and other assistance to the states to help them develop land-use programs. However, the House took no action on a somewhat similar bill.[a] Finally, on 12 October 1972 the Congress cleared for the President the Coastal Zone Management Act of 1972 after extensive committee discussion and the compromise on key issues. The Senate had wished to designate the Secretary of Commerce as the responsible agent, since the Act was basically water-related, believing that the actual administration would be delegated to the National Oceanographic and Atmospheric Administration. The House had wished to give authority to the Secretary of Interior as the head of the Cabinet department chiefly concerned with land use and management. However, the Senate view prevailed, although the conference report stated that "coordination and concurrence" with the Secretary of Interior would be required—and that once a national land use policy had been established the two secretaries would have to collaborate closely. Authority to designate estuarine sanctuaries extending beyond the U.S. coastal zone and to apply the federal management program to the contiguous zone beyond U.S. territorial waters was deleted.[38]

Under the Act, the Secretary of Commerce was authorized to make annual grants to coastal states (including the Great Lakes states) to help them to develop plans within federal guidelines and to administer such programs. Appropriations of $9 million a year for five years for development grants, up to $30 million a year for four years for administrative grants, necessary sums for estuarine sanctuaries up to $6 million for fiscal year 1974 only, and $3 million a year for five years for administration of the Act were authorized in 1972. On 19 December 1974 Congress increased the authorizations for program development from $9 million to $12 million a year for fiscal years 1975–1977, and authorized estuarine sanctuary grants for three years through fiscal year 1977 at $6 million annually. In the first year of the operation of the Act NOAA provided assistance to thirty-four states and territories that decided to establish coastal zone resource management plans.

---

[a]The line between those advocating an immediate coastal zone management act and those supporting a national land-use act was sharply drawn by the Chairman of the Subcommittee on Oceanography of the House Merchant Marine and Fisheries Committee in his opening remarks on hearings on three bills for coastal zone management: "Are we to sit idly by without establishing a national policy on coastal zone management, are we to wait until the problem is resolved through a Federal land use policy covering the entire United States with coastal zone policy as one element . . . ?" Gordon J. F. MacDonald, a member of the Council on Environmental Quality took another point of departure in his testimony: "We may . . . set up at the State level a fragmented institutional base for the longer-term development . . ."

In 1976 the Coastal Zone Management Act was amended to increase the federal share for the funding of state coastal zone program developments; to require that Outer Continental Shelf development and production plans be consistent with approved state coastal management programs; to set up funds for providing access to public beaches; and to authorize coastal research and personnel training. Moreover the Act (PL94-370), signed by the President on 26 July, created authority for $800 million in loans and bonds over a ten-year period and $400 million for direct grants until 1984 to coastal states affected by such energy activities as outer continental shelf oil and gas production.

It would be an error to suppose, however, that all marine policy—particularly in the conservation of the coastal zone and the prevention of pollution—was a consequence of federal action. The movement for the protection of the environment swept the nation from 1969 to 1972 and enlisted the support of both private and public groups at the local and state levels. By 1973 more than a third of all counties with populations over 400,000 and almost a fourth of all cities with more than 100,000 inhabitants had created citizens' environmental commissions.[39] Some states led the way of the federal government toward land-use planning and the protection of "critical" areas; other states, vitally concerned about their water supplies, waste disposal, and the pollution of their rivers and shores by oil, took action equal to or beyond the environmental legislation of the federal government.

Within five years after the National Environmental Policy Act of 1969, moreover, twenty-one states and Puerto Rico had adopted the requirement of an environmental impact statement for major actions or projects undertaken by state agencies. In some states the requirement for an environmental impact statement had been comprehensive, affecting every action at every level of government in the state and, sometimes, private actions; in other states the requirements have been less comprehensive. Even a city like New York, operating under executive order, may require an impact statement for certain city projects. Some of the most significant legislation affecting the marine environment has occurred in the sphere of land-use planning, which historically has been a prerogative of state and local government.

By 1974 states like California, Delaware, Maine, New Jersey, Rhode Island, and Washington, especially concerned over the abuse of their coastal zones, had enacted legislation placing great responsibility on state agencies for land-use decisions along the shores. Several other coastal states had moved specifically to protect their wetlands against draining, dredging, filling, or construction, while others, like the Great Lakes states of Wisconsin, Michigan, and Minnesota, had enacted laws to preserve their shorelands. The Coastal Zone Management Act of 1972 was an added inducement for the states to examine their entire structure of land use, which for so long had been left to local zoning and the overwhelming economic pressures of developers. It encouraged states to plan comprehensively an optimal allocation of the lake and seashores for residence, recreation, fish and wildlife, commerce, and industry.

The states also turned their attention to oil pollution policy. Although the Water Quality Improvement Act of 1970 had imposed absolute liability on owners and operators of vessels and onshore or offshore facilities for any oil spills in the navigable waters, territorial sea, and contiguous zone, with costs payable to the federal government, Florida passed its own Florida Oil Spill Prevention and Pollution Control Act in 1970. Terminal facilities, ships, and barges under the Act were held strictly liable to the state and to private parties for pollution damage within Florida's territory and territorial waters. Strong penalties were imposed for failure to report any spill, and a Florida Coastal Protection Fund was established to cover the costs of clean-ups. This fund was to be maintained by license fees against terminals and barges as well as by reimbursements from those responsible for discharges and their removal.

The Florida Act was quickly challenged and in *American Waterways Operators* v. *Askew* the District Court held that the Act infringed on federal admiralty jurisdiction under the Water Quality Improvement Act. But on appeal the Supreme Court reversed, citing the Act's own words that "nothing in this section shall be construed as preempting any state or political subdivision thereof from imposing any requirement or liability with respect to the discharge of oil into any waters within such state." Nevertheless, the problem of the costs of the operators of maintaining multiple liability protection, including the likelihood of third-party damage suits from private parties and their burden on the oil transport business (to be paid ultimately by the consumer), remained a political, if not a legal, issue.

The state of Maine went even further than Florida by passing in 1970 *An Act Relating to Coastal Conveyance of Petroleum.* Again discharges of oil were prohibited, but in this instance by the state of Maine as far out as twelve miles from the Maine coast. Furthermore, absolute liability was imposed for the clean-up of spills to the satisfaction of a new Maine Environmental Improvement Commission. The Commission was empowered to clean up oil discharges if the person responsible failed to do so. The Act also created a Coastal Protection Fund, up to four million dollars, initially supported by the imposition of an annual license fee based on one-half cent per barrel of petroleum products transferred over water during the licensing period. This fee was imposed on oil terminal facilities, which included both shore facilities and certain vessels within the twelve-mile zone used for off-loading of the products. Once the Fund was created, license fee reimbursements from responsible polluters would maintain it.

In 1973 a pipeline and terminal facility operator and the major oil companies operating terminal facilities challenged the Act in *Portland Pipeline Corp.* v. *Environmental Improvement Commission.* Arguments that the Act imposed liability on the oil terminal facilities for acts or omissions of vessels not under their control were denied by the Maine court as were other arguments on equal protection of the law, the commerce power, and admiralty jurisdiction, with the court partly relying on the Supreme Court ruling on *Askew.*[40]

Nevertheless, all the federal and state legislation to reduce marine pollution was bound to involve international law and organization, for the oceans mix with rivers and estuaries, their pollutants travel thousands of miles, their polluters come from many states, and their physical-chemical-biological dynamics recognize no political frontier.

International Cooperation to Prevent Marine Pollution

The maritime states that met in Washington in 1926 had failed to reach any international agreement on measures to reduce the pollution of the seas by oil. But the problem was hardly laid to rest. In 1934 the British government laid before the League of Nations the question of oil pollution of the seas. The Council of the League decided to hold an international conference in 1936 to consider a draft convention on the matter, which had been prepared by the League's Transit Organization in 1935 and was largely based on the work of the earlier Washington conference. However, Germany, Japan, and Italy refused to attend the conference, and it was cancelled.

Following World War II the United Nations again took up the question, issuing a background history as well as an attachment of the convention proposed by the League in 1935. Discussions were held on the subject in the UN Transport and Communications Commission during the spring of 1950, and member states were invited to give their views on oil pollution of the seas. The United States found no serious problem of oil pollution on its coasts. Admitting that the rupture of vessels might cause fouling of the seas, the U.S. Shipping Coordinating Agency—an interagency governmental group—said, " . . . the occurrence is infrequent and cannot be legislated against." Admitting that a heavy oil spread in marshes and on open water might make it impossible for waterfowl to "rise again" and might have a "deleterious effect" on fish, the Agency termed these occurrences as "unusual" and said it had "no data on the distances oily waters may drift and still appreciably contaminate beaches or fish." In the American view, national action for the control of pollution of the territorial seas seemed to be sufficient, particularly since data on ocean pollution was lacking. When the UN Secretary General asked the United States to furnish experts to assist him in further study of the problem, Washington politely refused.

Meanwhile the British government on 24 September 1952 had appointed a committee chaired by Percy Faulkner, Under Secretary in the Ministry of Transport and Civil Aviation, to study the pollution of sea water. The Faulkner report, published in 1953, then became the basis for an invitation by London to other maritime states to attend an international conference on pollution of the sea by oil from 26 April to 12 May 1954. At that point the United Nations postponed its actions with respect to marine pollution. It agreed to await the outcome of the conference, assuming that a central role would in any event be played by the Intergovernmental Maritime Consultative Organization (IMCO), when it came into legal existence—as it did in 1958.

The London conference was attended by forty-two states—thirty-two with official delegates and ten with observers. The Faulkner report and other papers by interested states served as a framework for the discussions in the committees and the plenary meetings from which emerged (1) an international convention, which was opened to the states for signature and acceptance on 12 May 1954, and (2) eight resolutions to be submitted to governments and other bodies for their appropriate consideration and action. At the conference the U.S. delegate was forthright in declaring, "Mr. President, the delegates to this Conference may differ as to procedure but they are unanimous on a common objective. The pollution of the seas must be cleared up promptly." Nevertheless, although ten states, of which five had at least 500,000 gross tons of tankers, had either signed or accepted the International Convention for the Prevention of the Pollution of the Sea by Oil by 26 July 1958, when it came into force, the U.S. Senate did not consent to its ratification by the President until 1961.[41]

The Convention provided for the first time that all states parties to the agreement would ensure that tankers registered under their flags would not discharge oil or oily mixtures (more than 100 parts of oil in 1,000,000 parts of the mixture) into prohibited zones, generally fifty miles from land, with certain exceptions in the Adriatic, North Sea, Atlantic, and the coasts of Australia. For other ships oily ballast waters or tank washings had to be discharged "as far as practicable from lands"; however, three years after the Convention came into force the prohibited zones would also apply to all ships—unless the port to which the ship was proceeding was not equipped with a reception facility for the wastes.

Twelve months after the Convention came into force, moreover, all ships of the contracting states were required to have fittings to prevent the escape of fuel oil or diesel oil into bilges that emptied into the sea without going through an oily-water separator. And all contracting states were required, within three years after the Convention came into force, to provide in their major ports facilities to receive "without causing undue delay to ships" the residues of oily ballast water or tank washings that had been retained as a result of oily-water separators or settling tanks on ships other than tankers.

Every vessel to which the Convention applied, that is, "registered" ships of 500 tons and over, (not naval auxiliaries, nor "for the time being" whalers and ships navigating the Great Lakes) had to carry an oil record in a form specified in an annex to the Convention. A contracting government had the right to inspect in any of its ports the oil record book of a vessel and to bring contraventions of the Convention to the attention of the vessel's flag state for investigation and appropriate action, with notification of such actions to the other contracting government and the Bureau. The Bureau, serving as an administrative-depositary-information exchange center, was designated as the government of the United

Kingdom, until IMCO came into being and took over its duties under the IMCO Convention of 1948.

The 1954 Convention for the Prevention of the Pollution of the Sea by Oil had lots of loopholes. It did not apply to public vessels. Notoriously it excepted the discharge of oil by all registered ships from the prohibitions "for the purpose of securing the safety of the ship, preventing damage to the ship or cargo, or saving life at sea." Investigation of any alleged offense by a vessel and possible prosecution could only be undertaken by the flag state, no matter where the contravention might take place on the high seas. Not a single word of the Convention spoke of damages. And acceptance by the maritime states of all its provisions took many years. Nevertheless, the Convention was the first step toward the international regulation of marine pollution by multilateral agreements. It became the foundation for amendments in 1962, 1969, and 1973 to further control the fouling of the seas as well as a stimulus for new conventions to end the abuse of the oceans as a sink for wastes of humankind.

In 1954 the U.S. State Department took the position that signature of the International Convention for the Prevention of Pollution of the Sea by Oil had not been possible, first, because so little time for study was available between the issuance of the invitation to the London conference (January) and its opening (April), and, second, because no draft convention had been submitted with the invitation. It took another seven years before the Senate consented to ratification of the Convention—with a reservation.

The International Convention for the Prevention of Pollution of the Sea by Oil did not come into force until 1958, and not until 1961 for the United States. In 1962 the Convention was amended to apply to ships, whether registered or unregistered, having the nationality of the contracting party. Furthermore, the provisions of the Convention were applied to all tankers over 150 tons (previously 500 tons), and every ship over 20,000 tons under contract at the time the amendments came into force was prohibited from the discharge of oil and oily mixtures everywhere—except when the master found it not reasonable or practical, in which case he could discharge outside the prohibited zones and make a report to the state of registry or nationality as well as to IMCO. Other provisions of the amendments indicated the need for marine pollution control and the hope for effective action, but they scarcely provided a mandate with condign punishment for breaches of any obligations. For example, in the Convention the carrying of water ballast in oil fuel tanks "shall be avoided if possible." Moreover, the original requirement that states should provide reception facilities at major ports for oil wastes was modified to read that states "shall take appropriate measures to promote" the provision of such facilities. As usual, ratifications of the amendments were slow in coming, and the United States only made them law in 1966.

Three years later a new set of amendments to the International Convention for the Prevention of the Pollution of the Sea by Oil were ready. The problem of marine pollution had gained increasing worldwide attention as the environmental protection movement mounted. Despite the Convention oil pollution of the seas had risen because of the immense tanker traffic. Permissible levels of discharge were found to be too slowly dispersed and oxidized when carried out by slow moving or stationary tankers, and heavy discharges still occurred outside the "prohibited zones." The 1969 amendments started from the premise that oil discharges ought to be totally prohibited at sea, but they were forced to recognize the state of technology, the costs, and the political drag in yielding national interests to international regulation. Over an entire ballast voyage tankers were prohibited from discharging more than a quantity of oil equal to 1/15,000 of the vessel's cargo capacity; and the rate of discharge of oil could not exceed 60 litres per mile travelled. No discharge of oil from cargo tanks was allowed within 50 miles of any land, while bilge discharges, for all tankers and other ships that could be fitted with separators, was limited to 100 parts per million of persistent oils—and then only "as far as practicable from land."

Whatever progress had been made by these articles to curb marine pollution, the states of the world were slow to ratify the amendments themselves. By 1975 only twenty-four states had approved the 1969 amendments, and thirty-two were required to give them legal force. Other amendments in 1971 pertaining to the Great Barrier Reef, defining it as "land," and prescribing construction standards for tankers were very far from being put into force by 1975.

Neither the basic Convention for the Prevention of Pollution of the Sea by Oil nor the subsequent amendments had dealt with the problems of casualties within the "prohibited zones," which included ocean areas contiguous to coastal states, but not within their territorial waters. True, the Geneva Convention on the Territorial Sea and Contiguous Zone (1958) had recognized that a state in a zone on the high seas contiguous to its territorial sea might exercise jurisdiction to prevent infringement of its customs and its fiscal, immigration, or sanitary regulations within its territory or territorial sea. But that contiguous zone could not extend beyond twelve miles from the baseline from which the breadth of the territorial sea was measured. The only other consensus to emerge from the first UN Law of the Sea Conference with respect to pollution had been embedded in the Convention on the High Seas (Article 25), which called on every State to take measures to prevent pollution of the seas, with radioactive wastes primarily in mind, and to cooperate with "competent international organizations" to prevent pollution resulting from any activities with radioactive materials "or other harmful agents."

The catastrophic wreck of the *Torry Canyon* on 18 March 1967 off the coast of the United Kingdom, but not in British territorial waters, brought worldwide attention to the need of a coastal state to take preventive action against a vessel on the high seas in order to protect its shores from drifting oil slicks. International law, however, generally forbids the arrest, boarding, or other actions against a vessel of one state by another on the high seas in time of peace without special agreement. Moreover, nothing in previous conventions nor in customary international law had provided an adequate norm for fixing liability for such accidents on the high seas that, negligently or not, damaged coastal states. In 1969, therefore, IMCO called for an International Legal Conference on Marine Pollution Damage, which met in Brussels from 10 to 29 November with 48 states officially represented and which formulated two conventions for signature: the International Convention Relating to Intervention on the High Seas in Cases of Oil Pollution Casualties and the International Convention on Civil Liability for Oil Pollution Damages.

Article One of the Convention Relating to Intervention on the High Seas began boldly by stating that parties to the Convention might take such measures on the high seas as may be necessary to prevent, mitigate, or eliminate grave and imminent danger to their coastline from oil pollution resulting from a maritime casualty, when there was a reasonable expectation of "major harmful consequences." However, no measures are allowed against any warships or other noncommercial public vessels of states. Moreover, before taking any measures a coastal state is obliged to consult with other states affected by the marine casualty, especially the flag state(s), and notify without delay all persons, physical or corporate, that have interests that could be reasonably affected. In "extreme urgency" a coastal state can take action without prior notification, but in any case all concerned must be advised as promptly as possible as to the measures taken. Whatever the coastal state does must be "proportionate to the damage actual or threatened." Should a coastal state take action contrary to the provisions of the Convention and cause damage to others beyond that "reasonably necessary" to achieve the prevention, mitigation, or elimination of grave and imminent danger to the coastline or related interests, it would be obliged to pay compensation for such damage. Expecting difficulties, the Convention provided for elaborate conciliation and arbitration procedures. In 1973 the provisions of the Convention were expanded by a protocol to include "substances other than oil."

Intervention on the high seas to prevent marine pollution of coastal waters and shorelines, however, hardly helped anyone who had suffered damage due to a casualty. The Convention on Civil Liability for Oil Pollution Damage, therefore, fixed strict liability on the owner of a ship for any pollution damage caused by oil which escaped or was discharged as a result of an "incident" that caused pollution damage. The Convention was only applicable to damages caused on the territory, including the territorial sea, of a contracting state; the owner could be freed of liability only if it was proved that the damage resulted from an act of war, a natural phenomenon of "exceptional, inevitable, and irresistible character," the act of a third party intending to cause damage, or by the negligence of a government or other authority responsible for navigational aids. Liability was limited to 2000 gold francs ($134) for each ton of the ship's net tonnage, not to exceed 210 million francs ($14 million) for any one incident.

This, however, was only if the owner constituted or guaranteed a fund equal to the maximum amount of liability that was acceptable to the contracting state where the fund was constituted or guaranteed and that was deemed adequate by a court or competent authority of that state. Under the Convention each contracting state guaranteed that any vessel of its registry carrying more than 2000 tons of oil as cargo would carry insurance or other financial security up to the limits of liability. Furthermore, each contracting state would require such security to be in force on every vessel carrying more than 2000 tons of oil, wherever registered, that entered or left a port of its territory, including offshore terminals in the territorial sea.[42]

Again the states of the world have been reticent in making these marine pollution conventions part of their law by acceptance, ratification, or accession once they have "adopted" them in an international conference. The International Convention Relating to Intervention on the High Seas in Cases of Oil Pollution Casualties required fifteen ratifications for entry into force. It took almost six years before it came into force—and the United States has become a party to the Convention. The International Convention on Civil Liability for Oil Pollution Damage, which required eight ratifications, five of which must be from states with at least one million gross tons of shipping, also came into force in 1975, but the United States had still not incorporated the Convention into its law at that time. Finally, the 1973 protocol that expanded the Intervention on the High Seas Convention to apply to substances other than oil had not come into force at the beginning of 1975.

The Civil Liability Convention, progressive as it was from its adoption in 1969 to its entry into legal force for some seventeen states in 1975, still left little recourse and no assurance of compensation for damages in a number of instances.[43] For example, if damages exceeded 210 million gold francs, the legal remedies for pollution of a shoreline by a foreign vessel on the high seas were the same as before the Convention—most uncertain. Moreover, acts of war or of a third party intending damage, or negligence by a government in providing navigational aids or natural phenomena (acts of God) could relieve the shipowner from liability under the Convention. Therefore, representatives from more than fifty countries met in Brussels again from 29 November to 28 December 1971 to conclude a new International Convention on the Establishment of an International Fund for Oil Pollution Damage.

The Fund to be established was designed for two reasons: (1) to ensure full compensation for all victims of oil pollution; and (2) to relieve some of the financial burden placed on the shipowners by the Civil Liability Convention. With the Fund and the Civil Liability Convention the aggregate amount collectible by victims can be as high as 450 million francs ($30 million) for a single incident and could, by action of the Assembly (all contracting states) be increased to 900 million francs ($60 million). Moreover, the Fund would cover damages due to exceptional, inevitable, and irrestible natural phenomena. But it would not compensate for acts of war, of a public vessel in noncommercial service, or the intentional omission of a third party.

Some relief was provided for the shipowners from their financial obligations under the Civil Liability Convention, but only on condition of full compliance with the requirements laid down in the International Convention for the Prevention of the Pollution of the Sea by Oil (1954), the Safety of Life at Sea Convention (1960), the Load Lines Convention (1966), and all their amendments in force at least twelve months prior to an incident. If the damages were not the result of willful misconduct by the owner or due to the fault of the owner by not following regulations under the conventions mentioned above, then the Fund would indemnify the owner (or guarantor) for that portion of aggregate liability under the Civil Liability Convention in excess of 1500 francs ($100) for each ton of the ship's tonnage or a total of 125 million francs ($8.3 million), whichever is less. Also it would not indemnify the owner for more than 2000 francs ($133) for each ton or a total of 210 million francs ($14 million), whichever was less.

Contributions to the Fund would come initially from "any person," including subsidiaries or commonly controlled entities, that receives in ports and terminal installations more than 150,000 tons of oil, with the levy during the first year fixed by the Assembly to obtain 75 million francs ($5 million) for the Fund. Future levies will be made by the Assembly. Plainly the Fund could not come into being before the Civil Liability Convention was in force—and states parties to the Fund must also be parties to the Convention. Moreover, the Fund will be in force only when at least eight states that have persons who received at least 750 million tons of oil in the preceding calendar year have ratified it.[44]

Neither the Civil Liability Convention nor the Fund met all the demands of the alarmed environmental public interest groups for protection against oil spills. For example, the limits of liability were held to be too low by them. Nevertheless, the conventions went far toward providing comprehensive remedies for marine casualties that caused damages which hitherto had been either ignored or repudiated. The test of the efficacy of these conventions still lies ahead, depending on (1) the number of states that ratify them, (2) the enforcement of the regulations by national agreements, and (3) the willingness of the contracting states to agree on fair charges to shipowners and oil receivers as well as a fair compensation for damages.[45]

Meanwhile, beyond the marine pollution conventions initiated through IMCO during these years, the United Nations itself took a broad interest in reducing pollution and made specific proposals both through the UN Conference on the Human Environment in 1972 and the Third UN Conference on the Law of the Sea, which began its meetings in 1973.

As indicated earlier, a tide of public opinion, especially in the developed countries, channelled through many scientific associations and organized interest groups, pushed the issue of environmental protection forward to governmental attention during the late 1960s. The Swedish Permanent Representative to the United Nations on 20 May 1968 proposed that the organization call a world conference on the human environment and, after a favorable recommendation by the Economic and Social Council, the idea was adopted by the General Assembly (Resolution 2398, XXIII). Stockholm was chosen as the place and the summer of 1972 as the date for the first UN Conference on the Human Environment. Although the Food and Agriculture Organization, the World Health Organization, UNESCO, and other specialized agencies of the United Nations had been concerned for some time with environmental issues limited to their own interests and competence, the Stockholm conference was the first major international effort to deal comprehensively with the pollution of the environment on a global scale, attempting to protect and maintain the entire ecosystem on the planet.

Preparations for the Human Environment Conference were intensive. The activities of many private groups, nationally or internationally linked to environmental concerns, proliferated as the United Nations geared itself for action. Maurice Strong, a Canadian, was designated as Secretary General of the Conference. A twenty-one nation preparatory committee beginning in 1970 decided to establish a number of intergovernmental working groups to develop proposals and bases for agreement for the agenda items, recognizing that a two-week international conference hardly would allow governments any time to adopt principles or recommendations unless there had been a previous opportunity to consider them closely. Among the various intergovernmental working groups established was the Intergovernmental Working Group on Marine Pollution. In addition, papers, statements, and views were invited by the preparatory committee from the private associations, scientific organizations, national agencies, and international groups concerned about the work of the conference.

When the Marine Pollution Working Group gathered in London in June 1971, the United States had ready a draft convention on "The Regulation of Transportation for Ocean Dumping" with the hope that such a convention might be ready for signature at Stockholm the following year. But many states regarded the American draft as inadequate, and at the next meeting of the Group in Ottawa in November 1971 they sought substantial amendments or revisions. Meanwhile a group of European countries had met in Oslo in September to prepare a regional agreement. On 15 February 1972 twelve of these states bordering either the Mediterranean, the Atlantic, or the Baltic seas adopted at Oslo the Convention for the Prevention of Marine Pollution by Dumping from Ships and Aircraft, the text of which was far more comprehensive, detailed, and apt than the original American draft convention before the UN Working Group. Under the Oslo Convention, the restrictions on ocean dumping applied only to a part of the Atlantic ocean. But the structure and language of the Oslo regional convention was virtually incorporated in the London International

Convention on the Prevention of Marine Pollution by Dumping of Wastes and Other Matter, which was opened for signature on 29 December 1972.[46]

The UN Conference on the Human Environment met in Stockholm from 5 to 16 June 1972. Delegates from 113 nations, often exhorted by dozens of nongovernmental groups that held their own meetings and issued their own manifestos, brought forth a major resolution that led the UN General Assembly on 15 December 1972 to create a UN Environmental Program (UNEP).[b] With a fifty-eight-member Governing Council and Maurice Strong as Executive Director, UNEP formed an Environmental Coordination Board to link the heads of the UN specialized agencies with the plans and programs of the new organization. Nairobi became the headquarters of UNEP. All this was abetted by the pledge of the United States at Stockholm to contribute up to 40 percent toward the five-year goal of a $100 million Environmental Fund.

The Stockholm Conference also issued a bold, broad philosophical Declaration on the Human Environment, which proclaimed that man was "both creature and moulder of his environment which gives him physical sustenance and affords him the opportunity for intellectual, moral, social and spiritual growth" and that a point had been reached in history "when we must shape our decisions throughout the world with a more prudent care for their environmental consequences." Of course, the developing countries of the world were far more concerned with raising their economic standards of living by intensive agriculture, industry, or commerce, and they were willing to accept, if need be, their peripheral pollution problems. The Declaration neatly covered that issue by stating that in the developing countries, "most of the environmental problems are caused by underdevelopment."

A set of twenty-six principles in the Declaration dealt not only with natural resources, nonrenewable resources, wildlife and nature conservation, the discharge of toxic substances into the air and seas, demography, science and technology, and education in environmental affairs, but also with the special needs of the developing countries for development, including stability of prices and earnings for primary commodities and raw materials, and even the condemnation of racial segregation, discrimination, colonial domination, "and other forms of oppression." More important were the actual recommendations of the Conference, several of which dealt specifically with marine pollution. The Conference urged governments (1) to support national research and monitoring efforts for international investigations to control marine pollution; and (2) to endorse collectively the principles of the Stockholm conference as guidelines for the

---

[b]The United States was by no means the first or only country conscious of the need to halt land, air, and water pollution. Many European environmental groups had been active in the 1960s and had aimed for a European Conservation Year in 1970. The call of the Swedish Permanent Representative in 1968 to the UN for an international human environment conference was part of that European movement.

UN Law of the Sea Conference and the IMCO meeting on Marine Pollution scheduled for 1973.[47]

Essentially the delegates at Stockholm agreed that the marine environment and all its resources were vital to humanity and that management was required to ensure that the quality and resources of the oceans were unimpaired. The Conference also recommended that governments, assisted and guided by appropriate UN bodies, accept and implement available instruments for the control of maritime sources of marine pollution, ensure the compliance with rules for controlling pollution by ships under their jurisdiction.

With respect to ocean dumping, the Conference specifically recommended that the draft articles and annexes that had been elaborated by the Inter-Governmental Working Group at meetings in Reykjavik, Iceland in April 1972 and in London in May 1972 be referred to (1) the UN Seabed Committee and (2) the conference on the prevention of marine pollution that Great Britain had planned to convene that year.[48]

Thus four months after the close of the Stockholm conference ninety-one nations assembled in London from 30 October to 13 November to fashion what U. Alexis Johnson, the acting Secretary of State of the United States, called the "first international treaty devoted to environmental protection on a global basis." The Convention on the Prevention of Marine Pollution by the Dumping of Wastes and Other Matter (the "Ocean Dumping Convention"), consisting of a preamble and twenty-two articles, was opened for signature simultaneously at London, Mexico City, Moscow, and Washington on 29 December 1972. Under the Convention the parties were pledged to take "all practical steps" to prevent the pollution of the sea by the dumping of wastes and other matter liable to create hazards to human health, to harm living resources and marine life, to damage amenities, and to interfere with other legitimate uses of the sea. Dumping was defined as the "deliberate disposal" at sea of wastes or other matter from vessels, aircraft or platforms, or other man-made structures at sea. Dumping did not include disposal incidental to the normal operations of vessels, aircraft, or platforms, nor disposal arising from or related to the exploration, exploitation, or offshore processing of any seabed mineral resources. Vessels entitled to sovereign immunity under international law were not covered by the Convention, although each contracting state agreed that such vessels under its jurisdiction would not act in ways inconsistent with the object or purpose of the Convention.

They key to the Ocean Dumping Convention, shaped ten months earlier by the regional Oslo Convention for the Prevention of Marine Pollution by Dumping from Ships and Aircraft, was two lists (Annex I and Annex II) of "wastes and other matter." The Convention prohibited the dumping of the first list of materials, including organohalogen compounds (DDT, PCEs, etc.); mercury and mercury compounds; cadmium and cadmium compounds; persistent plastics; crude, fuel, heavy diesel oils, etc.; high-level radioactive wastes;

and materials for biological or chemical warfare. The second list included "wastes containing significant amounts" of arsenic, lead, copper, zinc, organosilicon compounds, cyanides, fluorides, and pesticides not covered by Annex I; among large quantities of acids and alkalis scheduled for dumping, beryllium, chromium, nickel, and vanadium; bulky wastes likely to present obstacles to navigation or fishing; and radioactive wastes not covered by Annex I. States could allow the dumping of any of these wastes by a vessel under their registry or loading at one of its ports but only after the issuance of a special permit. Wastes not included in either the first or second list could be dumped under a general permit issued by the state.

Before any permit for ocean dumping can be issued by a contracting party, it must take into account (1) the characteristics and the composition of the matter to be dumped, including its amount, toxicity, persistence, accumulation, and so forth; (2) the characteristics of the dumping site, including its location in relation to other uses of the sea, dilution and dispersal characteristics, water and bottom characteristics; and (3) other general considerations or conditions. Among such considerations are "the practical availability of alternative land based methods of treatment, disposal, or elimination" for the materials.

Clearly under the Convention a state has considerable discretion in determining whether a particular dumping activity falls within the special permit list or the general permit category. Furthermore, the state has been allowed to make a cost-benefit judgment about the efficacy of ocean dumping as compared to alternative methods or sites for the disposal of many of its wastes. On the other hand, the state is bound to keep records of the nature and quantities of all the matter permitted to be dumped, including the locations, times, and methods. Also, a state must monitor, either by itself or in collaboration with other governments and international agencies, the condition of the adjacent seas. Each state is required to report all such information to the organization to be designated three months after the Convention comes into force. It should be noted, finally, that the prohibitions or constraints on ocean dumping set up by the Convention do not apply when dumping is necessary to secure the safety of human life, vessels, and platforms in exceptional cases of bad weather or other extraordinary circumstances.[49]

As indicated earlier, the United States had passed its own Ocean Dumping Act in October 1972 prior to signing the Ocean Dumping Convention in December. In August 1973 Washington ratified the Ocean Dumping Convention, whose provisions paralleled the domestic act. At the same time Congress approved amendments of a minor and technical character to the Act to bring it into conformity with the Convention. Ratification or accession by fifteen states was required to bring the Convention into force, and on 27 September 1975, two years and nine months after first being opened for signature, the Convention on the Prevention of Marine Pollution by Dumping of Wastes and Other Matter took legal effect.

Apart from the conventions on marine pollution developed regionally (or through the UN Conference on the Human Environment, or under the auspices of IMCO), the UN Committee on the Peaceful Uses of the Deep Sea Bed and Ocean Floor and the Subsoil thereof beyond the Limits of National Jurisdiction had also become involved in the broad international effort to reduce environmental degradation of the oceans.

As described in earlier chapters, the United Nations had considered the possibilities of a new ocean regime to enhance the uses of the oceans as early as 1966. Then the General Assembly, under Resolution 2172 (XXI) had requested the Secretary General to survey the activities of both national governments and the United Nations in marine science and technology and to formulate proposals for expanded international cooperation to develop marine resources. The Economic and Social Council in 1966 had also requested the Secretary General to appraise knowledge about ocean resources in the deep seas and ocean floor (excluding fish) and to identify which resources, if any, were capable of exploitation. In 1967 Malta, in the UN General Assembly, called for a draft treaty that would create an international agency to assume jurisdiction over the seabed beyond present national jurisdiction. The General Assembly first approved an ad hoc Committee to study the matter. Then, in December 1968 the ad hoc committee by resolution of the General Assembly became the UN Committee on the Peaceful Uses of the Sea-Bed and the Ocean Floor beyond the Limits of National Jurisdiction (the UN Seabed Committee).

The UN Seabed Committee began its work in 1969. Among its several mandates from the General Assembly, the Committee was charged with the task of proposing measures for the control of marine pollution in connection with the exploration and exploitation of resources beyond national jurisdiction. On 17 December 1970 the General Assembly overwhelmingly approved the Declaration of Principles Governing the Sea-Bed and the Ocean Floor, and the Subsoil thereof, beyond the Limits of National Jurisdiction. With respect to any activities in the area and in conformity with an international regime to be established, states were called upon to prevent pollution, contamination, and other hazards to the marine environment, conserve natural resources, and prevent damage to the flora or fauna of the marine environment. The Assembly had also called for the convocation of a conference on the law of the sea in 1973 to deal not only with an international regime for the seabed, but also with the territorial sea, the continental shelf, fisheries, international straits, and the preservation of the marine environment. Responding to this agenda the UN Seabed Committee on 12 March 1971 decided to organize its work under the three subcommittees. To Subcommittee III the UN Seabed Committee allocated, "the preservation of the marine environment (including, *inter alia,* the prevention of pollution) and scientific research, and to prepare draft treaty articles thereon."

During 1971 the Subcommittee held fourteen meetings in Geneva. In 1972 the Subcommittee held two sessions, one in New York from 28 February to 31 March and the other in Geneva from 17 July to 18 August. In 1973, on the eve of the beginning of the Third UN Law of the Sea Conference, the Subcommittee again held two sessions, one in the spring in New York and a second in the summer at Geneva. In plain fact, however, over the three-year period very little progress was made in gaining a consensus on specific draft articles for the control of marine pollution—or on freedom of scientific research, another item for which the Subcommittee was responsible. Five working papers on marine pollution and ten sets of draft articles on marine pollution had been submitted to the Subcommittee, but in 1972 and 1973 Working Group Two of the Subcommittee, which had the specific mandate of drafting textual articles, moved at a snail's pace. Some articles were elaborated, yet in virtually every case one or more delegations attached conditions, reservations, or qualifications. Thus, when the Third UN Law of the Sea Conference held its first organizational meeting in New York in the winter of 1973 precious little had been accomplished in the Third Subcommittee to guide the delegates.

In truth, the control of marine pollution and the provision of reasonable access of scientific expeditions to the continental shelf and the deep seabed were low-ranking interests of the UN Seabed Committee. Most delegates considered navigation, particularly through international straits, the catch of fish, or the exploitation of submarine mineral resources far more crucial to their national security and economic welfare. Moreover, as already described in this chapter, substantial international progress was being made through conventions on the prevention of pollution from oil and other harmful substances negotiated under the auspices of IMCO and through the Ocean Dumping Convention precipitated by the Human Environment Conference of 1972.

In 1974 at Caracas, no negotiating text had emerged from the long deliberations of the Conference, but in May 1975 the chairman of the Third Committee of the Conference at the close of the Geneva session presented a single negotiating text that largely dealt with the dumping of wastes into the ocean. Under the text coastal states were given the power to regulate all dumping by vessels, regardless of their nationality, within a certain distance from their shores, which was not specified. So far as pollution of the ocean from land-based sources, the text merely would have required states to establish laws to control such pollution, taking into account global standards but not being bound by them.

The Revised Single Negotiating Text that emerged from the 15 March–7 May 1976 session of the Third UN Law of the Sea Conference in New York did not change the strictures on land-based pollution. However, it continued to charge states with the responsibility of taking various measures to abate pollution of the oceans and prescribed that they pass national laws to prevent, reduce, or control pollution from seabed activities, including islands, installations, and structures, dumping of wastes, or vessels. These laws should "be no less effective than international rules, standards, and recommended practices and procedures."

With regard to vessels, states were to ensure that their flag vessels would not leave their ports unless in compliance with international rules and standards established by competent international organizations or conventions. Moreover, all states would be empowered to prevent any ship voluntarily in their ports or at an offshore terminal from sailing when not in compliance with applicable international rules and might cause proceedings against such vessels for violations of national laws or international standards. In the territorial sea, states might undertake physical inspection of a vessel when there were clear grounds for believing that a vessel had violated national laws or international standards, and undertake proceedings; and in the exlusive economic zone, states could require the vessel to give information about its registry, ports of call, and other information to establish whether a violation had occurred.

Under international law, however, the stopping and arrest of foreign ships transiting the territorial waters of a coastal state under innocent passage can provide diplomatic complications, and such interference with foreign vessels by a coastal state beyond the territorial sea can lead to serious international consequences. Additional safeguards were written into the text to ensure that criminal proceedings would be suspended against a foreign flag vessel if the flag state should assume jurisdiction over the case and that in any case where a violation was commited beyond the internal waters of a state, only monetary penalties might be imposed.[50]

Many specialists in marine transportation had come to believe that the 1954 Convention on Prevention of Pollution of the Sea by Oil, with its amendments, needed to be replaced by a comprehensive international convention applicable not only to oil, but also to other noxious, hazardous, and polluting substances. In October 1969 the IMCO Assembly decided [Resolution A176(VI)] to convene an international conference on marine pollution in 1973 to prepare an international agreement to place restraints upon the contamination of the sea, land, and air by ships, vessels, and equipment operating in the marine environment. Consultations and preparatory studies began under the auspices of the organization, while the Assembly, with grand euphoria, in 1971 set as its goal the achievement "by 1975, if possible, but certainly by the end of the decade . . . the complete elimination of the willful and intentional pollution of the sea by oil and noxious substances other than oil." Nine background studies were prepared by different member states of IMCO, covering load-on-top techniques for preventing marine pollution, segregated ballast tanks, double bottoms, and other devices, as well as an analysis of the cost and effectiveness of such means in order to guide the formulation of the convention. The U.S. Coast Guard, for example, prepared a study of the cost and effectiveness of segregated ballast tanks both with and without double hulls, while the United Kingdom made a comprehensive study of the costs or damages, both financial and environmental, arising from oil pollution by ships. A fifth and final draft text prepared by IMCO's Marine Safety Committee and its subsidiaries was approved in February–March 1973. Then, from 8 October to 2 November representatives from seventy-nine countries of the world worked to adopt the International Convention for the Prevention of Pollution from Ships, 1973. "Both in breadth of coverage and in methods of control of marine pollutants" said Russell E. Train, chairman of the U.S. delegation, "this Convention far surpasses any previous international agreement."[51]

The Convention itself consisted of twenty articles to govern five technical annexes and it included two protocols. Both Annex I, which set forth regulations for the prevention of oil pollution, and Annex II, which dealt with noxious liquid substances, were integral parts of the Convention. However, Annex III (harmful substances in packaged form), Annex IV (pollution from sewage), and Annex V (pollution from garbage) were optional, that is, open to acceptance by states or not without impairing the Convention. One protocol dealt with the reporting of incidents of pollution and the other provided arbitration procedures in the event of a dispute among the parties.

A major achievement of the Convention was to place stringent regulations on the discharge of light refined oil products into the marine environment, regulations that had previously been applied only to crude and heavier petroleum products. In the early 1970s refined products probably constituted about 15 percent of world oil trade and accounted for about 17 percent of the operational discharges into the sea. Another major achievement of the Convention was the requirement that all tankers over 70,000 deadweight tons, either contracted for after 31 December 1975 or delivered after 31 December 1979, be built with segregated ballast tanks. The object was to end the practice of loading seawater into empty oil tanks to ballast a ship and then flushing out both the seawater and the oily residues when the vessel was ready to load oil again. The United States also urged that the Convention include provisions making it mandatory that all new tankers be constructed with double bottoms, but a substantial majority in the Technical Committee of the Conference voted down that controversial reform.

In addition to its regulation of light refined oil products as well as crude and its requirement of segregated ballast tanks in new tankers, the Convention prohibited the discharge of all oil within fifty miles of land and, furthermore, prohibited the discharge of any oil whatsoever in the Mediterranean, Red, Black, and Baltic seas as well as in the Persian Gulf. Another step taken by the Convention to reduce marine pollution was the agreement by the governments to provide facilities for the reception of oily residues and mixtures remaining from oil tankers and other ships "at oil loading terminals, repair ports, and in other ports in which ships have oily residues to discharge." While the obligation would largely fall on the oil-loading terminals of exporting nations, ports with repair yards would also be affected. Finally, the discharge of noxious liquid substances other than oil were regulated for the first time under the Convention. An appendix to Annex II evaluated the harmful effects to the marine environment of some three hundred chemicals or mixtures and spelled out the quantity, rate of discharge, and distance from the shore permitted for the discharge of such chemicals or mixtures.

As an international agreement that had been drafted by many states over a period of years and that imposed decidedly new, complex, and often expensive obligations on the contracting states under international law, the Convention, of course, had its limitations. Some critics believed them to be weaknesses. First, following the 1954 Convention, the 1973 Convention did not apply to any warship, auxiliary vessel, or other ship owned or operated by a state "and used, for the time being, only on government non-commercial service." Second, both the regulations on the limitations of discharges of oil and the regulations preventing any oil discharge from ships while operating in the enclosed seas did not apply if discharges were necessary for "securing the safety of a ship or saving life at sea." The same kind of clause was also attached to the regulations on the discharge of noxious liquid substances. Third, and more debatable, was Article 6 of the Convention, which dealt with the detection of violations and the enforcement of the rules.

The United States had strongly urged that port states be given authority under the Convention to prosecute foreign vessels as well as their own flag ships for any violations of the Convention that took place on the high seas. But this concept, which would have been a radical change in existing international law, was rejected with the argument that such matters should be left to the Third UN Law of the Sea Conference about to begin its substantive work in 1974. Nevertheless, the flag state was required by the Convention to prosecute any violations by vessels of its registry wherever they might occur. And if information or evidence has been furnished by one of the parties to the Convention to another state about a violation by a vessel under its registry, the flag state is bound to notify the other contracting party of whatever action it takes. Coastal states party to the Convention, moreover, may inspect foreign vessels in their ports or at offshore terminals for assurance that the ship's construction and equipment are in compliance with the requirements of the Convention. The coastal state may detain such vessels until satisfied that the vessel presents no unreasonable threat to the marine environment or else is proceeding to a repair yard. Significantly the coastal state must take the same action against all foreign vessels—not just those of contracting parties—so that no competitive advantage can be gained by vessels not fitted or equipped according to the standards of the Convention.

As indicated earlier, the requirement for double bottoms on new tankers was decisively rejected. It was also felt either impracticable or too expensive to force all existing tankers to be refitted with segregated ballast tank systems. Thus, while new tankers must be launched with such systems, many old tankers without them will continue to ply the seas. In truth, the delegates did not start from an assessment of damages from discharges and then seek options through which the marginal cost of abatement would reach the marginal benefit of damage reduction. Rather they asserted an environmental quality objective, that is, the almost total elimination of discharges, and then prescribed what they considered the most cost-effective means of reaching it: namely, segregated ballast tanks, the provision of load-on-top facilities on vessels, an instantaneous rate of discharge outside prohibited areas not to exceed 60 liters per nautical mile, and a total quantity of discharge not to exceed 1/15,000 of the cargo for existing tankers and 1/30,000 for new tankers.

The 1973 International Convention for the Prevention of Pollution from Ships stipulated that it would come into force twelve months after fifteen states, whose combined merchant fleets exceed 50 percent of the world's merchant shipping, have accepted it. By 1977 it was still not in force.

Problems and Issues

The people of the United States had finally come to realize the impact of their enormous productive effort on the environment. Food stocks had multiplied prodigiously. Transportation had been revolutionized with amazing combination of speed and mobility. Millions of products, both of necessity and pleasure, had been manufactured, often utilizing ingenious chemical combinations. Giant urban centers, like black reticules, had mushroomed on the landscape, providing industry, bustling commerce, mass education, and popular amusements. As productive costs declined, utilizing the abundant natural resources of the country, American standards of living rose fabulously—the United States was the richest country in the world. But the expense of the soils and rock, the atmosphere, and the air that provided the essential environment for all human activity had scarcely been counted.

As indicated in this chapter public opinion about environmental costs in the early twentieth century had been apathetic, and remedial legislation had been sluggish. The first federal controls over the navigable waters of the United States that slightly reduced their abuse did not come until the very end of the nineteenth century. The first prohibition against oil pollution by ships within three miles of shore came a quarter-century later. No federal control over the quality of water was enacted until almost another quarter-century had elapsed. Then the gospel of protecting and preserving the environment burst on the scene through the warnings of scientists, the writing of journalists, and the organization of interest groups composed of rather well-educated and economically comfortable people. The President and Congress responded almost frenetically with Federal Water Pollution Control acts of increasing stringency from 1948 to 1972, and dramatic legislative innovations like the Ports and

Waterways Safety Act, the Marine Protection, Research, and Sanctuaries Act, and the Coastal Zone Management Act, all in 1972.

The rush to environmental legislation, accompanied by the outcries of the public interest groups seeking to save the rivers, save the fish, and save the seas, overwhelmed the critics who argued against precipitate action based on incomplete knowledge with an increase in taxes and prices. But by the mid-1970s, with soaring energy prices and general economic recession in the United States, assaults on the presumptions of the environmental movement became more widespread. Industry and labor called for a closer examination of what losses would be suffered by individuals in the form of higher prices, unemployment, and other restraints on transportation, commerce, and recreation in order to abate pollution.

There have been two inescapable problems with recommendations to abate pollution and maintain, protect, or preserve the environment. The first is one of cause and effect. By definition the environment is large, complex, and dynamic, whereas harm to rivers or oceans tends to be marginal, incremental, and long term. Screeching headlines often reveal "new scientific evidence" that some process, chemical, or waste can cause irreparable harm to life in the marine environment. But it sometimes is not clear to the layperson on what small samples, limited time, or laboratory control conditions such "evidence" has been based. Incomplete data and tentative conclusions modestly admitted by the scientist may scarcely be conveyed to the untutored and fearful public by journal accounts. Finally, the complexity of the scientific data, the careful weighing of uncertain conclusions, and the need for more time to achieve verification hardly meet the need of legislators who require a simplification of the issues and a partisan point of view to get political action.

A retrospect of recent years in the United States can find scores of journalistic exaggerations of very limited scientific findings about varying amounts of carbon dioxide in the atmosphere or the effects of DDT, mercury, and oil on the marine food chain, to name but a few. No one disputes the necessity of research and reasonable precautions to delay, avoid, or stop reasonably clear environmental damage. But often the consequences of alarms have been the rapid indictment of one process, practice, or pollutant without distinctions of quantity, rates of discharge, or the absorptive character of the ambient environment.

Federal legislation to stop or correct some alleged environmental harm usually exercises its force through administrative regulations that are universally applied by an agency. For example, the EPA in 1973 drafted regulations requiring the secondary treatment of all waste discharges, which meant either an 85 percent removal of biochemical oxygen demand (BOD) and suspended solids or less than thirty parts per million of BOD and suspended solid, whichever was more restrictive. It is a very expensive treatment. This requirement was to be applied regardless of whether the discharge occurred upstream, into an estuary, or in the open ocean. Off the coast of Southern California wastes were already being treated mechanically, with biological digestion of sludge, and then flowing into open ocean areas where a dilution of 100 parts of seawater to 1 of waste water took place at the outfalls. Furthermore, there had been no study that showed any problem with BOD or suspended particles in these areas. Finally, the EPA regulation not only failed to discriminate between upstream and open ocean areas, but it also drew no distinction between waste water treatment plants from which only 20,000 gallons flowed a day and plants from which 100,000,000 gallons a day spewed forth into nearby rivers, lakes, bays, or oceans.[52]

The second inescapable problem with recommendations to protect the environment has been an assessment of the damages caused by an allegedly noxious practice or process. In general the harmful effects occur over a long period of time in large areas like lakes, rivers, and oceans. And they affect, at least in the early years, populations of plants or animals that seem to bear little or no relationship to man's total productive activities. Obviously it is no easy matter to fix prices for the long-term depletion of phytoplankton, let alone the stench of a stagnant river or the blackening of a bay with hydrocarbon slicks. And even when values can be assigned through a market economy, such as the cost of losing the oyster harvest or the closing of an income-producing beach, the public may feel that it obtains greater benefit from cheap gasoline, good highways, and the cult of the automobile.

Economists would generally agree that the true costs to society of the petroleum industry, the disposition of human and industrial wastes, or river-ocean transportation, to name but a few activities, have hardly been calculated. Both public and private agencies utilize a common property resource, like water, which belongs to no one in particular, and they scarcely pay for its degradation and damage within the environmental system. Fixing these costs is difficult enough. Given the large number and variety of uses of the environment, the collection of such costs challenges both political tolerance and administrative skill.[53]

With such intricate problems of cause-effect and assessment of damages to the environment, the tendency of legislation in the United States has been to create general prohibitions to restore an idealized environment. One illustration of this was the Federal Water Pollution Control Amendments of 1972 that set forth as national goals the elimination of the discharge of pollutants into navigable waters by 1985, with an interim goal of water quality that would provide for the protection and propagation of fish, shellfish, and wildlife as well as recreation in and on the water, all to be achieved by 1983. At one point in the discussion of legislation Senator John V. Tunney of California wanted the nation's waterways to be fit for swimming by 1980!

Moreover, the permit system for discharges established by EPA, which can be delegated to state agencies, ultimately relies on the regulation of effluents by general formulas. For private industries it has meant a complicated system of regular, special, or interim permits, with both prolonged argument and periodic monitoring. For state and local water treatment plants it has meant politicallly popular large-scale federal appropriations to upgrade facilities to meet the arbitrary standards set by the legislation and by EPA for the treatment of sewage.

A second illustration of the regulatory approach to restore an idealized environment without a true analysis of the costs and benefits of the prohibitions was the 1973 Convention on the Prevention of Pollution from Ships. As with the Federal Water Pollution Control Act amendments, no place was allowed for economic incentives, such as the imposition of a graduated tax on polluting discharges to discourage potentially harmful or dirty effluents. Obversely, no attention was given to graduated tax reductions for the installation and utilization of more efficient equipment to reduce water pollution.

In any case, the control of pollution is likely to be expensive, the more so when tied to the restoration of an idealized environment by meeting such standards as "secondary treatment," "parts per million discharge," "best available technology," "no discharge," and so forth. At the end of 1975 the Council on Environmental Quality (CEQ) had estimated that from 1975 through 1984 the nation was expected to spend $258.8 billion for environmental improvements as a result of federal environmental legislation ($110.8 billion for water pollution control and $7.9 billion for solid waste disposal). The EPA grants program for waste treatment plants and sewers had become the second-largest federal public works program in terms of obligations. By 1977 it was expected to match such federal government programs as international affairs and finance, space research and technology, and agricultural-rural development.

While a report by the Environmental Policy Division of the U.S. Congressional research service in 1975 had said that the CEQ's estimates were too high, a report by the National Water Commission had placed the CEQ estimates on water pollution control as far too low. In truth, no one could do better than make estimates based on some very broad assumptions: for example, that manufacturers would spend for pollution abatement rather than substitute or abandon some of their products or processes. Not the least problem was the fact that no one knew what the cost of the "best available technology" would be in the 1980s and whether its requirement would be applied to individual plants or industries as a group. In the years ahead a perennial issue with regard to water pollution control will undoubtedly be the weighing of benefits and costs of particular programs, taking into account not only their impact on prices and employment but also the choice of goods and service available to the people. Inherent in this issue are the proper distribution of costs between federal, state, and private budgets as well as the gross expenses of bureaucratic management under regulatory schemes, which are bound to be slowly litigated and clumsily administered.[54]

Another central issue of marine pollution that had not been resolved was "the patchwork of Federal and State laws regarding liability for oil pollution from ocean-related sources within which there exists gaps, ambiguities, and conflicts." Although the Outer Continental Shelf Act of 1953 had not imposed liabilities in consequence of exploration and exploitation of petroleum resources, it had allowed the Secretary of Interior to do so. The Department, therefore, had issued appropriate regulations imposing strict liability on lessees for any clean-up and removal of oil as a result of their operations. Liability for all other damages has been determined by the laws of the adjacent state applied as federal law in federal courts. Not until the Water Pollution Control Act of 1970 did federal law provide specifically for a recovery of damages as a result of any *unintentional* discharge of oil from an ocean-related source. Moreover, since 1970 the Trans-Alaska Pipeline Act of 1973 and the Deepwater Port Act of 1974 have both imposed strict liability for the discharge of oil by vessels or facilities covered by those acts. These federal laws have been by no means consistent or integrated. For example, vessels covered by both the Trans-Alaska Pipeline Act and the Deepwater Port Act of 1974 have also been covered by the Federal Water Pollution Control Act, yet the defenses and the limits of liability in these acts have differed.

Meanwhile, a number of states, in addition to their common law remedies, have also clarified and expanded by legislation liability for oil pollution and have imposed strict liability for damages. Again their practices have varied. Some states specified the defenses against strict liability, others did not. Some state statutes applied strict liability not only to pollution from vessels, but also to onshore and offshore facilities handling oil, including exploration and exploitation of the adjacent seabed under the jurisdiction of the state; others did not. Many states created funds to pay for clean-up costs in an emergency, usually from license fees, penalties, and fines, or special appropriations, whereas Florida, Maine, and Maryland financed their funds by a levy on barrels of oil transported or handled.

To meet all these difficulties President Gerald Ford transmitted to Congress on 9 July 1975 proposed legislation entitled the "Comprehensive Oil Pollution Liability and Compensation Act of 1975," noting that the recovery ability of claimants damaged by spills (amounting to more than 13,000 in 1973, one-third of which were unidentified) had been hampered by widely inconsistent federal and state laws. Under the Administration's proposal strict liability was fixed for up to $20,000,000 in damages or $150 per gross ton of a vessel, whichever is less, and up to $50,000,000 for onshore or offshore facilities. There was no limit of liability for willful or grossly negligent damages. A single federal fund of $200,000,000, financed by a charge of 3¢ per barrel on oil produced or transported on or near navigable waters of the United States, would replace the separate funds already established under the FWPC Act, the Trans-Alaskan

Pipeline Act, and the Deepwater Port Act. The new act would preempt all state laws and funds for the areas covered by it.[55]

Enactment of the Liability and Compensation bill would essentially implement the International Convention for Civil Liability for Oil Pollution Damage and the International Fund for Oil Pollution Damage. However, neither of these conventions had received the Senate's consent for ratification by 1976.

On occasion Congress has moved rapidly on marine pollution control, sometimes too rapidly in the views of critics. On other occasions Congress has procrastinated under pressure of organized interests and with a rueful reflection on the costs both to private interests and the public budget. As an electoral issue marine pollution hardly awakens voter response. The ratification of treaties in this area, moreover, has never been rapid. Despite the admonition of the President that the Liability and the Fund conventions could provide remedies for U.S. citizens from the discharge of oil by ships that otherwise would not fall under the territorial jurisdiction of the United States, the Senate moved slowly from 1971 to 1976 to consider and approve their ratification.

Opportunities for the further control of marine pollution by international agreement will undoubtedly capture the attention of many nations in the future. Going beyond the problem of deliberate dumping of hazardous materials from vessels and the discharge of pollutants from vessels into the seas, negotiations may touch the delicate issue of regulating the runoffs—or even the blowoffs—of pollutants from one state that may affect the environment of another state.

The first illustration of the regulation of land-based pollution by a multilateral convention was the Convention on the Protection of the Marine Environment of the Baltic Sea Area signed at Helsinki on 22 March 1974 by Denmark, the Federal Republic of Germany, the German Democratic Republic, Poland, Sweden, and the Soviet Union. The Convention covered both dumping and discharges from vessels, and it also dealt with land-based pollution: "pollution of the sea caused by discharges from land reaching the sea waterborne, airborne, or directly from the coast, including outfalls from pipelines." The Convention placed obligations on the parties to treat their municipal sewage to prevent eutrophication and ensure the hygienic quality of the receiving sea, while minimizing both the polluting loads of industrial wastes and the effects of cooling waters from nuclear power plants.[56]

International regulation of marine pollution will proceed cautiously and slowly, for high economic and political stakes are involved. Unless the costs of pollution control fall equitably on all the owners, operators, and shippers in marine transportation throughout the world, an advantage in freight rates for one state or another could obtain. Often the United States has held back from imposing higher standards of pollution control on its vessels for fear of sacrificing a commercial advantage to other merchants marine. Moreover, states have shown extreme reluctance in allowing another state to detain, prosecute, and punish their flag vessels, whatever the crime, if the offense occurs on the open oceans. And little proof of progress in both the national and international efforts to regulate marine pollution can be cited by the texts of laws or conventions alone. Implementation and enforcement must become a matter of record before any sanguine hopes turn into reality. Nevertheless, on balance, the twentieth century has been remarkable in turning the attention of mankind to the condition of the earth's environment. Never before has the world witnessed such abundant legislation and international agreements—equivocal or even misdirected at times—to reshape the relationship between man and his productive activities and man in his relationship to the air, seas, and skies.

7

Marine Policy for the United States

In the preceding chapters I have sketched the role of the oceans, the seabed, and the coastal zone in the history of the United States. Through many pages the Navy and its part in U.S. defense, the operation of the American merchant marine, the importance of fisheries and submerged mineral resources, and the problems of marine pollution have been examined. However, it is helpful to summarize these points and to analyze the contemporary institution of government available for marine policy. A sure result will be to stress the need to educate all Americans about the importance of the oceans and about the key issues that will require public decisions to assure a safe, productive, and enjoyable marine environment.

The Importance of the Oceans

Created by a seafaring people, the United States and its energetic citizens have cultivated a continent, built great cities, and leaped into outer space. But the oceans, washing the Atlantic and Pacific shores, the Gulf of Mexico, and the Great Lakes, have filled the cup of national welfare and remain a key to international policy. In truth, victory for America in World War II came from the sea. The ability of the Allies to slow the ravages of the German submarines on vital ocean commerce and the capacity of the United States to ship to both Europe and the Soviet Union essential supplies heralded the triumph over the Third Reich. Thereafter Japan was defeated following its critical losses on the Pacific from naval planes and amphibious warfare.

Since 1960, moreover, the oceans have assumed an importance to American national security even greater in time of peace than in the past. The certainty of both Washington and Moscow that some submarine-launched ballistic missiles, positioned in the wide, deep, opaque, and quiet subsurface of the seas, will survive any first attack by either the United States or the Soviet Union and bring instant retaliation on their cities has entirely changed strategic warfare. Both great powers of the world today strenuously seek advantages at sea. First, they wish to limit the survivability of the other's nuclear submarines armed with ballistic missiles by improving their own tracking devices, their sensors, sonars, and other submarine perceptors, while developing planes, mothered by ships, perfectly armed to deliver the kill of such submarines. Second, skirting the possibility of outright nuclear warfare, Washington and Moscow plan to develop combinations of ships and planes that will ensure the safety of commerce between their allied ports and demonstrate political support in waters adjacent to governments friendly to them.

The size and capability of naval vessels must be fitted to these common sense security objectives. For the United States the annual parade of arguments to gain appropriations of more than $35 billion for the U.S. Navy ultimately depends on an hypothesis about some unforeseen, but always impending, global conflict in which the oceans play a crucial role. Yet such hypotheses cannot be left to the judgment of the military; they must involve the balance of political arguments before informed American citizens. With twelve large deck-aircraft carriers, four of them nuclear powered, American debate will rage about the survival of these behemoths against massive Soviet air attacks. Arguments will also be raised about the urgency of extending further and further the range of submarine-launched ballistic missiles, at horrendous cost, when almost every major city of the Soviet Union can now be destroyed at a blow from an invulnerable location. Adversarial positions will also be taken, like those of the outgoing Ford administration and the incoming Carter administration in 1977, about the virtues of nuclear-powered over conventionally powered vessels. Yet none of these marginal shifts in tactics or appropriations belies the extraordinary importance of the oceans to the national security of the United States.

The U.S. Navy hardly faces extinction. If the Soviet Union regards navies as a means for achieving political objectives, both in peace and war; for demonstrating Moscow's economic and military might beyond national frontiers; and if the Russian Commander in Chief of the Navy bluntly declares that great power stutus is impossible without a powerful navy, can the Pentagon think otherwise? The armada of U.S. strike cruisers, aircraft carriers, and submarines, girded with missile launchers and fighting aircraft with their own lethal weapons, supported by tenders, oilers, and other auxiliary craft, may be expanded or trimmed, reorganized, or amalgamated. Still, for the next decade, the Navy will remain as the silver key to America's defense posture. Intelligence about the shaping of that mighty instrument of foreign policy will be demanded, with shrewd estimates by the President and Congress of international relations and a full recognition of the groaning domestic costs of a mighty war machine that may never be used.

The merchant marine has supported American defense efforts in all previous wars: in earlier days by direct conversion to fighting ships, in later years by hauling across the oceans the vital feed, fuel, weapons, and man power into combat zones. In practice, moreover, the enormous international trade of commodities that contribute so much to the prosperity of the American economy mostly arrive or depart at seaports. In a single year of the mid-1970s the value of U.S. trade reached 230 billion dollars, of which about 70 percent in value and 95 percent in weight was floated on American and foreign flag vessels.

For the United States the merchant marine, although in serious decline from its glorious days of the nineteenth century, will continue to be regarded as an auxiliary to American naval defense and the essential carrier of foreign commerce. The privately owned merchant fleet, of course, reflected the rapid technological changes in ocean transportation in recent decades. By 1977 about 26 percent of some 530 ships in the merchant fleet had been built or modified as container ships, and about 30 percent of the total or 160 vessels were tankers. Ten of these were over 100,000 dead weight tons. Moreover, the shipping industry involves not only the marine systems for building and equipping vessels, training seamen, providing navigational aids, and safety controls, but also the bustling business of shipping brokers, ratemaking, marine insurance, packing, handling, or lightering cargo, and the whole interface of ports with pipelines, rail, and road transportation. In the United States alone in the mid-1970s there were about 48 ports handling more than 7,500,000 tons of shipments annually.

More than half a billion dollars a year of American public money has been going for direct subsidies of the merchant marine. Other millions of dollars of costs to the public have been disguised by legislation requiring American built ships for U.S. registry as well as the transport of government-owned or government-financed commodities aboard U.S. flag vessels. Plainly the importance of the merchant marine to American world trade cannot be viewed complacently, for foreign vessels in the 1970s were carrying the overwhelming part of the goods imported to and exported from the United States. Much is at stake: the security of the nation, the U.S. balance of payments, and the vitality of the domestic shipping industry, with its tens of thousands employed in ship construction, sailing, and servicing. How much of the costs of a merchant marine that must compete against the ships of other nations with their own subsidies and economical operation should be borne by the public—and why—will require far more explication by the President and Congress. On the international scene, the United States must be deeply concerned (1) that new legal regimes for straits connecting one part of the high seas to another do not unreasonably obstruct navigation and (2) that innocent passage by merchant vessels through foreign coastal waters is not unduly restricted.

With the establishment of a two-hundred-mile exclusive fisheries zone in 1977, the United States placed almost one-fifth of the world marine fish resources under its jurisdiction. Competition and the catch for this treasured foodstock can be expected to change under new management policies. Although the United States has dropped from the second-largest fishing country of the world to fifth over the last two decades, its landings of about 5 billion pounds of fin and shellfish annually have been fairly constant. Moreover, the total value of the catch, in which shellfish count for almost half, has more than doubled in the last ten years, approaching $2 billion in the late 1970s.

Fishing has never been a minor matter to U.S. policy. With imports of fish approaching two billion dollars annually in the late 1970s and exports tripling in a decade to well over a quarter of a billion dollars, and with about 15,000 boats of more than five net tons engaged in fishing, an important segment of the American economy will continue to be affected by domestic policies. The number of actual fishermen in the United States appears quite small, about 170,000 employed commercially, of whom only about 50 percent work full-time at the industry. But their political influence, concentrated in the coastal states of Alaska, Maine, California, Maryland, or Louisiana, coupled to their historical hold on the public in states like Massachusetts or Rhode Island, has made them formidable in legislation. To their loud voice in marine fisheries policy should be added the interests of another 70,000 Americans, almost as large in number as the full-time fishermen, who are engaged in the processing and wholesaling of fish for either human consumption or agricultural-industrial uses. Although the U.S. Fishery Conservation and Management Act of 1976 may have quieted their immediate concern about the depletion of stocks in American coastal waters, debate over fisheries policy has hardly been stilled.

Judgments by the eight regional fisheries management councils on the stocks and the quantity of fish that can be caught under a formula of "optimum sustainable yield" will be open to question. The allocation of part of this yield to Americans, based on their "harvesting capacity" and the rest to foreigners will also lead to extended debate. While U.S. fishermen will seek public subsidies to improve their capacity, thereby raising real costs to the consumers, foreign nations will not only press the State Department for greater shares of stocks in the 200-mile zone, but also enter into joint fishing ventures under American companies to circumvent the law. Fish that swim beyond the exclusive jurisdiction of the United States will have to be managed in concert with foreign governments, and the distant water fishermen of the United States will almost certainly clamor for assistance to reap the shrimp or tuna located in foreign coastal waters. Despite 200-mile conservation and management zones, the United States cannot escape many future years of negotiation about entry, licensing, shared catches, migrations of species, or conservation on the high seas.

Apart from the utility of the oceans for security, navigation, and food, the greatest wealth to be drawn from the waters bordering the United States has been the oil and gas extracted from the submerged lands or continental shelf. Only since World War II, which exhausted so many of the wells of petroleum that had been drilled through dry land in the United States, has the value of the offshore sources of hydrocarbon fuels been realized. By 1976 some 850 thousand barrels a day of oil (or about 10 percent of total U.S. production), and 9.2 billion cubic feet a day of gas, (or about 10 percent of total U.S. production) were being drawn from offshore reservoirs. In fact, the worth of offshore oil and gas had mounted to almost four billion dollars annually, and more was expected from the seabed.

The mounting anxiety of America about the availability of its energy supplies and their cost has not abated since the Arab embargo of 1973 first jolted the United States into reality about the nonrenewability of oil and gas resources. With an ever-increasing demand for petroleum products by a country already using about one-third of all the energy produced in the world and with domestic sources declining, the United States was forced to face unpleasant economic and political facts. By 1977 almost 50 percent of the oil and gas of America was coming from foreign countries, and the prices, mainly set by the Organization of Petroleum Exporting Countries, reflected the new bargaining stance of the developing countries, which could extract full value on the world market.

In April 1977 President Carter dramatically faced the nation with proposals for a national energy policy that emphasized conservation. Under his plan there would be increased taxes on gasoline, higher prices for domestic oil and natural gas, and tax credits for conversions to solar power or insulation to save fuel. Nevertheless the production of petroleum had to be maintained and hopefully increased to avoid even greater dependence on imported fuels, with the concurrent danger of political interruption and economic squeeze.

Proved reserves of oil and gas were ready to flow from the North Slope of Alaska, although delayed again and again by negotiation and litigation over environmental impacts. Efforts to reach the untapped resources within the Atlantic continental shelf were slowed by arguments over potential effects on marine biota and coastal communities. At every turn the public and their pliable representatives in a democratic republic were caught between earnest advocates of economic development and environmental protection, with more rhetoric than proof, more zeal than constructive progress toward a good society. In the same vein the urgency for greater reliance on nuclear reactors, several to be placed in estuaries or offshore, opened the floodgates of political resistance to those fearful of legality or explosion with ultimate contamination of the environment. Never was more intelligent leadership through a thicket of claims and public irritation required in the federal and state capitals.

On the international scene, the issue that divided the Third UN Conference on the Law of the Sea in 1977 most was the exploitation of the seabed beyond national jurisdiction. For the United States the right of private entrepreneurs to obtain licenses from some international authority to explore and mine the manganese nodules lying on the ocean floor—licenses that would be secure after initial risk investments and assure reasonable profits after operations began—seemed imperative. Year by year, however, the United States conceded that the international authority ought to be able to mine portions of the seabed itself, ought to be able to restrict mineral production from the seabed, and ought to be assured of both capital and technology so that the Authority could actually mine the manganese nodules. But as the Conference convened again in May 1977, how much further the United States—and other developed countries—would concede to the persistent demands of the developing countries for giving paramount power over the seabed and its resources to the International Authority was clouded in diplomatic negotiations and Congressional concerns.

In no area of marine policy, however, has the United States moved faster and with such effect in such a short time than in the protection of the marine environment. The reinterpreted National Refuse Act, the Federal Water Quality Act, the Marine Protection, Research, and Sanctuaries Act, and the Coastal Zone Management Act, with their various amendments, have completely transformed the regulation of discharges and dumpings into waterways and the oceans while prodding states into wiser land and beach management. In addition, the Ports and Waterways Act as well as certain international conventions regulating vessel construction and operations were designed to safeguard American waters and the contiguous seas from the pollution of tankers.

The Council on Environmental Quality in 1976 found the quality of air and water in the United States to be improving rapidly. But the basic question about any new legislation and improved standards will clearly be the costs to the American economy. With respect to point source pollution, a National Commission on Water Quality in 1976 recommended that (1) the application of the "best practicable technology" standard for all dischargers by 1977 be modified to permit extensions or even waivers on a case-by-case basis; and (2) the "best available technology" standard for 1983 be postponed for five or ten years.

Serious delays in implementing permits for point source dischargers, moreover, have been due to clumsy federal bureaucratic management and endless negotiation or litigation to satisfy protests by environmental groups. Some reforms may lie in the direction, recommended by the Commission, of turning over all regulatory and administrative functions to the states. In any case the price of environmental programs was high, for in 1977 some twenty-one federal agencies were expected to lay out $8.7 billion, of which almost half would go to municipal sewage treatment facilities.

Criticisms of the General Accounting Office (GAO) on water pollution control have dwelt on the failure of industrial discharge permits to incorporate final guidelines and the failure of some industrial dischargers to adhere to their permits. The GAO also found the grant program for municipal sewage plants to be operating inefficiently, with poor operation and maintenance of plants and inadequate environmental assessments. Enormous sums of money have been involved in water pollution control—with the prices of industrial products raised to pay for the installation and maintenance of devices and the states themselves paying 25 percent of the costs of the management of sewage plant programs funded by the federal government. Moreover, little or nothing yet has been done to track and control the very large amounts of water pollution due to the blow-offs of noxious substances into the atmosphere, which are later deposited in the seas, or worse, the runoffs from rural and paved land surfaces of pesticides, hydrocarbons and other chemical or metal deposits that flush into streams, rivers, and estuaries.

About 90 percent of all the deliberate dumping of waste materials into the oceans, which totals about 130 million tons a year, consists of material dredged and dumped under permits from the Army Corps of Engineers or by the Corps itself. Only in the mid-1970s was the systematic study and regulation of this potentially pernicious practice in the marine environment effected. Dredge spoils may present toxic health hazards by their collection of heavy metals and chlorinated hydrocarbons, but the 13.5 million tons of municipal and industrial wastes dumped along the Atlantic and Gulf shores have roused greater public protests. Here the problem lies in alternative sources for the disposal of sewage sludge from large cities and the chemical wastes of industry. Better knowledge about the biological degradation of such wastes in the marine environment and the cost effectiveness of landfill, combustion, or other disposal techniques could contribute more reason and less heat to the formulation of public policy.

Yet the darkest image of marine pollution projected on the American citizen has been oil spills from tankers on the rivers and the seas, usually with collision, explosion, and black water killing wildlife and fouling beaches. Although far fewer spills have occurred in recent years, the quantity of oil sloshed, leaked, or poured into U.S. waters has risen dramatically.

Strong penalties for negligent spills and the costs of clean-up have been well-fixed by federal law on vessel captains, owners, and operators. Nevertheless, Congress was considering in 1977 a bill to assure compensation for damage to the marine environment and property through a fund financed by charges on barrels of oil received at terminals or refineries, as well as a Tanker and Vessel Safety Act that would require large tankers to have double bottoms and other safety features. Not the least problem was the reconciliation of U.S. standards of seaworthy ships and tanker operations with international regulations or the weakness of regulation by other states over their flag ships. Precipitate American action to constrain foreign vessels transiting U.S. waters or entering U.S. ports could have international repercussion. The voluntary acceptance of the 1973 International Convention for the Prevention of Pollution from Ships, the ideal way to set minimum standards for worldwide regulation of tanker navigation, has been painfully slow and doubtful.

For Americans, angry at tanker disasters off Nantucket, in the Delaware River, and in the Chesapeake Bay within a single year, the cry for security and compensation will rise to legislative halls in Washington and state capitals. Indeed, the Supreme Court had been called again in 1977 to rule on state law (Washington) that would refuse entry to all tankers above 120,000 DWT and tightly control the navigation of smaller tankers in state waters. Arguments about the economic costs of these prescriptions for an energy-hungry society cannot be brushed aside, and evidence exists to show that the environmental damage of oil spills has been easily exaggerated. The American statesman will have to steer a steady course to reach sound policy in this turbulent debate over the protection of the marine environment with its escalating economic costs.

Integrated Policy?

The management of marine policy in the United States in 1977 was still spread across several different departments, bureaus, and offices of the federal government. Eleven years earlier the Marine Resources and Engineering Act had expressed the feeling in Congress that the time for a national ocean program had arrived and ought to include systematic attention to both American marine resources and the environment with expanded research in marine science and technology. The Commission on Marine Science, Engineering, and Resources (the Stratton Commission), established by the Act to study the whole matter, had finally recommended in 1969 that a new, strong federal focus for marine activity should be located in a National Oceanic and Atmospheric Agency (NOAA), which ought to report directly to the President.

In his reorganization plan of 9 July 1970, however, President Nixon placed NOAA within the Department of Commerce and left the Coast Guard within the Department of Transportation. Nevertheless, the Bureau of Commercial Fisheries, the Marine Game Fish Research Center, and the Marine Minerals Technology Center from Interior; the National Oceanographic Data Center from and National Oceanographic Instrumentation Center from Navy; the National Sea Grant Program from the National Science Foundation; and small programs from the Coast Guard and the Corps of Engineers were all transferred to NOAA, which also incorporated the large Environmental Science Service Administration already in Commerce.

Although the Marine Resources and Engineering Act of 1966 had also created a National Council on Marine Resources and Engineering Development to plan and coordinate federal marine activities for the President and to report to Congress annually, that high-level policy instrument languished after the arrival of the new Administration in 1969 and died in 1971. Meanwhile a National Advisory Committee on Oceans and Atmosphere (NACOA) was created by Congress under PL 91-125 on 16 August 1971. Composed of twenty-five members drawn from the states, scientists, industry, and other nonfederal sources, NACOA has reviewed the progress of marine and atmospheric science programs, advised the Secretary of Commerce, and delivered annual assessments on marine affairs to both the President and Congress.

Not satisfied with this approach to marine affairs, the U.S. Senate took the initiative by authorizing its own National Ocean Policy Study. It sought to determine the adequacy of federal ocean programs, to evaluate policies and laws affecting the oceans, especially in the conservation and management of living resources, mineral utilization, coastal zone management, and to help establish a comprehensive national policy for understanding and protecting the global ocean environment. Since 1972 the Senate National Ocean Policy Study has held extensive hearings, made several studies, and recommended legislation to the Senate.

By 1977, although NOAA remained the lead agency for marine affairs in the federal government, the extraordinary problem of collecting all the complex activities of the bureaucracy pertaining to the oceans, the seabed, and the coastal zone under one agency was apparent. While NOAA had moved ahead of other agencies in ocean science research, its managerial and regulatory functions had to be shared with, no fewer than eleven federal departments and agencies; indeed, some NOAA research was being duplicated by other agencies. For example, the Bureau of Land Management and the Geological Survey in the Department of Interior have had key responsibilities for leasing of outer continental shelf tracts for mining, which include the collection of geological and geophysical data about these submerged lands as well as the analysis of environmental conditions or constraints in areas scheduled for leasing. Such duties plainly require studies parallel or duplicative of NOAA's activities. Similarly the U.S. Fish and Wildlife Service and the National Park Service, also in the Department of Interior, have had overlapping responsibilities with NOAA. Inland fisheries under the Fish and Wildlife Service may spend part of their life cycle in the ocean where fisheries come under NOAA. The management of lakeshore and seashore areas by the Park Service is intertwined with the coastal and marine sanctuary interests of NOAA.

Moreover, the Maritime Administration, a sister agency of NOAA in the Department of Commerce, administers the subsidy programs for American shipping and, in this connection, conducts ocean research. The Coast Guard, in the Department of Transportation, engaged in the safety of life and property at sea, is expected to enforce maritime law, not only rules of navigation or customs, but also violations of fisheries or pollution regulations. In any arrangements for the oceans, seabed, or use of the coastal zone with foreign nations, the Department of State must take leadership, and the Army Corps of Engineers in the Defense Department, with its traditional purview over navigable waters, has had responsibilities for structures, pollution, and ocean dumping. The analytical work of the Council on Environmental Quality and the regulatory actions of the Environmental Protection Agency also impinge directly on research on the marine environment and its uses. The National Aeronautical and Space Administration (NASA) has "sensed" or photographed the oceans, gathering data and monitoring behavior, while the Energy Research and Development Agency (ERDA), whose functions were transferred to the new Department of Energy in 1977, has studied radioactive elements, waste heat, and other energy phenomena in the seas. A major research agency, the National Science

Foundation, was spending about 8 percent of its budget for marine science investigation in 1977, and minor ocean-related activities could be found in the Department of Health, Education, and Welfare.

What should an analyst of marine policy make out of all this? The growth in numbers, increase in powers, and control of funds in the U.S. federal bureaucracy over the last twenty years has been absolutely stunning. One of the warmest appeals in the American Presidential campaign of 1976 was a promise to the public that the number of government agencies and federal personnel would be reduced. In the management of marine affairs, stimulated by cries for benefits or regulation from the states, from fishermen, from shippers, from marine scientists, from environmental groups, and others, there has been a dazzling proliferation of laws, agencies, rules, budgets, and staff. NACOA reported to the President and Congress that there were too many actors and too many chains of command. In the profusion of budgets, appropriations, and programs, national priorities have had no perspective. The ability of the President and Congress to lead effectively and to demand accountability, therefore, has been frustrated, according to the Council.

Bureaucracy beyond Depth

In the history of American public administration, national issues have always generated new government agencies to minister to public concerns. Indeed, the creation of another agency—or the consolidation of several bureaus under a new title—has often been regarded as the solution to some transcending problem of the United States. The consequences have been the multiplication of departments, bureaus, divisions, offices, and sections in a tightly packed bureaucracy, with each unit vying for the attention of the Chief Executive. Thwarted in the climb through the pyramid of paper and checkpoints by directors and department secretaries, the head of a program seeks to raise his voice above the bureaucratic clatter and woo the Oval Office with the least static. In the process the span of control of the President continues to widen and weaken, while titles are inflated to impress peers. Where once Assistant Secretaries had access to a Secretary, now they have been duplicated and depressed to wait on undersecretaries and deputy undersecretaries. Where once a Secretary, such as Navy, could easily cross the sill of the White House door, he has been pushed down to make way for a super-Secretary of Defense; and even departmental secretaries must deal with callow White House staff or stand beside independent administrators, directors, chairmen, or advisors reporting directly to the President.

Not to be forgotten in the gyrations of American government bureaus is the oversight of Congress. No fewer than seven committees of the Senate and six committees of the House, all with subcommittees, scan marine affairs and doggedly review the departments or agencies that manage ocean-oriented research, production, or protection. Such committees manipulate the bureaucratic ups and downs of the federal hierarchy no matter how a President may cast the executive organization.

Should the U.S. government be organized around a geophysical medium like the oceans? Around cogent needs of the state like security, energy, and international relations? Around major functional activities like agriculture and transportation? Clearly there is no simple answer. Proponents of a sharp focus on the seas, a national marine policy, and a single powerful lead agency for marine affairs reporting directly to the President have a peculiar, if justifiable, perspective about American society. Hopefully the preceding chapters have forcefully demonstrated the complexity of the uses of the oceans for defense, shipping, fishing, and mineral resources, while illuminating a host of environmental policy issues that involve the seas and the coastal zone. To place all these responsibilities, whether analytical, productive, or regulatory, within a single agency might not only divide and beggar several Cabinet departments with proven competence but might also engender an octopus with fissiparous tendencies.

In 1978 NOAA may have over 13,000 permanent staff positions. If MARAD (1500) and the Coast Guard (6000) were transferred to NOAA, the ocean agency would have well over 20,000 employees—not counting unscheduled or consultant personnel. If then the EPA (9500) and the Fish and Wildlife Service with parts of the National Park Service, the Bureau of Land Management, and the Geological Survey (3000) were moved into NOAA, the agency would overflow with 33,000 scheduled permanent positions, a number larger than any other independent federal agency except the mammoth Veterans Administration. Some advocates of NOAA would undoubtedly expect the National Science Foundation, NASA, and HEW to yield certain programs to NOAA, while the more zealous might covet certain oceanographic activities of the Navy. In sum, the end would be a vast complex of bureaus within a huge agency, tantamount to a Cabinet department, with strikingly diverse orientations about the uses of the sea and the marine environment.

On the other hand most experienced observers believe that a better focus on national policies involving the uses of the oceans is desirable — at least to reduce duplication of effort and at best to ensure coherent policies that can be effectively transmitted into legislation. The means need not be a concentration of all "ocean" matters into one department or agency. Rather a transcending council or commission could concentrate on the exigencies of marine affairs, investigate the capacities and performance of the several agencies whose work involves the coasts and seas, and harry both the President and Congress to take the required remedial action.

Efficient organizations should be taut, woven with a mesh of vertical bureaus in hierarchical patterns of authority and lateral strands of reviews, investigation, assessments, and recommendations conducted by boards external to the actual administrators of policy. The National Council on Marine Resources and Engineering, which expired in 1971, was replaced by the Inter-agency Committee on Marine Science and Engineering (ICMSE) under the Federal Council of Science and Technology. Essentially an executive coordinating committee of thirteen members from different departments, agencies, and bureaus and chaired by the administrator of NOAA, ICMSE has been charged with the examination of the planning and coordination of federal activities in marine sciences, identifying and fostering appropriate studies, and reviewing marine science and engineering programs with their budgets. But a coordinating committee, composed of the very agencies whose programs may need revision, integration, or excision, can hardly be expected to do more than cautiously exchange information while protecting its bureaucratic hold on budget, personnel, and authority.

Far more satisfactory in forthrightly addressing major marine policy issues has been NACOA. Composed of nonfederal members, NACOA has been bold in analyzing the bureaucracy and eager to suggest new programs or reorganize agencies in the interests of better-endowed marine programs. Instead of advising the Secretary of Commerce and merely reporting to the President and Congress, this Committee could be transformed into a Commission to act as the primary advisor to the Chief Executive on federal marine policy and could coopt, as chairman, the Vice-President of the United States or a Special Advisor to the President for Marine Affairs.

The game of organizational arrangements can be played by anyone, yet the principle of vertical specialization for the application of policy and lateral review of performance by disinterested parties should not be forgotten. Marine affairs are no exception to the rule. Only detachment from the pardonable bureaucratic biases and courage to recommend a reallocation of resources throughout the government will ensure a flexible response to the emerging needs of the United States in its uses of the oceans.

Education for Marine Affairs

A sound public policy in a democratic society must rest on an informed people. Moreover, leaders need to be trained both to phrase the political choices and to implement electoral decisions. With respect to marine policy the American institutions of higher education have only recently begun to expand their curricula to encompass study of the several uses of the sea and analyze marine environmental issues. Specialized degrees, indicating expertise in marine affairs, have barely peeked through the academic crust of respectability.

Since the days of Aristotle, marine biology has been the lodestone drawing scholars to the beaches, bays, estuaries, and oceans. In the United States until the middle of the twentieth century the more recondite investigations of marine geophysics and the chemical characteristics of the seas had been confined to a few highly specialized research institutions, such as the Scripps Institution of Oceanography, the Woods Hole Oceanographic Institution, or the Lamont-Doherty Institution. However, the International Geophysical Year of 1957, the growth in tonnage of marine transportation, the rise in the fishing catch, and great oil gushes from offshore wells in the 1960s, as well as the use of nuclear ships and submerged missiles, roused national interest in the oceans and posed new issues for the international law of the sea. One response to all this was the awakening of higher education to the importance of marine science and marine affairs, not only stimulating teaching and research in natural sciences, but also evoking new programs in legal regulations, economic analysis, and political behavior. By 1977 a chain of universities stretching from Hawaii to Alaska, from Southern California to Washington, in Texas, Louisiana, Florida, and north to Delaware and Rhode Island had outstanding marine studies programs. Several other institutions on the Atlantic seaboard and around the Great Lakes had excellent ocean and coastal research underway. All of them contributed to the accumulation of knowledge about the marine environment—providing data, original theory about marine phenomena, and improved technologies to exploit the seas.

Although billions of dollars had been contracted or granted for marine science studies and technological research, including the expensive ocean-going expeditions, funds for marine policy analyses from public agencies or private donors tended to be quite small. They were often limited to studies of the commercial applications of technologies or to the transient issues of the law of the sea. The first Center for the Study of Marine Policy at an academic institution in the United States was established by the University of Delaware in 1973, and other centers, focused on policy or management, were rapidly founded at the University of Southern California, the University of Washington, the University of Virginia, the University of Rhode Island, and elsewhere. For the first time in American higher education, groups of historians, lawyers, economists, and political scientists began to work systematically with engineers, biologists, chemists, and physicists on common ocean problems. This promising interdisciplinary approach to marine policy was abetted by the demands of public officials for more facts and better options in formulating both domestic legislation and treaties with other nations. Partly precipitated by the UN law-of-the-sea discussions beginning in 1968 and partly stimulated by the national will to legislate safer navigation, better conservation of fisheries, sounder offshore mineral exploitation, and a country of clean rivers and bright beaches, education in marine affairs has flourished.

Yet the need to understand, develop, and conserve the American heritage of the seas cannot be confined to research universities. Knowledge about the oceans must be transferred into the life-stream of the United States and excite the imagination of all citizens whose protection, livelihood, and recreation depend so much on the vital marine environment. Plainly too much legislation dealing with the uses of the oceans and the environment has been ill-advised and hastily drawn under the twisted arguments of interest groups or the passionate surges of public opinion. The President, members of Congress, and American delegates to international conferences will only correct their errors by better advice founded on adequate data and wise reflection.

Hopefully the preceding pages have contributed something to a clarification of the historical development and principal issues of marine policy. Expertise in all uses of the sea and coast lands will be required in the next decades, combining the objective knowledge of the natural sciences with the perspective, methodological analysis, and political options that can be posed by skilled social scientists. But the matter is too important to the national interest to be left to scholars and sailors, to fishermen and miners, or to the parochial concerns of the environmental groups; it must be shared with all American citizens. On 29 February 1808 in a letter to the New York Society of Tammany, Thomas Jefferson wrote that the ocean, like the air, "is the common birthright of mankind." Such a resplendent trust ought not to be meanly breached by any nation of the world, and never by the United States.

Notes

Chapter 1
The United States as a Maritime Nation

1. Some of these voyages to America are beautifully described with luminous navigational detail by Samuel Eliot Morison in *The European Discovery of America – The Northern Voyages* (New York: Oxford University Press, 1971). Between 1608, when the first permanent settlement was made in Virginia, and 1660, the English colonies in New England, Maryland, and Virginia increased to about 85 thousand (white) people along the Atlantic coast. Geographic influences on American commerce and the beginnings of trade are fully described by Emory R. Johnson, "American Commerce to 1789" in *History of Domestic and Foreign Commerce in the United States* (Washington, D.C.: Carnegie Institution, 1915).

2. Statistics on the U.S. coastline have been taken from the National Oceanic and Atmospheric Administration, U.S. Department of Commerce publication, *The Coastline of the United States* (Washington, D.C.). The U.S. Coast and Geodetic Survey (since 1970 the National Ocean Survey) is the source of data on the continental shelf and has a continuous program of soundings, surveys, and seabed analyses. A good general description of the United States continental shelf can be found in A. L. Shalowitz, *Shore and Sea Boundaries*, U.S. Department of Commerce, Coast and Geodetic Survey [Washington, D.C., 1962 (vol. I) and 1964 (vol. II)].

3. For an introduction to the wonders of the seas, see Rachel L. Carson, *The Sea around Us* (New York: Oxford University Press, 1951) which interestingly enough did not have the word "pollution" in its index. A later, lively book that provided me with details on oceans, tides, currents, and climates, as well as other fascinating marine data, is William C. Walton, *The World of Water* (New York: Taplinger Press, 1970).

4. An extremely well written book with fifteen pages of bibliography on the history of oceanography is Susan Schlee, *The Edge of An Unfamiliar World* (New York: E. P. Dutton, Inc., 1973), and I have made generous use of its chapters on both nineteenth- and twentieth-century development in discovering and studying the marine environment as well as its narrative of institutional growth. Also useful has been John Lyman's "History of Oceanography" in *Ocean Sciences,* edited by Captain E. John Long, U.S. Naval Institute, Annapolis, Maryland, with all the important dates of voyages, instrument-invention, organization of marine stations, and oceanographic institutions.

5. Nothing tells about Matthew Fontaine Maury's work better than his own book, *The Physical Geography of the Sea* (New York: Harper and Brothers, 1855), which is still worth reading for breadth and tone and insight, even though

supplanted by modern science. Thirty-six years after the first edition, Sampson Low, Marston and Co., London, published the twenty-second edition of this popular work — essentially a revised eighth edition.

6. Following the Act of 1907 establishing a "Survey of the Coast," the Secretary of Treasury requested proposals to create an agency. Hassler's plan was deemed best of seventeen submitted. See Albert A. Stanley, "Hassler's Legacy," *NOAA*, vol. 6, no. 1 (January 1976), p. 52.

7. Edmund Fanning had first reached the South Seas aboard a sealing vessel in 1792. He captained an incredulously successful voyage in 1797–1798 that yielded a profit of $53,000 to the owners on a $7000 investment while making himself a rich man from the trade of sealskins for Chinese–South Sea Island goods. He was an agent for scores of later private trade voyages to the Pacific and his *Voyages Around the World* published in 1833 further helped in the campaign to get Congress to finance a public exploration expedition.

8. Charles Wilkes had conducted the first survey of Georges Shoal and Bank. He led the United States Exploring Expedition with an iron hand. In a letter to the Secretary of the Navy on 11 March 1840 Wilkes called the great southern land mass that he had spotted "the Antarctic Continent." The *Narrative of the United States Exploring Expedition* by Wilkes was printed in one-hundred copies by C. Sherman of Philadelphia in 1844; however, Wilkes secured the copyright and editions were issued by Lee and Blanshard, Philadelphia, in 1845, 1849, 1850, and in 1851 by G. Putnam, New York. Both G. W. Gorton of Philadelphia (1849) and G. P. Putnam (New York) also published abridged editions of *Voyage around the World*. Wilkes also wrote the *Meterology* (1851) and the *Hydrography* (1861) volumes based on the expedition. See also the study of William Stanton, *The Great United States Exploring Expedition of 1838–1842* (Berkeley: University of California, 1975).

9. The *Challenger* expedition, in contrast to the U.S. Exploring Expedition, was marked by cordial cooperation between the naval staff and the civilian scientists. In addition to Thompson, John Murray and John Young Buchanan, a chemist, both from the University of Edinburgh, Henry Nottidge Mosely, a British naturalist, and James John Wild, the artist and secretary, made up the civilian staff. At the last moment Rudolf von Willemoes Suhm from the University of Munich was substituted for another scientist who had resigned. Seventy-six scientists in several countries received samples from the *Challenger*. Between 1885 and 1895 fifty volumes of narrative and scientific reports were published under the superintendence of C. Wyville Thompson and John Murray by His Majesty's Government. In fact, Thompson died in 1882, and John Murray, appointed editor, devoted himself to the publication of the handsome volumes. Murray not only wrote partly or wholly seven volumes, but he also increasingly subsidized the publication of the series as the government stinted its outlays. See also Eric Linklater, *The Voyage of the Challenger* (Garden City, New York: Doubleday and Co., 1972) for a recent popular work filled with sketches and pictures.

10. For a list and brief description of oceanographic research voyages, see G. Wust, "The Major Deep Sea Expeditions and Research Vessels, 1873-1960" in M. Sears, ed., *Progress in Oceanography,* vol. 2 (Oxford: Pergammon Press, 1964). A handsomely organized story of the evolution of oceanographic ships used by the U.S. Navy and other agencies, with hundreds of sketches or photographs of actual vessels is Stewart B. Nelson, *Oceanographic Ships – Fore and Aft* (Washington, D.C.: Office of the Oceanographer of the Navy, 1971). See also Robert C. Cowen, *Frontiers of the Sea: The Story of Oceanographic Expeditions* (New York: Doubleday, 1960).

11. For theories of continental drift, sea floor spreading, and plate tectonics, see Schlee, *Edge of an Unfamiliar World,* pp. 317-362, from which I have borrowed much. Her bibliography has forty-five items of note, and I have perused the articles written by Heezen, Hess, and others that are cited.

12. The Navy was largely responsible for the establishment of ocean science programs at many universities, such as Johns Hopkins, Texas A&M, Oregon State, and the Massachusetts Institute of Technology as well as helping to expand the efforts of other institutions. For details of the history of Navy ocean science, see Maury Center for Ocean Science, U.S. Navy, *The Ocean Science Program of the U.S. Navy* (Washington, D.C., June 1975). A splendid coverage of "the state of the art" for this period is Henry B. Bigelow, *Oceanography – Its Scope, Problems, and Economic Importance* (Boston: Houghton Mifflin, 1931) which was part of the report submitted to the National Academy of Sciences by its Committee on Oceanography in November 1929. Thomas Wayland Vaughan et al *International Aspects of Oceanography* (Washington, D.C.: National Academy of Sciences, 1937) is a digest of the oceanic data then available for the different ocean basins and a catalogue of all the institutions in the world, national and international, engaged in any kind of oceanographic work during the 1930s.

13. The Introduction and Summary of the report *Oceanography–1960–1970* was first distributed on 15 February 1959. The last of the twelve chapters, *A History of Oceanography,* was issued in 1962. In between, the Committee covered: basic research needed in the next ten years, oceanic research for defense applications, radioactivity, engineering needs, education and labor force, oceanwide surveys, international cooperation, and other subjects.

14. "Oceanography and the Government" by Captain Steven N. Anastasion in E. J. Long, *Ocean Sciences* (Annapolis: U.S. Naval Institute, 1964), is a good chapter on the evolution of government participation in science and technology at high policy levels and particularly on the development of federal coordinating machinery for oceanography from 1957 to 1963.

15. An abridged chronology of events related to *Federal Legislation for Oceanography, 1956–66* was prepared by the Legislative Reference Service of the Library of Congress, Washington, 15 July 1965, revised 9 January 1967, and contains a summary of all bills and hearings during this period.

16. The Sea Grant program was originally lodged in the National Science

Foundation and given authority to make money grants to colleges and universities in 1967. The first universities actually designated "sea grant" were Rhode Island, Texas A&M, Oregon State, and the University of Washington. "Land Is Just an Island — The Birth of Sea Grant" by Athelstan Spilhaus, unpublished, 1972, was given to me by the author of the concept. See also James P. McNulty, "The National Sea Grant Program: Expectations vs. Reality," *Marine Affairs Journal*, no. 3, University of Rhode Island, Kingston (September 1975) pp. 1–27.

17. Data on U.S. marine science and ocean affairs activities have been drawn from the Message from the President, *Federal Ocean Program*, transmitting on 11 December 1975 the 1974 annual report on the Federal Ocean Program pursuant to PL 89–454 (Marine Resources and Engineering Development Act of 1966). The report was prepared by the Science and Technology Office of the National Science Foundation. I have also made use of the report to the Congress by the Controller General, *The Need for a National Ocean Program and Plan*, B–145099 (Washington, D.C.: United States General Accounting Office, 10 October 1975), which was the second report of the Controller General in response to a request from the Senate Commerce Committee for information to be used in its National Ocean Policy Study. The first report dealt with *Federal Agencies Administering Programs Related to Marine Science Activities and Oceanic Affairs*, GGd–75–61 (25 February 1975).

18. Hugo Grotius, *The Law of War and Peace*, Francis W. Kesley, trans., James Brown Scott, ed., *Classics of International Law* (New York: Oxford, 1925), Book II, Chapter III: "Of the Original Acquisition of Things with Special Reference to Seas and Rivers."

19. Cornelius van Bynkershoek, *On the Sovereignty of the Sea*, Ralph van Deman Magoffin, trans., James Brown Scott, ed., *Classics of International Law* (New York: Oxford, 1923), Chapter I: "Concerning the Origin of Ownership."

20. The letter to Genêt from Thomas Jefferson on the extent of U.S. protection of its coasts can be found in *State Papers and Public Documents of the United States*, 2d ed., 10 vols. (Boston: T. B. Watt's Sons, 1817), vol. 1, p. 195. For the Act of Congress giving cognizance of complaints for captures made within the waters of the United States or within marine league of the coasts or shores thereof, see *Laws of the United States of America*, 5 vols., John Bioren and W. John Duane, Philadelphia and R. C. Weightman, Washington City, 1815, Vol. II, p. 427.

21. The opinion of Sir William Scott (Lord Stowell) is taken from *The Anna*, 5C. Rob 373, 385.

22. Thomas Weymyss Fulton, *The Sovereignty of the Sea* (Edinburgh and London: William Blackwood and Sons, 1911) is an extraordinarily valuable account, drawn in the main from original sources, of the historical claims of England to dominion over British seas and the evolution of the territorial waters doctrine.

23. For a background in studying the range of legal issues affecting the oceans and seabed, see such works as Philip C. Jessup, *The Law of Territorial Waters and Maritime Jurisdiction* (New York: G. A. Jennings, 1927); Gilbert Gidel, *Le Droit International Public de la Mer,* 3 vols. (Chateauroux, 1932-34); M. S. McDougal and W. T. Burke, *The Public Order of the Oceans,* (New Haven: Yale University Press, 1962); H. A. Smith, *The Law and Custom of the Sea,* 3d ed. (London: Stevens and Son, 1959); C. J. Colombos, *The International Law of the Sea,* 6th rev. ed. (London: Longmans, 1967). Other more specialized works will be referred to in later chapters.

24. The Hague Conference documents, plenary meetings, committee reports, and so forth can be found in League of Nations, *Acts of the Conference for the Codification of International Law* (The Hague, 1930), while the conclusions of the Conference are also gathered in the *American Journal of International Law,* vol. 24, 1930, Supplement, pp. 234 ff. See also Jesse S. Reeves, "The Codification of the Law of Territorial Waters," *American Journal of International Law,* vol. 24 (1930), p. 486, and League of Nations, Secretariat, "Codification of International Law," in *Ten Years of World Cooperation,* Chapter IV (Geneva, 1930).

25. The first fifteen years of the organization and work of the UN International Law Commission have been well traced by Herbert W. Briggs, *The International Law Commission* (Ithaca, N.Y.: Cornell University Press, 1965). Details on the Commission's work with respect to law of the sea can be found in the annual reports, beginning in 1949, to the UN General Assembly and the *Yearbook of the International Law Commission,* beginning in 1956.

26. On the Law of the Sea Conference at Geneva in 1958, two excellent summaries and analyses are: Arthur H. Dean, "The Geneva Conference on the Law of the Sea: What Was Accomplished," *American Journal of International Law,* vol. 52 (1958), p. 607, and Philip C. Jessup, "The United Nations Conference on the Law of the Sea, *Columbia Law Review,* vol. 59 (1959). The four conventions adopted at Geneva are in UN Docs. A/Conf. 13/L. 52; L.54; and L.55. The Final Act of the Conference was UN Doc. A/Conf. 13/L.58. For the work of the Second UN Law of the Sea Conference in 1960 see Arthur Dean, "The Second Geneva Conference on the Law of the Sea: The Fight for Freedom of the Seas," *American Journal of International Law,* vol. 54 (1960), p. 751 and Philip Jessup, "The Law of the Sea Aground," vol. 55 (1961), p. 104.

27. Developments of the treaty prohibiting the emplacement of weapons of mass destruction on the seabed can be conveniently traced through J. F. Leonard's articles in the *Department of State Bulletin,* vol. 61 (3 November 1969, 17 November 1969, and 1 December 1969).

28. For the work of the UN Seabed Committee, see United Nations, General Assembly, *Official Records,* 28th Session (1973), "Report of the Committee on the Peaceful Uses of the Sea-Bed and Ocean Floor beyond National Jurisdiction" (Oct-Nov 1973), 6 vols. (A/9021).

29. The literature, both descriptive and analytical, of the Caracas-Geneva sessions of the Third UN Law of the Sea Conference is extensive. For an overview from the American point of view by the Special Representative of the President to the Conference who headed the delegation and by the Assistant Legal Adviser for Oceans, see John R. Stevenson and Bernard H. Oxman, "The Third United Nations Conference on the Law of the Sea: The 1974 Caracas Sessions," *American Journal of International Law,* vol. 69 (1975), pp. 1-30 and, by the same authors, "The Third United Nations Conference on the Law of the Sea: The 1975 Geneva Session," *American Journal of International Law,* vol. 69 (1975), pp. 768-797. See also Bernard H. Oxman, "The Third United Nations Conference on the Law of the Sea: The 1976 New York Session," *American Journal of International Law,* vol. 71 (1977), pp. 247-269. For a detailed political interpretation of the Conference, see Edward Miles, "An Interpretation of the Caracas Proceedings," in Francis Christy et al., eds., *The Law of the Sea: Caracas and Beyond* (Cambridge, Mass.: Ballinger Publishing Co., 1975), pp. 39-94, and by the same author, "An Interpretation of the Geneva Proceedings, Part I," *Ocean Development and International Law,* vol. 3 (1976), pp. 187-224.

30. In addition to the three main Committees of the Law of the Sea Conference an "informal working group on the settlement of disputes" had been active in Caracas and in Geneva as well as through a number of informal meetings and consultations. The group produced a single working paper for information purposes, which was distributed by the President of the Conference some months after the adjournment of the 1975 Geneva session. For the informal single negotiating texts of Committees I, II, and III see UN Doc. A/Conf.62/WP.8/ Part I; Part II; and Part III, all 7 May 1975. For the working paper of the group on the settlement of disputes, see SD.Gp/2nd Session/No. 1/ Rev. 5, 1 May 1975.

31. At the 15 March-7 May 1976 session of the Third UN Law of the Sea Conference some 1,000 informal amendments were proposed for the Single Informal Negotiating Text that had been prepared at Geneva. Close to 4,000 statements were also made, nearly all supporting the parts of the text. A *Revised Single Negotiating Text* was prepared for the next session beginning 2 August 1976. UN Document A/CONF.62/WP.8/Rev.1/ Parts I, II, III.

32. Henry Kissinger's remarks were taken from his speech before the Foreign Policy Association, the U.S. Council of the International Chamber of Commerce, and the UN Association of the U.S.A. in New York, 8 April 1976, reprinted by the Department of State's Bureau of Public Affairs, Washington, D.C.

33. The quick catalogue of contemporary American interests in the ocean comes from several statistical sources, but the earliest best compilations came from the annual reports *Marine Science Affairs,* 1967-1971, by the President to Congress prepared by the National Council on Marine Resources and Engineering (now defunct), Washington, D.C. and the *Report of the President on*

the Federal Ocean Program, 1974, submitted to Congress pursuant to Public Law 89-454. Budget figures, of course, have been extracted directly from the *Budget of the United States Government,* Fiscal Years 1976 and 1977.

Chapter 2
The Navy, The Oceans, and American Security

1. The British fleet had run down considerably after the end of the Seven Years War in 1763 and was in poor shape in 1776. France sent a fleet of twelve ships of the line plus five frigates from Toulon to America on 13 April 1778; seven ships of the line, three frigates, and thirty-six transports carrying five thousand troops from Brest to Newport, R.I. on 2 May 1778; and twenty ships of the line from Brest to America on 22 March 1781. Facing Lord Cornwallis of Great Britain at Yorktown in 1781 were eight thousand French and seven thousand American troops under Washington, while Admiral de Grasse with twenty-four battleships and two frigates forced the British fleet of nineteen battleships and seven frigates to break off their engagement and support of Cornwallis. See the original accounts and reports in Frank Ensor Chadwick, *The Graves Papers and Other Documents Relating to the Naval Operations of the Yorktown Campaign, July to October, 1781* (New York: Naval Historical Society, 1916).

2. For the development of the U.S. navy one can begin with Harold and Margaret Sprout, *The Rise of American Naval Power,* 1776-1918 (New Jersey: Princeton University Press, 1939) and follow with Donald W. Mitchell, *History of the Modern American Navy* (New York: Alfred Knopf, 1946). I have found J. W. King, *Warships and Navies of the World,* (Boston: A. Williams & Co., 1880), valuable for nineteenth century figures, especially Chapter XXVI. The Naval History Division of the Department of the Navy has published several editions of *United States Naval History: A Bibliography* since 1956, which contain over a thousand items by period and subject matter on the U.S. Navy.

3. An excellent study of relations between Washington and London through the nineteenth century, showing the benefits of reconciliation to the diplomacy of both states and the protective role of the British fleet is H. C. Allen, *Great Britain and the United States: A History of Anglo-American Relations 1783-1952* (New York: St. Martins Press, 1955).

4. The American-China trade began in earnest with the sailing of the 360-ton *Empress of China* directly from New York to Canton in 1784. Although never large in terms of total U.S. commerce, the China trade was profitable. In 1805-1806, for example, 37 American vessels carried away 11 million pounds of tea, about one-half of the British haul. American merchants, however, had none of the benefits of the European traders who utilized their colonies en route to China and enjoyed the presence of their navies for military support. In 1826

Captain Thomas Jones of the U.S. Navy had negotiated the first agreements with chiefs at Hawaii, the Society Islands, and Tahiti for the friendly treatment of American trading vessels; seven years later Edmund Roberts was commissioned by President Andrew Jackson to sign treaties with Cochin-China, Siam, Muscat, and Japan, but he died in Macao before reaching Japan; following the Opium War between China and Great Britain, Commodore Lawrence Kearney of the U.S. Navy in 1842 secured equal treatment for American nationals in the five trading ports opened to English merchants, and Caleb Cushing obtained these rights by treaty in 1844 as well as extraterritorial rights for both civil and criminal cases involving Americans. Japan not only stood athwart the Chinese trade route, but there was good reason to believe that great trade possibilities for the United States lay in that country itself. Commodore James Biddle called with a United States naval expedition at Tokyo bay in 1846 requesting Japan to open itself to American trade, but the shogunate refused and Biddle left, only to be followed by Perry six years later with a slightly veiled demand. Some of my references have been drawn from Tyler Dennett, *Americans in Eastern Asia* (New York: Macmillan, 1922); Kenneth S. Latourette, *The History of Early Relations between the United States and China* (New Haven, Conn.: Yale University Press, 1917); Paul Hibbert Clyde, *The Far East, A History of the Impact of the West on Eastern Asia* (New York: Prentice Hall, 1948); and Arthur Wolworth *Black Ships Off Japan, the Story of Commodore Perry's Expedition* (New York: A. A. Knopf, 1946).

5. Alfred Thayer Mahan's lectures were published as *The Influence of Sea Power upon History, 1660-1783* (Boston: Little, Brown, 1890), which ran into 14 editions by 1898 and brought Mahan international fame. Theodore Roosevelt, who was Assistant Secretary of the Navy from 1897 to 1898, was one of his many powerful American advocates, but Mahan's doctrine had a profound effect on every great power of the world. He was on the strategy board for the Spanish-American War and became a U.S. delegate to the first Hague Peace Conference in 1899—where he opposed compulsory arbitration and the outlawing of gas in warfare. See William D. Puleston, *Mahan: The Life and Work of Captain Alfred Thayer Mahan* (New Haven, Conn.: Yale University Press, 1939).

6. In 1898 the Spanish navy, by comparison with the American, had only one first-class battleship, thirteen years older than the U.S. ships of the same class, in a bad state of repair. The Spaniards had a number of armored cruisers and several destroyers, but almost all were poorly equipped and manned. Before the Spanish American war began, Rear Admiral Cervera estimated for Madrid that the Spanish navy was only one-third as strong as the American. John D. Long, *The New American Navy*, 2 vols. (New York: The Outlook, 1903); and French E. Chadwick, *The Relations of the United States and Spain: The Spanish American War* (New York: Charles Scribners, 1911), have full details on the U.S. Navy and naval events in the war.

7. For the "great white fleet" and Theodore Roosevelt's advocacy of naval power, see G. C. O'Gara, *Theodore Roosevelt and the Rise of the Modern Navy* (Princeton: Princeton University Press, 1943).

8. For German goals and plans in 1914, see Fritz Fischer, *Germany's Aims in the First World War* (original work *Griff nach der Weltmach* published in 1961) (New York: W. W. Norton, 1967).

9. The only major fleet engagement of the belligerents during World War I was the mighty battle of Jutland in which 254 ships totalling 1,600,000 tons faced each other. The British lost 14 ships and suffered 6784 casualties; the Germans lost 11 ships and suffered 3029 casualties. However, the strategic dominance of the Atlantic by the British was unchanged. A good account of the World War I struggle for the oceans is William S. Sims and Burton J. Hendrick, *The Victory at Sea* (New York: Doubleday, Page, 1921) and more particularly R. H. Gibson and Maurice Prendergast, *The German Submarine Warfare, 1914–1918* (New York: Richard R. Smith, 1931).

10. The 1922 Washington conference on naval disarmament is fully covered by Raymond Leslie Buell, *The Washington Conference* (New York: Appleton-Century-Crofts, 1922), while the hindsight of thirty years on the achievements—or lack of them—can be found in John Chalmers Vinson, *The Parchment Peace* (Athens: University of Georgia Press, 1955). Other than the naval disarmament convention, the Anglo-Japanese alliance was abrogated, and the sovereignty and independence of China was guaranteed, while the United States, Great Britain, France, and Japan agreed to respect one another's rights in the Pacific.

11. There is voluminous literature on the neutrality policy of the United States from 1935 to 1939 and the gradual slide of the United States in 1940 toward support of the Allies against Germany. Excellent studies are William L. Langer and S. Everett Gleason, *The Challenge to Isolation and the Undeclared War* (New York: Harper and Bros., 1952 and 1953). See also E. R. Stettinius, *Lend Lease: Weapon of Victory* (New York: The MacMillan Co., 1944).

12. Herbert Feis, *The Road to Pearl Harbor* (Princeton: Princeton University Press, 1950) is a scholarly detailed analysis of diplomacy and preparations by the United States and Japan before 7 December 1941. For naval operations during World War II, see S. W. Roskill, *The War at Sea, 1939–1945,* 3 vols. (London: His Majesty's Stationers Office, 1954-1961); and Samuel Eliot Morison, *History of U.S. Naval Operations in World War II,* 14 vols. (Boston: Atlantic Monthly, Little, Brown, 1947-1960), with Supplement and General Index (1961). A shorter, but good study is John Creswell, *Sea Warfare, 1939–1945* (Los Angeles: U. of California Press, 1967).

13. On the U.S. Fleet organization the best account for the 1930-1945 period is Ernest J. King and Walter Muir Whitehill, *Fleet Admiral King: A Naval Record* (New York: W. W. Norton, 1952). See also the U.S. Office of the Comptroller of the Navy, *The Naval Establishment, Its Growth and Necessity for Expansion, 1930–1950* (Washington, D.C., 1951).

14. In the immediate postwar period Congress responded to the administration's call for universal military training by strengthening the Air Force, which, like the Navy a half-century ago, seemed a wonderful and relatively inexpensive way of being powerful without getting involved in the international politics of Europe or Asia. W. W. Rostow, *The United States in the World Arena* (New York: Harper and Bros., 1960) contains an extremely lucid review of American policy and the military services in this period in Book Two, Part II.

15. For the Korean War and other naval conflicts, see E. B. Potter and Chester W. Nimitz, eds. *Sea Power: A Naval History* (Englewood Cliffs, N.J.: Prentice Hall, 1960). In Lebanon 10,000 American troops were landed in a week and effectively quelled a revolution with international implications; when Quemoy and Matsu were threatened by Peking, the 7th Fleet appeared on the scene, calmed tempers, and thwarted a potential invasion.

16. For the section on "New Strategic Uses of the Oceans," I have drawn data from the U.S. Secretary of Defense, *Annual Report to the President,* including the annual reports of the Secretaries of the Army, Navy, and Air Force published semiannually from 1949 to 1958 and annually since Fiscal Year 1959. Statements by the Chairman of the Joint Chiefs of Staff before the U.S. Senate Armed Services Committee have also been used. Other data on naval forces of the United States and the Soviet Union have been taken from the Stockholm International Peace Research Institute, *World Armaments and Disarmament,* 1968/69 and 1969/70 and the Center for Strategic and International Studies, *Soviet Seapower,* Special Report Series no. 10 (Washington, D.C.: Georgetown University, 1969).

17. Valuable studies of naval post-World War II defense planning and the politics of policy-making in the Navy are Vincent Davis, *Postwar Defense Policy and the U.S. Navy, 1943-1946* (Chapel Hill: University of North Carolina Press, 1966) and *The Admiral's Lobby* (Chapel Hill: University of North Carolina Press, 1967).

18. During the Cuban missile crisis, the Joint Chiefs of Staff were unanimous in recommending immediate military action to destroy or displace the armaments that had been installed on the island by the Soviet Union. Secretary of Defense Robert S. McNamara disagreed, favoring a blockade, but made ready for an attack on Cuba that required 500 sorties against all targets. Congressional leaders like Senators Richard B. Russell of Georgia and J. William Fulbright of Arkansas urged military action stronger than a blockade. President Kennedy's decision to use a naval blockade as the instrument for exerting pressure on the Soviet Union and Cuba to reverse their actions included the deployment of 180 ships into the Caribbean, dispersion of the Strategic Air Command, and a full alert of B-52's flying continuously with atomic weapons. See Robert F. Kennedy, *Thirteen Days* (New York: W. W. Norton & Co., 1969).

19. Regarding the attacks on the U.S. destroyer *Maddox,* see U.S. Senate Foreign Relations, *Hearings,* "Gulf of Tonkin 1964 incidents," 90th Congress,

2d session, with Robert S. McNamara, Secretary of Defense, 20 February 1968.

20. Information on the history of Navy ocean science and the Navy ocean science program has been taken from Office of the Oceanographer of the Navy, *The Ocean Science Program* of the U.S. Navy, Alexandria, Virginia, 1970, updated by the Maury Center for Ocean Science, Department of the Navy, Washington, 1975.

21. A few outstanding works on seapower in the 1970s and the Soviet Navy are Edward N. Luttwak, *The Political Uses of Seapower* (Baltimore: Johns Hopkins University Press, 1974); Michael MccGwire, ed., *Soviet Naval Developments: Capability and Context* (New York: Praeger Publishers, 1973), and Normal Polmar, *Soviet Naval Power: Challenge for the 1970s,* rev. ed. (New York: Crane, Russak, and Co., 1974). A mine of information, of course, are the annual hearings before the U.S. Congress, House of Representatives, Armed Services Committee with testimony from naval officers and queries from Committee members on all aspects of naval plans and operations.

22. Texts of the treaty on the limitation of ABM systems, the interim agreement and protocol on the limitation of strategic offensive arms, and agreements on environmental protection, medical science and public health, cooperation in space, science and technology, and incidents at sea are in U.S. Department of State, *Bulletin,* vol. LXVI, no. 1722, Washington, D.C. (26 June 1972). A report of Secretary of State William P. Rogers to the President, with agreed interpretations and unilateral statements are in the *Bulletin,* vol. LXVII, no. 1728, Washington, D.C. (3 July 1972). A statement urging favorable consideration of the two SALT agreements was made by Gerard Smith, Director of the U.S. Arms Control and Disarmament Agency, who headed the delegation to SALT, before the U.S. Senate Committee on Armed Services on 28 June 1972.

23. On the matter of comparing U.S. and Soviet forces, as well as defining the mission of the U.S. Navy in the light of foreign policy objectives, two excellent articles are Stanfield Turner, "The Naval Balance: Not Just a Numbers Game," and Michael Krepon, "A Navy to Match National Purposes," in *Foreign Affairs,* vol. 55, no. 2 (January 1977), New York: Council on Foreign Relations. Another short, but cogent analysis is Julien S. Le Bourgeois, "What Is the Soviet Navy Up To?" *Policy Paper,* Atlantic Council of the United States, Washington, D.C. (1977).

24. The *1952 Yearbook of the International Law Commission,* vol. II, "Documents of the Fourth Session, including the report of the Commission to the General Assembly," pp. 29–30 contains a list of fifty-five states and their legislation on territorial seas and contiguous zones as of 1952. During the first UN Conference on the Law of the Sea in 1958, the Secretariat prepared a "Synoptical Table of the Breadth and Juridical Status of the Territorial Sea and Adjacent Zones," which was further amended and revised in light of comments and additions by governments during the following year, and then

published as DOC. A/CONF. 19/4 in the *Second United Nations Conference on the Law of the Sea Official Records,* Annexes, pp. 157–163. The United Nations published several volumes in its legislative series dealing comprehensively with laws, regulations, and treaties relating to the high seas, territorial sea, contiguous zones, continental shelf, and fishing, such as: *Laws and Regulations on the Regime of the High Seas,* vol. I, ST/LEG/SER.B/1 (1951); *Supplement to Laws and Regulations on the Regime of the High Seas,* vol. I, ST/LEG/SER.B/8 (1959); *Laws and Regulations on the Regime of the Territorial Sea,* vol. II, ST/LEG/SER.B/6 (1957); and *National Legislation and Treaties Relating to the Territorial Sea, the Contiguous Zone, the Continental Shelf, the High Seas, and to Fishing and Conservation of the Living Resources of the Sea,* ST/LEG/SER.B/15 (1970). National claims to maritime jurisdiction in 1971 for 123 countries were listed in detail by the Geographer of the U.S. Department of State, "National Claims to Maritime Jurisdiction," *International Boundary Study,* Series A, Limits in the Seas, no. 36, Washington, D.C. (3 January 1972). Claims to the territorial sea, continental shelf, exclusive fishing zones, and other areas of special marine jurisdiction were noted, with sources of the legislation, decrees, proclamations, treaties, or other acts supporting the claims.

25. *The Corfu Channel Case,* 1949 International Court of Justice, *Reports,* 17.

26. See the Third United Nations Conference on the Law of the Sea, *Revised Single Negotiating Text* (Doc. A/CONF.62/WP.8/Rev. 1/Part II, 6 May 1976, Articles 33–42. For a valuable geographic analysis of articles of the text dealing with baselines, delimitation between states, islands, archipelagoes, and so forth, see Robert D. Hodgson and Robert W. Smith, "The Informal Single Negotiating Text (Committee II): A Geographical Perspective," *Ocean Development and International Law,* Crane, Russak & Co.), vol. 3 no. 3 (1976), p. 225.

27. Frederic G. De Rocher, *Freedom of Passage through International Straits: Community Interest Amid Present Controversy,* University of Miami Sea Grant Program, Sea Grant Technical Bulletin, no. 23, (November 1972), is an excellent study of straits issues.

28. Admiral Sergei Gorshkov, the architect of the modern Soviet navy, survived the political regimes of Stalin, Kruschchev, and Brezhnev by professional ability and dedication to the Russian fleet. Short, energetic, and single-minded about the importance of the Soviet Navy, Gorshkov wrote many books and articles on naval strategy, including *Red Star Rising at Sea* (Annapolis: Naval Institute Press, 1974).

29. For a vivid, personalized insight on the politics of defense and particularly naval affairs at the presidential level, few books can match the candid work of Elmo R. Zumwalt, Jr., *On Watch* (New York: Quadrangle, New York Times Books, 1976). Zumwalt, the youngest Chief of Naval Operations ever appointed in the United States, served under Secretary of Defense Melvin Laird

and his successor, James Schlesinger through the dark days of President Nixon after the Watergate affair.

30. An extensive analysis of the budgetary process, of the role of Congress, and of American seapower has been made by James K. Oliver, summed up in "The Future of American Seapower: The Role of Congress," *Marine Policy Reports,* vol. 1, no. 1 (January 1977), Center for the Study of Marine Policy, University of Delaware, Newark.

Chapter 3
The American Merchant Marine

1. The most detailed and extensive work about the development of the American colonies and the United States with respect to the merchant marine under sail is William Armstrong Fairburn's *Merchant Sail,* 6 vols. (Center Lowell, Maine: Fairburn Marine Educational Foundation, 1945-1955). A flowing comprehensive story of the origin and growth of the American Merchant from Colonial America to the Civil War is Carl C. Cutler, *Queens of the Western Ocean* (Annapolis: United States Naval Institute, 1961) with appendices containing all sailing lines, their ships, both oceanic and coastal tonnage, and masters, as well as data on shipowners, schooners of 300 tons and upward, fast packet passages, and sailing plans. For the early American merchant marine, I have used the excellent Samuel Eliot Morison, *Maritime History of Massachusetts,* (Boston: Houghton Mifflin, 1921), John R. Spears, *The Story of the American Merchant Marine* (New York: Macmillan, 1919), and *Historical Statistics of the United States: Colonial Times to 1957* (Washington, D.C.: Bureau of the Census, U.S. Department of Commerce, 1960. Daniel Henderson, *Yankee Ships in China Seas* (New York: Hastings House, 1946) is a popular, romantic book based on an excellent three-page bibliography of source materials; E. Kemble Chatterton, *The Mercantile Marine* (Boston: Little, Brown, 1923) was very helpful too. The specialist will want to consult, Robert Greenhalgh Albion, *Naval and Maritime History, An Annotated Bibliography,* 3d ed. (Mystic, Conn.: Marine Historical Association, 1963) with 212 pages of references divided into seven major subjects. *The American Neptune,* a quarterly journal of maritime history, Peabody Museum of Salem, Salem, Massachusetts contains many fine articles and some documents on the maritime industry. *The Mariners Mirror,* published quarterly by the Society for Nautical Research, founded in 1910, National Maritime Museum, Greenwich, London is also valuable for articles on shipping and marine transport from ancient times to the present.

2. For the glory of a great commercial center in American history, see James Duncan Phillips, *Salem and the Indies* (Boston: Houghton Mifflin, 1947).

3. "Tonnage" for vessels is a word used rather indiscriminately. The origin is "tun," a large wine-vessel or cask which in the 15th century held 100 to 140 gallons of wine. By the 17th century "tun" and "ton" were distinguished, the latter coming to mean the space of 40 cubic feet or a maritime ton. For registry purposes, however, the tonnage of ships has in modern times been calculated in numbers of 100 cubic feet spaces, which may be gross if all space is included or net if only actual cargo space is included. The amount of water tonnage a vessel displaces is still another measure but generally "deadweight tonnage," that is, the difference between the weight of the ship unloaded and loaded to the waterline is used. Unless otherwise indicated "tons" in this book are intended to mean gross registered tons for 19th and 20th century ships. Bankers Trust Co., *American Merchant Marine* (New York, 1920) has among other things, documented tables on the tonnage of the merchant marine, percentage of foreign trade carried by American flagships, etc., for more than a century.

4. Problems for American shipping and trade with foreign countries dated back to the Navigation Acts of 1660 and 1663. Parliament required certain American exports (sugar, tobacco, cotton, etc.) to be laid on the English shore before shipment to any foreign country and forbade any imports to America not carried in an English vessel. The result was a rise in the price of imports to America, a drop in the price of exports arriving in English ports, and the beginnings of the American revolution. In the Treaty of Peace with England in 1783 there was no commercial clause. The Americans found themselves treated like foreigners, that is, discriminated against or shut out completely from British trade and British colonial ports, especially the West Indies. Treaties of amity and commerce with the Dutch, French, and Swedes were not worth much since the overwhelming trade of the Americans had been with Great Britain. Every effort was made by Congress and the President after 1815 to liberalize trade with Great Britain through reciprocal concessions. Just before the Civil War, by treaty or by informal agreement, the United States had complete trade reciprocity with twenty-nine nations. Lloyd W. Maxwell, *Discriminating Justice and the American Merchant Marine* (New York: H. W. Wilson Co., 1926) has an extensive treatment of tariffs and their effect on the American merchant marine.

5. There are several good books on the American packets, but the first and best scholarly study is Robert Greenhalgh Albion, *Square Riggers on Schedule* (Princeton: Princeton University Press, 1938). See also Arthur H. Clark, *The Clipper Ship Era* (New York: G. P. Putnam's Sons, 1911).

6. Warren Armstrong examines the packet monopoly of the Americans in *Atlantic History* (London: George C. Harrap, 1969) and traces the rise of Samuel Cunard's steamship lines. Adam W. Kirkaldy, *British Shipping* (New York: E. P. Dutton, 1914) deals with the history, organization, and importance of nineteenth century steam navigation. The United States was the slowest of the mercantile nations to switch to steam propulsion. In 1900 about 49 percent

of American tonnage was still borne by sailing vessels, while only 32 percent of foreign tonnage was carried by the force of wind. The Civil War further hastened the decline of American merchant marine. Ship owners, in fear of loss, sold their ships or laid them up in safe harbors. About 750,000 tons of shipping were sold while the armed cruisers of the South destroyed some 110,000 tons at sea. In 1866 Congress forbade American vessels sold or transferred to foreign registry from readmission to U.S. registry.

7. The first extensive source about shipping conferences is the *Report of the Royal Commission on Shipping Rings*, 5 vols. (London: 1909) and next the U.S. Congress, House of Representatives, Committee on Merchant Marine and Fisheries, *Investigation of Shipping Combinations*, 4 vols. (Washington, D.C.: 1913 and 1914). Both these investigations are exhaustive with ample candid testimony from shipowners and operators as well as exporters and importers. The U.S. Congressional investigation included a description of eighty shipping conference agreements. Daniel Marx, Jr., *International Shipping Cartels*, (Princeton: Princeton University Press, 1953) is the best scholarly study of its day of shipping conferences. The 1916 Shipping Act originally placed the regulation of the rates and practices of coastal and intercoastal water-borne vessels (as well as ocean carriers) under the U.S. Shipping Board, but in 1940 these domestic functions were transferred to the Interstate Commerce Commission.

8. A historical narrative of the problems and the achievements of the U.S. Shipping Board and the Emergency Fleet Corporation is W. C. Mattox, *Building the Emergency Fleet* (Cleveland: Penton Publishing Co., 1920). See also Paul Maxwell Zeis, *American Shipping Policy* (Princeton: Princeton University Press, 1938); and John G. B. Hutchins, *The American Maritime Industries and Public Policy*, Harvard Economic Studies, vol. LXXI (Cambridge, Mass: Harvard University Press, 1941).

9. In its report on the original version of the Merchant Marine Act of 1936 the Senate Commerce Committee was almost evenly divided between those encouraging private enterprise and those calling for public ownership. The minority views of ten senators, out of a twenty-member Committee, alleged that the bill had been framed entirely in the interest of private shipbuilders and operators without regard to the costs to the taxpayers. 74th Congress, 2d Session, *Congressional Record—Senate*, p. 4888. In the House of Representatives the minority report railed against the Act's violation of the shipping lessons of the past six years as pointed out by the President, its failure to correct evils and abuses of steamship companies with regard to subterfuges, subsidies, and profits at public expenses, and its lack of assurance in providing an adequate merchant marine. 74th Congress, 2d Session, *Congressional Record—House*, p. 1533.

10. For a study of whether ship subsidies should be offered by the government, see Walter T. Dunmore, *Ship Subsidies* (Boston: Houghton Mifflin, 1907), with a bibliography addressed to the policy issue then before Congress as framed

by the majority of the Merchant Marine Commission appointed by President Theodore Roosevelt. William S. Benson, *The Merchant Marine* (New York: MacMillan, 1924) gives many details on government aid to the American merchant marine up to 1920 in Chapters X and XI. In Chapters III, IV, and V, Wytze Gorter, *United States Shipping Policy* (New York: Council on Foreign Relations, 1956) deals with assistance to shippers, operating aid, and cargo preferences in the 1940s and 1950s.

11. A good study of the World War II shipbuilding effort is F. C. Lane, and others, *Ships for Victory* (Baltimore: Johns Hopkins Press, 1951). Figures on the logistics of beachheads and maintenance during World War II have been drawn from Stewart R. Bross, *Ocean Shipping* (Cambridge, Md.: Cornell Maritime Press, 1956). The book contains excellent descriptive chapters on ocean trade, routes, types of ocean vessels, liner organization, and so forth in the postwar period. During World War II a high tonnage was hauled by the Liberty-type and later Victory-type prefabricated vessels, but they were obsolescent very soon after 1945.

12. A valuable collection of articles and data on the condition of the Merchant Marine as of 1961 can be found in Fifteenth Ocean Shipping Management Institute, School of Business Administration, American University, *Merchant Marine Policy* (Cambridge, Maryland: Cornell Maritime Press, 1963).

13. Samuel A. Lawrence, *United States Merchant Shipping Policies and Politics,* (Washington, D.C.: Brookings Institution, 1966) is a thorough study of the industry's problems with proposals for change at the time of President Lyndon B. Johnson's administration. His later work, excellent and up-to-date, is *International Sea Transport: The Years Ahead* (Lexington, Mass.: D.C. Heath, 1972).

14. For PL87-346, see 87th Congress, 1st session, *United Statutes at Large,* p. 762. The Amendment to the amended Shipping Act of 1916 authorized ocean carriers and conferences to enter into effective and fair dual rate contracts with shippers. Enacted 3 October 1961.

15. For details about various international conventions on safety at sea, salvage, and other maritime matters, see Marjorie M. Whiteman, *Digest of International Law,* vol. 9 (1968), U.S. Department of State Publication 8419, Washington D.C.

16. See Union of International Associations, *Yearbook of International Organizations,* Brussels for the structure, officers, program, and publications of the International Hydrographic Bureau.

17. For a summary of the work of the Committee for Communications and Transit, see League of Nations Secretariat, *Ten Years of World Cooperation* (Geneva: 1930), Chapter VI.

18. The *Yearbook of the United Nations,* New York gives a summary of the developments of the Intergovernmental Maritime Consultative Organization. See also the *Annual Reports* of the Intergovernmental Maritime Consultative Organization, London.

19. The work of the UN Conference Trade and Development's Committee on Shipping has been extensive. See, in particular, *Review of Maritime Transport, Current and Long Terms Aspects,* UN Document TD/B/C.4/125 (1975).

20. Very valuable for its 207 pages of text and tables, 33 pages of appendices, and bibliography of some 100 books, articles, and documents is Earl W. Clark, Hoyt S. Haddock, and Stanley J. Volens, *The U.S. Merchant Marine Today* (Washington, D.C.: The Labor-Management Maritime Committee, 1970). For the Merchant Marine Act of 1970, see the "Message from the President of the U.S. Transmitting Recommendations for New Ship Building Program, 23 October 1969," U.S. House of Representatives, Committee on Merchant Marine and Fisheries, *Hearings.* Serial No. 91-17, Washington, D.C., (1970). For a detailed explanation of the bill, see U.S. House of Representatives Committee on Merchant Marine and Fisheries, *Hearings,* "President's Maritime Program," Serial No. 91-17, Washington, D.C., (1970).

21. For basic data about the Maritime Administration I have made use of the *Annual Report* of the Secretary of Commerce (Washington, D.C.: U.S. Government Printing Office), beginning with fiscal year 1951. This is the regular, official source for developments of the American merchant marine through government assistance and administration. The annual reports contain current statistics on the size of the merchant marine, subsidy payments, percentage of U.S. flag vessels in American trade, and so forth.

22. Some idea of the enormous size of modern tankers can be gained from the *Globtik Tokyo.* The vessel was 477,000 deadweight tons, 1250 feet long, equivalent to a 22-storey building, and had deck space that could accommodate 49 tennis courts. For a graphic, fascinating account of the operations of a very large crude oil carrier, see Noel Mostert, *Supership* (New York: Alfred Knopf, 1974). Even the *Globtik Tokyo* was not the limit of crude carriers at sea; in 1977 the Royal Dutch Shell Group was operating two mammoth tankers of 542,000 deadweight tons.

23. For a strategy of developing nuclear-powered merchant ships, see National Research Council *Nuclear Merchant Ships* (Washington, D.C.: National Academy of Science, 1974).

24. The Deepwater Port Act of 1974 was enacted as PL93-618. Debate centered on which federal agency ought to have the licensing power and how much influence or control the states ought to have in determining whether a license should be granted.

25. For a fine study of the problem of subsidizing merchant marine, see Gerald E. Jantscher, *Bread Upon the Waters* (Washington, D.C.: Brookings Institution, 1975).

26. For some of the motivation for "flags of refuge," see Richard E. Madigan, *Taxation of the Shipping Industry* (Cambridge, Md.: Cornell Maritime Press, 1971), which has a very useful explanation of the taxation of shipping in the United States and in foreign countries that register American-owned vessels. On the legalities, see the study of Boleslaw Adam Boczek, *Flags of*

Convenience: An International Legal Study, (Cambridge, Mass.: Harvard University Press, 1962).

27. A thorough report that describes the development and status of the U.S. Merchant Marine at the beginning of 1976 is National Research Council, *Toward an Improved Merchant Marine* (Washington, D.C.: National Academy of Sciences, January 1976), which includes a recommended program of studies on trade policy, marketing, labor relations, government activities, and training. A most valuable source for merchant marine issues is the *Proceedings of the American Merchant Marine Conference* organized each year since 1934 by the Propeller Club of the United States, Washington, D.C.

Chapter 4
Fisheries and Foreign Policy

1. For the first section of this chapter, I have drawn on Edward Channing's great work, *History of the United States,* 6 vols. (New York: Macmillan, 1905-1925), especially Chapter XVIII; Harry J. Carman, *Social and Economic History of the United States,* 2 vols. (Boston: D.C. Heath, 1930), particularly Chapter III; and Emory R. Johnson and others, *History of Domestic and Foreign Commerce of the United States* (Washington, D.C.: Carnegie Institution of Washington, 1915), especially "American Fisheries" by T. W. Van Metre.

2. John Cabot's news about the wealth of fish to be found in the New World traveled rapidly. Small, sturdy European vessels crossed the Atlantic annually to take their seasonal catch. Prior to 1550 there already were about 128 ships in these fleets, 93 of them French, sailing to the Newfoundland banks. Later in the century the English interests began to increase. The fishing for cod was especially valuable to the west counties of England, abetted by acts of Parliament that forbade the eating of flesh on certain days of the week. The English pushed the Dutch out of the lucrative carrying trade in exhanging cod for Mediterranean cargoes then sold to northern Europe. Thus, Newfoundland became the key that opened the Spanish treasure chest of gold to London, while further strengthening the English navy. Harold A. Innis, *The Cod Fisheries: The History of an International Economy* (New Haven, Conn.: Yale University Press, 1940) is a superb study of the cod, markets, commercial policy, and their effects on both domestic and foreign policy in England, Canada, and Newfoundland.

3. At the request of the U.S. House of Representatives, Secretary of State, Thomas Jefferson reviewed the American fisheries to enable Congress "to see with what a competition we have to struggle." His detailed report is in U.S. Congress, *American State Papers,* vol. VII, no. 5, Walter Lowrie and Matthew St. Clair Clarke, eds., 1st Congress, 3d Session, 2 February 1791 (Washington, D.C.: Gates and Seaton, 1832).

4. Data on the early fisheries of New England have been drawn from the comprehensive Raymond McFarland, *A History of New England Fisheries* (New York: D. Appleton and Co., 1911). Although the civilian farmers of the rebellious United States suffered less than the soldiers and sailors of the Revolution and although the town dwellers managed to obtain the essentials of life, the hardness of the war was felt in the northern and middle states, especially in the shore towns of New England. Profiteering and wanton luxury, as in all wars, existed side by side with penury and suffering. To illustrate the grief of the Revolution for New England ports, the number of voters in Marblehead went from 12,000 in 1772 to 544 in 1780, with 458 widows and 966 fatherless children in this one little town, a leader in the fishing industry.

5. For many statistics in this section, see the United States Commission of Fish and Fisheries, *Bulletin of the United States Fish Commission*, beginning with vol. I (1881) (Washington, D.C.: Government Printing Office), until 1903 when it became the *Bulletin of the Bureau of Fisheries* in the new Department of Commerce and Labor and then continued as a publication of the separate Department of Commerce until 1939 when the Bureau was transferred to the Department of the Interior. I have also made extensive use of the U.S. Secretary of Commerce, Bureau of Fisheries, *Annual Report* (Washington, D.C.: U.S. Government Printing Office, Washington, D.C., 1921–1939) for details on employment, value of catch, and policy questions. A retrospect of the 1920–1940 period was helped greatly by U.S. Department of the Interior, Fish and Wildlife Service, A. W. Anderson and E. A. Power, *Fisheries Statistics of the United States,* 1945 (Washington, D.C.: Government Printing Office, 1949).

6. For the second section of this chapter I have used the U.S. Commission of Fish and Fisheries, *Annual Report of the Commission* (Washington, D.C.: U.S. Government Printing Office, from 1871 to 1903), the Department of Commerce and Labor, Bureau of Fisheries, *Annual Report* (Washington, D.C.: U.S. Government Printing Office, from 1904 to 1913), and the Secretary of Commerce, Bureau of Fisheries, *Annual Report* (Washington, D.C.: U.S. Government Printing Office, from 1913 to 1939).

7. A. L. Burt, *The United States, Great Britain, and British North America from the Revolution to the Establishment of Peace after the War of 1812* (New Haven: Yale University Press, 1940), deals extensively with the negotiations of the Peace of Paris, 1783, the Treaty of Ghent, 1814, and the Convention of 1818, particularly the arrangements on fishing. A syllabus on the North Atlantic Fisheries Case in 1910, summarizing the history, the seven questions presented to the Permanent Court of Arbitration, and the decision itself can be found in Carnegie Endowment for International Peace, *The Hague Court Reports,* James Brown Scott, ed., (New York: Oxford University Press, 1916).

8. The award of the Tribunal of Arbitration of 15 August 1893, which denied the jurisdiction of the United States over the fur seals in the Bering Sea, can be found in *The American Journal of International Law,* vol. 6 (1912),

Washington, D.C., p. 233. The text of the Convention between Japan, Great Britain, Russia, and the United States for the Protection and Preservation of Fur Seals and Sea Otters in the North Pacific Ocean, Washington, 7 July 1911 is, among other places, in the *American Journal of International Law-Supplement,* vol. 5 (1911), Washington, D.C., p. 267.

9. For details on the resources of the fur seals, the Pacific halibut, and the sockeye salmon and their regulation before World War II, I have drawn from the excellent work of Jozo Tomasevich, *International Agreements on Conservation of Marine Resources* (Stanford, Calif.: Stanford University, Food Research Institute, 1943).

10. The citation of the Christiania Newspaper on whaling protection was taken from U.S. Fish Commission, *Bulletin,* vol. 1 (1881), (Washington, D.C.: Government Printing Office, 1882), pp. 17-19. For the whaling industry prior to World War II, see the fine monograph of Karl Brandt, *Whale Oil: An Economic Analysis,* (Stanford, Calif.: Stanford University, Food Research Institute, 1940); for international regulation prior to World War II see L. Larry Leonard, "Recent Negotiations toward the International Regulation of Whaling," *American Journal of International Law,* vol. 35 (1941), pp. 80-113, which has citations from M. Arnold Raestad, Philip C. Jessup, and other writers on this subject as well as quotations from the League of Nations study, the British "Discovery Committee" study, and some statements from the international whaling regulation conferences.

11. For this section I have made extensive use of the U.S. Secretary of Interior, Bureau of Fisheries, *Annual Report,* for the fiscal years ending 1945 to 1969 (Washington, D.C.: Government Printing Office), including the annual reports of the Fish and Wildlife Service, and *Fishery Statistics of the United States,* published by the Department of Interior from 1939 to 1967 and thereafter by the National Oceanographic and Atmospheric Administration in the Department of Commerce. In addition to a series of research reports and special reports on fish and the fishing industry, the Department of Interior, Fisheries and Wildlife Service continued the scientific *Fisheries Bulletin,* dating from the inception of the U.S. Fish Commission, until 1969 when publication was assumed by the Department of Commerce. In addition to scientific data, articles dealing with the fishing industry are nicely digested in *Commercial Fishing Abstracts* and I have made use of this source for some of the material on Japanese and Russian fishing efforts.

12. Observations on changes in the processing and marketing of fish over a thirty-year period were drawn from Wilbert McLeod Chapman, "Seafood Supply and World Famine-Positive Approach" presented to the American Association for the Advancement of Science, 29 December 1969, unpublished. This was reproduced as testimony before the U.S. Senate Committee on Interior and Insular Affairs, 4 March 1970.

13. For a short, useful study of tuna, including abbreviated figures on catch, canning, distribution, equipment used, and national fleets, see J. L. Kask, "Tuna—A World Resource," an occasional paper of the Law of the Sea Institution, University of Rhode Island, Kingston, R.I., n.d.

14. Figures on the expansion and intensity of sports fishing have been taken from the Department of Interior, Fisheries and Wildlife Service, *National Survey of Fishing and Hunting* (1970) (Washington, D.C.: Government Printing Office, 1971).

15. Wilbert McLeod Chapman became the first Special Assistant for Wildlife and Fisheries in the Office of the Undersecretary of State. "We set up this special assistant because the industry wanted it set up this way, and I think our organizational people even question whether it should be, but we were getting unfavorable editorials in the trade magazines two years ago, and now we are getting favorable editorials," said Carlisle H. Humelsine, Deputy Assistant Secretary of State for Administration. See U.S. 81st Congress, 2d Session, Senate Subcommittee on Appropriations, *Hearings, Department of State, Justice, Commerce, and the Judiciary* (20 February 1950), p. 884.

16. The discontent of U.S. fishing interests with the Fish and Wildlife Service and some of the bills introduced to Congress to reorganize the agency can be found in U.S. 84th Congress, 2d Session, House Committee on Merchant Marine and Fisheries, Subcommittee on Fisheries and Wildlife Conservation, *Hearings, Establishment of a National Policy for Commercial Fisheries* (May 10, 21, 22, and June 8, 1956). Senator Warren G. Magnuson of the state of Washington said of the 1956 Fish and Wildlife Act, ". . . this is my Act. I wrote the Act myself practically." Senator Henry C. Dvorshak of Idaho wryly noted, "I have no objection to (the Assistant Secretary for Wildlife and Fisheries) sitting at a table, but I wonder why he needs 117 employees to back him up?" See U.S. 86th Congress, 1st Session, Senate Subcommittee on Appropriations, *Hearings,* Interior Department and Related Agencies.

17. During the 1964 passage of fishing legislation by Congress, Senator Edward Kennedy of Massachusetts said, "This is a good day for the fishing industry . . . because we have before us two fishing bills . . . one designed to stimulate fish research and development projects and to rehabilitate a part of the fishing industry; and the other to provide strong enforcement provisions to prevent foreign encroachment within our territorial waters." Kennedy observed that 50 percent of the fish consumed in the United States was then coming from foreign countries, that modern methods of processing and harvesting fish had to be achieved by American fishers particularly since the Russian fishing fleets had the advantage of factory, supply, passenger, and refrigeration vessels working in concert. He also hinted that their "electronic rigging" might constitute a threat to U.S. national security. 88th Congress, 2d Session, *Congressional Record,* vol. 110, part 8 (May 4, 1964, to May 18, 1964), p. 10179.

18. As late as 1947 only 141,000 pounds of the king crab had been taken in the Bering Sea. Ten years later ten million pounds of king crab a year were taken and by 1964 over 100 million pounds. With Russian and Japanese fleets swarming into the waters contiguous to the American shores, the local fishers were understandably vexed. Up to 1964 no legislation regarding creatures of the continental shelf, as defined by Article 2, Convention on the Continental Shelf, Geneva, 1958 had been enacted in the United States. Public Law 88–308 then authorized the Secretary of Interior to publish in the Federal Register a list of the sedentary species that were considered U.S. continental shelf fishery resources and, therefore, prohibited from capture by foreign vessels. Eight crustacea (crabs), four mollusks (abalones, conches, clams), and four sponges were listed in the *Federal Register,* vol. 33, p. 16114. Six other crustacea, two other mollusks, and two coleonterata (corals) were listed in 1971.

19. For the issues on the width of the territorial sea and contiguous fishing zones, summarized lucidly and authoritatively, see Arthur H. Dean, "The Geneva Conference on the Law of the Sea; What Was Accomplished" and "The Second Geneva Conference on the Law of the Sea: The Fight for the Freedom of the Seas," 52 (1958) and 54 (1961) *American Journal of International Law,* p. 607–659 and p. 751–789. I have made special use of Myres S. McDougal and William T. Burke, *The Public Order of the Oceans* (New Haven: Yale University Press, 1962), which contains a fine chapter on "Claims to Determine the Width of the Sea" with detailed analysis of the Geneva conferences and the citations of UN documents that cover the discussions and the votes on the contiguous fisheries zone issue.

20. Accounts of Japanese and Russian fishing in waters close to American shores as well as data on the seizure of American fishers by Latin American countries with the problems of resolving both near-shore and distant-water U.S. fishing problems in the early 1960s can be found in 88th Congress, 2d Session, House Committee on Merchant Marine and Fisheries, *Hearings, Fishing in U.S. Territorial Waters* (February 19, 20, 25, 26, 1964) and 89th Congress, 2d Session, Senate Commerce Committee Subcommittee, on Merchant Marine and Fisheries, *Hearings, Twelve Mile Fishery Zone* (May 18–20, 1966). I have also borrowed from a splendid short article by Guenter Weissberg, "Fisheries, Foreign Assistance, Custom and Conventions," *The International and Comparative Law Quarterly* (July 1967), which describes the pressure by Congress on the President to cut off foreign economic assistance to states that were seizing American fishing vessels.

21. The recommendations of the Stratton Commission about U.S. fisheries and international law and organization for the management of fisheries have been drawn from Commission on Marine Sciences, Engineering, and Resources, *Our Nation and the Sea: A Plan for National Action* (Washington, D.C.: Government Printing Office, January 1969), pp. 87–118. Greater detail of the Commission's analysis on fisheries policy can be found in the Commission's Panel

Report on *Marine Resources and Legal-Political Arrangements for Their Development,* vol. 3. It contains an extensive analysis, with tables, of American fisheries and their harvests. The evaluation of the Bureau of Commercial Fisheries is at Section VII-44–VII-48.

22. In the discussions of Reorganization Plan 4 creating NOAA in the Department of Commerce, Congressman John D. Dingell of Michigan was one of a few conservationists who stoutly objected to placing natural resource functions within a Cabinet department dedicated to business development and trade. He introduced a bill to create a Department of Natural Resources. He felt that the Plan was "going to turn over the custody of the chicken coop to the fox." See *Congressional Record–House* (24 September 1970), p. 33893.

23. The literature on international fisheries agreements and commissions is extensive. The annual reports and proceedings of the Inter-American Tropical Tuna Commission (La Jolla), International Commission for the Northwest Atlantic Fisheries (Halifax and Dartmouth), International North Pacific Fisheries Commission (Vancouver), International Pacific Halibut Commission (Vancouver), International Pacific Salmon Fisheries Commission (New Westminster), International Whaling Commission (London), and North Pacific Fur Seal Commission (Washington) are primary references. Some of the more recent books that I have consulted are Douglas M. Johnston, *The International Law of Fisheries* (New Haven: Yale University Press, 1965), which has a bibliography of close to 600 items dealing with history, politics, and diplomacy of fishery disputes, administrative aspects of fisheries management, international law of fisheries, and other geographic, scientific, and commercial aspects of fishing. See also Francis T. Christy and Andrew Scott, *The Common Wealth in Ocean Fisheries,* published for Resources for the Future (Baltimore: Johns Hopkins Press, 1965), which has a bibliography of some seventy-five books and more than 80 articles dealing with fisheries. Chapter 2 deals specifically with fishery treaties and commissions.

24. See three FAO *Fisheries Technical Papers,* no. 50 (Rome, 1965), and no 60 (Rome, 1968), all by J. E. Carroz, which cover in detail the Indo-Pacific Fisheries Council, the Inter-American Tropical Tuna Commission, and the Regional Fisheries Advisory Commission for the Southwest Atlantic. For the documentary citations of some twenty intergovernmental fishery bodies, see J. E. Carroz and A. G. Roche, "The Proposed International Commission for the Conservation of Atlantic Tunas," *American Journal of International Law,* vol. 61, no. 3 (July 1967), pp. 674-678.

25. I have drawn extensively from Albert W. Koers, *International Regulation of Marine Fisheries* (London: Fishing News (Books), 1973), which contains an excellent chronology of international fisheries organizations, their structure and functions, with the author's policy proposals for the future as well as his bibliography of more than 300 books, articles, and documents relating to fisheries management.

26. For some parts of this section dealing with whaling and the International Whaling Commission, I am particularly indebted to J. L. McHugh, former Chairman of the Commission, for his unpublished article, "Role and History of the International Whaling Commission" presented at the International Conference on Whale Biology, Luray, Virginia (10 June 1971). Data can be found in *International Whaling Statistics,* which has been published annually since 1930 by the Bureau of International Whaling Statistics, Sandefjord, Norway. For some parts of this section dealing with the International Council for the Exploration of the Sea, the International Commission for Northwest Atlantic Fisheries, and the Northeast Atlantic Fisheries Commission see C. E. Lucas, *International Fishery Bodies of the North Atlantic,* Law of the Sea Institute, University of Rhode Island, Occasional Paper no. 5 (April 1970).

27. Donald L. McKernan, U.S. 92d Congress, 1st Session, Senate Subcommittee on Appropriations, *Hearings,* Departments of State, Justice, Commerce, the Judiciary, and Related Agency for FY 1972 (7 July 1971), p. 1142. For background to the International Convention for the High Seas Fisheries of the North Pacific Ocean, see William W. Bishop, Jr., "The Need for a Japanese Fisheries Agreement," *American Journal of International Law,* vol. 45 (1951), pp. 712-719; for commentary, see Charles B. Selak, Jr., "The Proposed International Convention for the High Seas Fisheries of the North Pacific Ocean," *American Journal of International Law,* vol. 46 (9152), pp. 323-330 and William C. Herrington, "International Issues of Pacific Fisheries," U.S. Department of State *Bulletin,* vol. LV, no. 1428 (3 October 1966), pp. 500-504.

28. The U.S.-Canadian Great Lakes Commission had to face the lamprey parasite after it was well entrenched. In 1947 conservationists had already sounded the alarm, but with little result. See U.S. Department of Interior, Director of Fisheries and Wildlife Service, *Annual Report for Fiscal Year Ending 1947,* p. 308. The Lake trout of Lake Huron alone dropped from an annual harvest of 1,345,000 to 41,000 pounds.

29. The problem of merely limiting the catch season and the total catch of a fishery has been well illustrated in Francis T. Christy, "New Dimensions for Transnational Marine Resources, *American Economic Review,* Vol. LX (May 1970) Number 2. In 1967, when limits were imposed by the Inter-American Tropical Tuna Commission on yellowfin tuna, the U.S. tropical tuna fleet was 37,000 tons; by 1970 it approached 65,000 tons as larger, faster vessels were used to get the greatest number of fish in the shortest possible time.

30. The world fisheries catches and the percentages of the American catches have been drawn from the data in U.S. Department of Commerce, National Marine Fisheries Service, *Fisheries of the United States,* published annually, especially the 1971-1975 issues, Washington, D.C. and the UN Food and Agriculture Organization, *Yearbook of Fishery Statistics,* Rome, 1947-.

31. For the work of the Pacific (Portland, Oregon), Atlantic (Washington,

D.C. and Gulf (New Orleans) marine fisheries commissions, see their *Annual Reports,* which contain information about their recommendations on fisheries and subsequent action by the states or the federal government.

32. Philip M. Roedel, U.S. Department of Commerce, National Marine Fisheries Service, *Commercial Fisheries Review,* vol. 34, No. 1-2 (January-February 1972). Reflecting the creation of the National Marine Fisheries Service within the National Oceanographic and Atmospheric Administration, Department of Commerce, and its new orientation, the *Commercial Fisheries Review* was retitled *Marine Fisheries Review* beginning with vol. 34, no. 7-8 (July-August 1972).

33. For data and views on the economic resource zone the primary reference is the UN General Assembly, *Report of the Committee on the Peaceful Uses of the Sea-Bed and the Ocean Floor beyond the Limits of National Jurisdiction,* Official Records, 26th Session and 27th Session, A/8021 and A/8721, which describes the work of Subcommittee II with regard to fisheries. The *Report* also includes documents in the Annex of special interest, such as the text of the Declaration of Santo Domingo, 7 June 1972, approved by the Meeting of Ministers of the Specialized Conference of the Caribbean Countries on Problems of the Sea; the Conclusions in the General Report of the African States' Regional Seminar on the Law of the Sea, Yaounde, 20-30 June 1972; and draft articles or working papers on fisheries by the USSR, the U.S.A., Japan, Australia, and other states. I have also consulted the summary records of Subcommittee II, which give greater detail and paraphrase the speakers' actual remarks. The quotations from the Alternate United States Representative to the UN Sea-Bed Committee setting forth the change of American fishery policy for the high seas contiguous to coastal states were taken from the statement by Donald L. McKernan before Subcommittee II and released by the United States mission in Geneva (4 August 1972).

34. See the Revised Single Negotiating Text, UN Document A/CONF.62/WP.8/Rev. 1/Part II (9 May 1976), Articles no. 50-57 that give the coastal state control over fisheries in its exclusive economic zone.

35. For the papers and proceedings of a conference of fishery economists, with many useful analyses of the problems of managing stocks and calculating optimum yields, see Lee G. Anderson, ed., *Extended Fisheries Jurisdiction* (Ann Arbor, Mich.: Science Press, 1977).

36. Of exceptional value to me in this section was the report to the Congress by the Comptroller General of the United States, *The U.S. Fishing Industry-Present Condition and Future Condition of Marine Fisheries,* vol. 1, Washington, D.C. (23 December 1976), which examined all aspects of the fishing industry, including federal involvement, and pointed out some of the difficulties in managing fisheries and in expanding industry with some proposed solutions.

Chapter 5
Mineral Resources of the Seas

1. For the description and comments on the importance of salt, I have drawn on L. G. M. Baas-Becking, "Historical Notes on Salt and Salt Manufacturing," *Scientific Monthly,* vol. 32 (1931), pp. 434–466, the scholarly treatise of A. R. Bridbury, *England and the Salt Trade in the Later Middle Ages* (Oxford: Clarendon Press, 1945), Harry B. Weiss and Grace M. Weiss, *The Revolutionary Saltworks of the New Jersey Coast* (Trenton: Past Times Press, 1959), and the lively account of fact and anecdote in Garnett Laidlaw Eskew, *Salt: The Fifth Element* (Chicago: J. G. Ferguson Associates, 1948). Contemporary salt production figures are found in Stanley M. J. LeFond, ed., *Handbook of World Salt Resources* (New York: Plenum Press, 1969).

2. For the growth of the sand and gravel industry in the twentieth century, see Shirley F. Colby, "Development of Sand and Gravel Industry," *Information Circular 7203* (March 1962), U.S. Department of the Interior, Bureau of Mines, Washington, D.C.

3. Most of the continental shelf of the northeastern United States is covered with fine-coarse grained sands. Scientific theory holds that most of the sand and gravel with it were brought down to the shelf by rivers and glaciers in earlier geologic eras when the sea level was lower. The commercial value of these deposits is enhanced by their nearness to the great urban centers of the east. See John Schlee, *Sand and Gravel on the Continental Shelf of the Northeastern United States* (1968), U.S. Dept. of Interior, Geological Survey Circular 602, Washington, D.C.

4. Some of my sources on the development of lighting were Leroy Thwing, *A History of Domestic Lighting Through the Ages* (Rutland, Vermont: Charles E. Tuttle, 1958), Henry O'Connor, *Gas Manufacturing and Lighting,* Walter King, Office of "The Journal of Gas Lighting, London, 1910, Louis Stotz, *History of the Gas Industry* (New York: Stettiner Brothers, 1938). I have also used Samuel Harris Daddow and Benjamin Bannan, *Coal, Iron, and Oil* (Philadelphia: J. Lippincott, 1866), which, while filled with the scientific inaccuracies of that day, is valuable for its historical detail, and K. Neville Moss, "A General Survey of the History of the Coal Mining Industry," Mining Association of Great Britain, *Historical Review of Coal Mining* (London: Fleetway Press, n.d.). Pertinent data were also taken from the excellent articles on coal, gas, fuel, and lighting in the 11th edition (1910) of the *Encyclopedia Brittanica.*

5. R. J. Forbes, *Studies in Early Petroleum* (Leiden: E. J. Brill, 1958) and R. J. Forbes, *More Studies in Early Petroleum* (Leiden: E. J. Brill, 1959) are valuable sources for the early records of petroleum recovery, speculations about the nature and origin of petroleum, and the variety of manufactures, use, and distribution of bituminous products prior to the nineteenth century. The

report to the Rock Creek Oil Co. of B. Silliman, Jr., the professor of chemistry at Yale University, is to be found in J. T. Henry, *The Early and Later History of Petroleum,* vols. 1 and 2 (New York: Burt Franklin), originally published in Philadelphia, 1873: "The Crude Oil was tried as a means of illumination . . . It produced nearly pure carburetted hydrogen gas, the most highly illuminating of all the carbon gases . . . It burned with an intense flame, smoking in the ordinary gas jet, but furnishing the most perfect flame with the Argand burner . . ." See also Paul H. Giddens, *The Birth of the Oil Industry* (New York: Macmillan, 1938). Data and descriptions on the subsequent development of the petroleum industry have been drawn from "Petroleum Panorama," *Oil and Gas Journal,* vol. 57, no. 5 (28 January 1959).

6. Excellent detailed studies of the life and the achievements of Gottlieb Daimler and Karl Benz can be found in the work of Eugene Diesel, Gustav Goldbeck, and Friedrich Schildberger, *From Engines to Autos* (Chicago: Henry Regnery, 1960), which contains an excellent history of five pioneers in engine development and their contributions to the automobile. Daimler had first applied his engine to a bicycle, but he also installed one on a coach as an experiment and driven it in his factory yards. He then installed a gas engine on a motorboat in 1886 and on a balloon in 1887. All these engines worked successfully in propelling the bicycle, carriage, boat, and balloon.

7. Some of the useful books that I have consulted with regard to the development of gasoline motors and the automobile are W. Worby Beaumont, *Motor Vehicles and Motors* (Westminster: Archibald Constable and Co., and Philadelphia: J. B. Lippincott, 1900); H. L. Barber, *Story of the Automobile* (Chicago: A. J. Munson, 1917); William Greenleaf, *Monopoly on Wheels* (Detroit: Wayne State University, 1961), which is of particular interest for its account of the patents of George Selden; and Anthony Bird, *The Motor Car, 1765-1914* (London: P. T. Botsford Ltd., 1960).

8. The quotation of Samuel Wrigley was taken from Leonard M. Fanning, ed., *Our Oil Resources* (New York: McGraw-Hill, 1945), pp. 123-124. Other statistics on domestic and foreign production in the early twentieth century have also been taken from this work.

9. Several paragraphs and notes in this section on the Continental Shelf have been copied, with revisions, from my monograph, *The United Nations, International Law, and the Bed of the Seas* (Washington, D.C.: Woodrow Wilson International Center for Scholars, 1972).

10. For Roman legal practice on rivers, see *Roman Water Law* translated from the *Pandects of Justinian* by Eugene F. Ware, (St. Paul: West Publishing Co., 1905), which contains all the Roman law concerning fresh water to be found in the *Corpus Juris Civilis* of the Emperor Justinian.

11. For the quotation on the legal status of the seabed in the early twentieth century, see John Westlake, *International Law,* 2d ed (Cambridge: University Press, 1910), part I, p. 188. For the reference to the American Institute

of International Law see League of Nations, *Committee of Experts for the Progressive Codification of International Law,* C.196.M.70, 1927, Vol. V, pp. 31, 32. No treaty on the territorial sea was actually concluded by the 1930 Hague Conference, but certain articles obtained provisional agreement. For the documents, see League of Nations, *Acts of the Conference for the Codification of International Law,* The Hague, 1930, especially vol. 1, *Plenary Meetings,* 1930, V. 14, Annel 10, *Report of the Second Committee: Territorial Sea* and Annex II, Final Act, as well as vol. III, *Minutes of the Second Committee,* 1930, V. 16.

12. For references on the origin of the "continental shelf" I have used Gérard de Rayneval, *Institutions de droit de la Nature et Gens,* 2d ed. (Paris, 1803), Otto Krummel, *Handbuch der Ozeannographie,* Band I, Stuttgart, 1907, mentions Hugh Robert Mill, pp. 103-104; Odon de Buen was cited by the League of Nations Committee of Experts for The Hague Codification Conference in 1930 in a report to the Council [C.196.M.70.1927,V., C.P.D.I. 95(2) Geneva, 1927].

13. An important and well-known article that directly addressed the issue of property rights in the seabed was C. J. B. Hurst, "Whose is the Bed of the Sea?" 4 *British Yearbook of International Law 1923-1924.* A prize-winning, comprehensive work that includes a wealth of citations on this subject is M. W. Mouton, *The Continental Shelf* (Martinus Nijhoff: The Hague, 1952), and valuable for the same period is Jose Luis de Azcarraga y Bustamente, *La Plataforma Submarina y el Derecho Internacional* (Madrid, 1952). The most comprehensive private work of this period on international law for the oceans and seabed is Gilbert Gidel, *Le Droit International Public de la Mer,* 3 vols. (Chateauroux, 1932-1934). For the early twentieth-century legal view on the subsoil of the seas, I have taken L. Oppenheim, *International Law,* 3d ed., Ronald F. Roxburgh, ed., (London: Longmans Green, 1920), pp. 451-455, which was essentially confirmed by the UN International Law Commission Summary Record, 66th Session (Doc. A/CN4/SR66), 12 July 1950 and embodied in Article 7 of the Convention on the Continental Shelf signed at Geneva in 1958: "The provisions of these articles shall not prejudice the right of the coastal state to exploit the subsoil by means of tunneling irrespective of the depth of water above the subsoil."

14. The first true seabed and subsoil boundary agreement occurred in 1942 between Venezuela and the United Kingdom, using the equidistant principle in dividing the Gulf of Paria between them, including land not geographically parts of the continental shelf. 205 League of Nations Treaty Series 121. Later in signing the 1958 Geneva Convention on the Continental Shelf, Venezuela specifically mentioned the special circumstances to be considered with respect to the Gulf of Paria. Trinidad and Tobago, which gained independence from Great Britain, assumed the obligations of the Paria treaty, and ratified the Geneva Convention on the Continental Shelf in 1968. In the Abu Dhabi Arbitral

Award, arising from a 1939 concession to the Petroleum Development (Trucial Coast) Ltd. by the Sheik, Lord Asquith of Bishopstone in 1951 found that "there are in this field so many ragged ends and unfilled blanks, so much that is merely tentative and exploratory, that in no form can the doctrine (on the continental shelf) claim as yet to have assumed hitherto the hard lineaments or the definitive status of an established rule of international law." 1 *International and Comparative Institute Quarterly* 247 (1952). For the background of the Truman proclamations, see Marjorie M. Whiteman, *Digest of International Law,* vol. 1V (Washington, D.C.: U.S. Department of State Publication 7825, April 1965). For the texts, see Presidential Proclamation 2667, 28 September 1945, with Respect to Natural Resources of the Subsoil and Sea-Bed of the Continental Shelf, 10 *Federal Register 12303,* and Proclamation 2668, 10 *Federal Register 12304* asserting the right of the United States to establish conservation zones for fish in the high seas contiguous to the coast.

15. The press release accompanying the Truman proclamations stated: "Generally, submerged land which is contiguous to the continent and which is covered by no more than 100 fathoms (600 feet) of water is considered as the continental shelf." Although 200 meters in depth has generally been considered the average point where the slope descended more precipitately toward the ocean floor, in fact, the average lies between 130-140 meters, and even then is misleading as to the true contours of the continental shelf. Edges of the continental shelf can be found anywhere from 20 to 550 meters under water; moreover, measured from the shore, the distance to the edge of the continental shelf can be anywhere from 0 to 1500 kilometers, with an average of about 78 kilometers. See A. L. Shalowitz, *Shore and Sea Boundaries* (Washington, D.C.: U.S. Department of Commerce, 1962-1964), 2V; K. O. Emery, "The Continental Shelves," *The Oceans,* an issue of the Scientific American Magazine (1969); Hollis Hedberg, "Continental Margins from the Viewpoint of the Petroleum Geologist," *American Association for Petroleum Geology Bulletin,* vol. 54 (1970), p. 3; Andre J. Guilcher, "The Configuration of the Ocean Floor and Its Subsoil: Geopolitical Implications," *Proceedings of the Symposium on the International Regime of the Sea-Bed* (Rome: Academia Nazionale dei Lincei, 1970).

16. For a compilation of national decrees, laws, and constitutional acts for the 1945-1958 period with respect to territorial seas and the continental shelf, see United Nations, Laws and Regulations on the Regime of the High Seas, vol. 1, ST/LEG/SER.B/1 with Add. 1 (1956) as well as ST/LEG/SER.B/8 (1959). Later data are in UN General Assembly, *Survey of National Legislation Concerning the Sea-Bed and the Ocean Floor, and the Subsoil Thereof, Underlying the High Seas Beyond the Limits of Present National Jurisdiction,* A/AC.135/11 and A/AC.135/11 Add. 1, 13 (August 1968).

17. The Inter-American Specialized Conference on the Conservation of Natural Resources, the Continental Shelf, and Marine Resources in 1956 had a

six-year background. The Inter-American Council of Jurists at its first meeting in 1950 in Rio de Janeiro had asked its Permanent Committee to report on territorial waters and other questions. Draft articles were placed before the Council, which quickly revealed a division between those states asserting a wide area of coastal jurisdiction and those states wishing to limit jurisdiction over the marginal seas and the continental shelf. In 1953 the Council was still divided on a compromise resolution which, without dealing with details, indicated that states had the right to protect, conserve, and exploit their territorial waters and continental shelves with new technological developments, which international law recognized. At the same time the Council recommended that a special conference on the subject be called. This recommendation was endorsed by the Tenth Inter-American Conference at Caracas in 1954 and led to the conference in Ciudad Trujillo. For the text of the final act, see Pan American Union, *Ciudad Trujillo Conference* (15–28 March 1956), Final Act, Washington, D.C. (1956).

18. A detailed study of the background to the formulation of the definition of the continental shelf found in Article 1 of the *Geneva Convention on the Continental Shelf (1958)* is Bernard H. Oxman, "The Preparation of Article 1 of the Continental Shelf," PB 182100, Clearinghouse for Federal and Scientific Information, U.S. Department of Commerce, Washington, D.C., which has extensive verbatim quotations from the records of the International Law Commission. For the activities and draft articles cited here, see UN General Assembly, *Official Records,* Documents A/1316, A/1858, A/2163, A/2456, A/2693, A/2934 and A/3159, all reports of the International Law Commission that deal with the regime of the sea between 1950 and 1956.

19. For the text of the Geneva Convention on the Continental Shelf, adopted in 1958, see 15 U.S. Treaty Series 473 (1964).

20. *Pollard* v. *Hagan* dealt with the ejectment of Pollard from property to which he claimed title by virtue of a U.S. patent, but which had been covered by high tide of the Mobile river at least between 1819 and 1823. "To give the United States the right to transfer to a citizen the title to the shores and soils under navigable waters would be placing in their hands a weapon which might be wielded greatly to the injury of state sovereignty and deprive the states of the power to exercise a numerous and important class of police powers." 3 *Howard* 212 (1845). See also the fine article of Davis S. Browning, "Some Aspects of State and Federal Jurisdiction in the Marine Environment" in *Proceedings, Third Annual Conference of the Law of the Sea Institute,* the University of Rhode Island, Kingston, Rhode Island (24–27 June 1968), pp. 89–141.

21. The joint resolution of Congress vetoed by the President that would have originally given title to the offshore resources of the United States to the coastal states was H. J. Resolution 225, 79th Congress, 2d Session, 1946. For the petition of the United States to the Supreme Court to declare its rights and enjoin California "from continuing to trespass" on the submerged lands, see

United States v. *California*, 332 *U.S.* 19 (1947). Justice Felix Frankfurter vigorously dissented from the Court ruling, believing that the United States had "imperium" over the area, but that the states had "dominium." For the subsequent litigation over the offshore resources in the Gulf of Mexico see *United States* v. *Louisiana*, 339 *U.S.* 699 (1950) and *United States* v. *Texas*, 339 *U.S.* 707 (1950).

22. Data on outer continental shelf figures for the number of wells and the income they have produced for the United States have been drawn from U.S. Department of the Interior, Geological Survey, Conservation Division, *Outer Continental Shelf, Oil, Gas, Sulfur, Salt, Leasing, Drilling, Production, Income and Related Statistics*, Washington, D.C. (April 1971), compiled by Walter M. Harris, Alta L. Lane, Bruce E. McFarlane. During this period, unproven submerged areas, after lease by competitive bidding, either rented for or paid minimum royalties at $3.00 per acre; proven areas (drainage sales) paid $10.00 an acre. In addition, royalties were paid to the United States by the private firms exploiting the seabed petroleum resources at the rate of $16^2/_3$ percent in the amount or value of the production saved, removed, or sold from the leases. Included in the total income cited are some very small amounts for salt and sulfur exploitation.

23. The fifty volumes of the *H.M.S. Challenger* report consists of two volumes of narrative of the voyage, two volumes on physics and chemistry, one volume on deep-sea deposits, two volumes on botany, forty volumes on zoology, and a two-volume summary. See C. Wyville Thomson and John Murray, *Report on the Scientific Results of the Voyage of H.M.S. Challenger*, published by order of Her Majesty's Government, (Edinburgh, 1895). I have taken data from several of these volumes as well as from C. Wyville Thomson, *The Voyage of the "Challenger": The Atlantic*, 2 vols., (London: Macmillan and Co., 1877).

24. At the turn of the century Alexander Agassiz dredged extensively in the eastern Pacific ocean from the *Albatross*, and he recovered manganese nodules from almost every station. Reports of his expedition can be found in *Memoirs of the Museum of Comparative Zoology* (Cambridge: Harvard College, 26, 1901), pp. 1-111 and (33, 1906), pp. 1-50; John Murray and G. V. Lee also wrote "The Depth and Marine Deposits in the Pacific," *Ibid.* (38, 1909), pp. 1-171. After a long gap, fundamental studies of the mineral composition and the agglomeration process of manganese nodules began again in the 1950s, with the work of such people as E. D. Goldberg, W. Buser, A. Grütter, and others who studied iron assimilation by marine diatoms, chemical scavengers of the sea, mineralogical aspects of deep-sea sediments, and particularly in 1956 the nature of manganese nodules.

25. The key to the future economic value of manganese nodules to the world was presaged by John Murray and A. F. Renard when they wrote in 1891 "To what mineral species or ore of manganese are these nodules to be referred? . . . a hydrated oxide of manganese, mixed with variable quantities of

limonite, clay, and other earthy and sandy matters. Among the associated substances there are several which are in a way peculiar to the concretionary and reniform manganese ores, for instance, copper, cobalt, nickel, &c." "Deep Sea Deposits," *Report on the Scientific Results of the Voyage of H.M.S. Challenger,* p. 368.

26. John L. Mero's first published interest in manganese nodules is to be found in "Manganese," *North Dakota Engineer,* vol. 27 (1952), pp. 28–32. For the Institute of Marine Resources he completed "The Mining and Processing of Deep-Sea Manganese Nodules" in 1959 and a good summary of some of the findings of study can be found in *Scientific American,* vol. 203 (December 1960), pp. 64–72, from which I have drawn the quotations in my text. Mero used this study and other materials, such as "The Economics of Mining Phosphorites from the California Borderland Area," which he completed for the Institute of Marine Resources in 1960, to finish the work that caught worldwide attention, *The Mineral Resources of the Sea* (Amsterdam: Elsevier Publishing Company, 1965). He suggested that even if only 1 percent of the nodules of the Pacific ocean proved economic to mine, the reserves of several metals in the nodules could be measured in thousands of years at present rates of free world consumption.

27. Information on the initiative of the Newport News Shipbuilding and Dry Dock Company in 1962 (which John Mero joined as a consultant) to recover manganese nodules and the formation of Deepsea Ventures, Inc. have been taken from testimony of John E. Flipse, President, Deepsea Ventures, Inc., before the U.S. Senate Commerce Committee, (23–24 September 1969). The Committee dealt with policy considerations germane to the peaceful, beneficial, and economic exploitation of the resources of the deep ocean floor. Details on the Deepsea Ventures company and the *R/V Prospector* voyage of 1970 have been taken from press releases and reprint articles as well as photographs of manganese nodules recovered supplied to me by Richard J. Greenwald, Special Counsel of Deepsea Ventures, Inc.

28. For comprehensive scientific studies of the location of manganese nodules on the ocean floor and their mineral composition, see J. E. Frazier and B. Arrhenius, *World-Wide Distribution of Ferromanganese Nodules and Element Concentrations in Selected Pacific Ocean Nodules,* Technical Report no. 2, Seabed Assessment Program, International Decade of Ocean Exploration (Washington, D.C.: National Science Foundation, 1972); D. R. Horn, M. N. Delach, and B. M. Horn, *Metal Content of Ferromanganese Deposits of the Oceans,* Technical Report no. 3, and *Ocean Manganese Nodules: Metal Values and Mining Sites,* Technical Report no. 4, NSF GX33616, International Decade of Ocean Exploration (Washington, D.C.: National Science Foundation, 1973).

29, For this section on the mining ferro-manganese nodules from the ocean floor, I have perused many issues of *Mining Engineering* and *Engineering and Mining Journal.* Both periodicals have yielded a number of relevant articles too numerous to cite. Typical of some of the better analyses have been H. D. Hess,

"The Ocean: Mining's Newest Frontier," *Engineering and Mining Journal,* vol. 166 (August 1965), pp. 79-96, C. Richard Tinsley, "Mining of Manganese: An Intriguing Legal Problem," *Ibid,* vol. 174, no. 10 (October 1973), pp. 84-87, Chester O. Ensign, Jr., "Economic Barriers Delay Underseas Mining, *Mining Engineering,* vol. 18 (September 1966), p. 59, and A. A. Archer, "Progress and Prospects in Marine Mining" *Ibid.,* vol. 25, no. 12 (December 1973), p. 31 (condensed from a larger paper presented at the 1973 Fifth Annual Offshore Technology Conference in Houston, Texas). Archer, head of the Mineral Resources Center at the Institute of Geological Sciences, London, suggested that a one-million-ton per year manganese nodule mining operation might yield about 13,000 tons of nickel, 11,000 tons of copper, 2500 tons of cobalt, and 270,000 tons of manganese.

30. Several studies and reports of the Secretary General of the United Nations on manganese nodules have been made, and they contain collected information of considerable technological, economic, and legal value. For some of my data I have drawn on *Possible Impact of Sea-Bed Mineral Production in the Area Beyond National Jurisdiction on World Markets, with Special Reference to the Problems of Developing Countries: A Preliminary Assessment* (A/AC. 138/36/) (28 May 1971), *Additional Notes on the Possible Economic Implications of Mineral Production from the International Sea-Bed Area* (A/AC.138/73/) (12 May 1972) *Economic Significance, in Terms of Sea-Bed Mineral Resources, of the Various Limits Proposed for National Jurisdiction,* (A/AC.138/87/) (4 June 1973), and *Sea-Bed Mineral Resources: Recent Developments* (A/AC.138/90) (3 July 1973).

31. John Mero testified on 18 August 1965 before the Subcommittee on Oceanography of the U.S. House of Representatives Committee on Merchant Marines and Fisheries, 84th Congress, 1st Session. The idea of an international regime for the seabed, however, can be traced at least ten years further back, particularly to George Scelle in 1955. Scelle, who was elected to the UN International Law Commission in 1948, 1953, and 1956, had proposed that an international agency be created within the United Nations system to (1) define the conditions to be followed by concessions granted on the continental shelf in order to guarantee the freedom of navigation and other uses of the high seas; and (2) act itself as the international administrative authority with power to grant concessions, in place of the state authorities. See, "Plateau Continental et Droit International," *59 Revue generale de droit international public* (1955), p. 59. The Commission to Study the Organization of Peace, an eminent group of scholars and public leaders, had also recommended in 1955 that the General Assembly of the United Nations "declare the title of the international community" to the bed of the sea beyond the continental shelf and "to establish appropriate administrative arrangements."

32. In 1966 the Commission to Study the Organization of Peace, following a chapter on "Shared Resources of the World Community" written by Francis T. Christy, Jr and David B. Brooks, reiterated its position and recommended that

no nation be allowed to appropriate the sea or seabed beyond a twelve-mile limit for fish or beyond the continental shelf for minerals. It urged that the United Nations take title to these marine areas and establish a special agency for their control and administration to be known as a United Nations Marine Resources Agency. See Commission to Study the Organization of Peace, Seventeenth Report, *New Dimensions for the United Nations: The Problems of the Next Decade* (New York: Dobbs Ferry, Oceana Publications, 1966). Another early article of seminal importance was Lieutenant Commander Richard J. Grunawalt, "The Acquisition of the Resources of the Bottom of the Sea — A New Frontier of International Law," *Military Law Review,* vol. 34 (October-November 1966), pp. 101-133. Grunawalt's recommendations included a redefinition of the continental shelf to extend to 200 miles or a maximum depth of 1000 meters, a conference to be convened to develop an international convention on the deep ocean floor, placement of deep ocean mineral resources under the jurisdiction of the United Nations, and a fair and equitable system of leasing submarine area, rents, or royalties "for the betterment of mankind."

33. I am particularly indebted in this section to the carefully researched study of Louis Henkin, *Law for the Seas Mineral Resources* (New York: Institute for the Study of Science in Human Affairs, Columbia University, 1968), a monograph prepared at the request of the U.S. National Council on Marine Resources and Engineering Development. Henkin succinctly examined the interests of the United States and suggested both guiding principles and eventual law favoring a narrow definition of the continental shelf, possibly with a buffer zone beyond the shelf. He urged support of the principle that the bed of the deep sea was not subject to national occupation or national claims of sovereignty for any purpose and that the United States endorse the creation of a UN Committee to study the problems of deepsea mining as well as make recommendations on new international legal regime, including a permanent international machinery to license mineral exploitation in the seabed beyond national jurisdiction. Many of these suggestions were eventually incorporated into U.S. policy formulations.

34. A note by John E. Dombroski, "Exploitation of Seabed Mineral Resources" in *Cornell Law Review,* vol. 58, no. 3 (March 1973), pp. 575-601 is an excellent brief, analytical exposition of the faults of the contemporary international framework for ordering the exploitation of seabed mineral resources and proposals to remedy the defects. The note has 149 footnotes, which cite some of the most relevant books, monographs, articles, testimony, and documents on the subject. Several articles from 1970 to 1977 in the *San Diego Law Review* and the *Natural Resources Lawyer,* in particular, have covered the issues of an international regime for the seabed.

35. For the activities of the *Ad Hoc* and the Committee on the Peaceful Uses of the Sea-Bed and the Ocean Floor beyond the Limits of National Jurisdiction from 1968 through 1973, I have made extensive use of the UN General

Assembly, Official Records, 23d Session through the 28th Session, *Report of the Ad Hoc Committee to Study the Peaceful Uses of the Sea-Bed and the Ocean Floor beyond National Jurisdiction* (A/7230) and *Report of the Committee on the Peaceful Uses of the Sea-Bed and the Ocean Floor beyond National Jurisdiction* (A/7622, A/8021, A/8421, A/8721, and A/9021). These documents contain summaries of all the work of the subcommittees and include draft proposals, draft articles, various working papers, and other documents submitted by states as well as by the Secretariat plus consolidated and comparative texts of articles up to the time of the opening of the Third UN Law of the Sea Conference in New York in December 1973.

36. A valuable summary of the preliminaries for the Third UN Law of the Sea Conference in Caracas in 1974 is John R. Stevenson and Bernard H. Oxman, "The Preparations for the Law of the Sea Conference," *American Journal of International Law,* vol. 68, no. 1 (January 1974), pp. 1-32. The article reviewed the work of Subcommittee 1 as "The Seabed beyond Jurisdiction," Subcommittee 2 as "Coastal State Jurisdiction," and Subcommittee 3 as "Pollution and Scientific Research." Summaries of the proposals of the various states on the main issues were included with an elaboration of U.S. policy. The article concluded that "If agreement is not reached in the time schedule elaborated by the UN General Assembly, it is problematic whether agreement can ever be achieved for a long time to come, and then only after much unnecessary conflict and waste."

37. For the text of Senator Claiborne Pell's "Ocean Space Treaty" and Senate Resolution 263, as well as his comment on the timeliness of the treaty, see U.S. 90th Congress, 2d Session, *Congressional Record,* vol. 114 (5 March 1968), p. 5181. The Executive Branch acted on the report of the Commission on Marine Science, Engineering and Resources, *Our Nation and the Sea* (Washington, D.C.: U.S. Government Printing Office, 1969).

38. On 23 May 1970 the White House released a comprehensive statement from President Nixon on U.S. policy for the use of the oceans. This was transmitted by the Representative of the United States to the UN Seabed Committee. See U.S. Department of State, *Bulletin,* vol. 62 (1970), p. 737.

39. The text of the General Assembly Declaration of Principles Governing the Seabed may be easily found in Jovan Djonovich, *UN Resolutions,* Series 1, General Assembly, vol. XIII (1976), (New York: Oceana, p. 240).

40. U.S. Department of State *Bulletin,* vol. 72 (1975), p. 785. Stevenson, an exceptionally able lawyer, headed the U.S. delegation at Caracas in 1974 and Geneva in 1975. He was succeeded by Carlyle E. Maw in 1975 and T. Vincent Learson in 1976. In 1977 President Carter appointed Elliot Richardson his representative to the Third UN Law of the Sea Conference.

41. See Part 1 of the *Revised Single Negotiating Text,* UN Document A/CONF.62/WP.8/Rev.1/Part I (6 May 1976), especially Article 9 and Appendix 1, paragraph 21, dealing with production controls.

42. On 1 September 1976 Secretary of State Kissinger at the second New York session of the Law of the Sea Conference said that the United States would be prepared to agree to a means of financing the Enterprise so that it could either begin to mine concurrently with a state or private enterprise or within an agreed time span. See U.S. Department of State, *Bulletin,* vol. 75 (1976), pp. 395–399.

43. For many of my figures and projections of U.S. mineral resources, I am particularly indebted to U.S. Geological Survey, *United States Mineral Resources,* Professional Paper 820, Donald A. Brobst and Walden P. Pratt, eds. (Washington, D.C.: U.S. Government Printing Office, 1973). Especially useful in this volume were essays by V. E. McKelvey, "Mineral Resource Estimates and Public Policy," and T. H. McCulloh, "Oil and Gas." The American Petroleum Institute, the American Gas Association, and the Canadian Petroleum Association annually publish *Reserves of Crude Oil, Natural Gas Liquids, and Natural Gas in the United States and Canada and United States Productive Capacity.* See vol. 28, (1974). I have also benefited from the group study led by Don E. Kash and Irvin L. White, *Energy under the Oceans,* a technology assessment of outer continental shelf oil and gas operations, (Norman, Okla.: University of Oklahoma Press, 1973), which examined many problems of developing U.S. oil gas resources from the outer continental shelf, including engineering, management, jurisdictional, and environmental factors.

44. The continued drive to exploit the offshore oil and gas reserves around the world can also be traced through statistics on drilling rigs. In the mid-1970s there were more than two-hundred active platform rigs drilling for oil or gas, most of them in the Gulf of Mexico and Lake Maracaibo, with a score each off California, Europe, and the Middle East, perhaps a dozen each off Alaska, the Caribbean, Africa, and Australia. Some idea of technological progress can be seen from a 1974 contract in which the Mitsubishi Heavy Industries of Japan signed a contract with Ocean Drilling and Exploration Co. of New Orleans to supply a super-class self-propelled semisubmersible rig. The design provided for a platform-vessel, 391 feet long, 262 feet wide, with twin lower hulls, and 8 vertical columns. It could drill from a floating position in depths of water up to 1500 feet and, with modifications, up to 3500 feet. For its mooring the vessel-rig would carry twelve 45,000-pound anchors held by chains 3.5 inches thick. Current information on offshore drilling can be found in *Engineering and Mining Journal,* New York, *Offshore, The Journal of Ocean Business,* Houston, and the *Oil and Gas Journal,* Tulsa.

45. For the U.S. proposal of draft articles for a chapter on the Rights and Duties of States in the Coastal Seabed Economic Area, see UN Document A/AC.138/SC.11/L.35. On 13 August 1973 John Norton Moore, Vice-Chairman of the U.S. delegation to the UN Seabed Committee, told the Main Committee "we are prepared to accept broad coastal state economic jurisdiction in adjacent waters and seabed areas beyond the territorial sea as part of a satisfactory

overall Law of the Sea settlement." But he warned that if coastal state jurisdiction over pollution were to include general jurisdiction over vessel-source pollution, the rights of states to navigate the high seas freely would be seriously threatened, especially if coastal states were to exercise independently such jurisdiction as far out as two hundred miles to sea.

46. See Articles 44-49 of the *Revised Single Negotiating Text* for the rights, jurisdiction, and duties of the coastal state in the exclusive economic zone. UN Document A/CONF.62/WP.8/Rev.1/Part II (6 May 1976).

47. Data on offshore leasing have been drawn from 94th Congress, 2d Session, House of Representatives, Ad Hoc Select Committee on Outer Continental Shelf, *Effects of Offshore Oil and Natural Gas Development on the Coastal Zone* (March 1976), a study by the Congressional Research Service made for the Chairman, John M. Murphy, which found that outer continental shelf petroleum production would be less harmful to the environment than importation of similar quantities and that the impact of such exploitation would not be significant to onshore communities if careful planning, including effective emission and effluent control were done. See also U.S. Department of the Interior, Mineral Resource Management of the Outer Continental Shelf, (Washington, D.C., n.d.).

48. In 1973 the American Mining Congress postulated that if nickel, copper, and cobalt were the major products obtained from manganese nodules, in addition to other volume byproducts, it would probably require about three million tons of dry nodules for a mine to be economical. Assuming certain inefficiencies of dredge collection, the lack of accessibliity of the dredge to some areas, and the need to have nodules of a high grade of mineral content, even the 10,000 square kilometer block that would remain to the entrepreneur after divestment of 75 percent of the original 40,000 square kilometer license, would barely sustain a commercial yield over 40 years. For the observations of industry and government as well as private environmental and international groups on S.1134, see U.S. Senate, Sub-Committee on Minerals, Materials, and Fuels, Committee on Interior and Insular Affairs, *Mineral Resources of the Deep Seabed, Hearings* (May 17, June 14, 15, 18, and 19, 1973).

Chapter 6
Marine Pollution

1. See Clarence G. Glacken, *Traces on the Rhodian Shore* (Berkeley and Los Angeles: University of California Press, 1967). The bibliography alone runs to 32 pages and contains some 600 citations of classical Greek and Roman items as well as medieval monographs and special studies or works on medicine, architecture, agronomy, general science, philosophy, and so forth. I have borrowed heavily from this monumental book while referring to the original writings of Montesquieu and Buffon on man and his environment.

2. George Perkins Marsh, *Man and Nature,* David Lowenthal, ed., (Cambridge, Mass.: Belknap Press, Harvard University Press, 1965), was my source for the ideas of the intellectual father of the conservationist movement in the United States. Marsh substantially revised and added some new materials to *Man and Nature* in 1873, which was copyrighted in 1874 by Scribner, Armstrong & Co., and published as *The Earth as Modified by Human Action.*

3. For the conservation movement in the United States in the early twentieth century, see the excellent study of Samuel P. Hays, *Conservation and the Gospel of Efficiency* (Cambridge, Mass.: Harvard University Press, 1959), the story of the progressive conservation movement from 1890 to 1920.

4. I am indebted to Lynton K. Caldwell for his book, *In Defense of Earth* (Bloomington: Indiana University Press, 1972), especially his chapter on "Discovering the Biosphere," which fixed my attention on the work of such men as Henderson, Blum, Vernadsky, and Teilhard. Caldwell's footnotes and references are extensive on man as an unecological animal, on ecosystems, international conservation efforts, and the need to understand the danger. See Lawrence S. Henderson, *The Fitness of the Environment* (New York: The Macmillan Co., 1913) and Harold F. Blum, *Time's Arrow and Evolution* (Princeton: Princeton University Press, 1951), especially pp. 208 and 212; second and third editions were published in 1955 and 1968 respectively. See also Pierre Teilhard de Chardin, *The Appearance of Man,* translated by J. M. Cohen (New York: Harper & Row, 1965) and *The Phenomenon of Man,* translated by Barnard Wall (New York: Harper & Brothers, 1959).

5. William Voigt, *The Road to Survival* (New York: William Sloane Associated, 1948), Fairfield Osborn, *Our Plundered Planet* (Boston: Little Brown, 1952), and Samuel H. Ordway, Jr., *Resources and the American Dream* (New York: Ronald Press Co., 1953) offer a good picture of certain American concerns about the relationship of humans and their environment, perhaps epitomized by Ordway's words, "Success has led us to believe that the earth is a cornucopia and the machine a god. It has led to a false faith in man's omnipotence." It might be noted that these were the years in which a number of other apocolyptic works advocating world government were popular in the United States, offering a choice between "peace or anarchy."

6. The key ideas of Barry Commoner in this period may be found in his *Science and Survival,* first copyrighted in 1963 (New York: Viking Press, 1966). Some of his data were based on the President's Science Advisory Committee, *Restoring the Quality of Our Environment* (Washington, D.C.: Government Printing Office, 1965). In *The Closing Circle: Nature, Man and Technology* (New York: Alfred Knopf, 1971), Commoner wrote, "I learned about the environment from the United States Atomic Energy Commission in 1953." Until then he had taken the air, water, soil, and the natural surroundings mostly for granted, but, having worked for the U.S. war program in World War II, he was deeply concerned about the enormous destructive forces of nuclear energy.

7. In a beautifully written, calm, and analytical style, filled with many references from philosophy, science, and literature, René Dubos in *Man Adapting* (New Haven: Yale University Press, 1965) set forth the theme that "the states of health or disease are an expression of the success or failure experienced by the organism in its efforts to respond adaptively to environmental challenges." He covered man and nature, man in the physical world, man's food, the microbial diseases, environmental pollution, and population. A more popular work, *So Human an Animal* (New York: Scribner, 1968), concluded, ". . . the various aspects of biological and social nature constitute such a highly integrated system that they can only be altered within a certain range."

8. The figures on the increase of U.S. production between 1950 and 1960 have been drawn from the *Statistical Abstract of the United States* (Washington, D.C.: U.S. Government Printing Office, 1951-1961).

9. I have taken some of the background of the environmental movement with respect to the alarms of the scientists over the atomic bombs following World War II from John Maddox, *The Doomsday Syndrome* (New York: McGraw-Hill, 1972). Maddox refutes or deflates some of the allegations of the alarmist writers, like Barry Commoner and Rachel Carson, about harmful effects on the environment and unproven consequences for both man and nature.

10. Rachel Carson's first of three articles entitled, "Silent Spring" appeared under a frequent section of the *New Yorker* magazine entitled, "A Reporter at Large" (16 June 1962). The book, *Silent Spring* (Boston: Houghton Mifflin, 1962) contains the three articles, but with some alterations in language, rearrangements, and additions. Carson certainly was not the only one alarmed over pesticides in 1960, as the long list of sources cited in *Silent Spring* demonstrates, but she effectively dramatized the problem for an attentive audience of influential Americans. My figures on the rise of U.S. agricultural productivity, the increased manufacture of synthetic pesticides, and the enlargement of aerial spraying with liquid compounds have been drawn from both the *Statistical Abstract of the United States* and *Silent Spring.*

11. For some of the early history of sewerage I am indebted to the introductory chapter of Leonard Metcalf and Harrison P. Eddy, *Sewerage and Sewage Disposal,* 2d ed. (New York: McGraw-Hill, 1930), which, like the first edition, was condensed and extensively rewritten from the three-volume treatise of the authors, *American Sewerage Practice,* first published in 1914-1915. I have also had recourse to The Selden Society, *Public Works in Medieval Law,* C. T. Flower, ed., (London: Bernard Quaritch, 1915) for a number of illustrations of indictments against landowners and townships for the poor maintenance of sewers in England during the reigns of Edward III and Richard II, particularly during the latter half of the fourteenth century.

12. For the *Seventh Annual Report of the State Board of Health of Massachusetts,* which includes *A Special Report on the Pollution of Rivers,* I have used James P. Kirkwood, *A Special Report on the Pollution of River Waters,*

Arno and the New York Times, 1970, which reprints entirely the document taken from Public Documents of Massachusetts: *Annual Reports of Public Officers and Institutions for the Year 1875,* vol. V., nos. 30 and 31, (Boston: Wright and Potter, State Printers, 1876). Only in 1875 did Great Britain pass a public health act that placed responsibility for health on the country as a whole, although local authorities actually supervised the disposal and treatment of sewage. A year later the Rivers Pollution Prevention Act, applying to England, Wales, and with some modifications, to Scotland and Ireland, forbade putting solid matter into a stream if it could be shown that it interfered with flow or that pollution was caused. Discharging solid or liquid sewage into a stream was also forbidden. But with regard to industrial pollutants there was no obstacle if no "reasonably" practical means were available to render the pollutants harmless. Enforcement was originally in the hands of sanitary boards, who were often themselves polluters. See Louis Klein, *Aspects of River Pollution* (London: Butterworth's Scientific Publications, 1957).

13. Missouri first sought an injunction against the Sanitary District of Chicago in 1900 to ban "the receiving or permitting any sewage to be received or discharged into the artificial channel or drain constructed by the Sanitary District." (*Missouri* v. *Illinois and the Sanitary District of Chicago,* 180 *U.S.* 208.) After almost five years of delay and the demurrer to the complaint had been dismissed, the merits were tried early in 1906 (*Missouri* v. *Illinois and the Sanitary District of Chicago,* 200 *U.S.* 496).

14. In 1888 the Supreme Court had held that there was no common federal law prohibiting obstructions or nuisances in the navigable waters of the United States. *Willamette Iron Bridge Co.* v. *Hatch* 125 *U.S.* 1. The texts of the rivers and harbors appropriations bill have been taken from *Statutes of the United States,* vol. XXIV, p. 329, and vol. XXX, p. 1152. Text of the Public Health Service Act was from ibidem, vol. XXXVI, part 1, p. 309.

15. For information about the 1924 Oil Pollution Act and the investigation of the U.S. government preparatory to calling an international conference to prevent the pollution of navigable waters by oil-burning and oil-carrying steamers, I have made use of the Interdepartmental Committee Report to the Secretary of State, *Oil Pollution of Navigable Waters* (13 March 1926) (Washington, D.C.: U.S. Government Printing Office, 1926).

16. In the United Kingdom the Oil in Navigable Waters Act was passed by Parliament in 1922. It prohibited discharges from vessels or from any place on land into navigable waters, and, furthermore, prohibited any transfer of oil by night unless specific permission had been granted by the harbor master. By 1926 Canada, Australia, and a few other countries had legislation that could be interpreted as a national prohibition against the discharge of oil into their navigable waters. But neither France, Germany, Japan, Norway, nor several other states had national legislation to stop such pollution. In some of these states local ordinances or port rules either forbade or mitigated the gross

discharge of oil and oil wastes into harbor waters. The difference between the law and its regular, timely enforcement, of course, could be substantial.

17. The data on the U.S. population served by sewage systems and the lack of treatment of wastes has been drawn from U.S. 89th Congress, 1st Session, House Committee on Government Operations, *Disposal of Municipal Sweage,* House Report no. 204 (24 March 1965), (Washington, D.C.: U.S. Government Printing Office, 1965).

18. The testimony cited for and against the Federal Water Pollution Control Act of 1948 has been taken from the U.S. 80th Congress, Senate Hearings, Subcommittee of the Committee on Public Works, *Stream Pollution Control* (April and May, 1947), (Washington, D.C.: U.S. Government Printing Office, 1947).

19. Data and materials used to illuminate the progress of water pollution control from 1945 to 1962, as well as contrasting opinions on the role of the federal government in bringing about improvements in the treatment of sewage, were taken from the U.S. 89th Congress, 1st Session, House of Representatives, Report no. 204, *Disposal of Municipal Sewage* (24 March 1965), in *House Reports,* vol. 3-5 (Washington, D.C.: U.S. Government Printing Office, 1965). I have also drawn from the U.S. 89th Congress, Senate Subcommittee on Air and Water Pollution Control, Committee on Public Works, *Hearings, Water Pollution Control–1966* (Washington, D.C.: U.S. Government Printing Office, 1966) and House of Representatives Committee on Public Works, *Hearings, Federal Water Pollution Control Act–1966* (Washington, D.C.: U.S. Government Printing Office, 1966).

20. The example of the use of chromatography in the detection of chlorinated hydrocarbons was taken from Harvey Brooks, "Can Science Survive the Modern Age," *Science,* vol. 174, no. 4004 (1 October 1971).

21. The UN definition of marine pollution was originally formulated by a mixed working group of scientists (SCOR/ACMRR) for an outline of "Enlarged and Long Term Program for Oceanographic Research," UN Document A/7750 (10 November 1969). It was accepted with slight amendments by the Group of Experts for Atmospheric and Marine Pollution (GESAMP), and adopted by the UNESCO International Oceanographic Commission. My phrasing of the definition of marine pollution is not quite the same as the English rendition in UN documents, but closer to the literal French version.

22. A valuable study was made by a number of environmental scientists, under the chairmanship of Edward D. Goldberg, of transuranic elements, synthetic organic chemicals, metallic and medicinal wastes, and marine litter as potential sources of marine pollution. Their report contains very useful information on the properties, production, mode of entry into the environment, and the effects of such wastes. See National Academy of Sciences, *Assessing Potential Ocean Pollutants,* a report of a study panel to the Ocean Affairs Board, Commission on Natural Resources, National Research Council, Washington, D.C. (1975).

23. The figures on the use of water and the rates of wastewater have been taken from various sources, including the *Handbook of Environmental Control,* 4 vols. (Cleveland: CRC Press, 1972-1974) and the *Statistical Abstract of the United States* (Washington, D.C.: U.S. Government Printing Office, 1971-1976); the figures on ocean dumping were taken from the first systematic analysis of how the seas were being used as a depository for U.S. wastes, Council on Environmental Quality, *Ocean Dumping: A National Policy,* a report to the President (October 1970), Government Printing Office, Washington, D.C. Figures on the suspended solids loads and their treatment came from a paper by T. D. Hinesly, "Practices, Economics, and Effects of Municipal Sludge Utilization on Land as an Alternative to Ocean Dumping" in U.S. Environmental Protection Agency, *Ocean Disposal Practices and Effects,* a report by the President's Water Pollution Control Advisory Board from a meeting held in New York City (26-29 September 1972), Washington, D.C. For an overview of ocean dumping and ocean pollution as of 1974, I have profited from the 84-page publication of the National Oceanic and Atmospheric Administration *Report to the Congress on Ocean Dumping and Other Man-Induced Changes to the Ocean Eco-Systems, October 1972 Through December 1973,* U.S. Department of Commerce, Washington, D.C.: (March 1974).

24. Three major sources for the inputs of oil into the oceans are Study of Critical Environmental Probe (SCEP), *Man's Impact on the Global Environment* (Cambridge, Mass.: MIT Press, 1970); U.S. Coast Guard, *Draft Environmental Impact Statement for the International Convention for the Prevention of Pollution from Ships,* Washington, D.C., 1973; and National Academy of Sciences, *Petroleum in the Marine Environment,* a workshop on inputs, fates, and effects of petroleum in the marine environment, held at Airlie House, Virginia (21-25 May 1973), Washington, D.C.: 1975. The last includes very valuable tables and charts, as well as some forty to eighty references after each section, and to date is by far the most objective and comprehensive American assessment of petroleum in the marine environment.

25. For a clear and useful statement on "The Environmental Impact of Manganese Nodule Mining" I am indebted to the testimony of Oswald A. Roels, submitted on 18 February 1974 to the Minerals Sub-Committee of the U.S. Senate at its hearings on 5-6 March 1974 on Ocean Mining Bill, S.1134, in an unpublished paper that I received from the author.

26. Much of my data on the effect of radioactive materials in the ocean on the marine environment has been taken from the extended U.S. 93d Congress, Senate Subcommittee on Oceans and Atmospheres, Committee on Commerce, *Ocean Pollution, Hearings* (June 12, 13, and 28, 1973), Government Printing Office, Washington, D.C., 1974. Especially valuable was the testimony of Dr. Herbert Volchok of the Atomic Energy Commission. In the *Hearings* the comments of Dr. Thomas Owen of the National Science Foundation were germane to the problem of assessing the dangers of heavy metals to the marine environment.

27. W. Eugene Smith and Aileen M. Smith, *Minamata* (New York: Holt, Rinehart, and Winston, 1975) tells the harrowing story of the Minamata tragedy, with photographs, and the long struggle to fix liability for damages on the Chisso company. Only in 1973, after a four-year trial, was the company ordered by the Japanese court to pay compensation, which through 1975 amounted to more than $80 million for damages, living allowances, and medical care. In 1976 the former President and former manager of the company went on trial for involuntary manslaughter, the first trial of its kind in Japan.

28. A list of hundreds of references on the behavior of petroleum in the marine environment and its effects on marine organisms can be found in National Academy of Sciences, *Petroleum in the Marine Environment.* This extraordinary report of a fourteen-member workshop under the chairmanship of E. Bright Wilson of Harvard University stemmed from the work of some 60 distinguished scientists and engineers from both American and foreign academic, government, and industrial organizations. A very fitting conclusion is, "The ocean may be able to accommodate petroleum hydrocarbon inputs far above those occurring today. On the other hand, the damage level may be within an order of magnitude of present inputs to the sea . . . it seems wisest to continue our efforts in the international control of inputs and to push forward research."

29. While public attention has been focused on tanker operations and continental shelf drilling as sources of oil pollution of the marine environment, it should be noted that about 1.5 billion gallons of spent lube oils and greases from vehicle crankcases and industrial plants were generated annually in the United States in the early 1970s. About half of these wastes were probably disposed of without any safeguard against their entry into surface or subsurface waters. Precise quantities and locations of waste oil have been difficult to pinpoint, especially since many of the activities have been illegal. U.S. 93d Congress, 1st Session, House Committee on Public Works, *Waste Oil Study,* a preliminary report from the Administrator of the Environmental Protection Agency, U.S. Government Printing Office, Washington, D.C., 1973.

30. The Convention for the Prevention of Pollution of the Sea by Oil was opened for signature on 12 May 1954, when it was signed by twenty states, but not the United States. The Convention came into force in 1958. The U.S. Senate gave its consent to ratifying the Convention on 16 May 1961. Although the Senate refused to accept the requirement of installing waste reception facilities at each major port, it urged U.S. port authorities to construct them. Moreover, the Senate recommended that consideration be given to (1) international uniformity in penalties and enforcement of the Convention; (2) a more realistic definition of what constitutes oil pollution; and with an eye toward evasion of the rules by other countries, suggested that (3) each contracting government ought to have right of access to the official records filed with the International Maritime Consultative Organization. See. *U.S. Treaties and Other International Agreements.* TIAS 4900 for the text of

the Convention, the resolution of the Senate, and the action of the President. See *Statutes of the United States,* vol. 75 (1961), p. 402 for P.L. 87 167, Oil Pollution Act, 1961.

31. The Water Quality Improvement Act of 1970, PL 91-224, was enacted 3 April 1970. The text is in 84 *United States Statutes at Large* 91. Title II established the Office of Environmental Quality under the Chairman of the Council on Environmental Quality and called for environmental quality reports to be sent to the appropriate committees of Congress.

32. For Senator Warren Magnuson's introduction of the Tanker Safety Improvement Act, see *U.S. Congressional Record* (23 January 1975), S 707 in which he cited the position of the U.S. Coast Guard at the International Conference on Marine Pollution from Ships and appended a table of double-bottom tankers either in service or under construction as of January 1975. Reasonable critics of the requirement of double bottom construction for tankers have argued that, beyond the additional cost, such vessels are less responsive in navigation, that there can be a greater threat to marine pollution when a puncture of the bottom hull leads to rapid water filling of the space between hulls and sinking or, even worse, an explosion of the "gassy" space between the two hulls. For the regulations of the U.S. Coast Guard with respect to vessel design and operations in force 31 July 1974, see 33 *Code of Federal Regulations* 155.100. For the proposed rules under the Ports and Waterways Safety Act of 1972, see U.S. 39 *Federal Register* 24150 (28 June 1974).

33. In *U.S.* v. *Pennsylvania Industrial Chemical Corporation,* 411 *U.S.* 655, 1972, the defendant had been found liable to criminal prosecution under the 1899 Refuse Act by the District Court for the discharge of wastes that had never been regarded by the Corps of Engineers as harmful to navigation. The Court of Appeals reversed the District Court, but the Supreme Court upheld. In 1965 the Supreme Court in an opinion by Justice Douglas, with three dissents, had already forbidden "a narrow, cramped reading" of discharges into the navigable waters of the United States and had included "all foreign substance and pollutants," in that case an accidental spill of aviation gasoline, *U.S.* v. *Standard Oil Co.,* 383 *U.S.* 226.

34. The text of the Federal Water Pollution Control Act Amendments of 1972 ran to almost 45,000 words. The legislative history can be found most conveniently in U.S. Environmental Protection Agency, *Legal Compilation,* Supplement I, vols. I–III (1972–1973) (Washington, D.C.: U.S. Government Printing Office). This series includes all statutes and legislative history, executive orders, regulations, guidelines, and reports of the EPA on all environmental matters within its purview.

36. For developments in amending legislation and implementation of both the Federal Water Pollution Control Act Amendments and the Ocean Dumping Act of 1972, I have consulted the report prepared by the Environmental Policy Division of the Congressional Research Service for the 94th Congress, 1st

Session, U.S. Senate Committee on Public Works. *Environmental Protection Affairs of the 93rd Congress,* Serial no. 94-2 (February 1975) (Washington, D.C.: U.S. Government Printing Office, 1975). The Ocean Dumping Act was further amended by P.L. 93-254 of 18 December 1974, which allowed deductions of spaces used aboard ships for collecting, processing, or carrying shipboard-generated wastes from gross tonnage in calculating the net tonnage of a vessel. Taxes and other charges on a ship have often been based on net tonnage. I have also used figures and language from the U.S. Council on Environmental Quality, Annual Reports, *Environmental Quality* (1974–1977) (Washington, D.C.: U.S. Government Printing Office), about the progress of water pollution and ocean dumping controls.

36. In addition to incipient Congressional concern over the fate of the wetlands in the 1950s and 1960s, special legislation provided for three new national parks, two national seashores, five national recreation areas, two national lakeshores, three national scenic rivers, and a score of historical parks, sites, and monuments between 1969 and 1972. For the recommendation of the Commission on Marine Science, Engineering, and Resources, see *Our Nation and the Sea* (January 1969) (Washington, D.C.: U.S. Government Printing Office). Descriptions of the legislation introduced, with House and Senate actions, and other details on land use planning from 1966 to 1972 have been taken from the excellent *Congress and the Nation,* vol. II (1965–1968) and vol. III, (1969–1972), Congressional Quarterly Service, Washington, D.C., (1969 and 1973).

37. The testimony of Walter J. Hickel was taken from U.S. 91st Congress, 1st Session, House Committee on Public Works, Subcommittee on Rivers and Harbors, *Hearings, Coastal Zone Management* (3 December 1949).

38. The conference report on the Coastal Zone Management Act of 1972, with a joint explanatory statement of agreements and disagreements between the Senate and House and their resolution, can be found in U.S. 92d Congress, 2d Session, House of Representatives *Report,* No. 92-1544.

39. Figures on the formation of citizens environmental commissions in state and local governments have been taken from Steve Carter et al., *Environmental Management and Local Government,* prepared by the International City Manager's Association for the Environmental Protection Agency (Washington, D.C.: U.S. Government Printing Office, 1974).

40. For *American Waterways Operators* v. *Askew,* see 411 *U.S.* 325 (1973). For *Portland Pipeline Corporation* v. *Environmental Improvement Commission,* see 307 *A.2d* 1 (1973).

41. For background to the London conference in 1954 and the creation of the Convention for the Prevention of the Pollution of the Sea by Oil, I have used John W. Mann (who was vice-chairman of the U.S. delegation of six), "The Problem of Sea Water Pollution," U.S. Department of State *Bulletin,* vol. 29 (1953), pp. 775–780 and Rear Admiral H. C. Shepheard (chairman of the

delegation) and John W. Mann, "International Conference on Pollution of the Seas and Coasts by Oil," *Bulletin,* vol. 31 (1954), pp. 311-314, as well as Office of International Conferences, Department of State, *Participation of the United States Government in International Conferences,* (Washington, D.C.: U.S. Government Printing Office, 1955). The text of the treaty was examined in UN *Treaty Series,* vol. 327 (1959), p. 4.

42. The International Convention for Prevention of the Pollution of the Sea by Oil text can be found in 12 *UST* 2989 (1961); the 1962 amendments, which were approved 4-11 April 1962 in London, can be found in 17 *UST* 1523 (1966). A convenient composite of the 1954 Convention and the amendments of both 1962 and 1969 can be found in IX *International Legal Materials* 1 (1970) published by the American Society of International Law. In the same volume are the texts of the International Convention Relating to Intervention on the High Seas in Cases of Oil Pollution Casualties (p. 25), and the International Convention on Civil Liability for Oil Pollution Damage (p. 45), as well as the three resolutions of the Conference (p. 65).

43. I have made use of several very throughful booklets and articles on this subject, including Jack Plano *International Approaches to the Problem of Marine Pollution,* Institute for the Study of International Organization, University of Sussex, England, 1972; L. F. E. Goldie, "International Principles of Responsibility for Pollution," *Columbia Journal of Transnational Law,* vol. 9, no. 2 (Fall 1970), pp. 283-330; Vincent Petaccio, "Water Pollution and the Future Law of the Sea," *International and Comparative Law Quarterly,* vol. 21 (January 1972), pp. 15-42; Robert M. Hallman, *Towards an Environmentally Sound Law of the Sea,* a report of the International Institute for Environment and Development, Washington, D.C., 1974; also, by the same Institute, *Critical Environmental Issues on the Law of the Sea,* Robert E. Stein, ed., 1975.

44. The text of the International Convention on the Establishment of an International Fund for Compensation for Oil Pollution Damage can be found in XI *International Legal Materials* 284 (1972).

45. William M. Ross, *Oil Pollution as an International Problem* (Seattle: University of Washington Press, 1973) has investigated state, provincial, national, and international law relating to oil pollution, with special reference to Puget Sound and the Strait of Georgia. His book also describes the Tanker Owners Voluntary Agreement Concerning Liability for Oil Pollution Damage (TOVA-LOP), a private insurance scheme to compensate governments for clean-up efforts.

46. The text of the U.S. Draft of "Regulation of Transportation for Ocean Dumping Convention" can be found at X *International Legal Materials* 1021 (1971). The concept that some materials would be abolutely prohibited from dumping and some materials would be permitted to be dumped only by special license, as well as a detailed list of such materials, was incorporated at Ottawa into draft articles. The text of the Oslo Convention for the Prevention of Marine

Pollution by Dumping from Ships and Aircraft can be found at XI *International Legal Materials* 262 (1972). Poland and the USSR were invited to join in adopting that Convention, but they declined.

47. Elaborate preparation went into the UN Conference on the Human Environment. In the United States, for example, the State Department had a twenty-seven-member advisory committee, which held public hearings in seven cities of the United States and also received hundreds of letters and written comments. Panels and study groups were established by such organizations as the National Academy of Science and the American Society of International Law; new thrusts into environmental problems were made by the creation of such organizations as the International Institute for Environmental Affairs (later International Institute for Environment and Development) and the Aspen Institute of Humanistic Studies. One of several studies of this subject is Thomas C. Wilson, Jr., *International Environmental Action* (Boston: Dunellen, 1972).

48. For the Report of the *United Nations Conference on the Human Environment* (1972), see UN Document A/Conf.48/14 and Corr. 1, which the UN General Assembly considered and adopted by Res. 2997 (XXVII) on 15 December 1972. Additional resolutions 2994-2996 specified the criteria under which the new UN Environmental Program should function and set priorities for its work.

49. For background to the Ocean Dumping Convention, see Lawson A. W. Hunter, *The Question of an Ocean Dumping Convention,* the conclusions of a working group formed by the Committee on International Marine Science Affairs, (Washington, D.C.: 1972). It contains both the U.S. revised draft circulated at Reykjavik and the draft convention produced there by the Inter-Governmental Meeting in April 1972. See also Charles A. Pearson, *International Marine Environment Policy* (Baltimore: Johns Hopkins University Press, 1974), a keen analysis of the Ocean Dumping Convention from an economist's point of view, and the book contains the text of the Convention. It can also be found in XI *International Legal Materials* 1291 (1972). The comment of U. Alexis Johnson was taken from U.S. Department of State *Bulletin,* vol. LXVIII, no. 1752 (22 January 1973), p. 96.

50. See Third UN Conference on the Law of the Sea, *Revised Single Negotiating Text,* Articles 17–42, New York (10 May 1976). UN Document A/CONF. 62/WP.8/Rev.1/Part III.

51. The testimony of Russell E. Train, Chairman of the U.S. Delegation to the International Marine Pollution Conference in 1973, and Admiral Chester E. Bender, Commandant of the U.S. Coast Guard, on the International Convention for the Prevention of Pollution from Ships, 1973 can be found in U.S. 93d Congress, 1st Session, Senate Committee on Commerce, *Hearing on 1973 IMCO Conference on Marine Pollution from Ships* (14 November 1973, U.S. Government Printing Office, Washington, D.C. The document also contains the completed text of the Convention.

52. My example of the lack of discrimination in EPA regulations for

wastewater treatment was drawn from the detailed testimony of Erman Pearson, Professor of Sanitary Engineering at the University of Berkeley, whose experience spanned more than twenty-four years. "It is popular to talk about no waste discharge. What that means is yet to be defined, but it will probably never occur as long as man is on the Earth." U.S. 93d Congress, 1st Session, Senate Committee on Commerce, Subcommittee on Oceans and Atmospheres, *Hearings on Ocean Pollution* (12, 13, and 28 June 1973), U.S. Government Printing Office, Washington, D.C. (1974), p. 112 *et seq.*

53. In his book *The Doomsday Syndrome* (New York: McGraw-Hill, 1972), John Maddox gives several illustrations of mistaken calculations and unsupported cause-effect relationships between a product or process and the human environment, (see Chapter 4).

54. A valuable study of the costs of pollution control is the report of the Environmental Policy Division of the Congressional Research Service, U.S. Library of Congress, prepared for the U.S. 94th Congress, 1st Session, Senate Committee on Public Works, *The Status of Environmental Economics* (June 1975), U.S. Government Printing Office, Washington, D.C., 1975. I am much indebted to Allen V. Kneese and Charles L. Schultze for their book, *Pollution, Prices, and Public Policy* (Washington, D.C.: The Brookings Institution, 1975) for data and analysis on the costs of pollution and how to frame policy based on incentives rather than blanket regulation. Estimates of the CEQ for costs of environmental improvement are to be found in the agency's annual reports, *Environmental Quality,* Washington, D.C. My figures are taken from the seventh annual report, 1976.

55. The quote on the inconsistency of federal and state laws with the difficulty for claimants in obtaining recompense for pollution damages has been taken from the message of the President transmitting the proposed legislation, "Comprehensive Oil Pollution, Liability, and Compensation Act of 1975," U.S. Department of State, *Bulletin,* vol. LXIII, no. 1886 (18 August 1975), pp. 262–263. Text of the proposed legislation is in U.S. 94th Congress, 1st Session, *House Document 214.*

56. For the text of the Convention on the Protection of the Marine Environment of the Baltic Sea Area, see XIII *International Legal Materials* 544 (May 1974).

Index

Index

About the Author

Gerard J. Mangone is H. Rodney Sharp Professor of International Law and Organization in the graduate professional College of Marine Studies, and Director of the Center for the Study of Marine Policy, at the University of Delaware. He has been Coordinator of Ocean Studies at the Woodrow Wilson International Center for Scholars, and Executive Director of the President's Commission on the United Nations. Mangone has been a consultant to the State Department, White House, and United Nations, and is an author or editor of more than twenty books on public and international affairs.